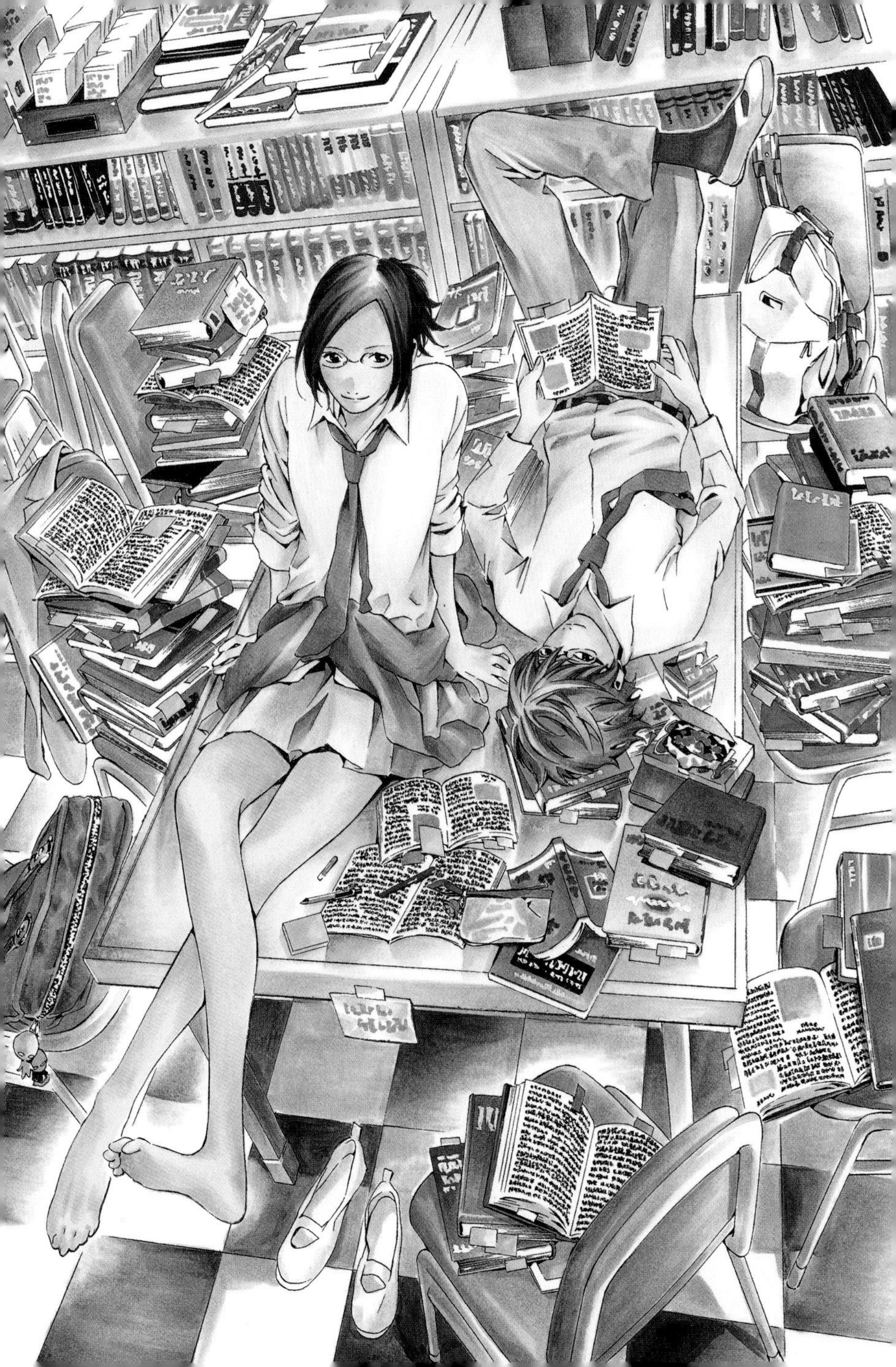

A School Frozen in Time ③

Art by Naoshi Arakawa

Story by Mizuki Tsujimura

Contents

WARNING: This volume contains references to suicide. If you or someone you know has suicidal thoughts or feelings, you are not alone, and there is free, 24/7 help.

National Suicide Prevention Lifeline offers specific resources and confidential support for those in crisis or emotional distress. You can call 1-800-273-TALK (8255) or go to SuicidePreventionLifeline.org at any time for free, 24/7 help when you or anyone you know needs help.

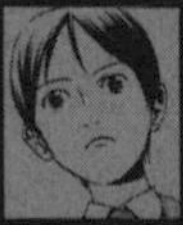

Mitsuru

Third-year at Seinan Gakuin.
Has a somewhat timid personality, which makes him an easy target for bullies. He has feelings for Rika.

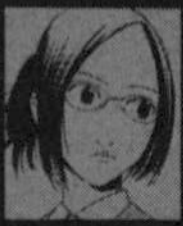

Shimizu

Third-year at Seinan Gakuin.
A hardworking model student who gets the highest scores in her grade.

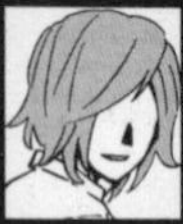

Sakaki

Homeroom teacher to Mizuki and the others. Despite being Takano's cousin, his personality is not even remotely close to Takano's.

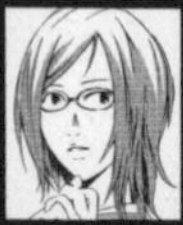

Haruko

Third-year at Seinan Gakuin.
She was Mizuki's best friend until she abruptly started to give Mizuki the cold shoulder.

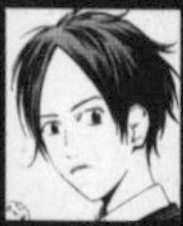

Suwa

Third-year at Seinan Gakuin and the student council president.
He's a popular guy with a cheeky personality.

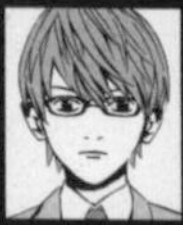

Takano

Third-year at Seinan Gakuin.
A popular guy with a sharp mind and outstanding athletic abilities.

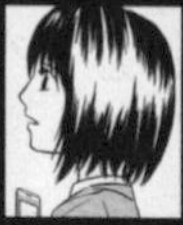

Mizuki

Third-year at Seinan Gakuin.
A bright and kindhearted girl. She is childhood friends with Takano.

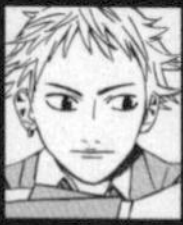

Sugawara

Third-year at Seinan Gakuin.
A mischievous brat who was suspended from school for gambling with mahjong.

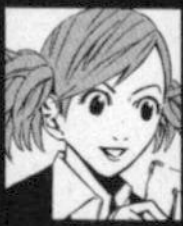

Rika

Third-year at Seinan Gakuin.
An energetic girl who's so talkative that some could find her annoying. She is in love with her homeroom teacher, Sakaki.

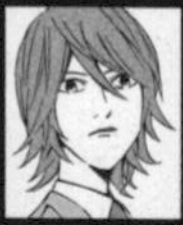

Akihiko

Third-year at Seinan Gakuin.
A cool and collected realist. But he actually has a softhearted side.

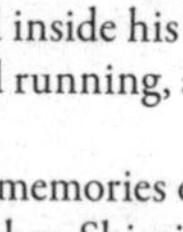

Keiko

Third-year at Seinan Gakuin.
A calm girl with a strangely intimidating air.

Story

On a snowy school day, Takano becomes trapped inside his school building with seven friends. Their phones don't work, the clocks have stopped running, and the other students and teachers are nowhere to be found...

The group is disturbed to realize that their memories of a suicide that occurred at the last school festival have become strangely vague. But then Shimizu proposes a theory:

"What if we're inside the mind of the person who took their own life that day?"

As they hunt for answers, Takano's friends start to disappear from the frozen school one after another. First Mitsuru, then Shimizu...and each time, at the chime of the bell...

Why are they trapped inside the school building? Who was it who took their own life? Determined to escape this nightmarish reality, Takano and Akihiko begin to speculate, and both arrive at the same thought: "It was Mizuki who took her own life. And it was the conflict she had with her best friend, Haruko Tsunoda, that led to it..."

It pains them to implicate their friend. But the school building shows no mercy as the bell rings again...!

A School
Frozen
in Time

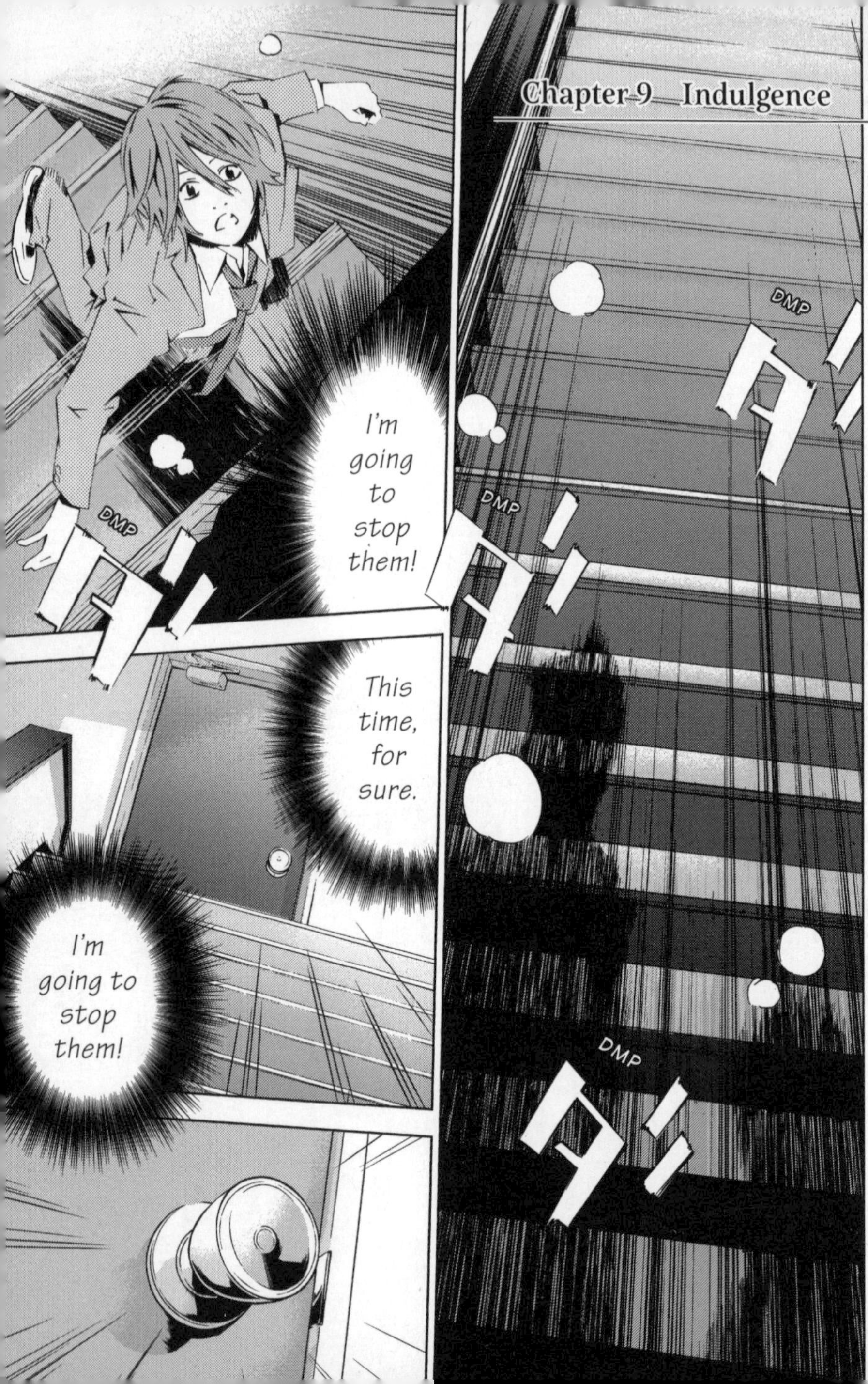
Chapter 9 Indulgence
DMP
DMP
DMP
I'm going to stop them!
DMP
This time, for sure.
I'm going to stop them!

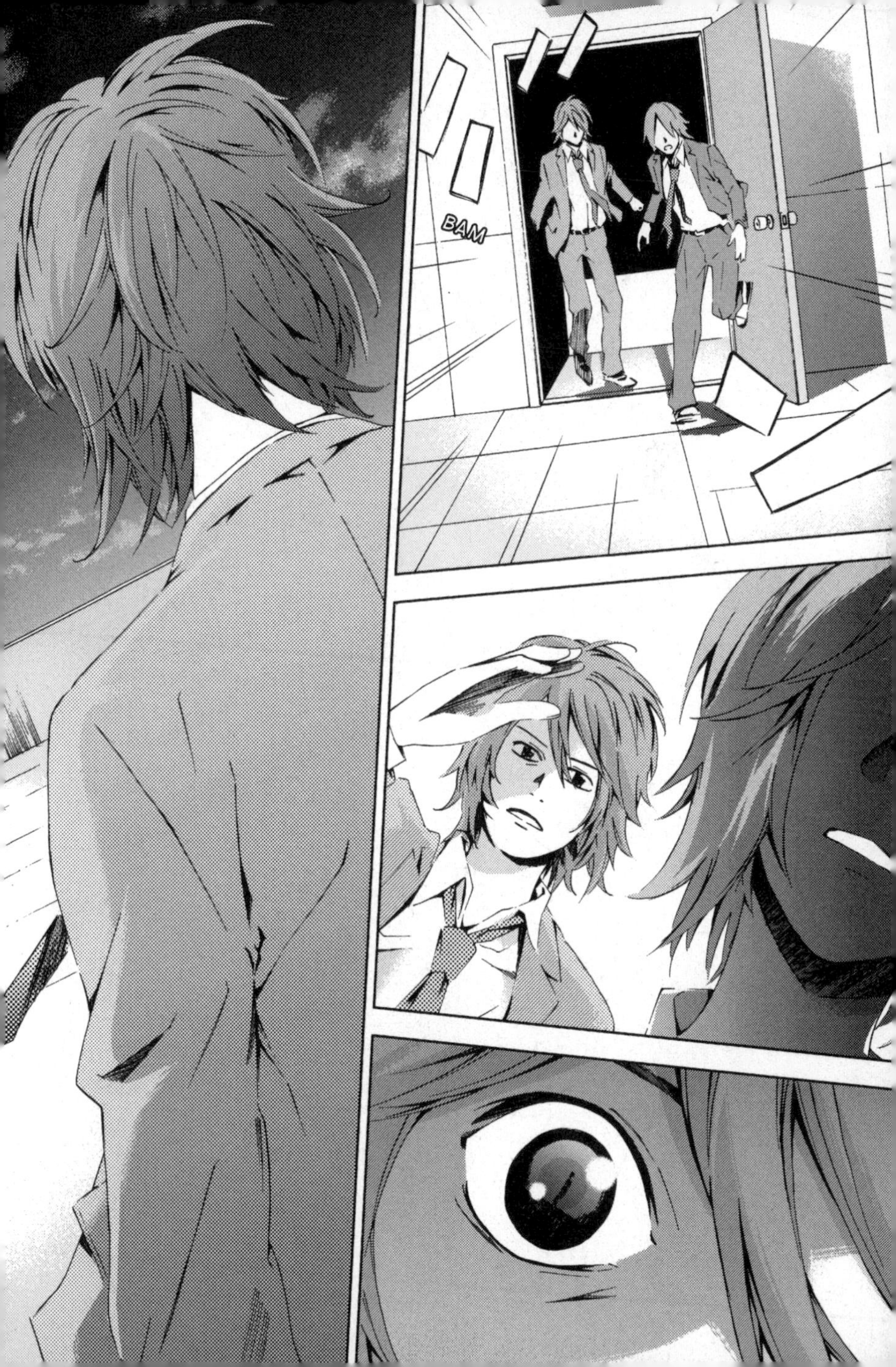
BAM

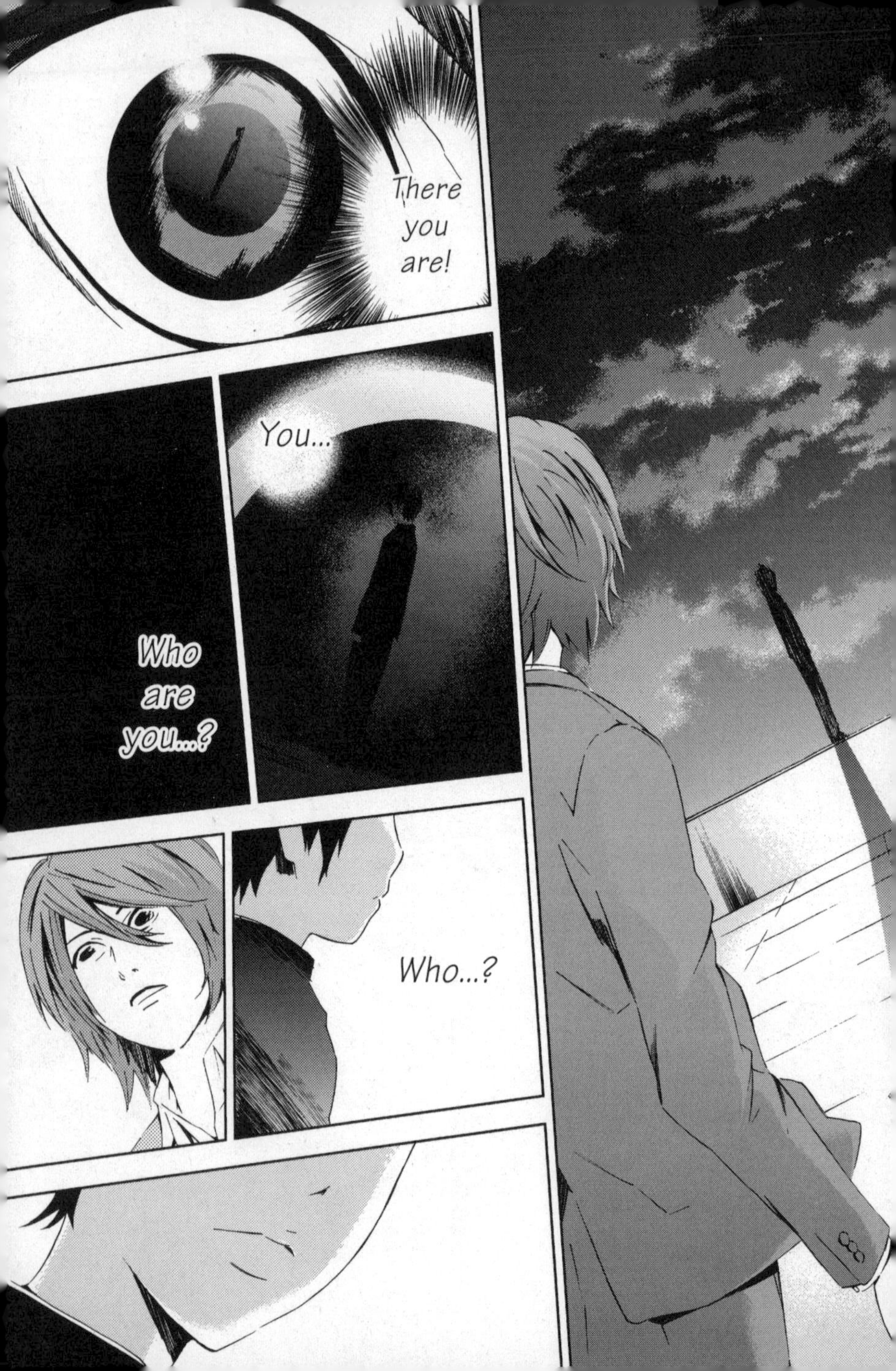
There you are!
You...
Who are you...?
Who...?

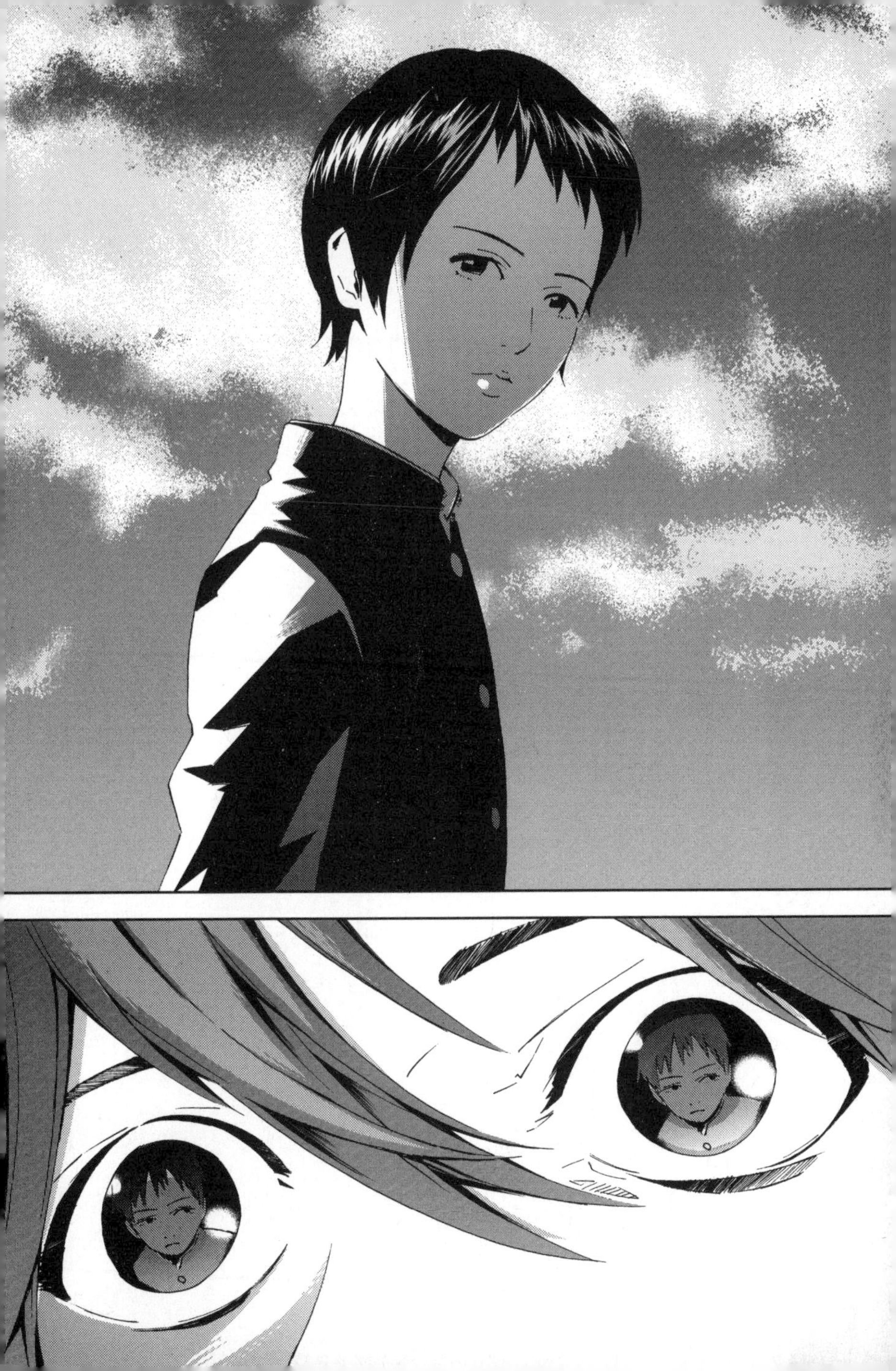

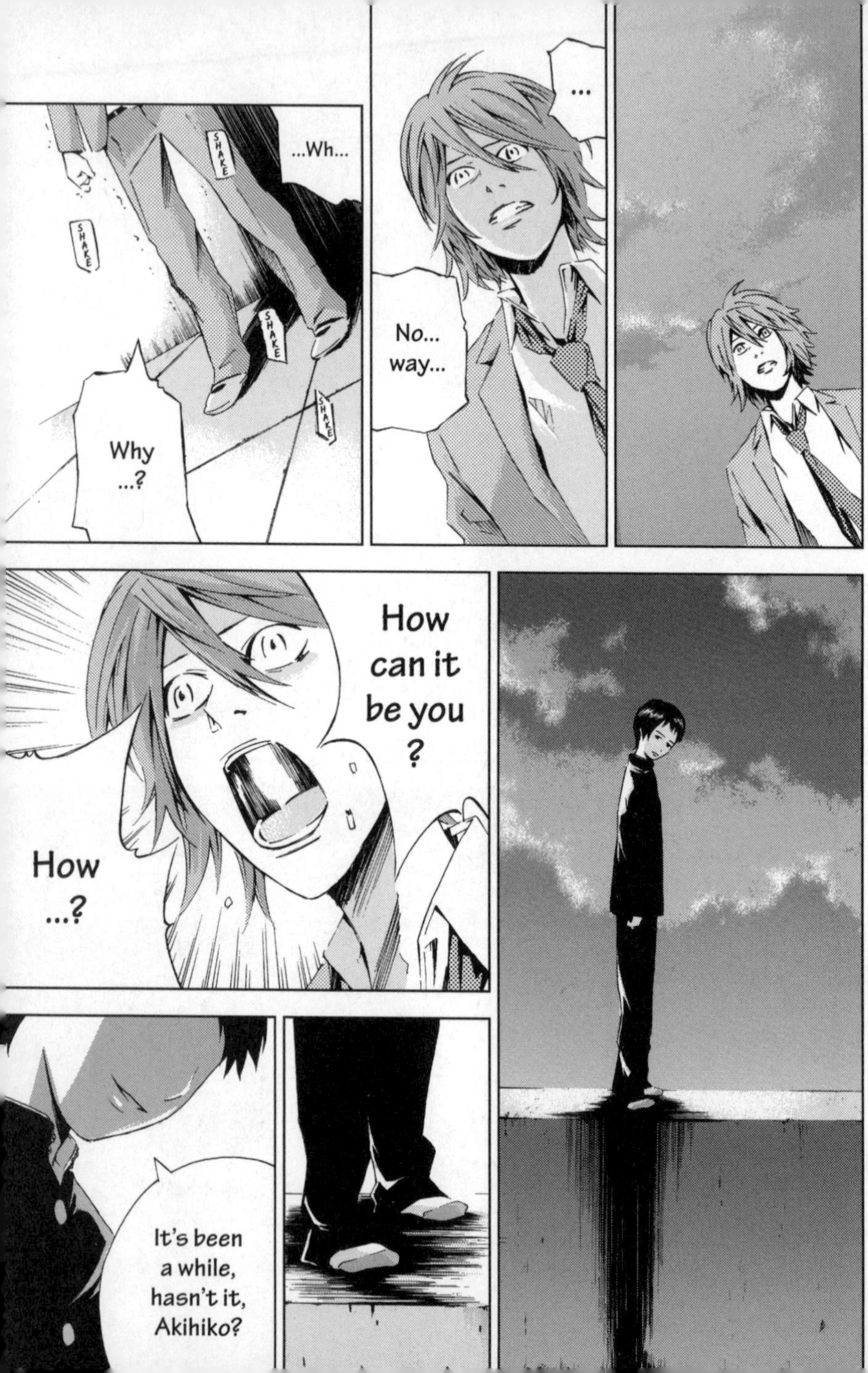
...
No... way...
...Wh...
SHAKE
SHAKE
SHAKE
SHAKE
Why ...?
How can it be you?
How ...?
It's been a while, hasn't it, Akihiko?

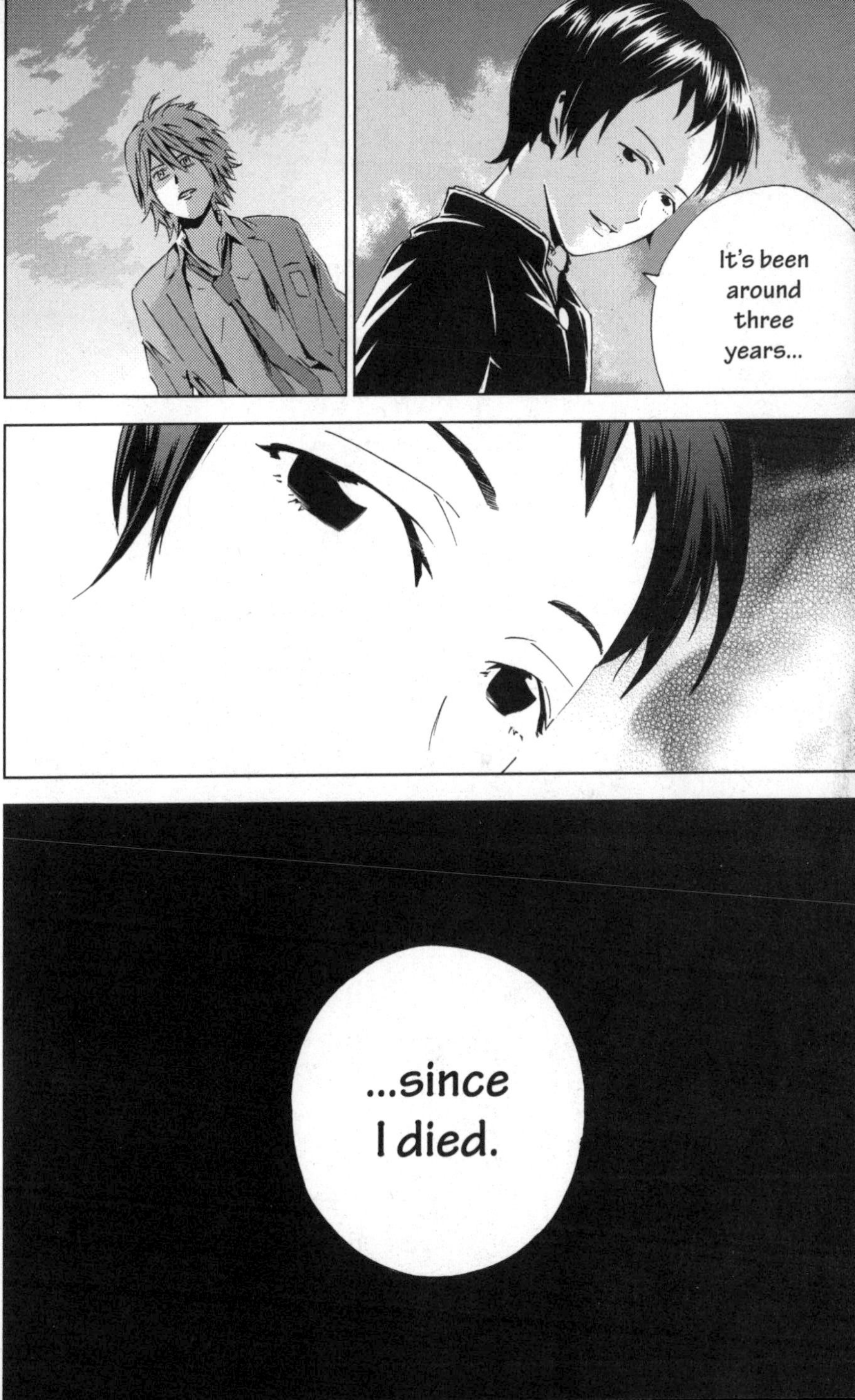
It's been around three years...
...since I died.

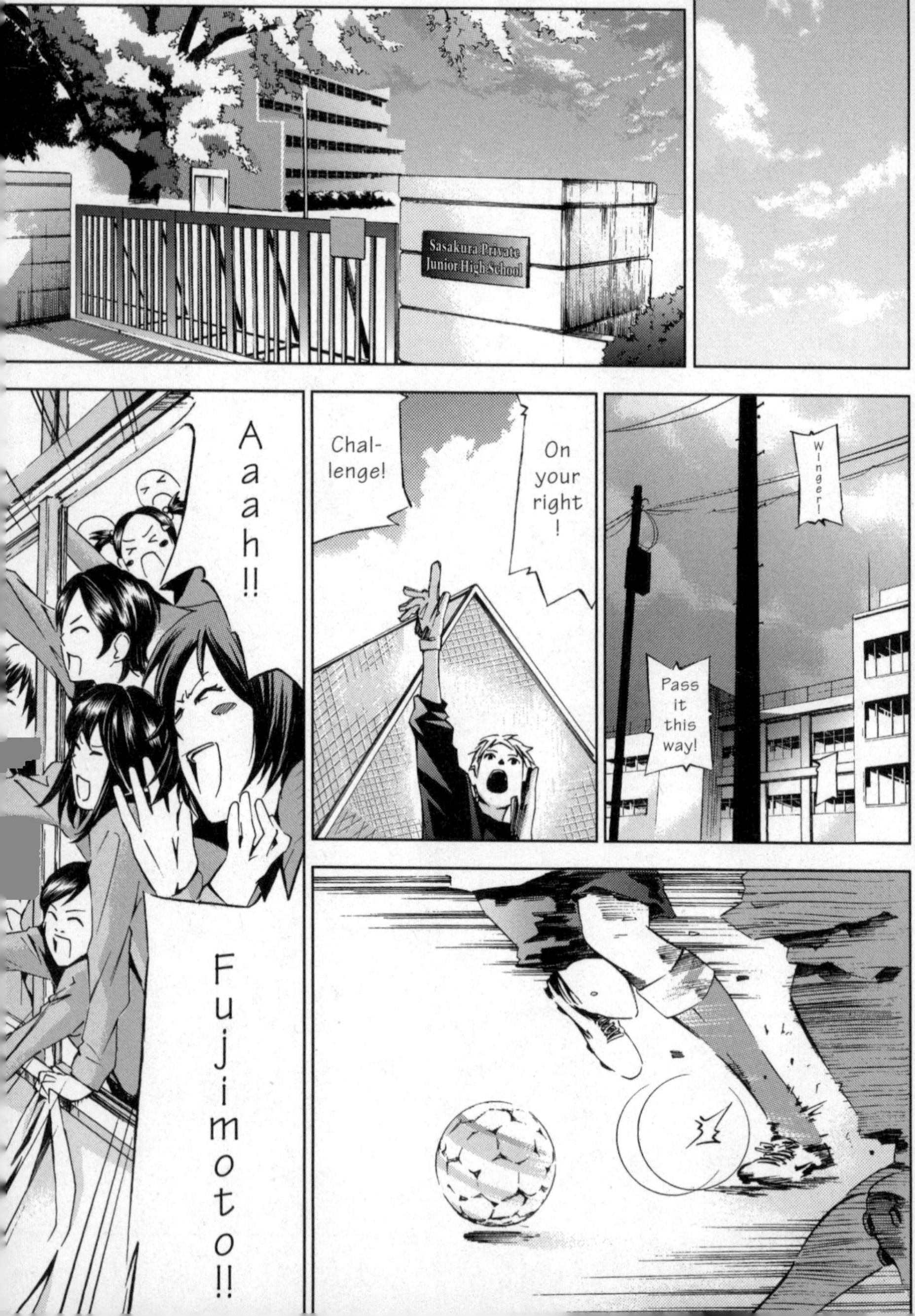
Sasakura Private Junior High School
Winger!
Pass it this way!
On your right!
Challenge!
Aaah!!
Fujimoto!!

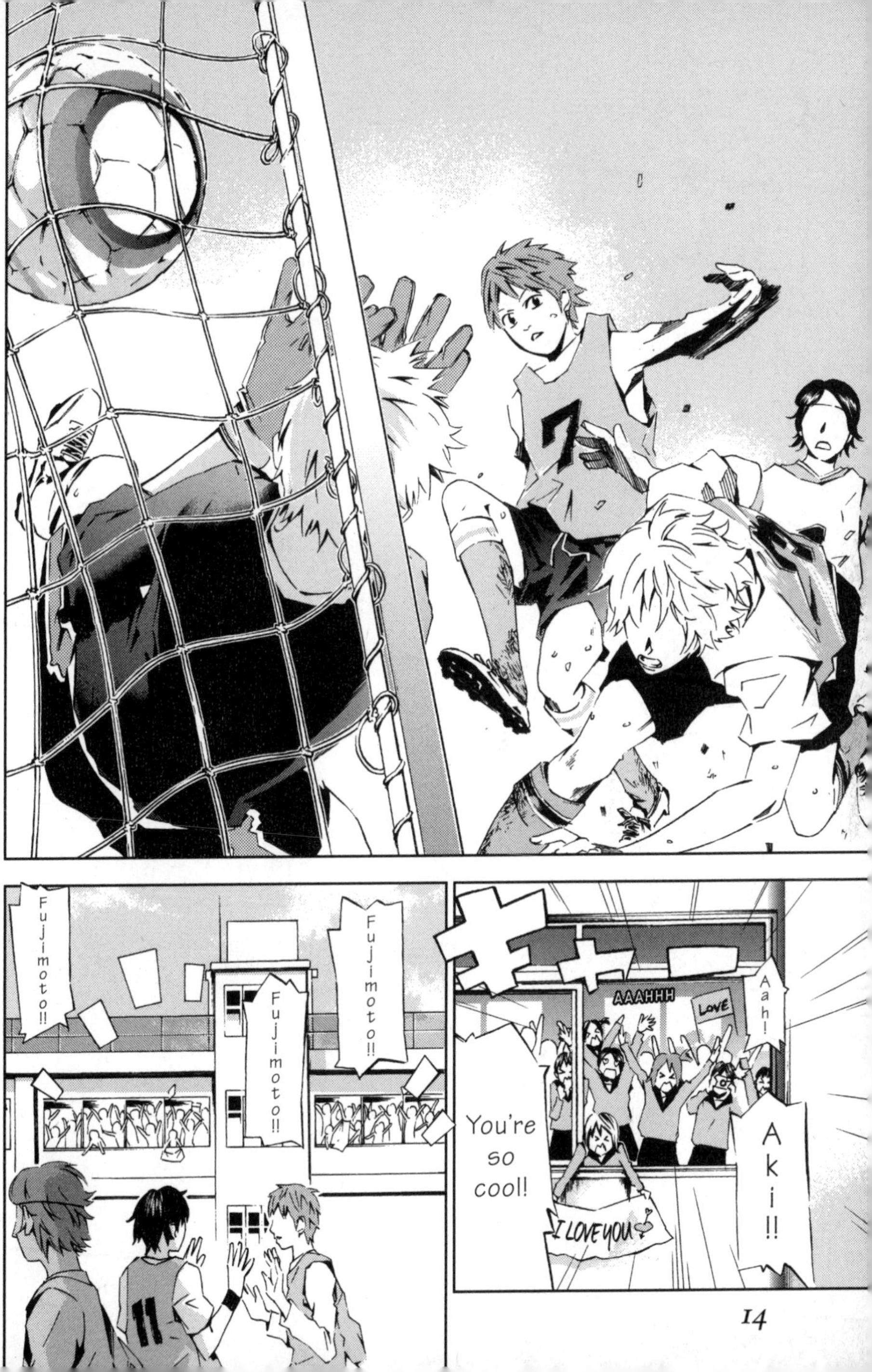
Aah!
AAAHHH
LOVE
Aki!!
You're so cool!
I LOVE YOU
Fujimoto!!
Fujimoto!!
Fujimoto!!

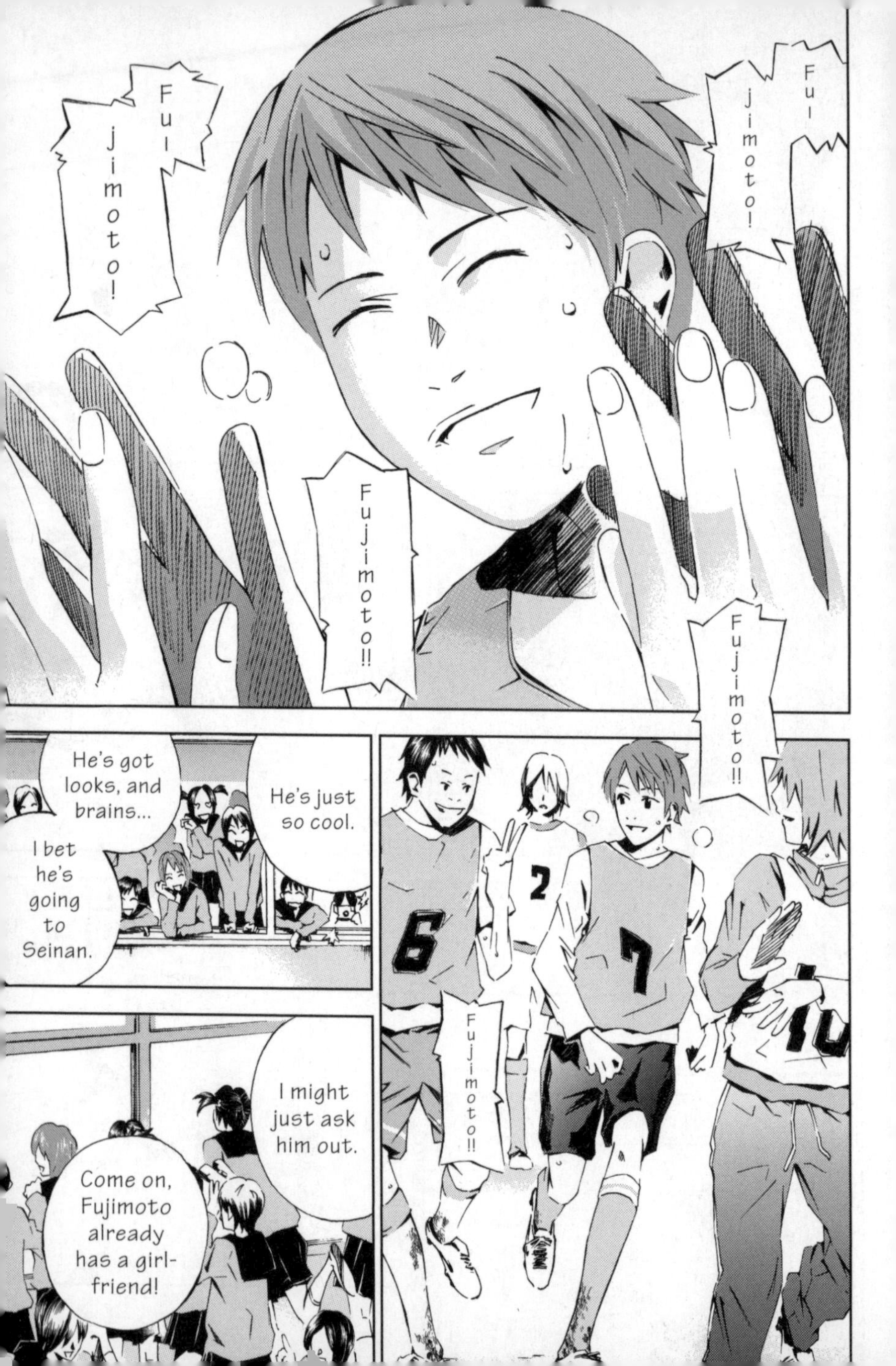
Fu-jimoto!
Fu-jimoto!
Fujimoto!!
Fujimoto!!
Fujimoto!!
He's just so cool.
He's got looks, and brains...
I bet he's going to Seinan.
I might just ask him out.
Come on, Fujimoto already has a girl-friend!

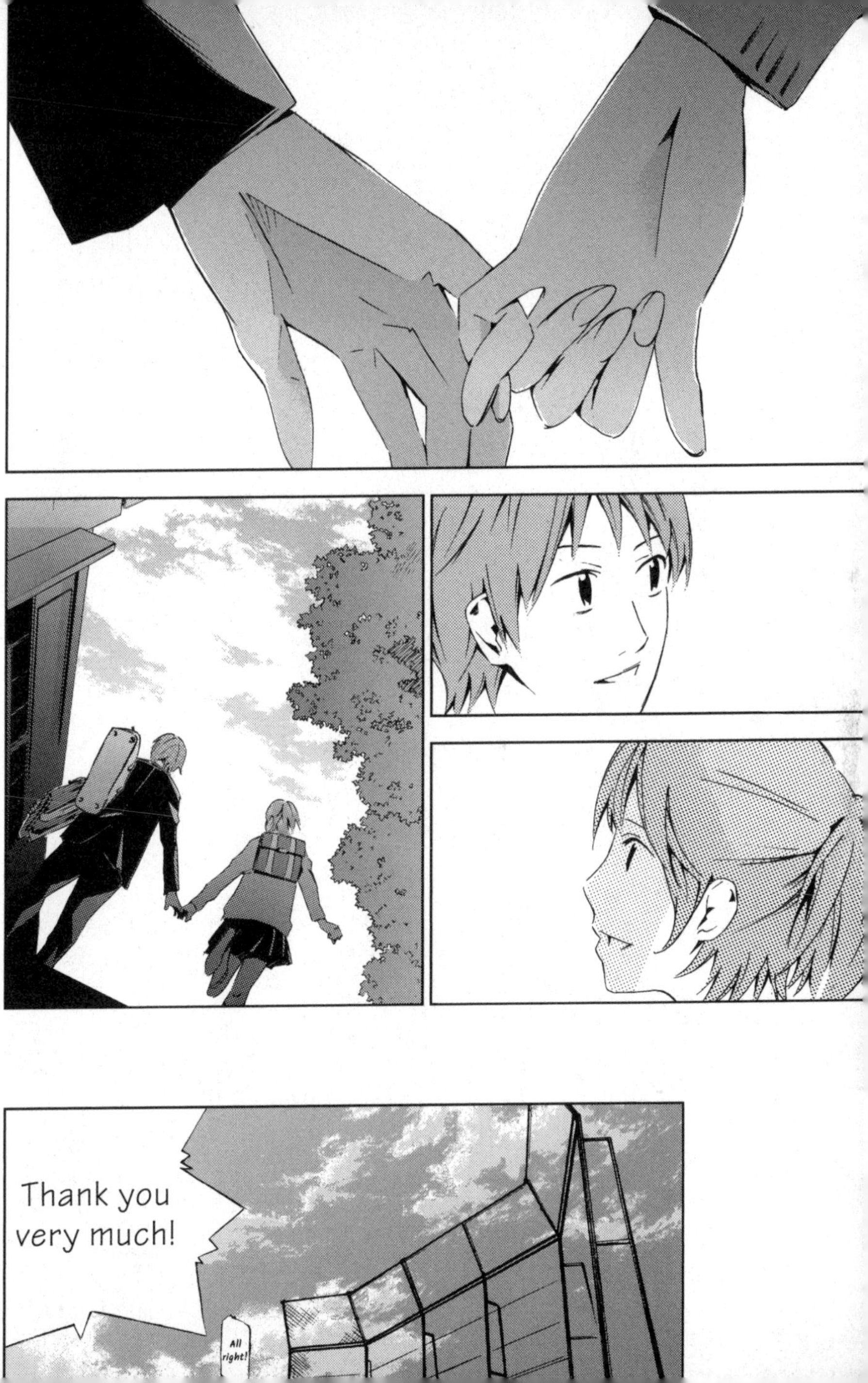
Thank you very much!
All right!

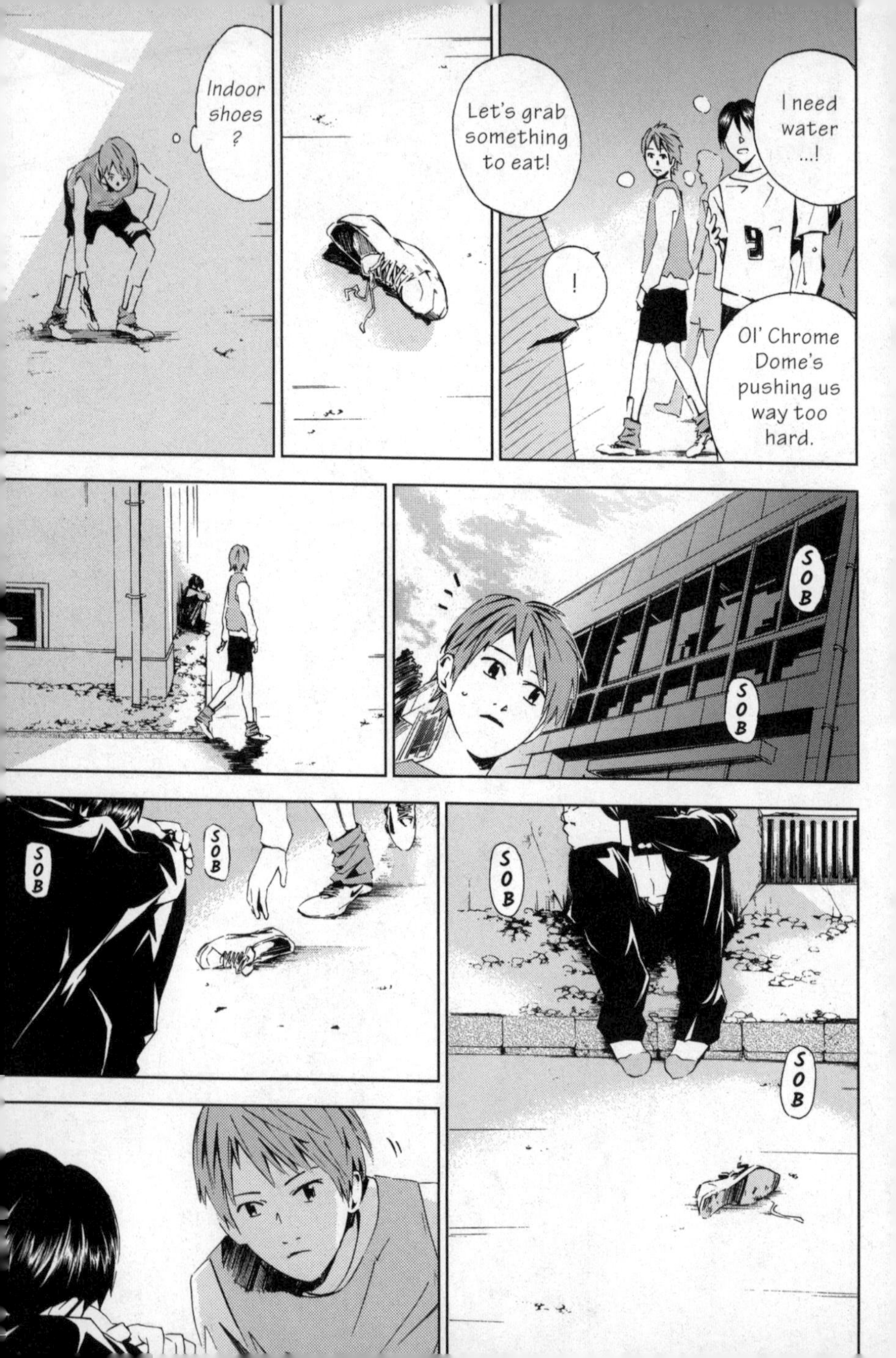
I need water ...!
Let's grab something to eat!
Ol' Chrome Dome's pushing us way too hard.
!
Indoor shoes ?
SOB
SOB
SOB
SOB
SOB
SOB

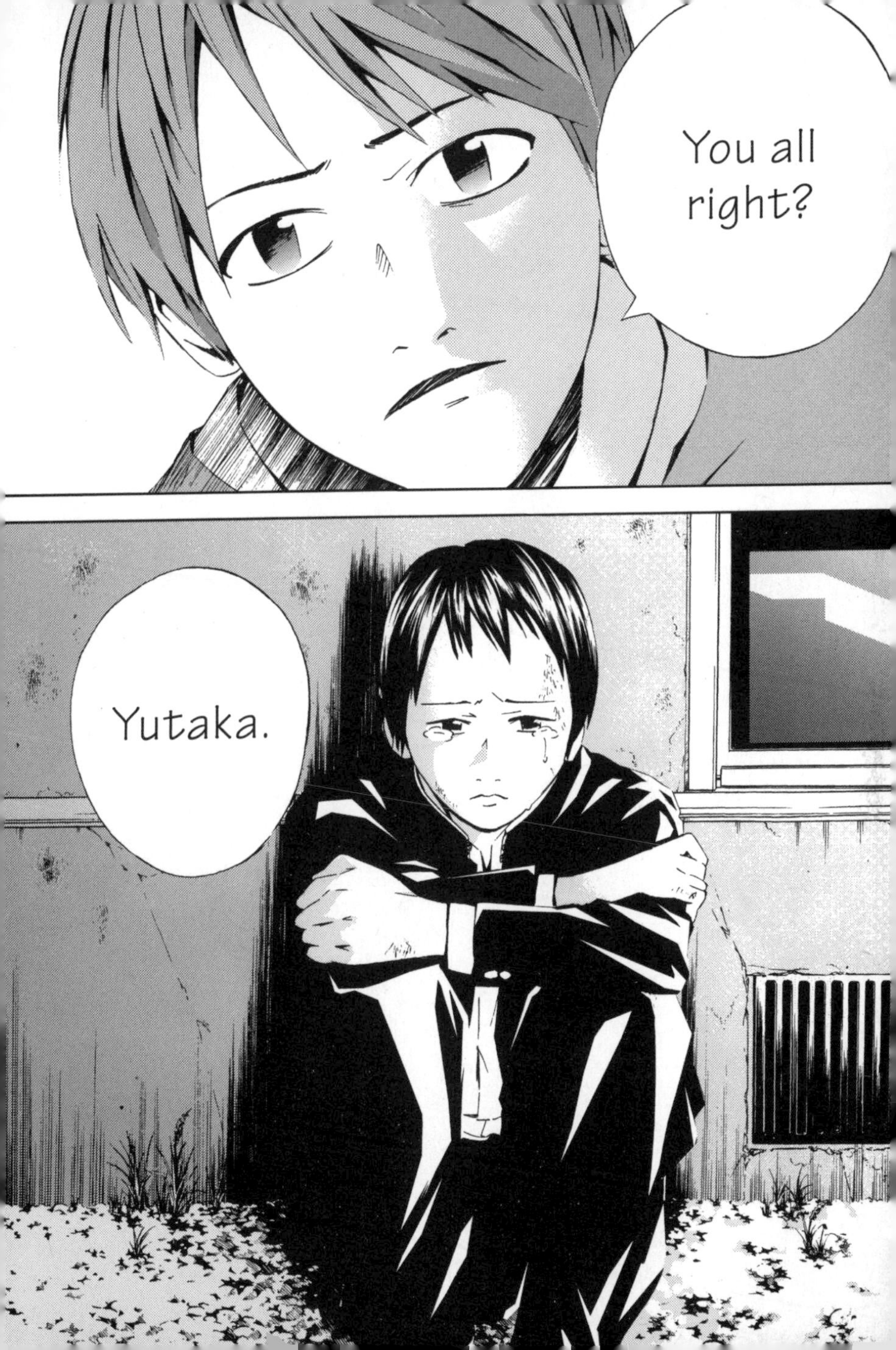
You all right?
Yutaka.

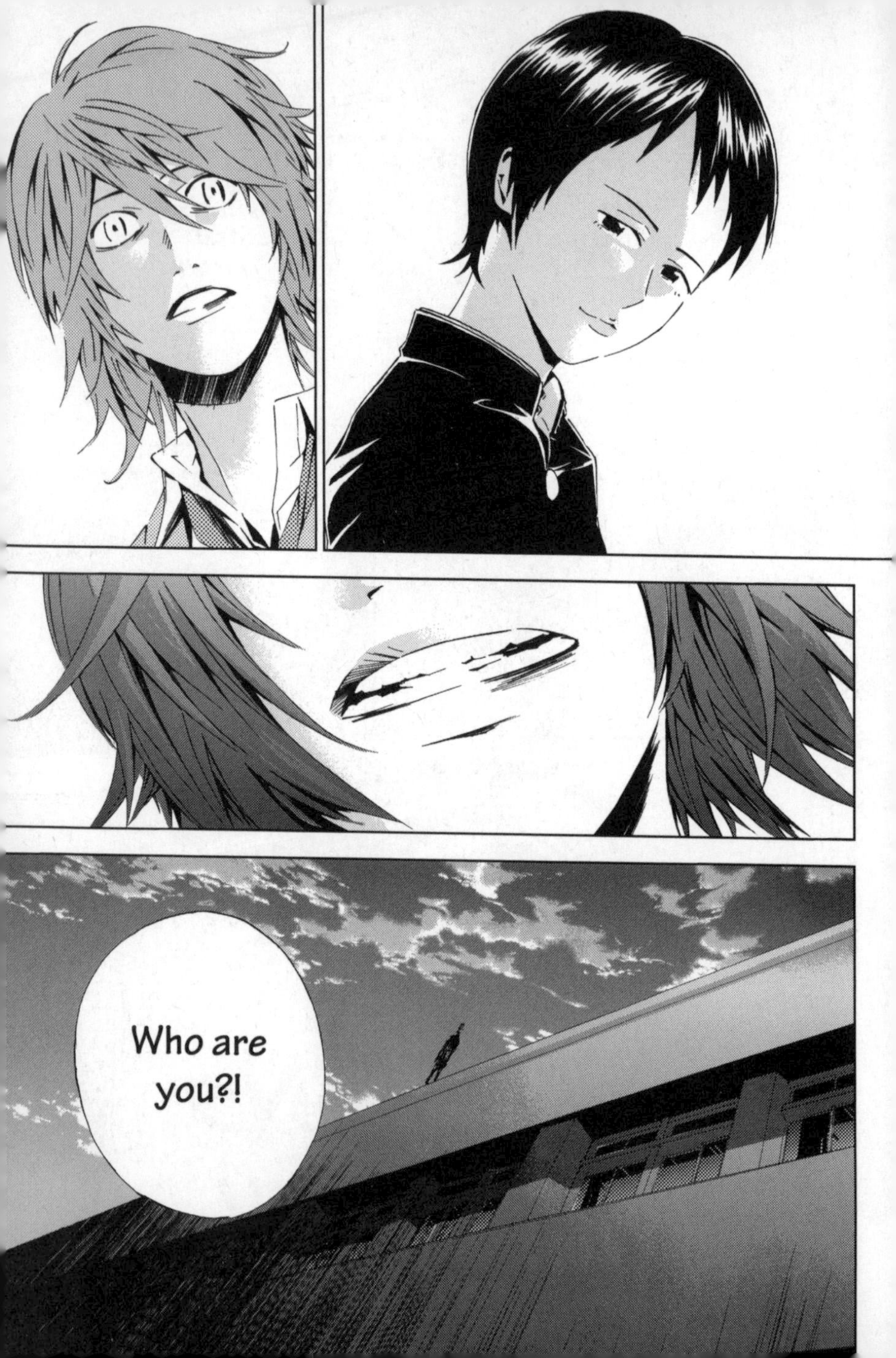
Who are you?!

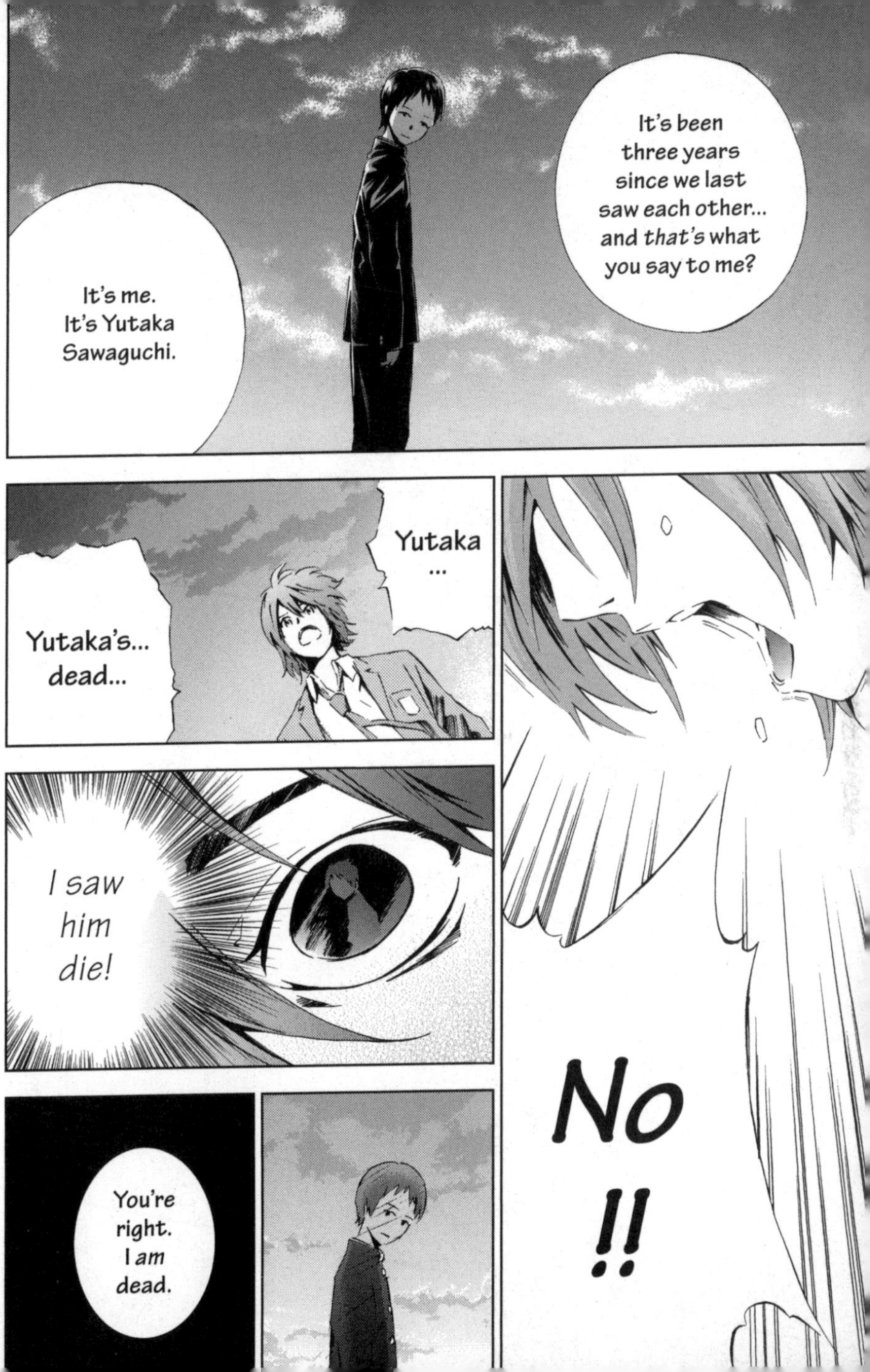
It's been three years since we last saw each other... and *that's* what you say to me?
It's me. It's Yutaka Sawaguchi.
No !!
Yutaka ...
Yutaka's... dead...
I saw him die!
You're right. I am dead.

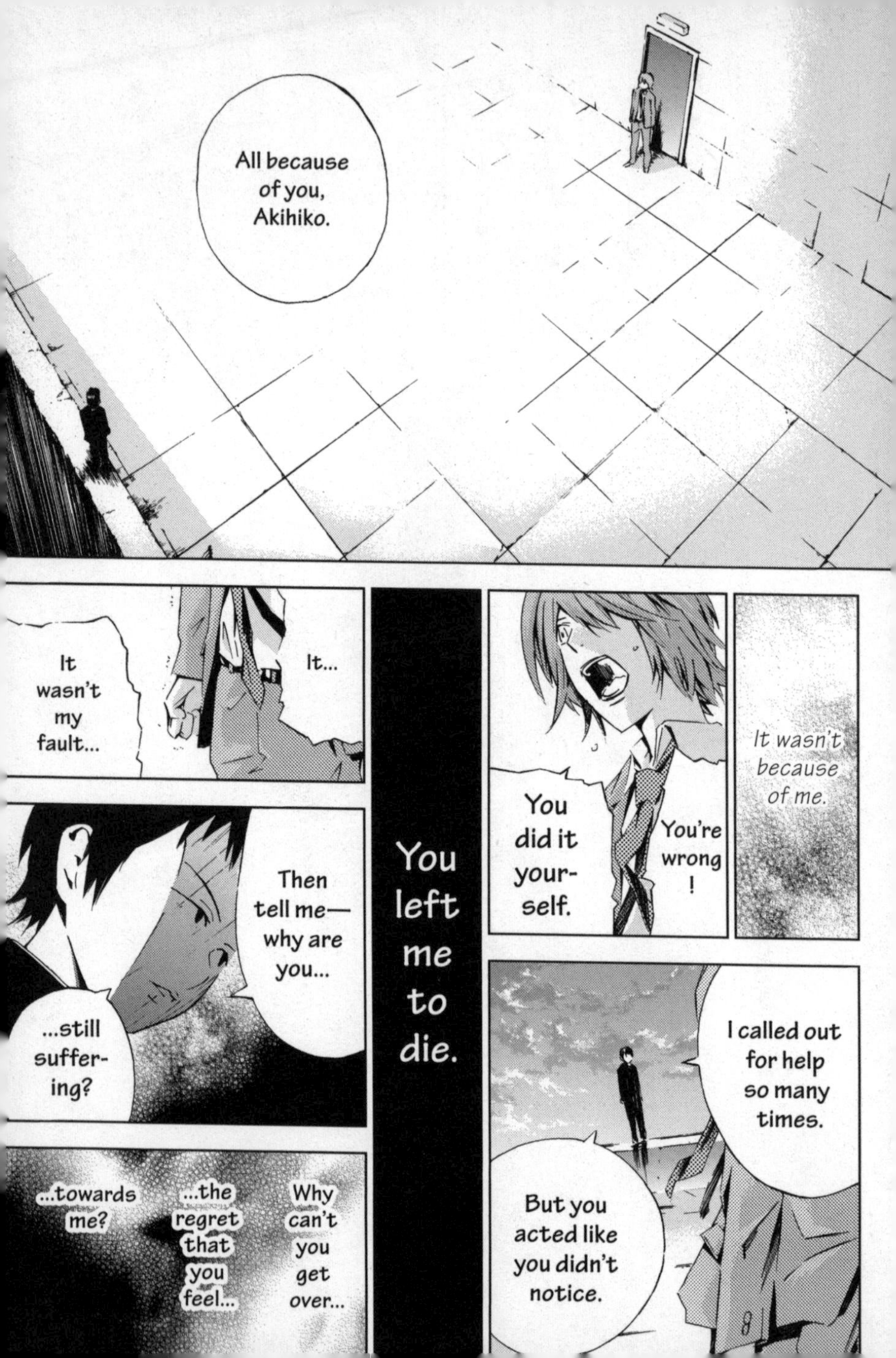

All because of you, Akihiko.
It wasn't because of me.
You're wrong!
You did it yourself.
I called out for help so many times.
But you acted like you didn't notice.
You left me to die.
It...
It wasn't my fault...
Then tell me—why are you...
...still suffering?
Why can't you get over...
...the regret that you feel...
...towards me?

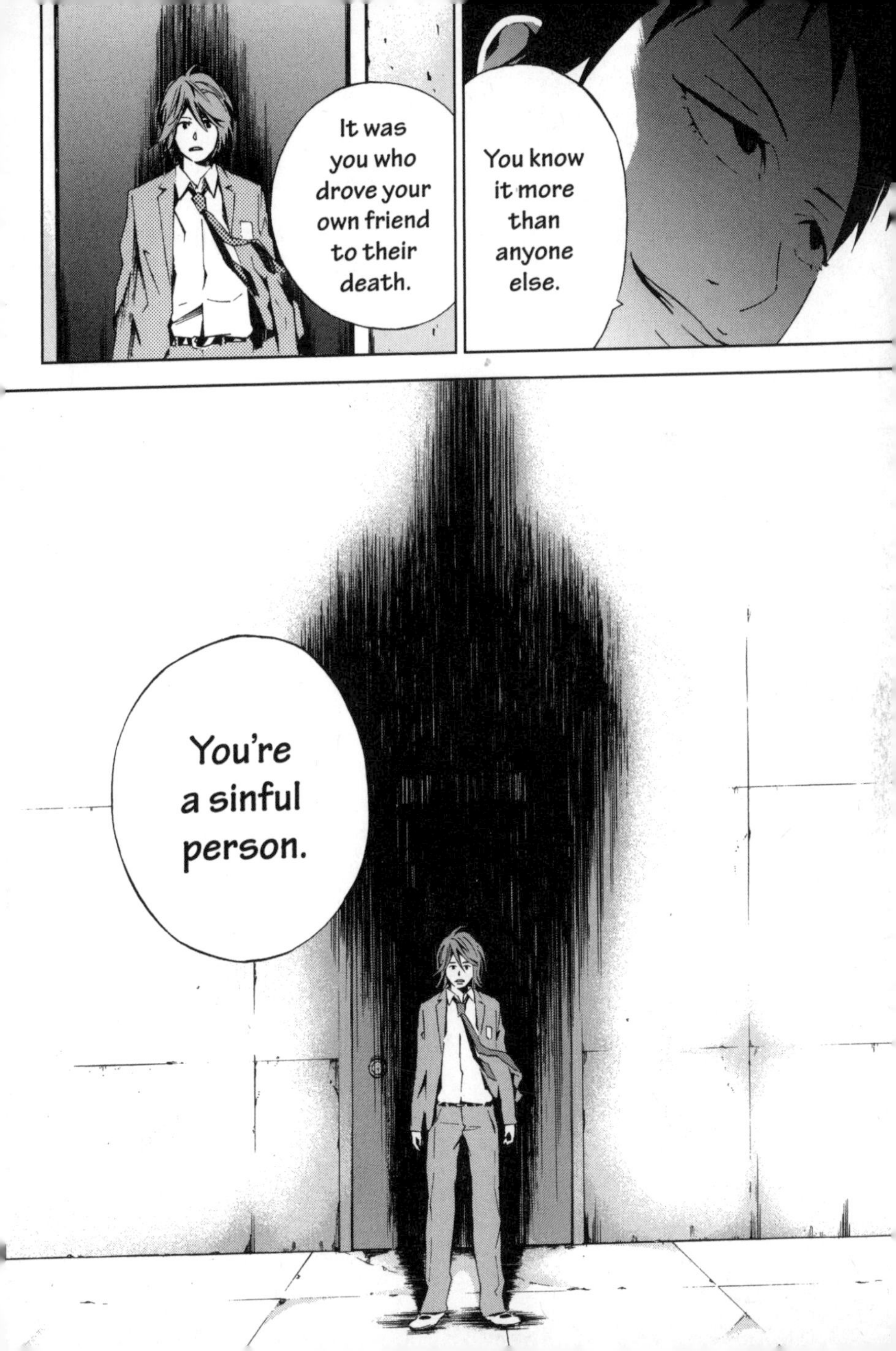
You know it more than anyone else.
It was you who drove your own friend to their death.
You're a sinful person.

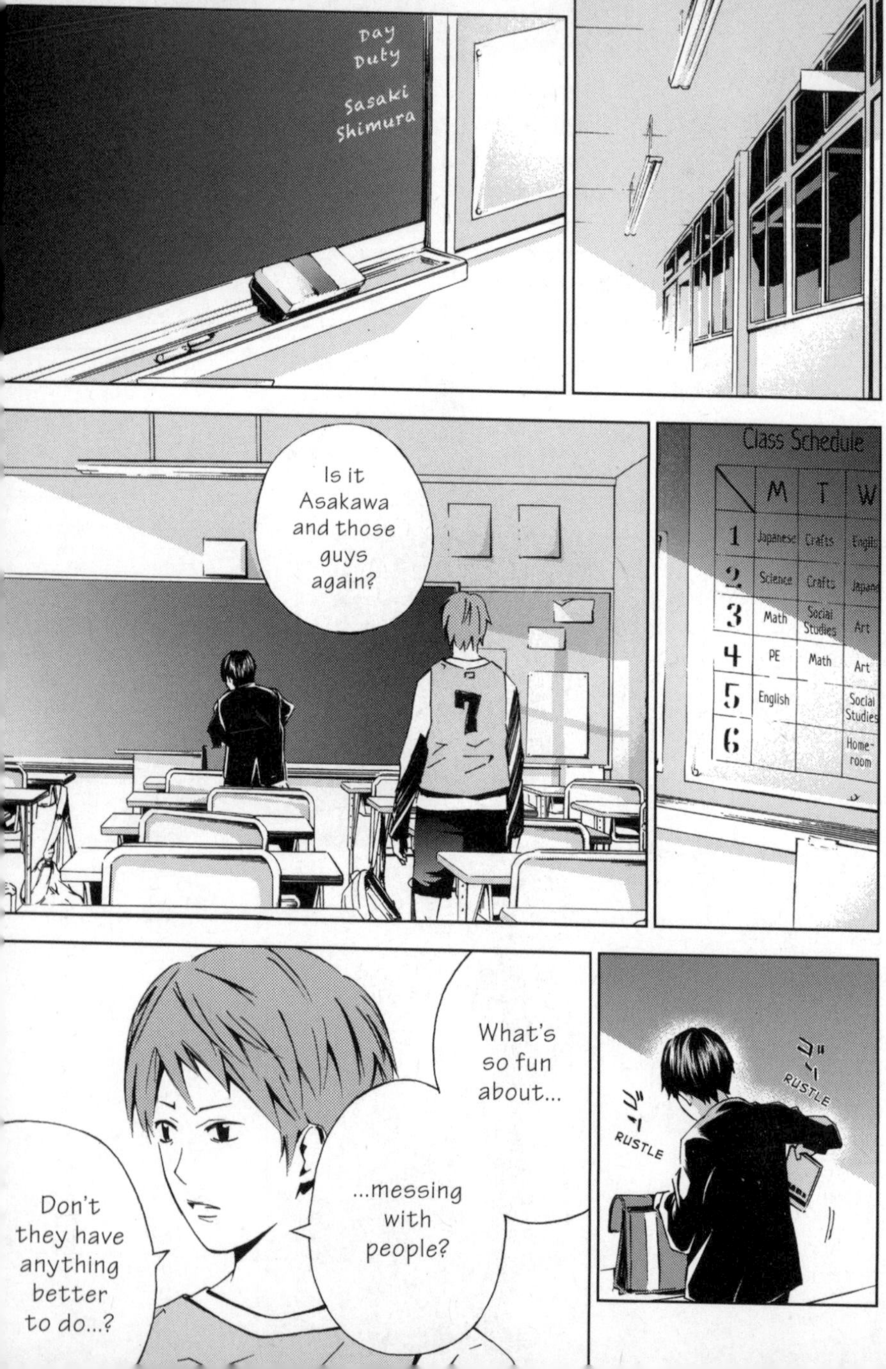
Day Duty
Sasaki
Shimura
Class Schedule
M T W
1 Japanese Crafts
2 Science Crafts
3 Math Social Studies Art
4 PE Math Art
5 English Social Studies
6 Home-room
Is it Asakawa and those guys again?
RUSTLE
RUSTLE
What's so fun about...
...messing with people?
Don't they have anything better to do...?

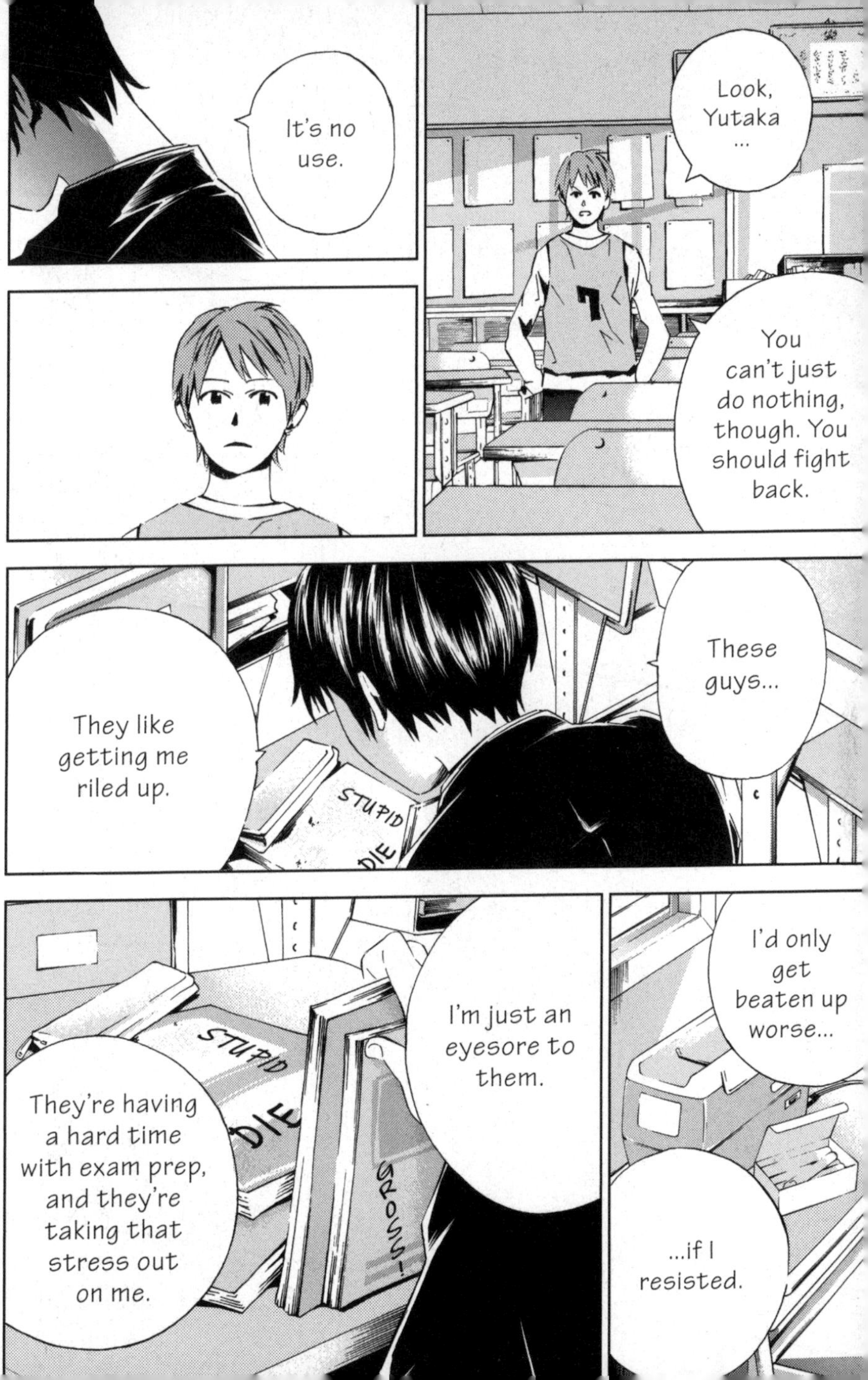

Look, Yutaka ...
You can't just do nothing, though. You should fight back.
It's no use.
These guys...
They like getting me riled up.
STUPID
DIE
I'd only get beaten up worse...
...if I resisted.
I'm just an eyesore to them.
They're having a hard time with exam prep, and they're taking that stress out on me.
STUPID
DIE
GROSS!

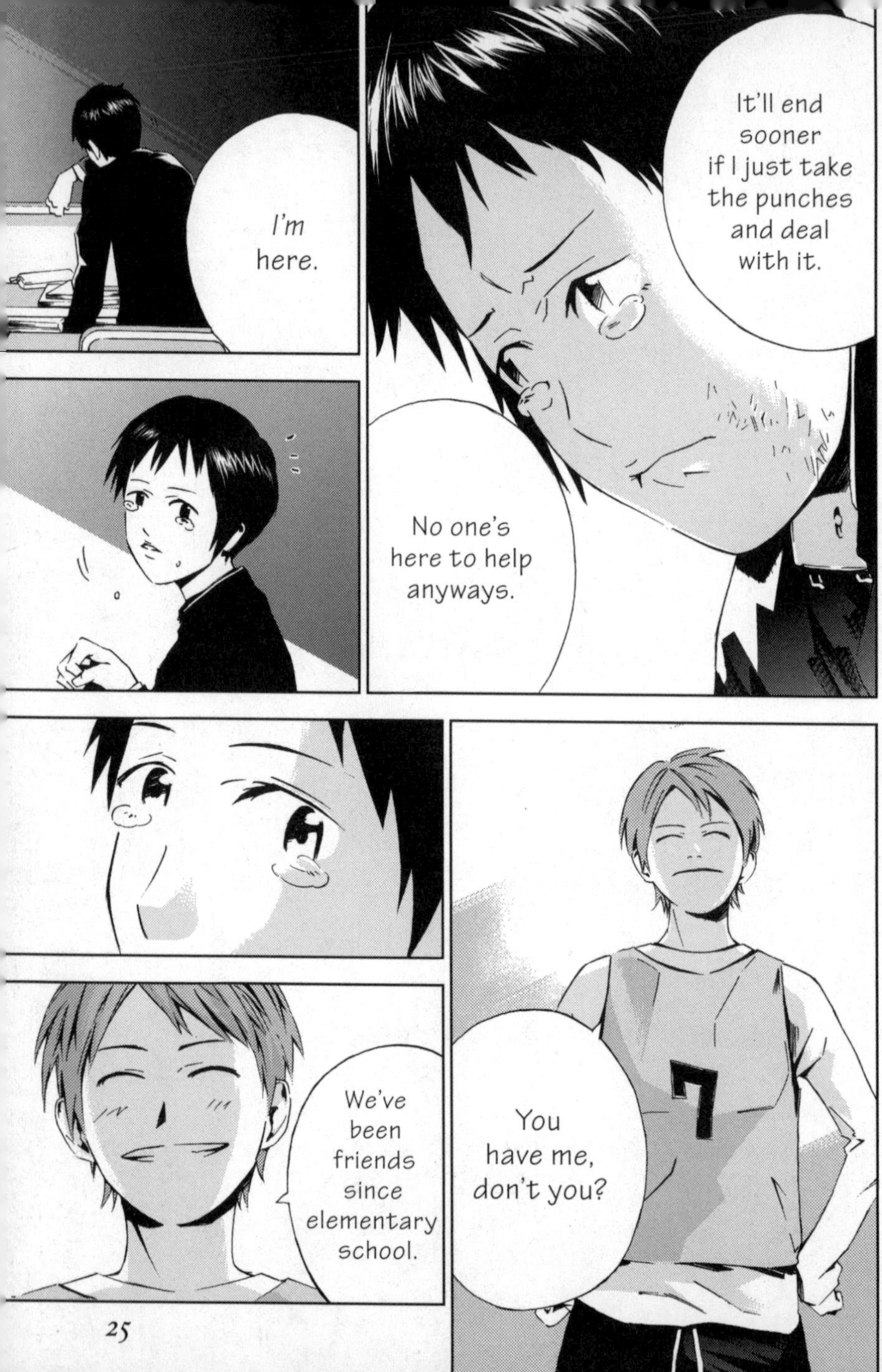
It'll end sooner if I just take the punches and deal with it.
No one's here to help anyways.
I'm here.
You have me, don't you?
We've been friends since elementary school.

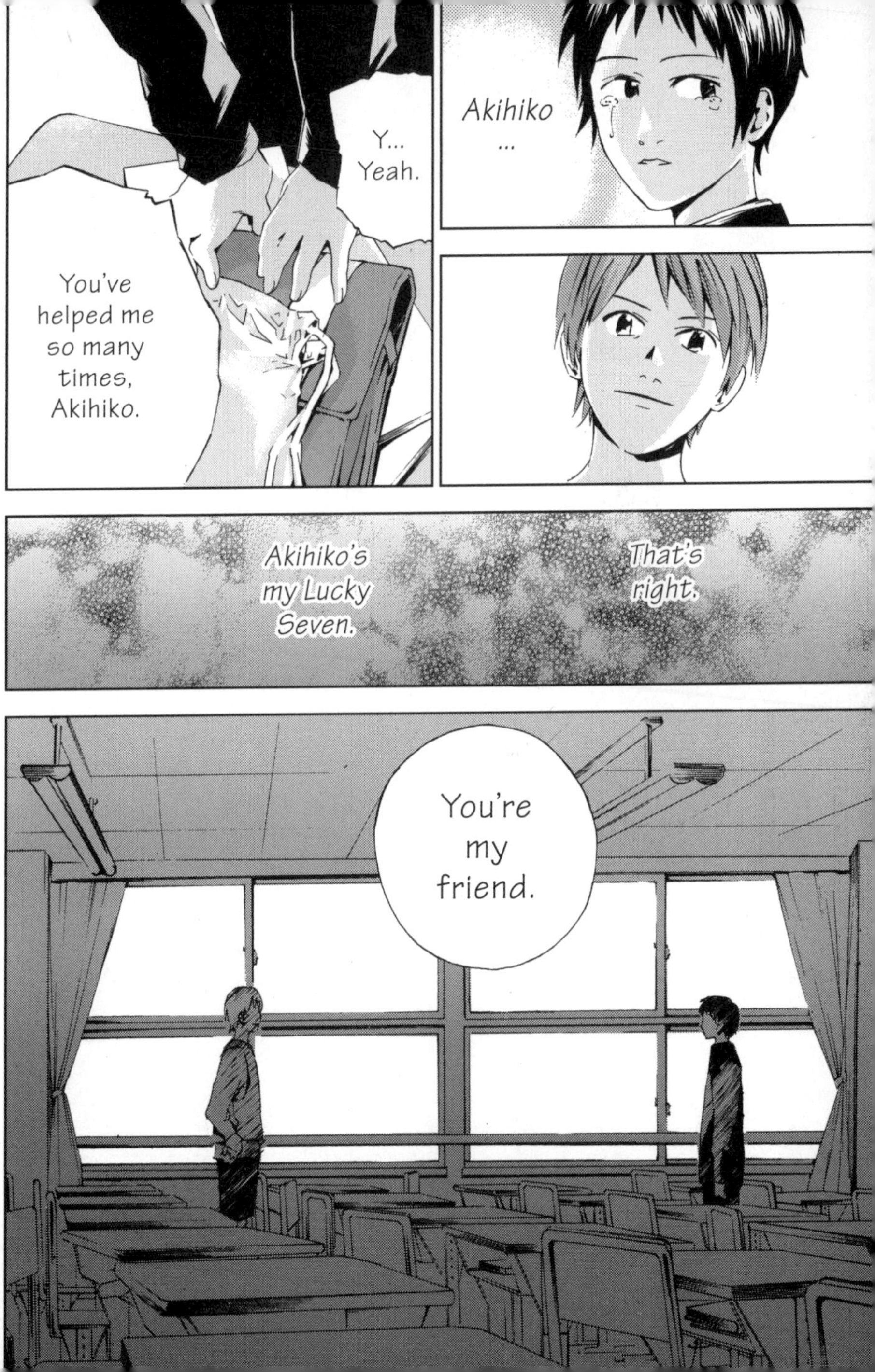
Akihiko ...
Y... Yeah.
You've helped me so many times, Akihiko.
That's right.
Akihiko's my Lucky Seven.
You're my friend.

BWAM

What an idiot!

I'm sorry!

I'm sorry!

Unghh!

Ha ha ha

This is the kind of bread you buy for us?!

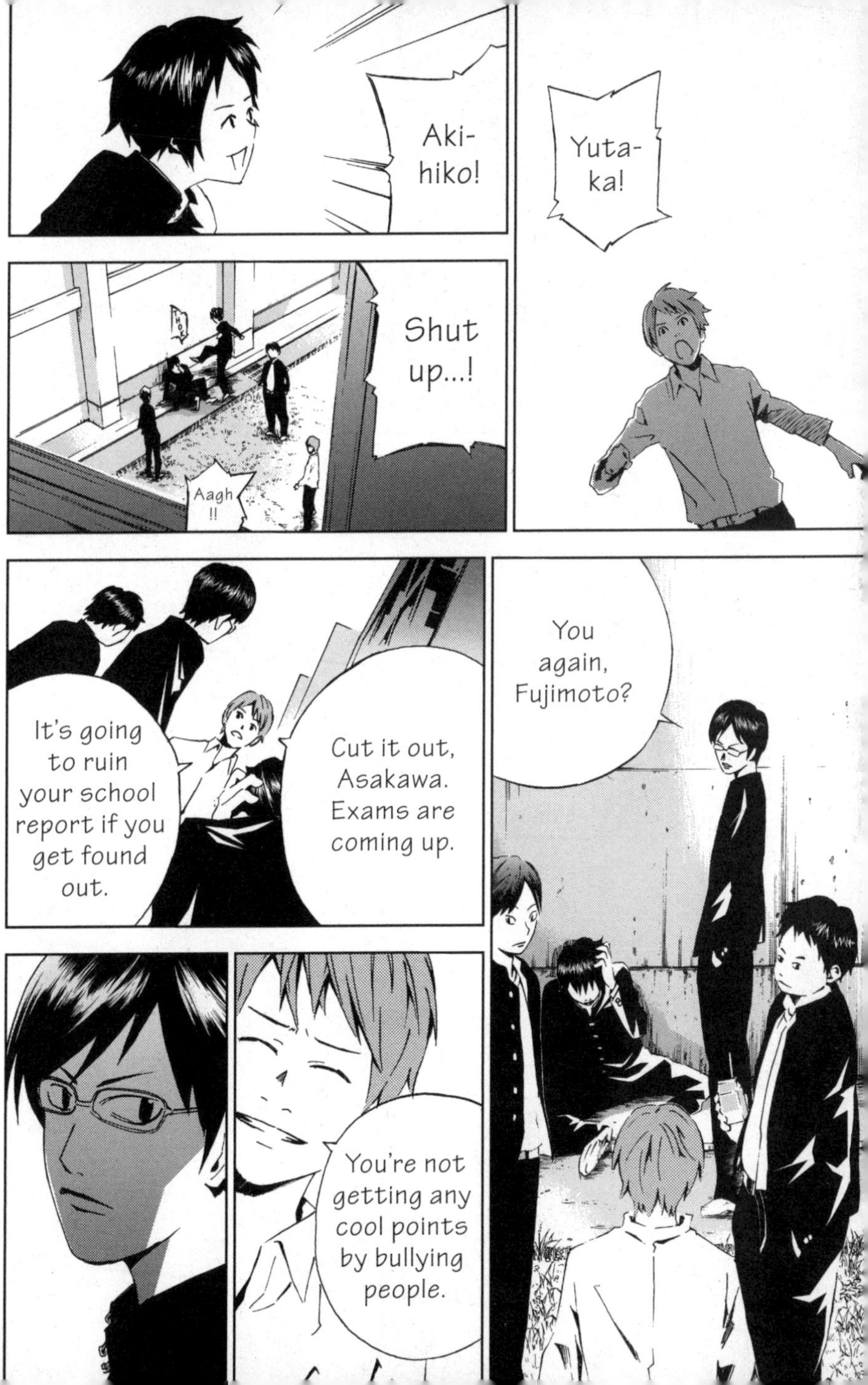
Yutaka!
Akihiko!
Shut up...!
Aagh !!
You again, Fujimoto?
Cut it out, Asakawa. Exams are coming up.
It's going to ruin your school report if you get found out.
You're not getting any cool points by bullying people.

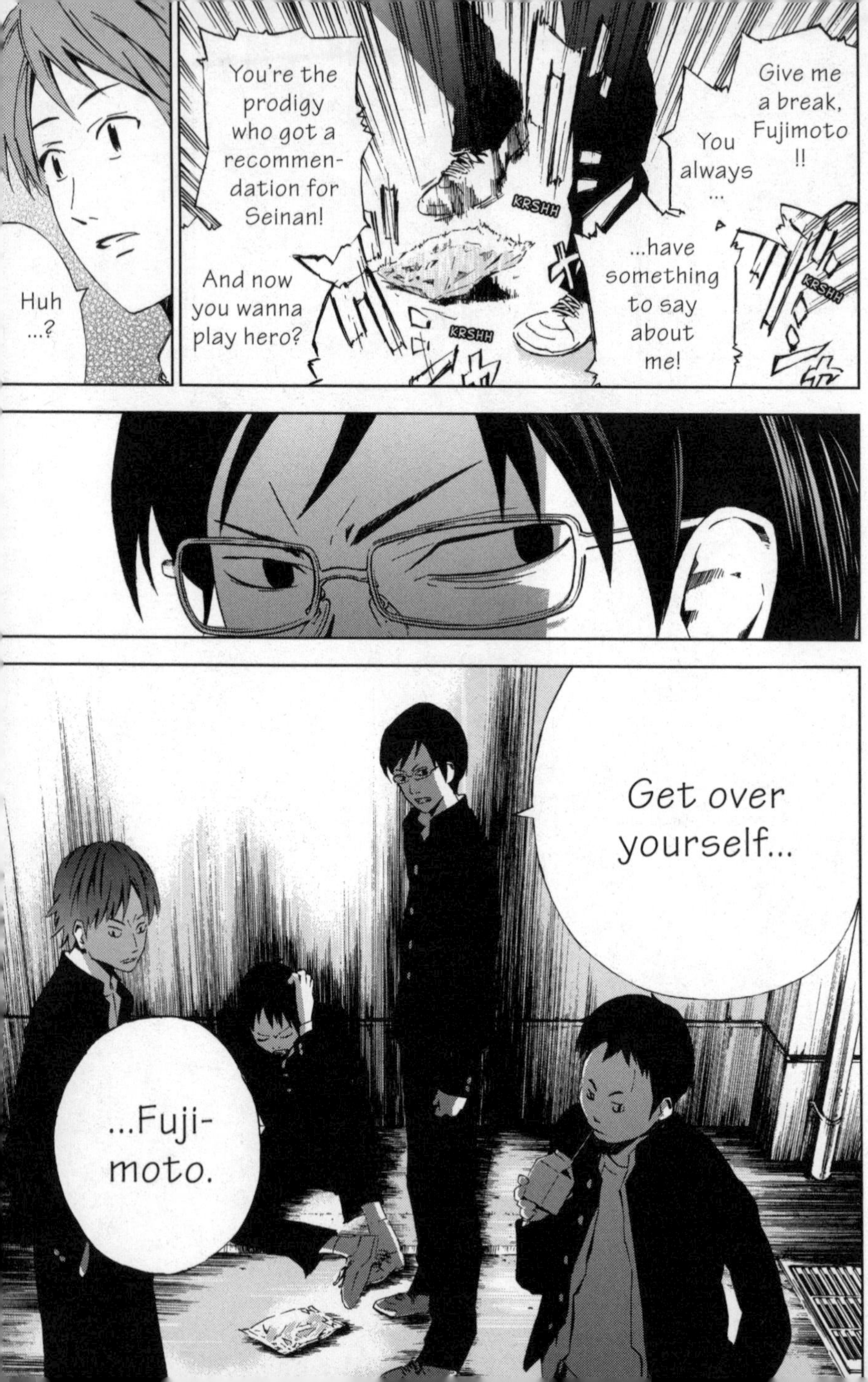
Give me a break, Fujimoto!!
You always...
...have something to say about me!
KRSHH
You're the prodigy who got a recommendation for Seinan!
KRSHH
And now you wanna play hero?
KRSHH
Huh...?
Get over yourself...
...Fuji-moto.

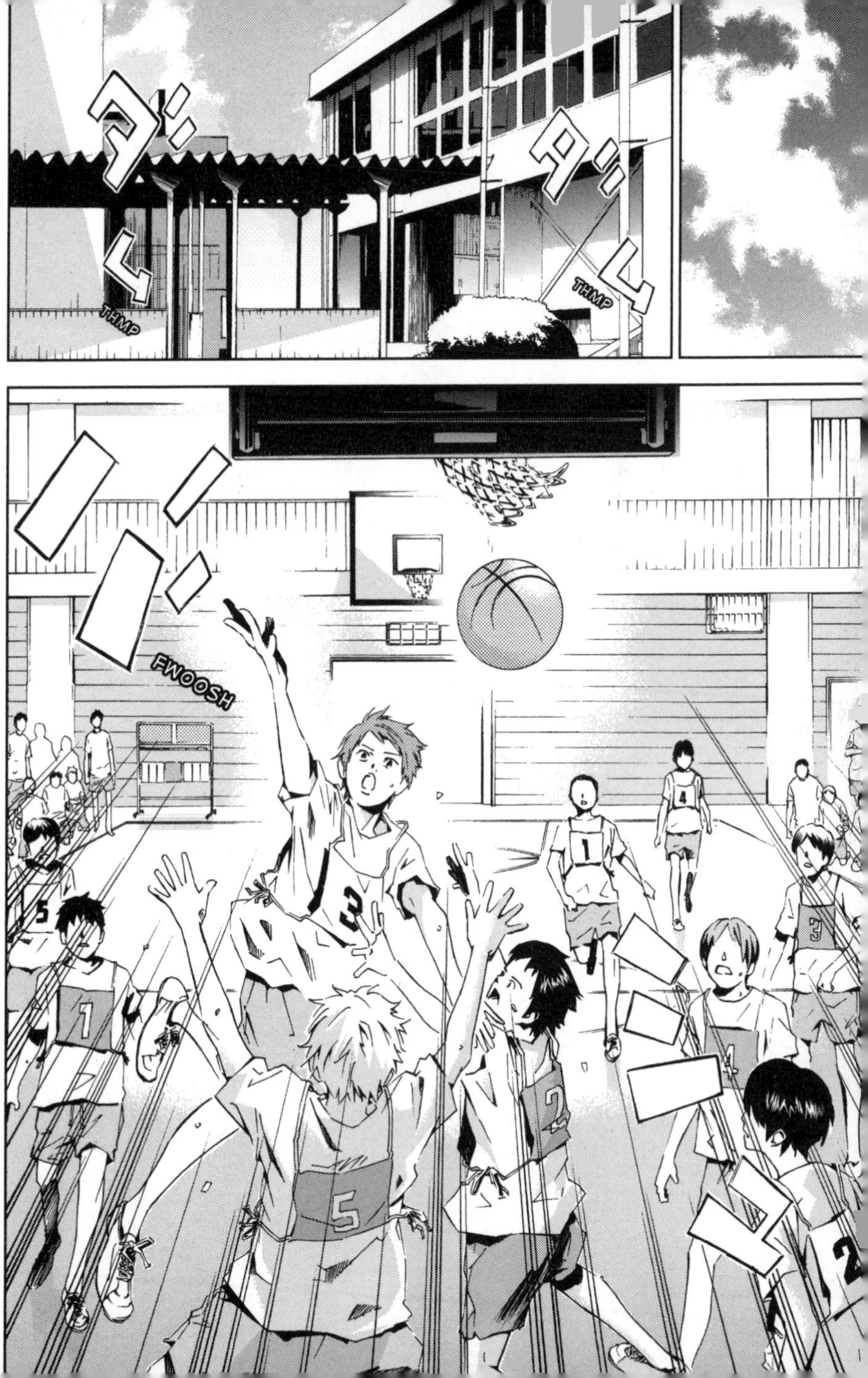
THMP
THMP
FWOOSH

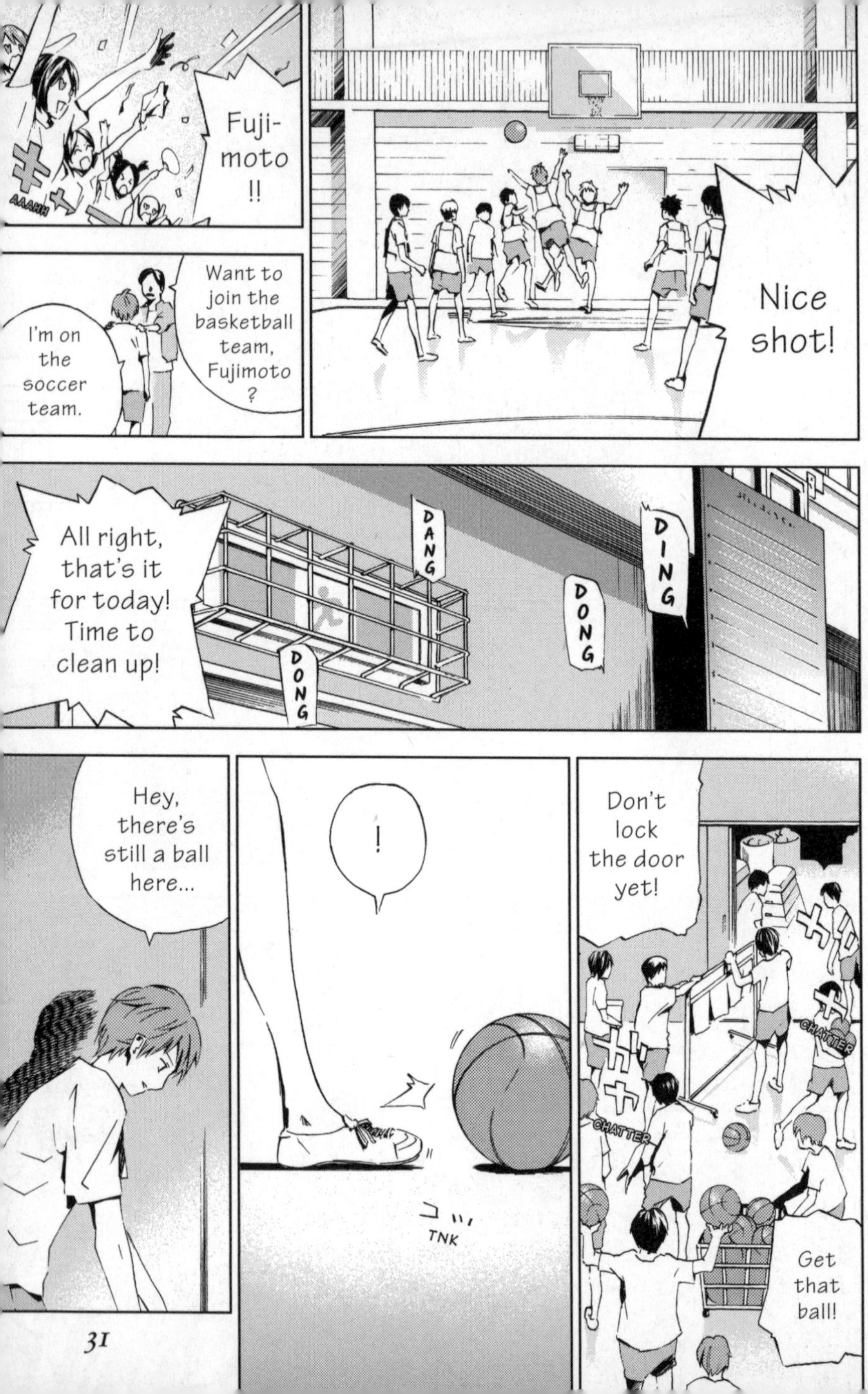
Nice shot!
Fuji-moto !!
AAAHH
Want to join the basketball team, Fujimoto?
I'm on the soccer team.
DING
DONG
DANG
DONG
All right, that's it for today! Time to clean up!
Don't lock the door yet!
CHATTER
CHATTER
Get that ball!
!
TNK
Hey, there's still a ball here...

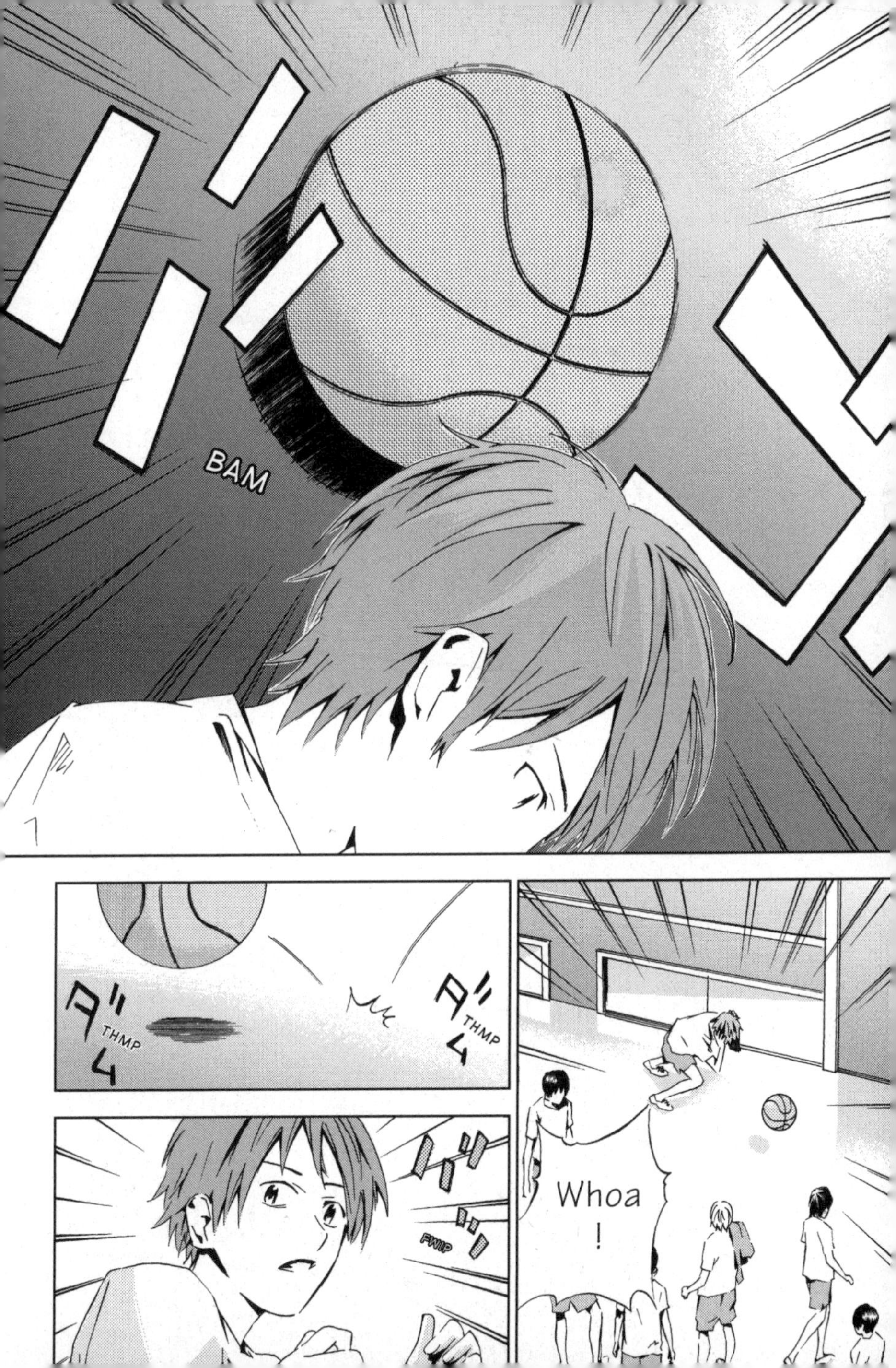
BAM
Whoa!
THMP
THMP
FWIP

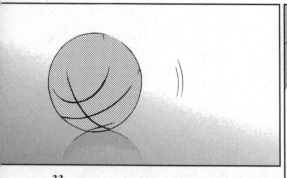

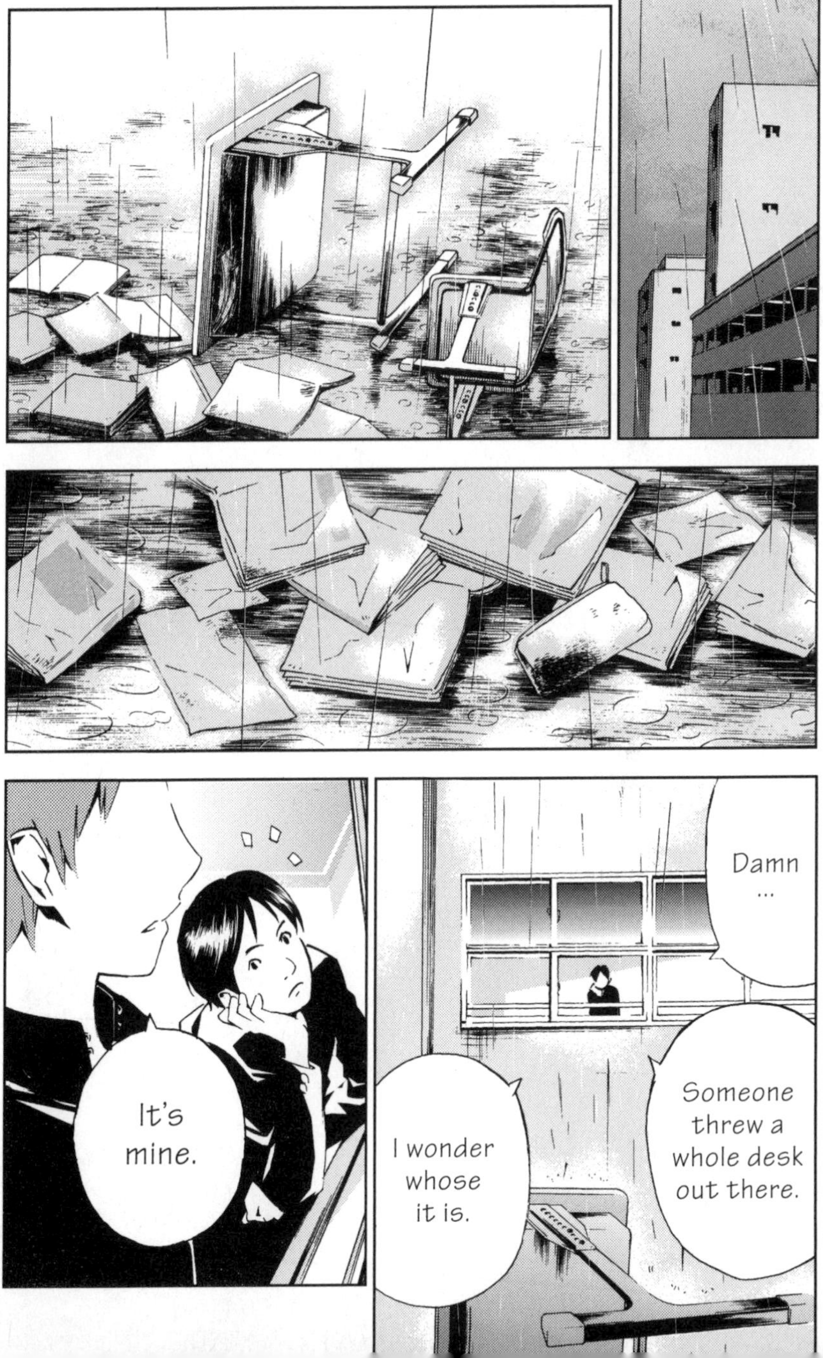
Damn ...
Someone threw a whole desk out there.
I wonder whose it is.
It's mine.

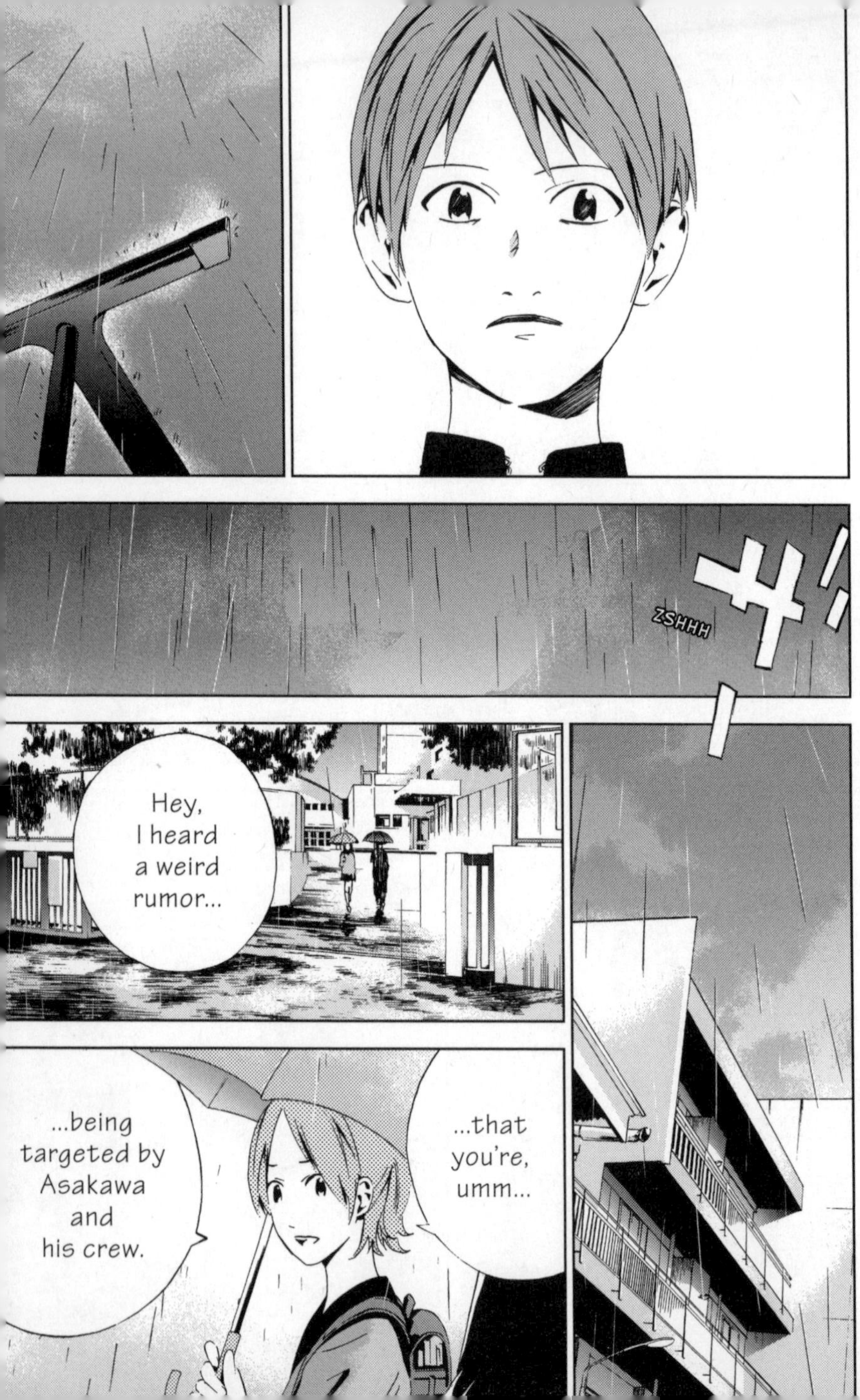
ZSHHH
Hey, I heard a weird rumor...
...that you're, umm...
...being targeted by Asakawa and his crew.

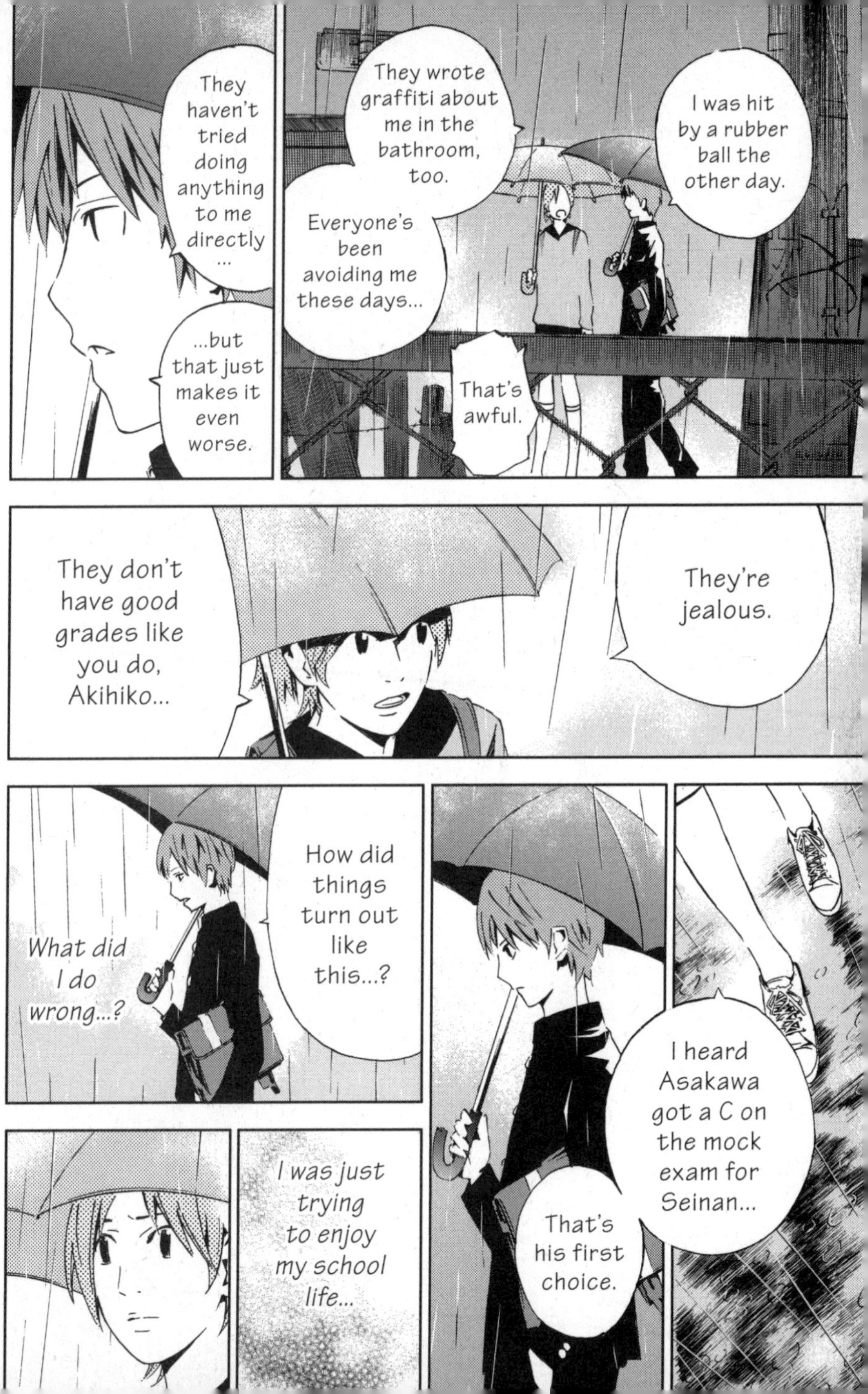
I was hit by a rubber ball the other day.
They wrote graffiti about me in the bathroom, too.
Everyone's been avoiding me these days...
That's awful.
They haven't tried doing anything to me directly...
...but that just makes it even worse.
They're jealous.
They don't have good grades like you do, Akihiko...
I heard Asakawa got a C on the mock exam for Seinan...
That's his first choice.
How did things turn out like this...?
What did I do wrong...?
I was just trying to enjoy my school life...

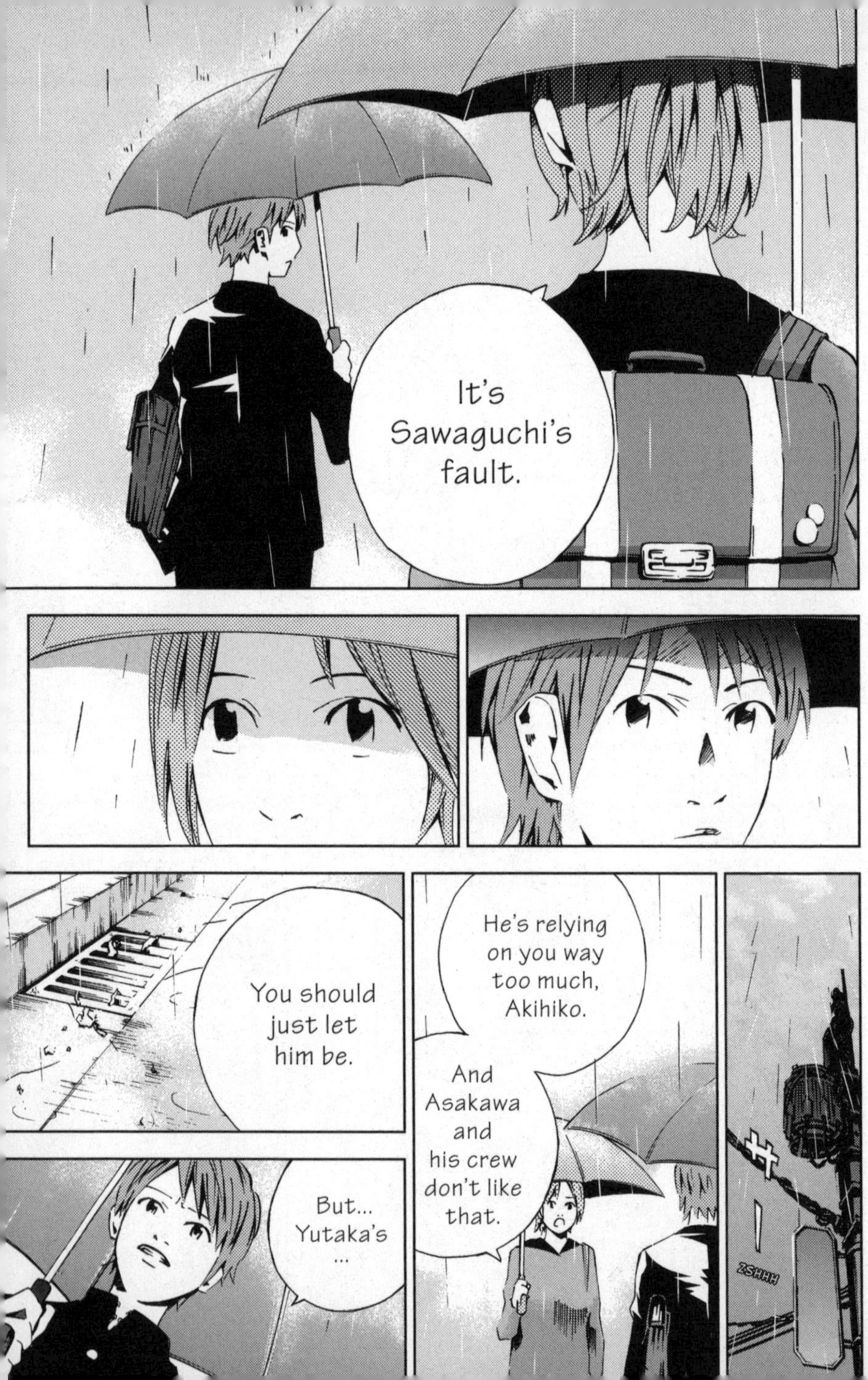
It's Sawaguchi's fault.
ZSHHH
He's relying on you way too much, Akihiko.
And Asakawa and his crew don't like that.
You should just let him be.
But... Yutaka's ...

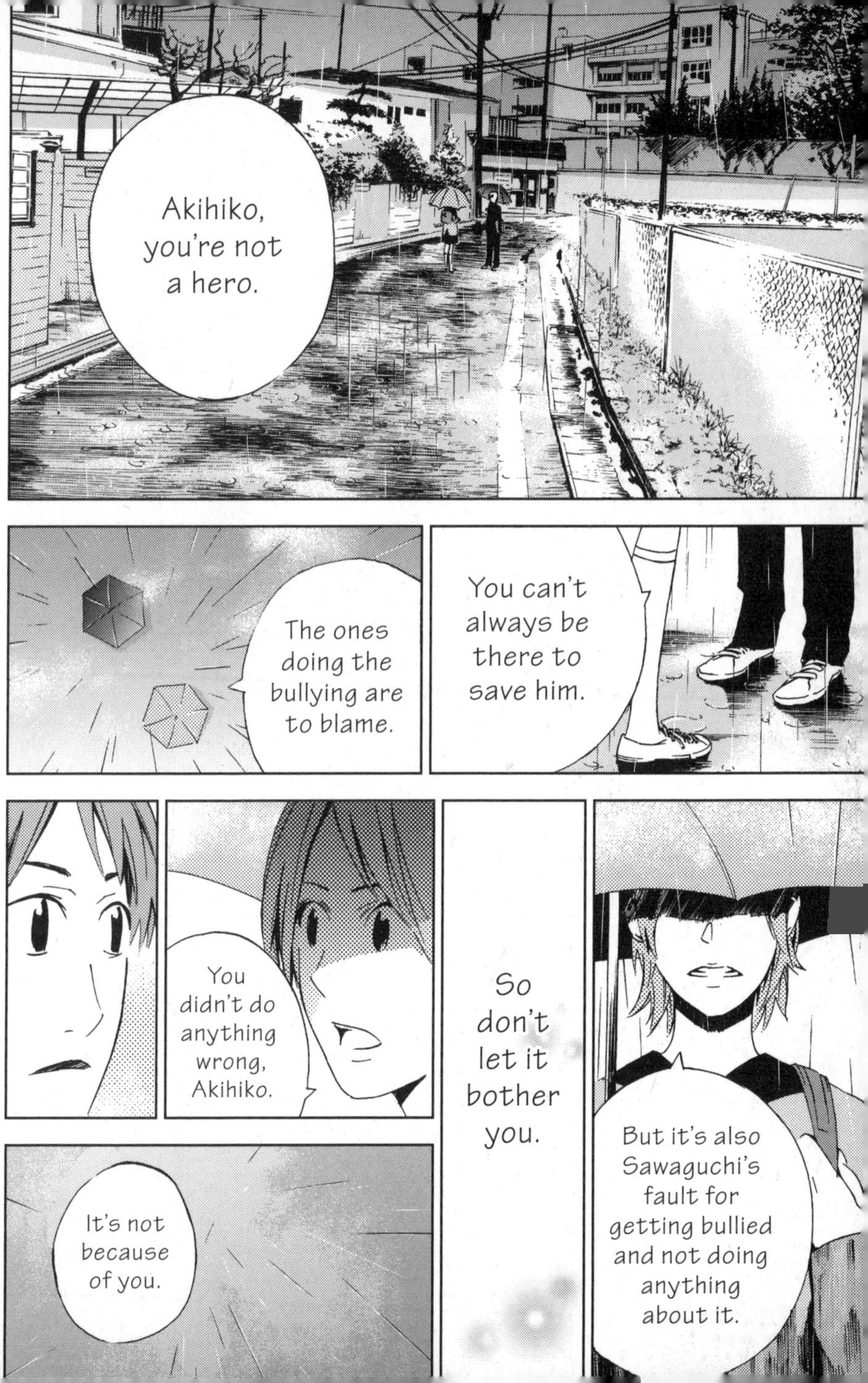
Akihiko, you're not a hero.
You can't always be there to save him.
The ones doing the bullying are to blame.
But it's also Sawaguchi's fault for getting bullied and not doing anything about it.
So don't let it bother you.
You didn't do anything wrong, Akihiko.
It's not because of you.

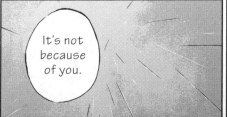

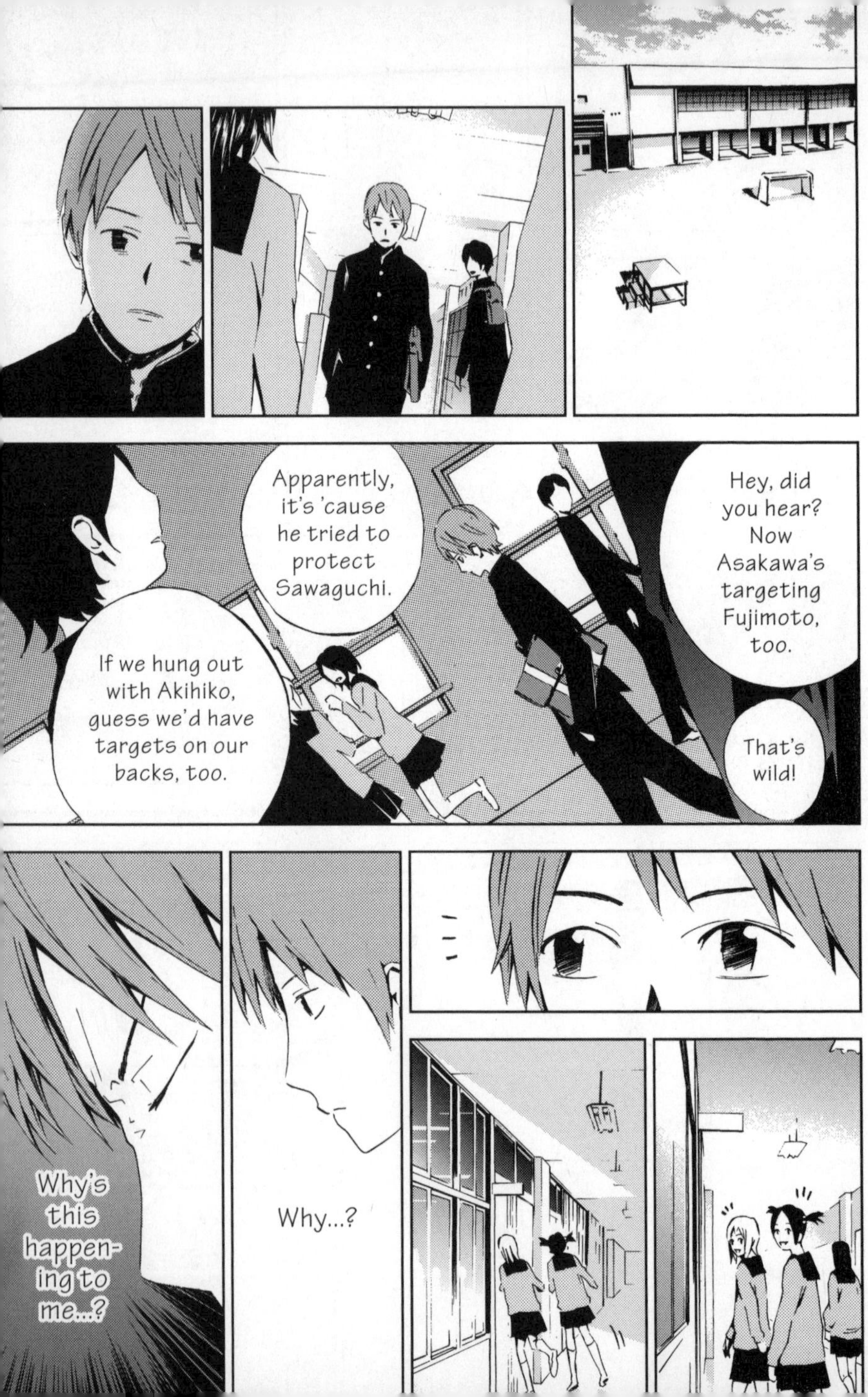
Hey, did you hear? Now Asakawa's targeting Fujimoto, too.
That's wild!
Apparently, it's 'cause he tried to protect Sawaguchi.
If we hung out with Akihiko, guess we'd have targets on our backs, too.
Why...?
Why's this happen-ing to me...?

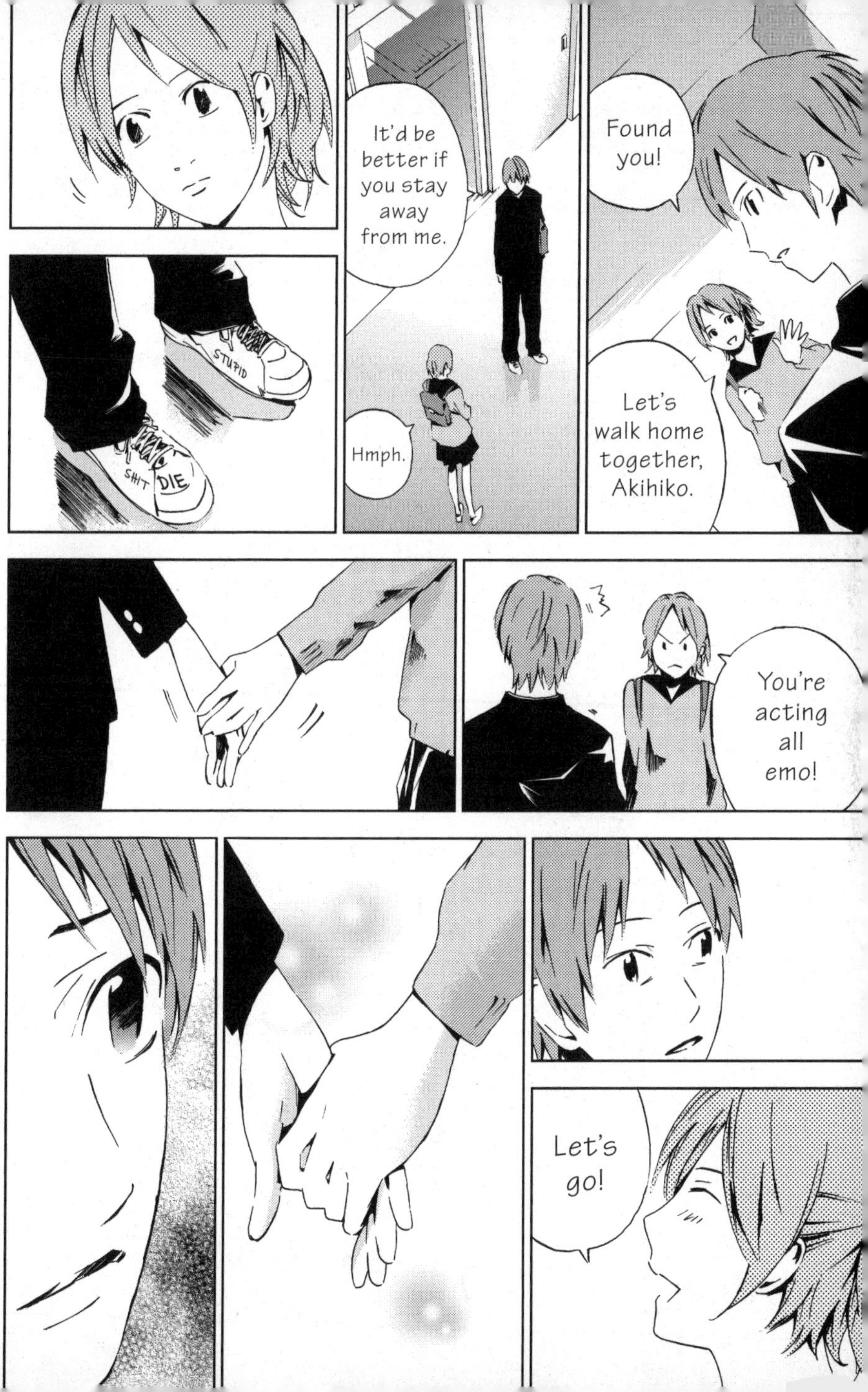
Found you!
Let's walk home together, Akihiko.
It'd be better if you stay away from me.
Hmph.
STUPID
SHIT
DIE
You're acting all emo!
Let's go!

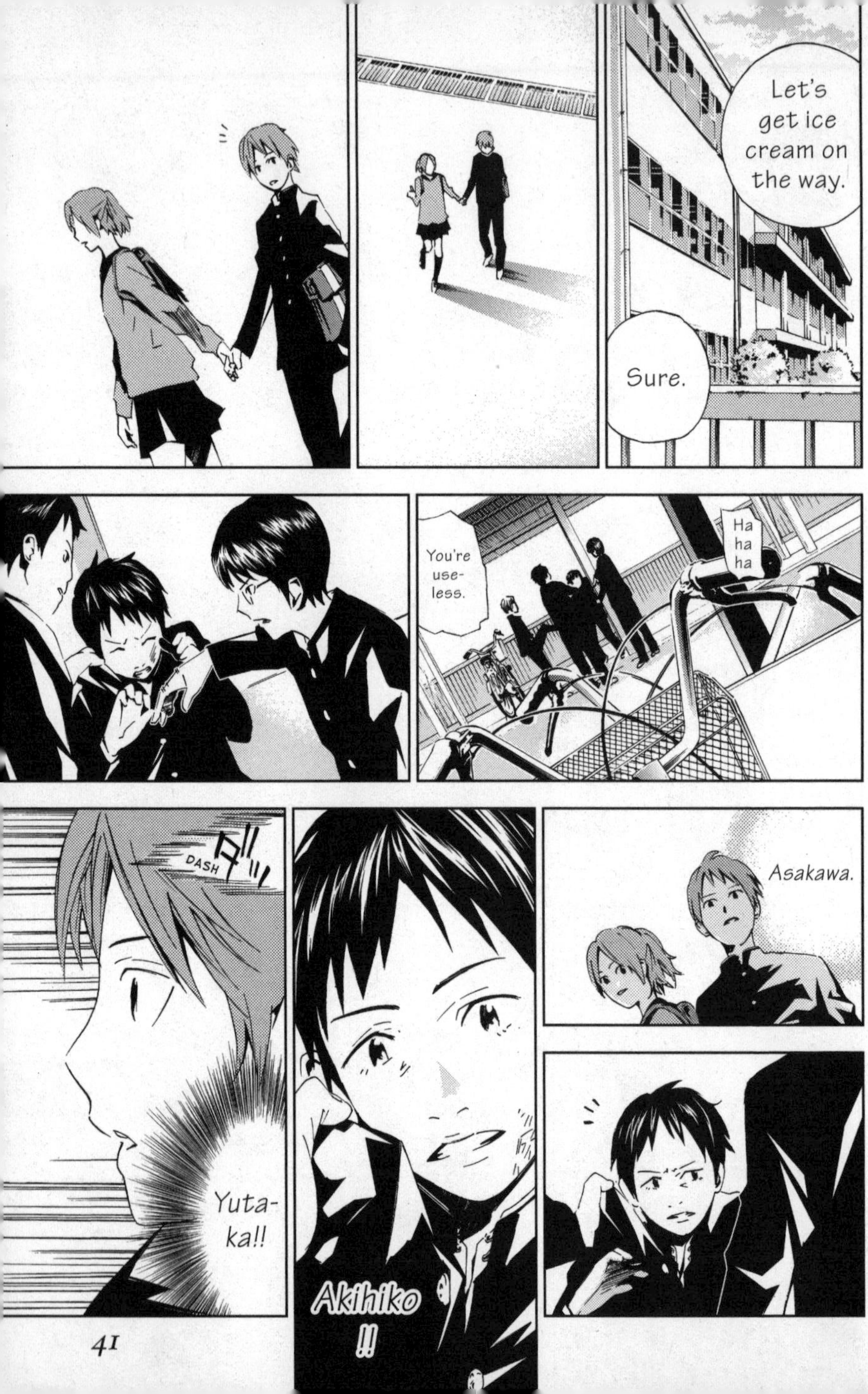

Let's get ice cream on the way.
Sure.
Ha ha ha
You're useless.
Asakawa.
Akihiko !!
DASH
Yuta-ka!!

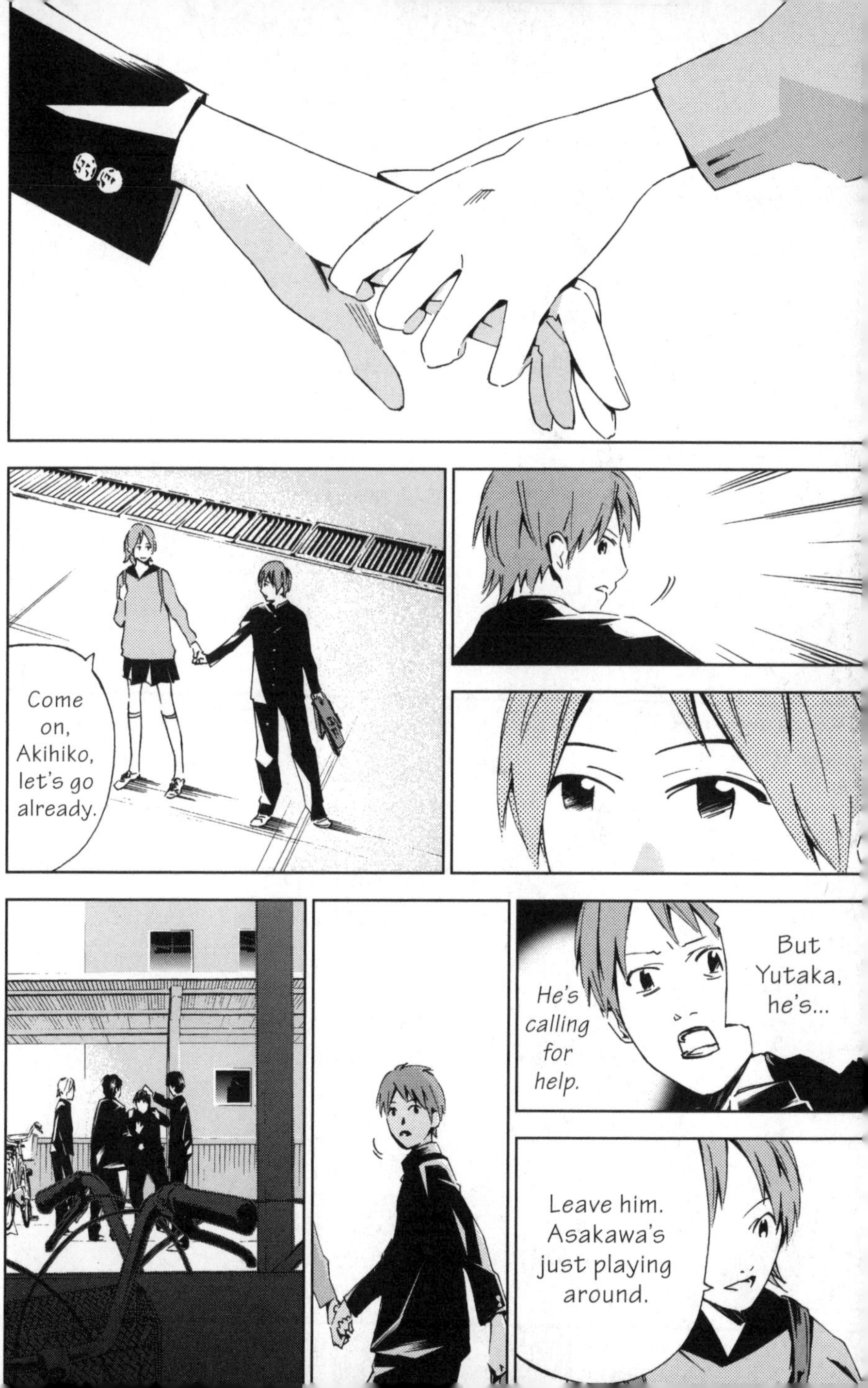

Come on, Akihiko, let's go already.
But Yutaka, he's...
He's calling for help.
Leave him. Asakawa's just playing around.

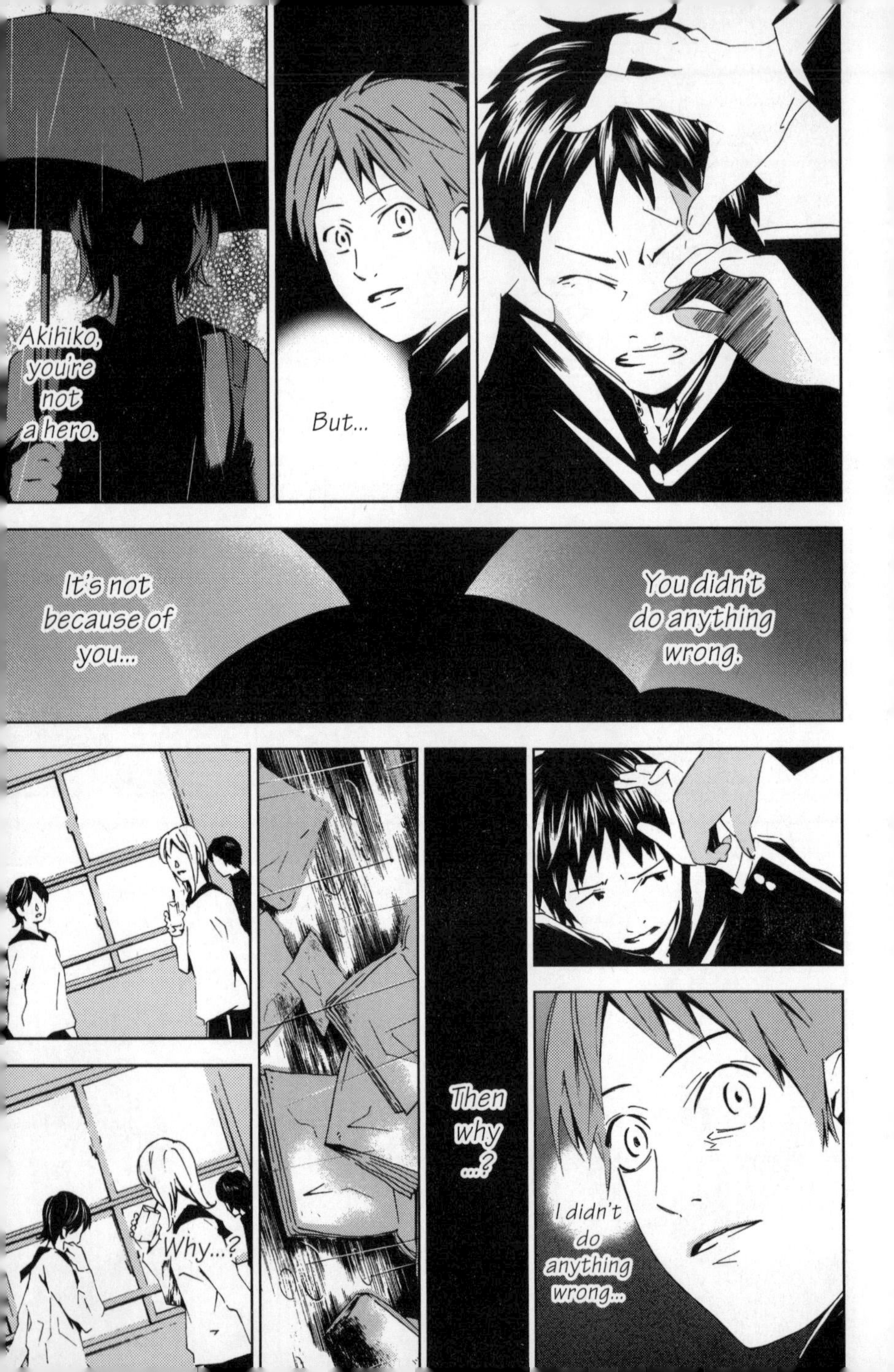
But...
Akihiko, you're not a hero.
You didn't do anything wrong.
It's not because of you...
I didn't do anything wrong...
Then why ...?
Why...?

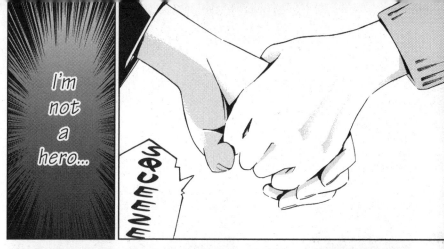

I'm not a hero...

SQUEEZE

Me, saving you doesn't do you any good.

That's right, Yutaka...

You have to handle these guys yourself.

YANK

Let's go.

I can't help you, Yutaka.

It won't help.

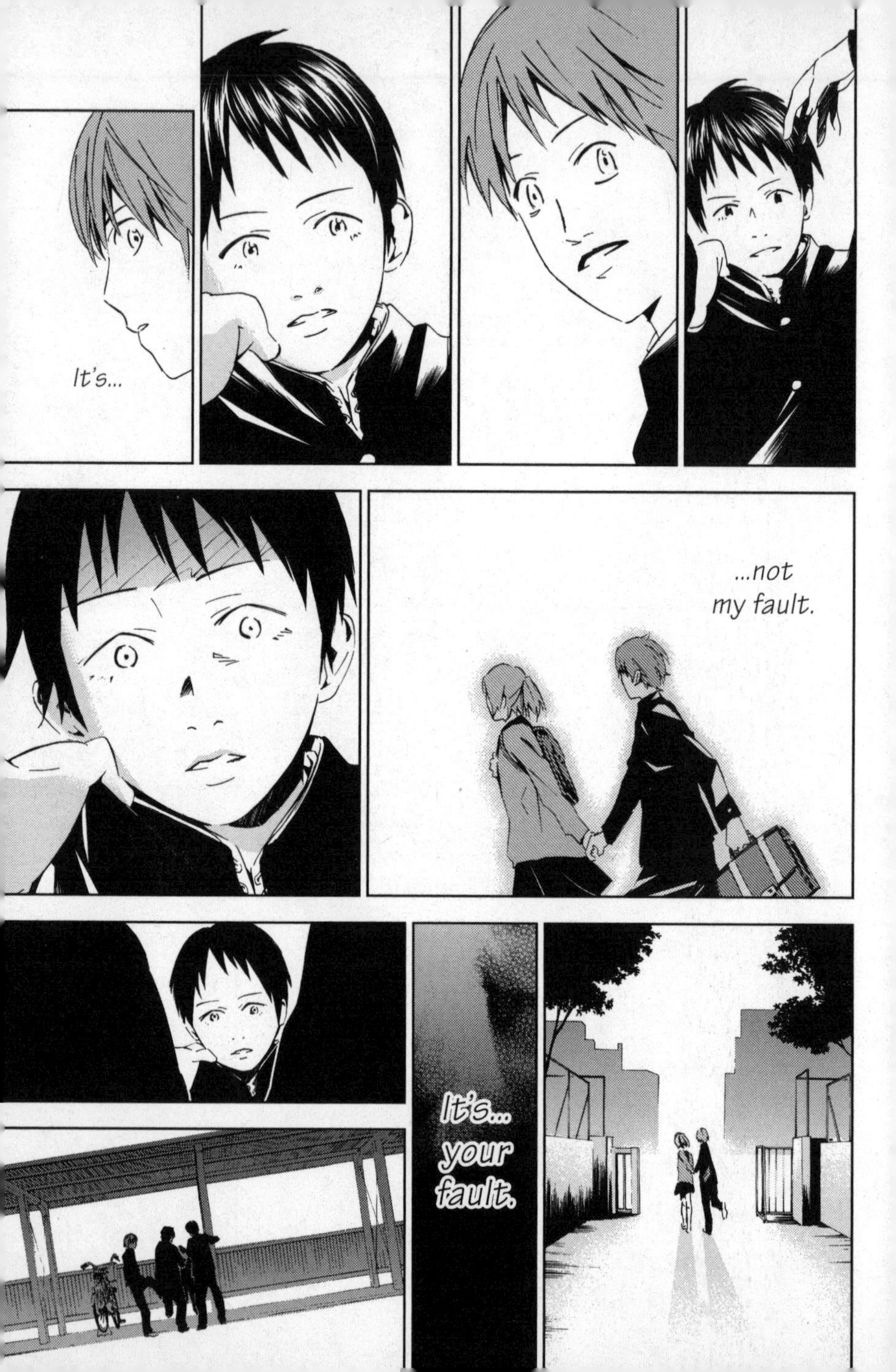
It's...
...not
my fault.
It's...
your
fault.

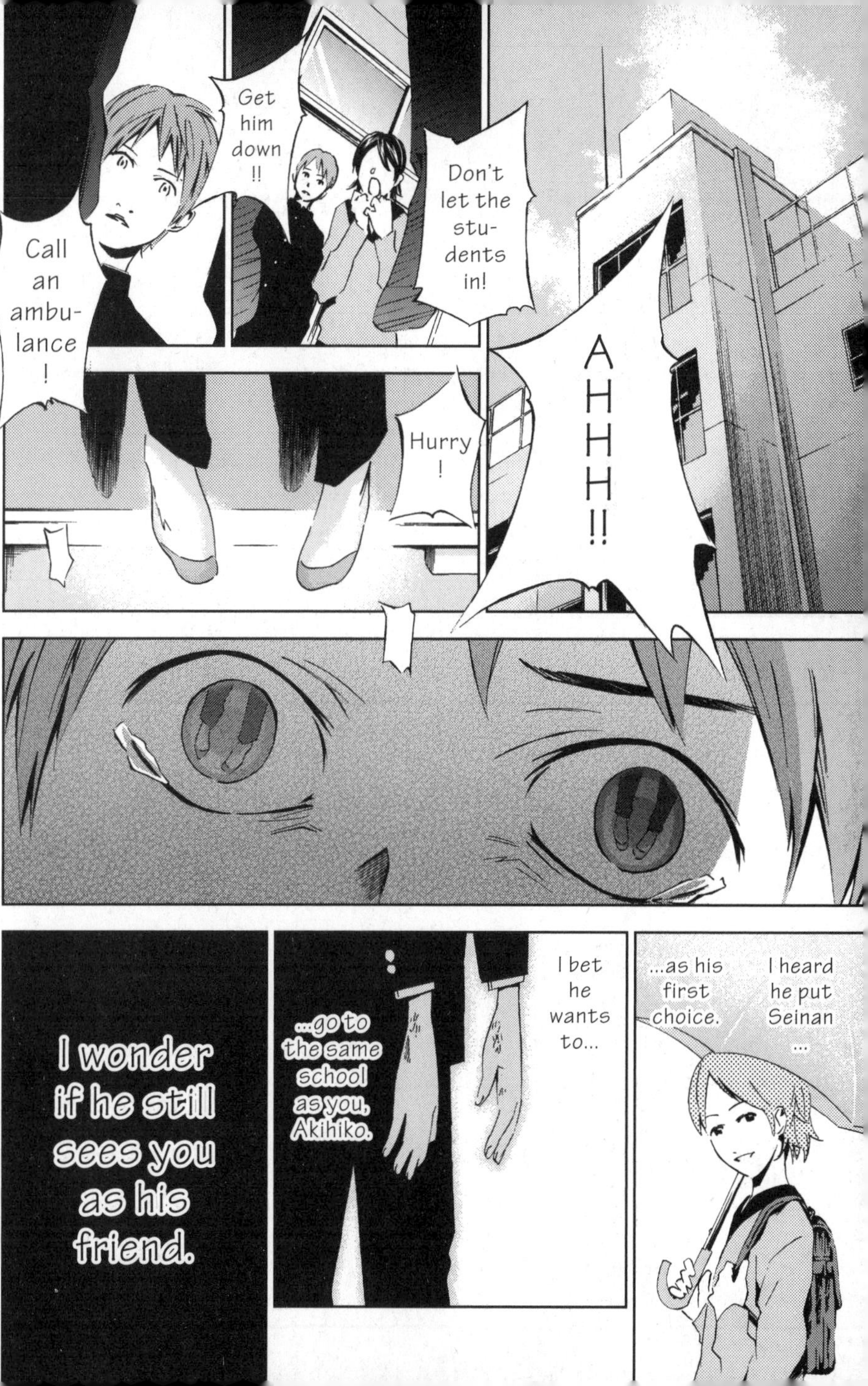
AHHH!!
Don't let the stu-dents in!
Get him down!!
Call an ambu-lance!
Hurry!
I heard he put Seinan...
...as his first choice.
I bet he wants to...
...go to the same school as you, Akihiko.
I wonder if he still sees you as his friend.

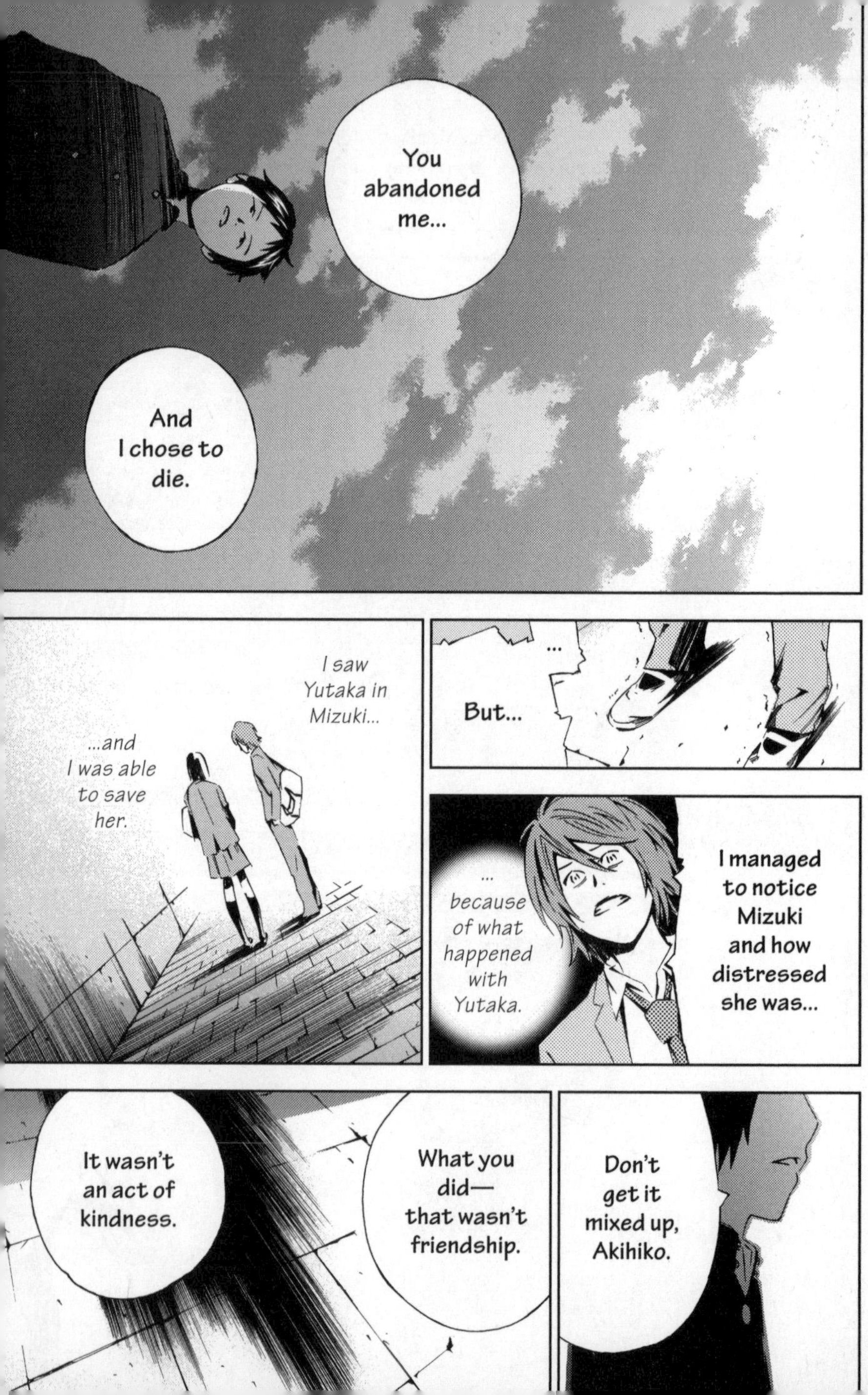
You abandoned me...
And I chose to die.
...
But...
I managed to notice Mizuki and how distressed she was...
...because of what happened with Yutaka.
I saw Yutaka in Mizuki...
...and I was able to save her.
Don't get it mixed up, Akihiko.
What you did—that wasn't friendship.
It wasn't an act of kindness.

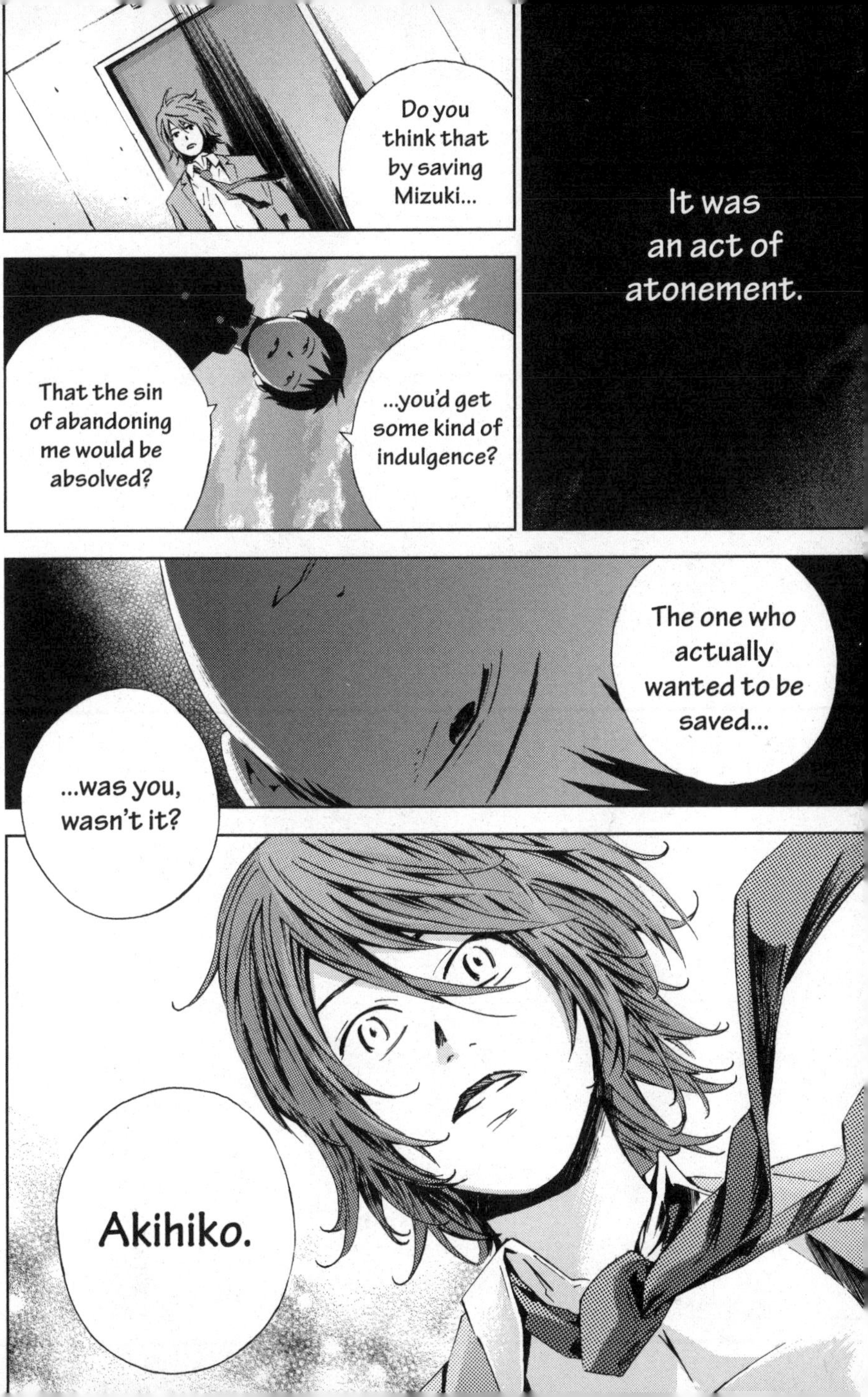
It was an act of atonement.
Do you think that by saving Mizuki...
...you'd get some kind of indulgence?
That the sin of abandoning me would be absolved?
The one who actually wanted to be saved...
...was you, wasn't it?
Akihiko.

I finally understand now.

You're...

I see ...

You're my pain.

You're the thoughts in my head that I don't want anyone to hear...

...me.

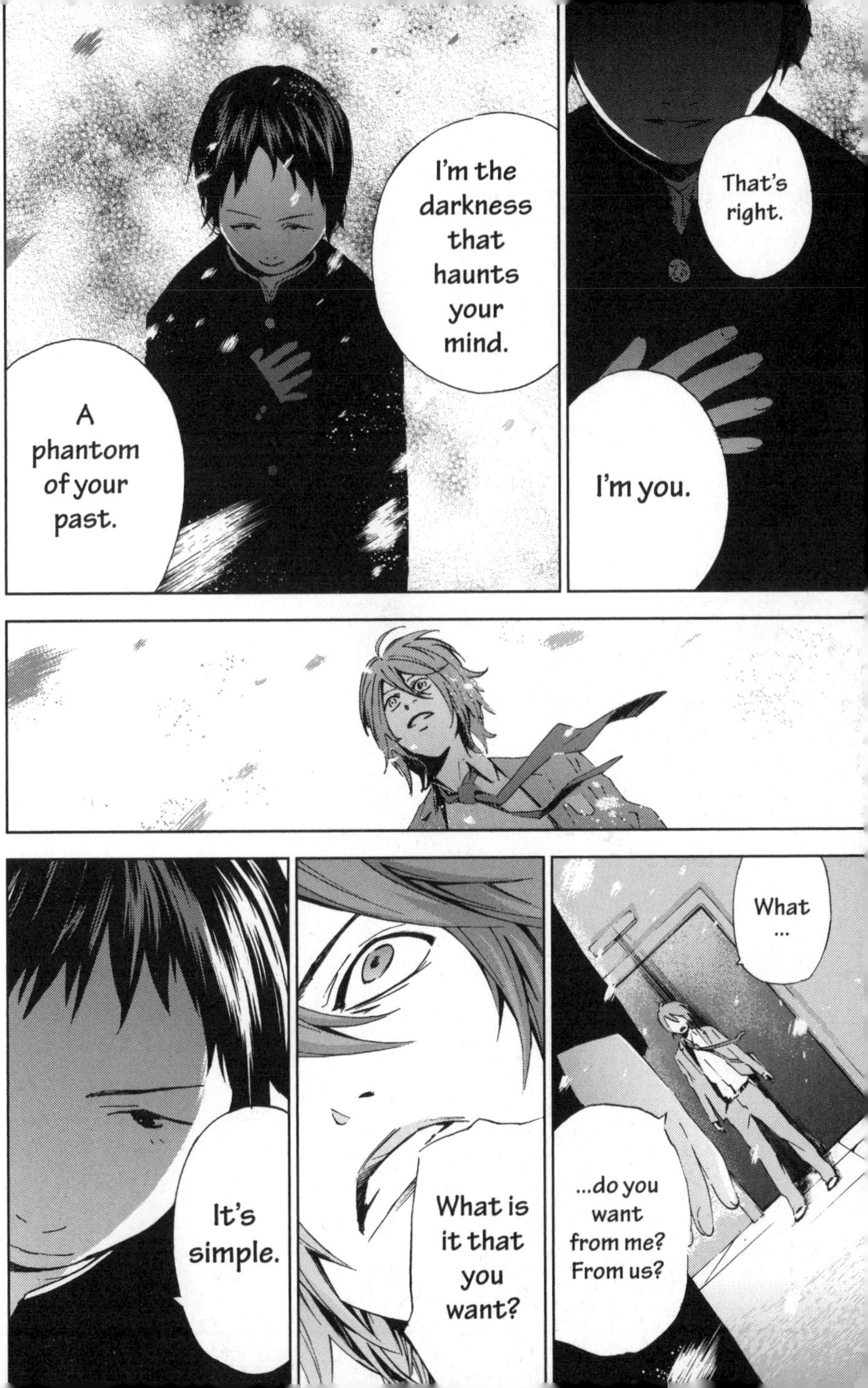
That's right.
I'm you.
I'm the darkness that haunts your mind.
A phantom of your past.
What ...
...do you want from me? From us?
What is it that you want?
It's simple.

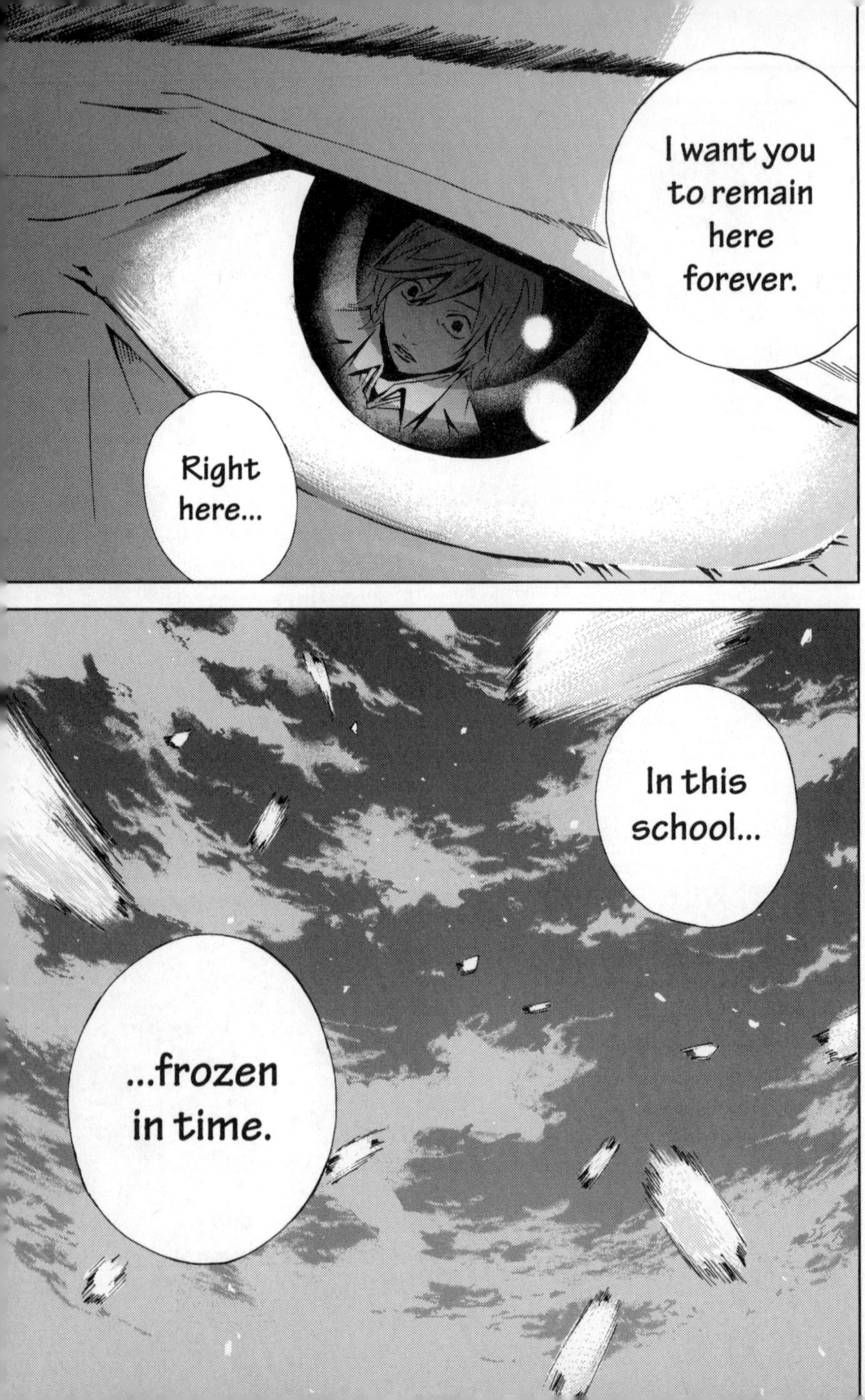
I want you to remain here forever.
Right here...
In this school...
...frozen in time.

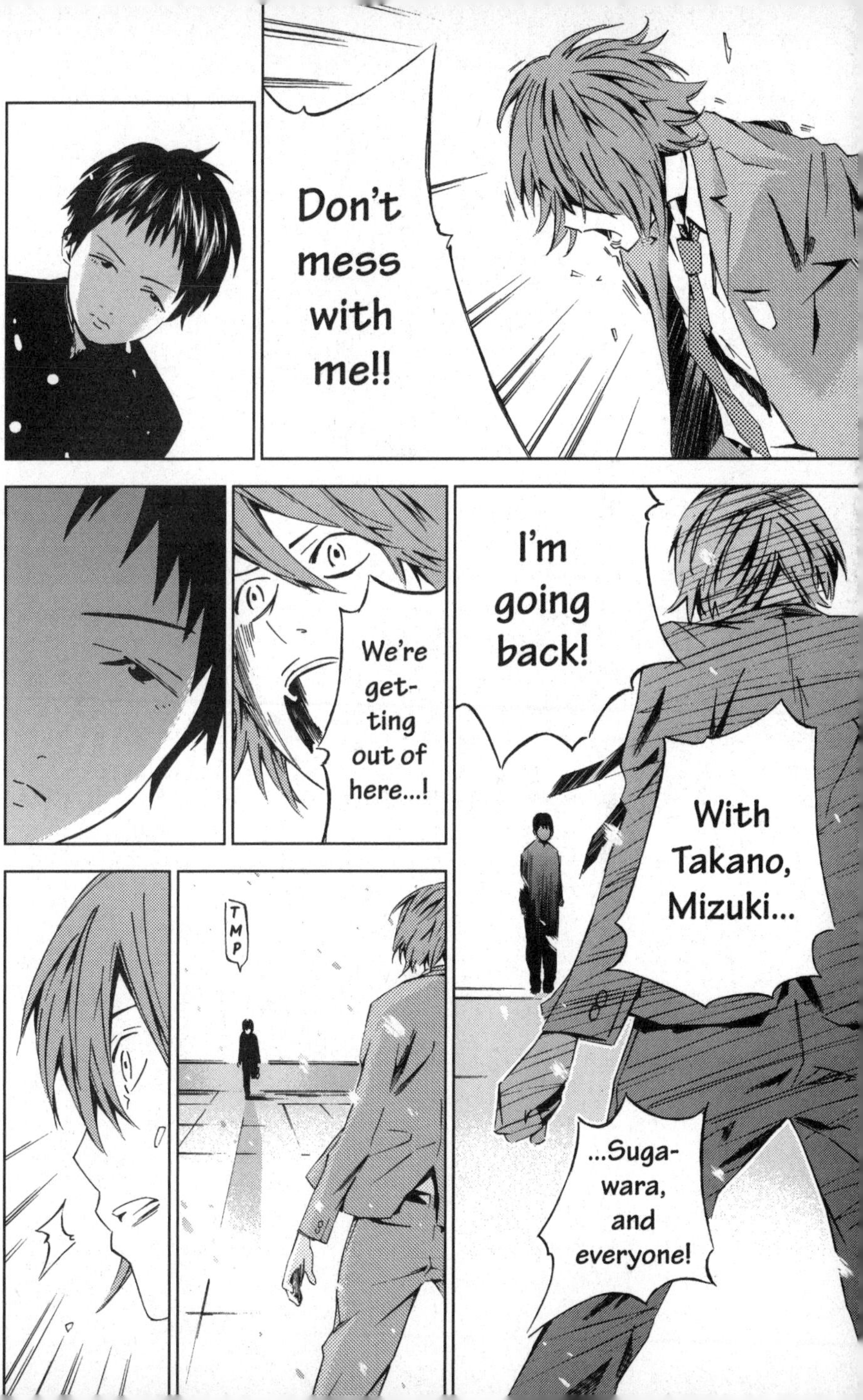
Don't mess with me!!
I'm going back!
With Takano, Mizuki...
...Sugawara, and everyone!
We're get-ting out of here...!
TMP

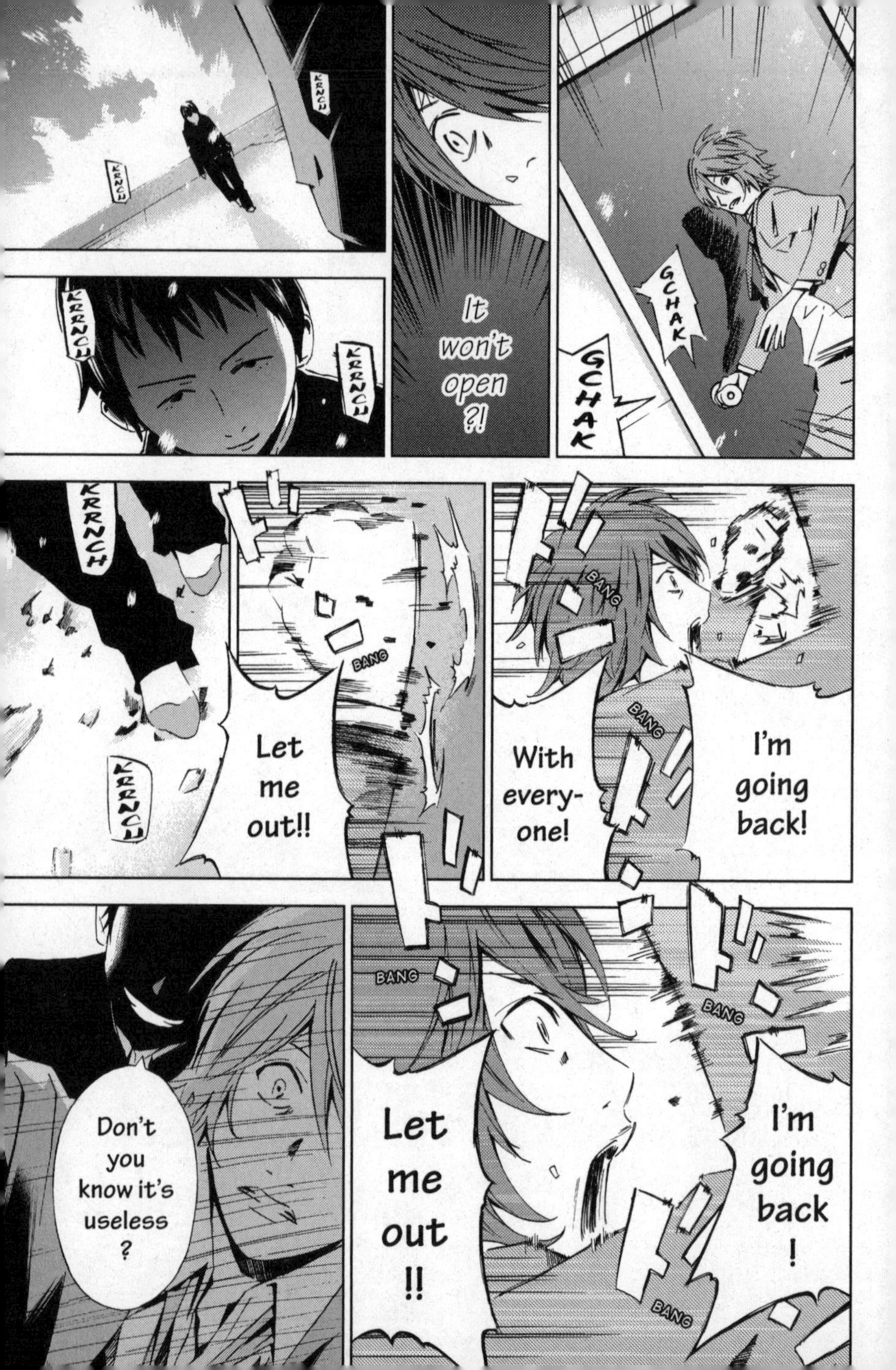
GCHAK
GCHAK
It won't open?!
KRNCH
KRNCH
KRRNCH
KRRNCH
BANG
BANG
I'm going back!
With everyone!
BANG
Let me out!!
KRRNCH
KRRNCH
BANG
I'm going back!
BANG
Let me out!!
BANG
Don't you know it's useless?

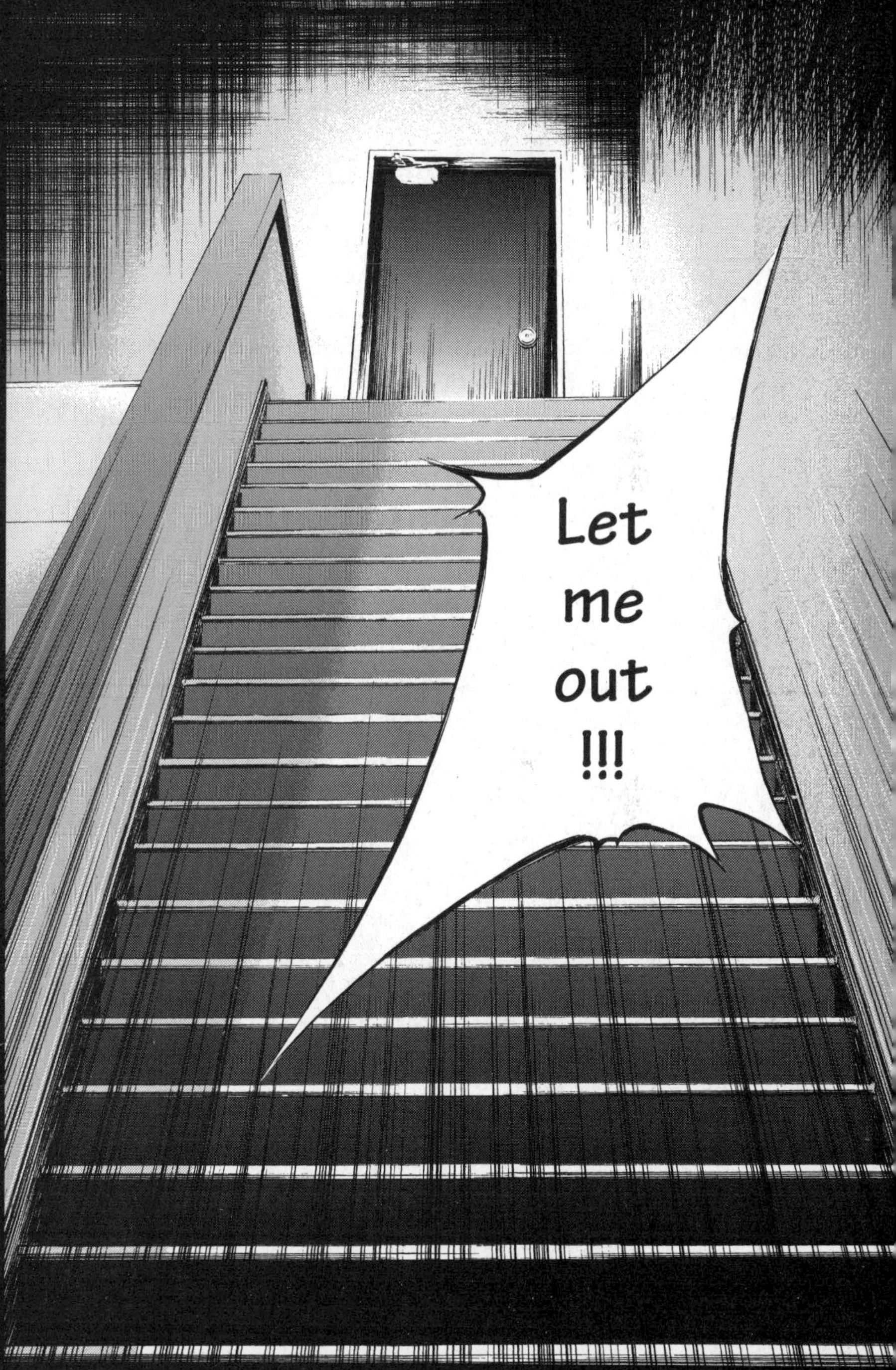
Let me out !!!

A School
Frozen
in Time

A School
Frozen
in Time

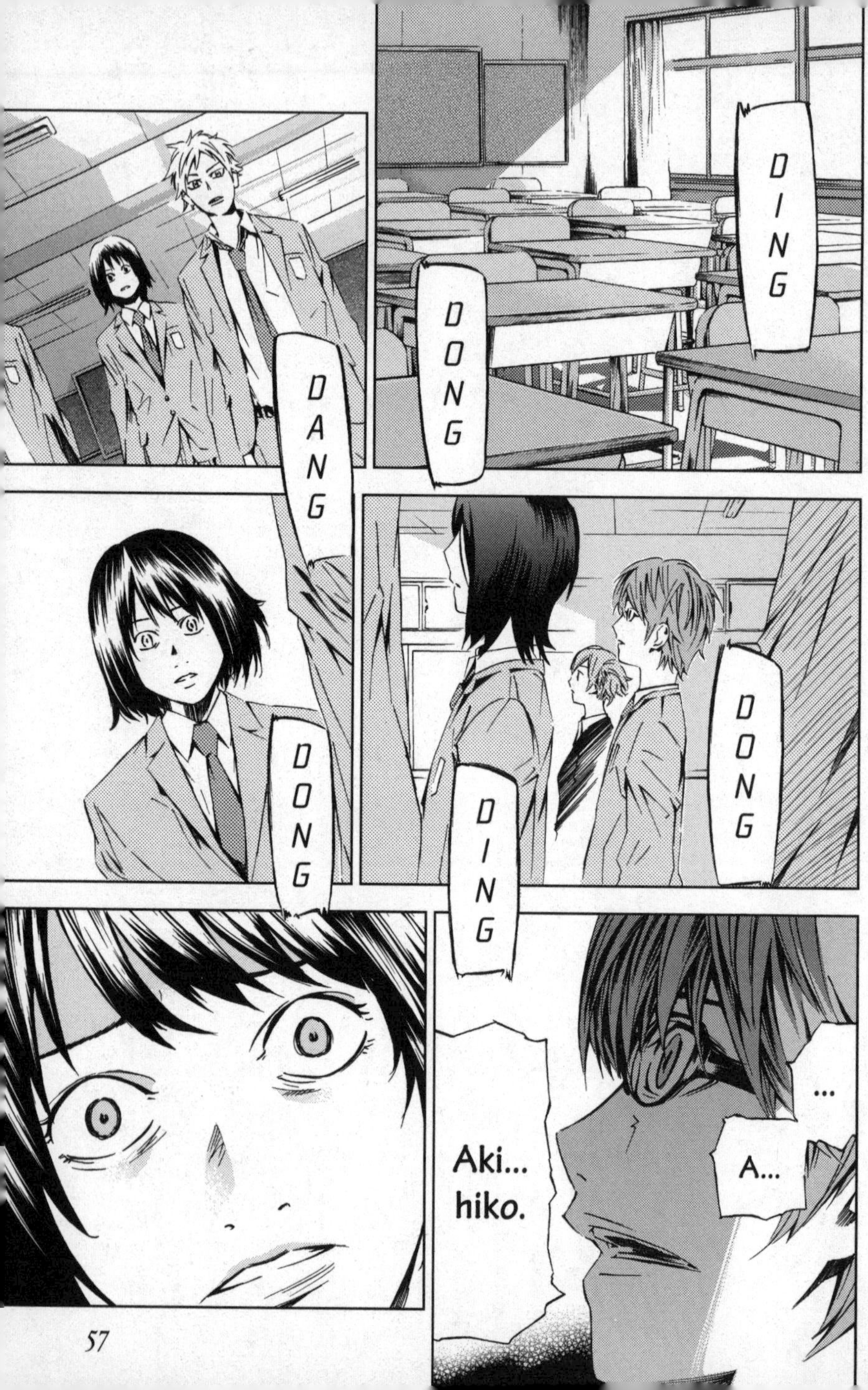

DING
DONG
DANG
DONG
DONG
DING
...
A...
Aki... hiko.

Chapter 10 You'll Believe

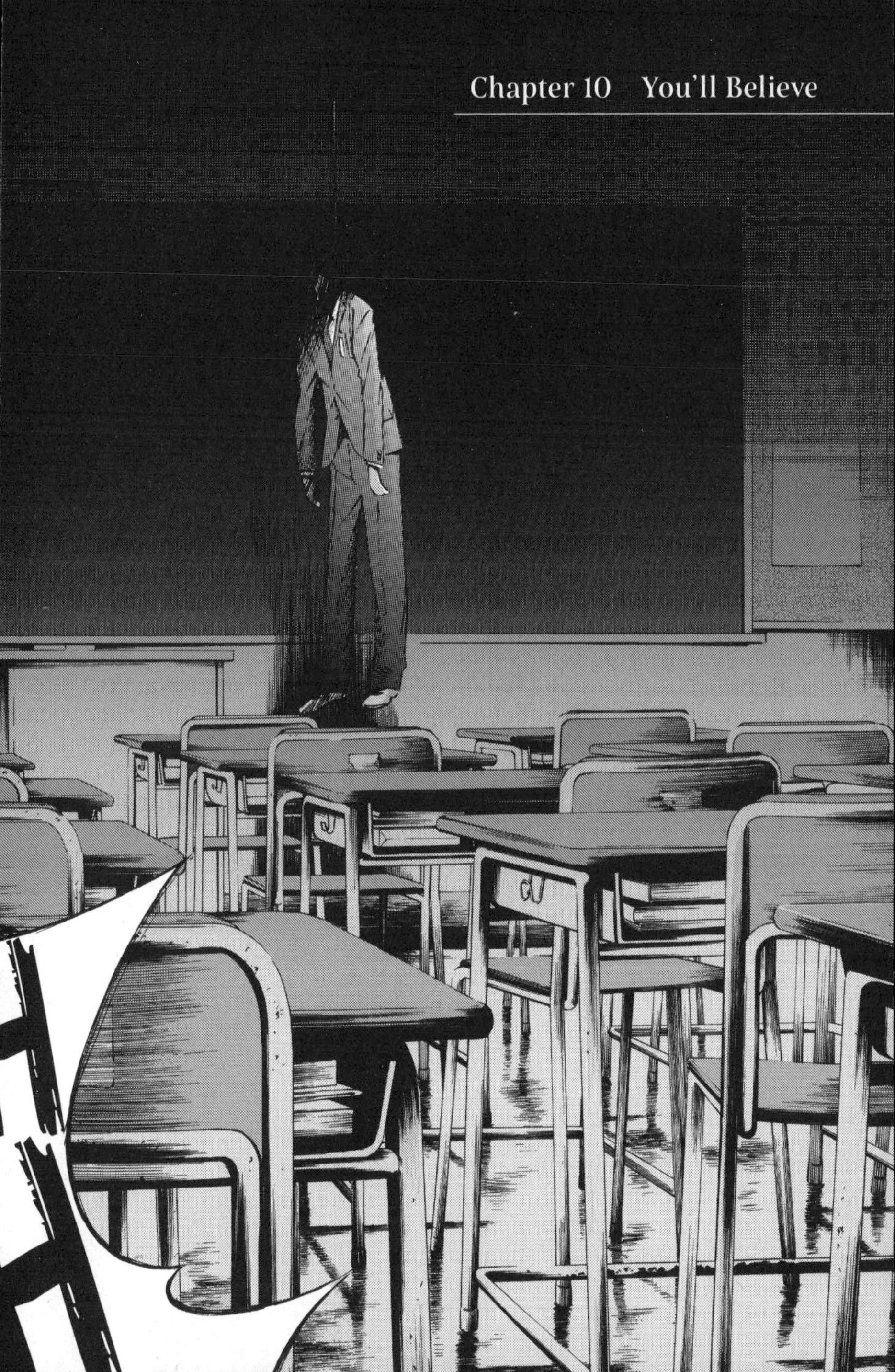

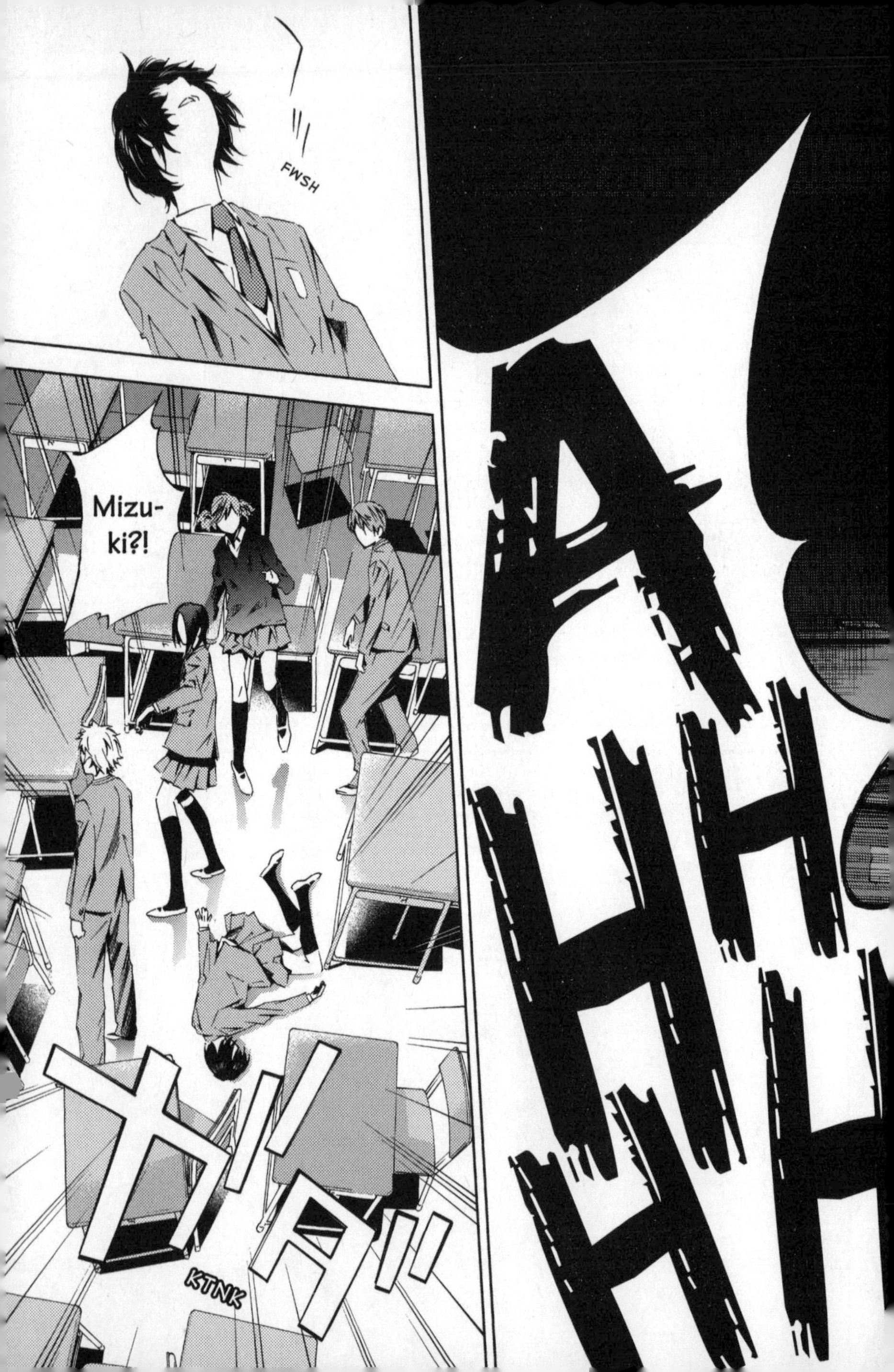
AHHHHH
FWSH
Mizu-
ki?!
KTNK

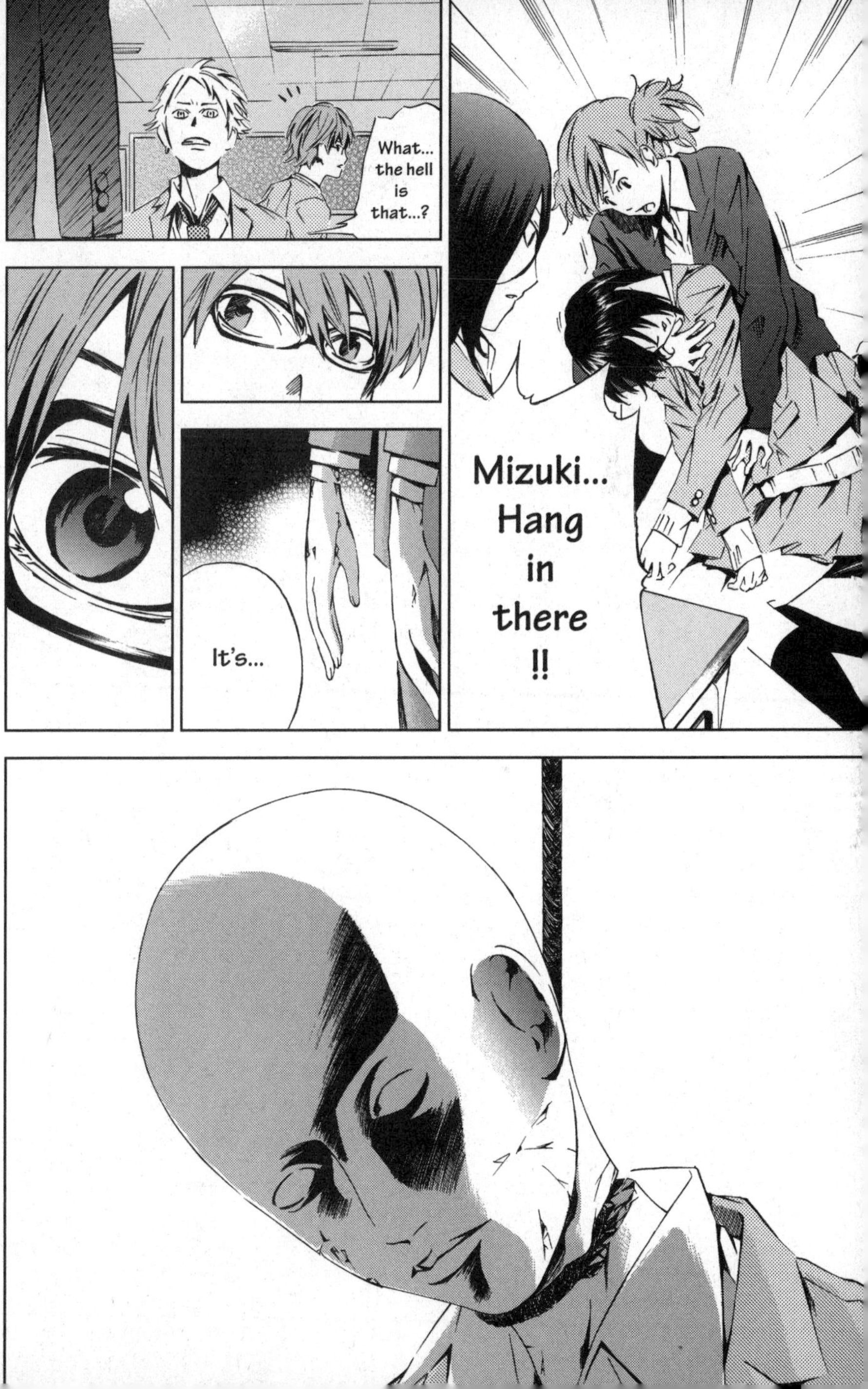
Mizuki... Hang in there!!
What... the hell is that...?
It's...

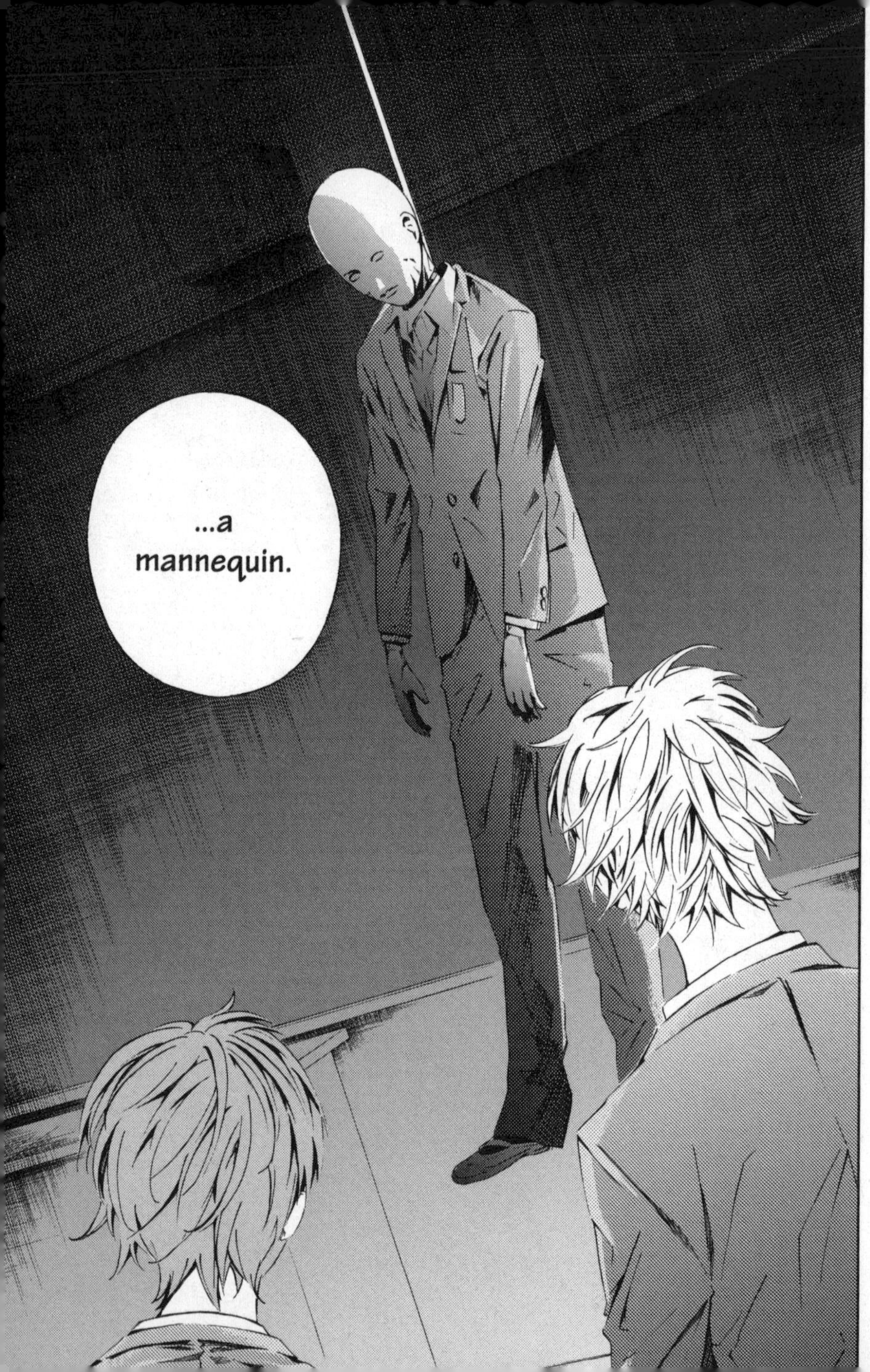
...a mannequin.

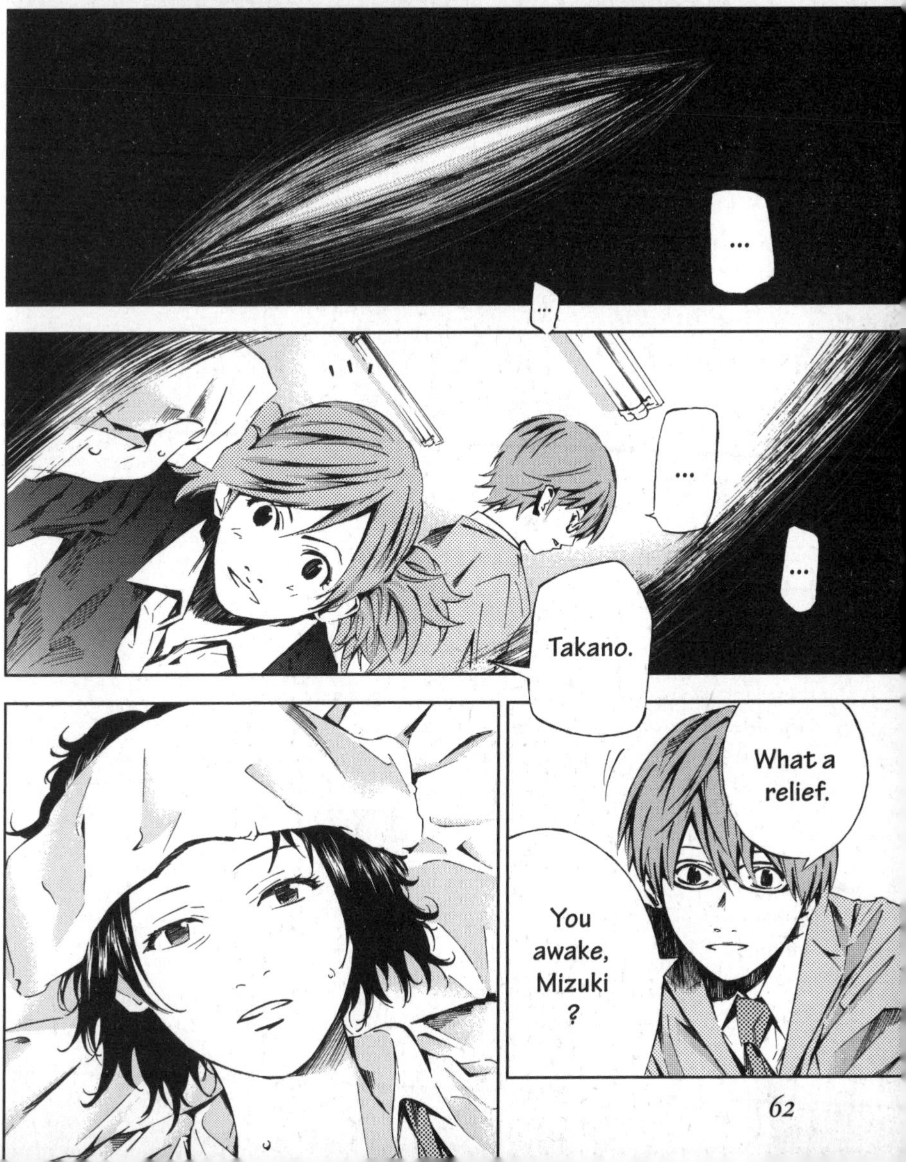
...
...
...
...
Takano.
What a relief.
You awake, Mizuki?

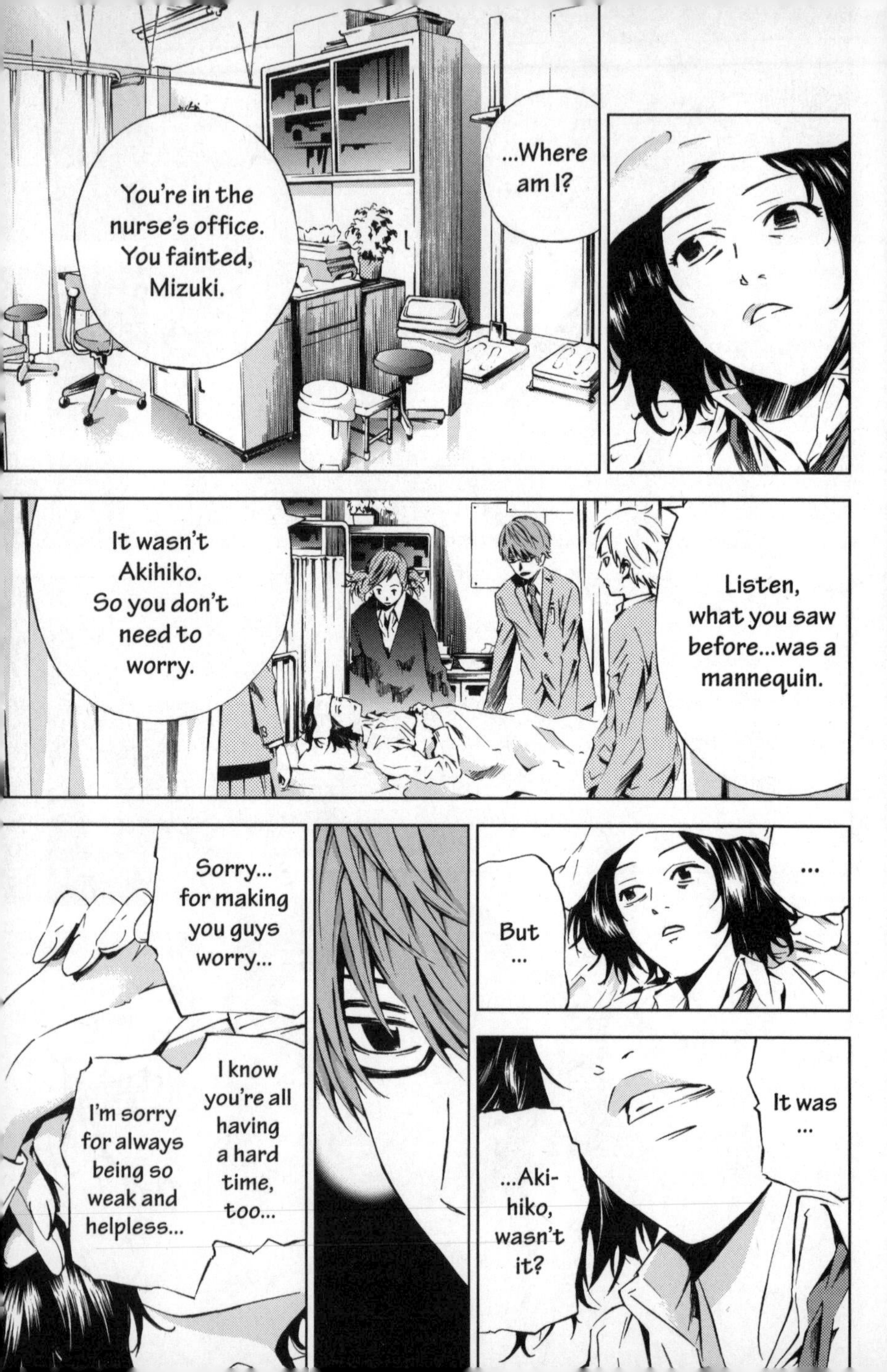
...Where am I?
You're in the nurse's office. You fainted, Mizuki.
Listen, what you saw before...was a mannequin.
It wasn't Akihiko. So you don't need to worry.
...
But ...
It was ...
...Aki-hiko, wasn't it?
Sorry... for making you guys worry...
I know you're all having a hard time, too...
I'm sorry for always being so weak and helpless...

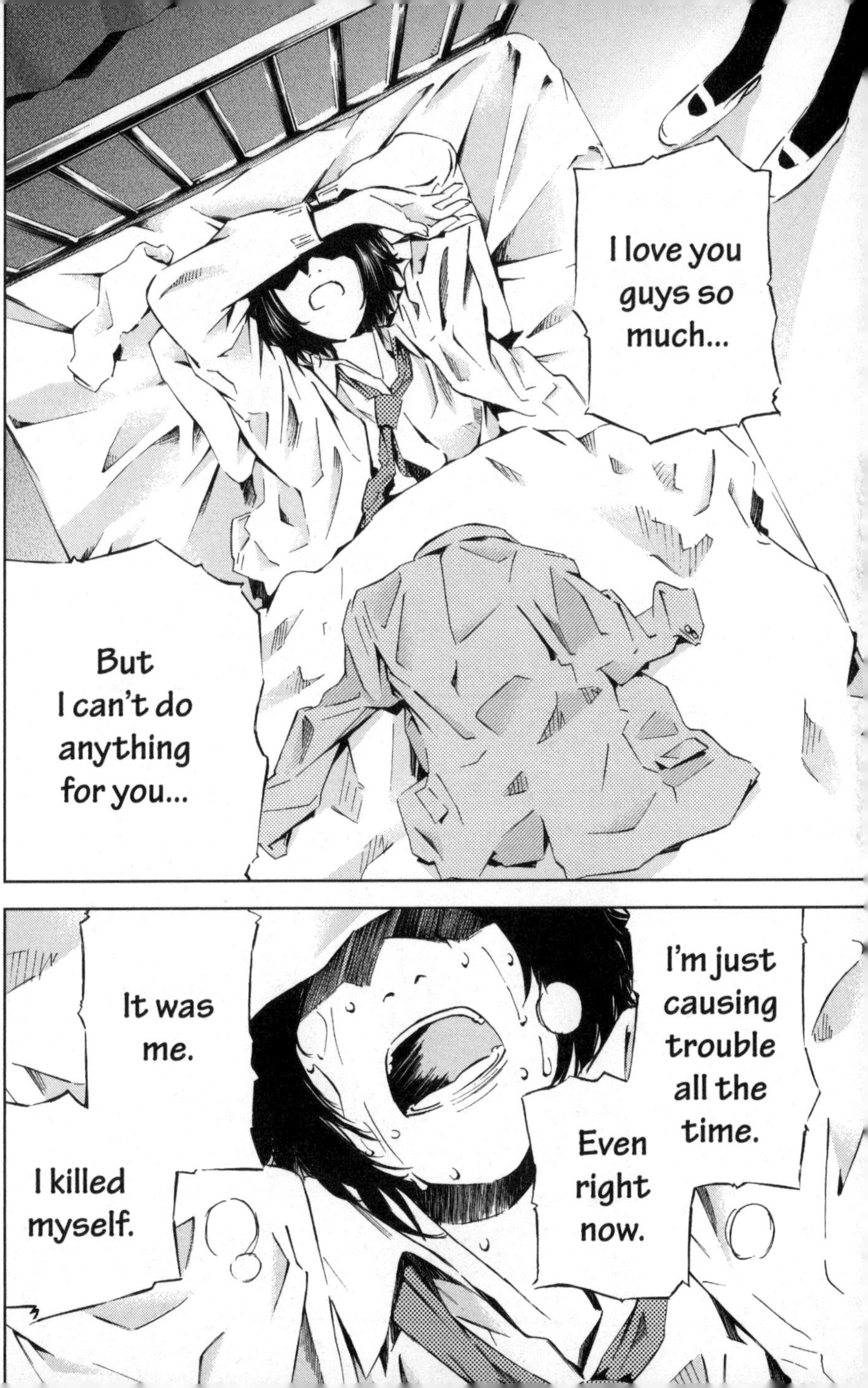
I love you guys so much...
But I can't do anything for you...
I'm just causing trouble all the time.
Even right now.
It was me.
I killed myself.

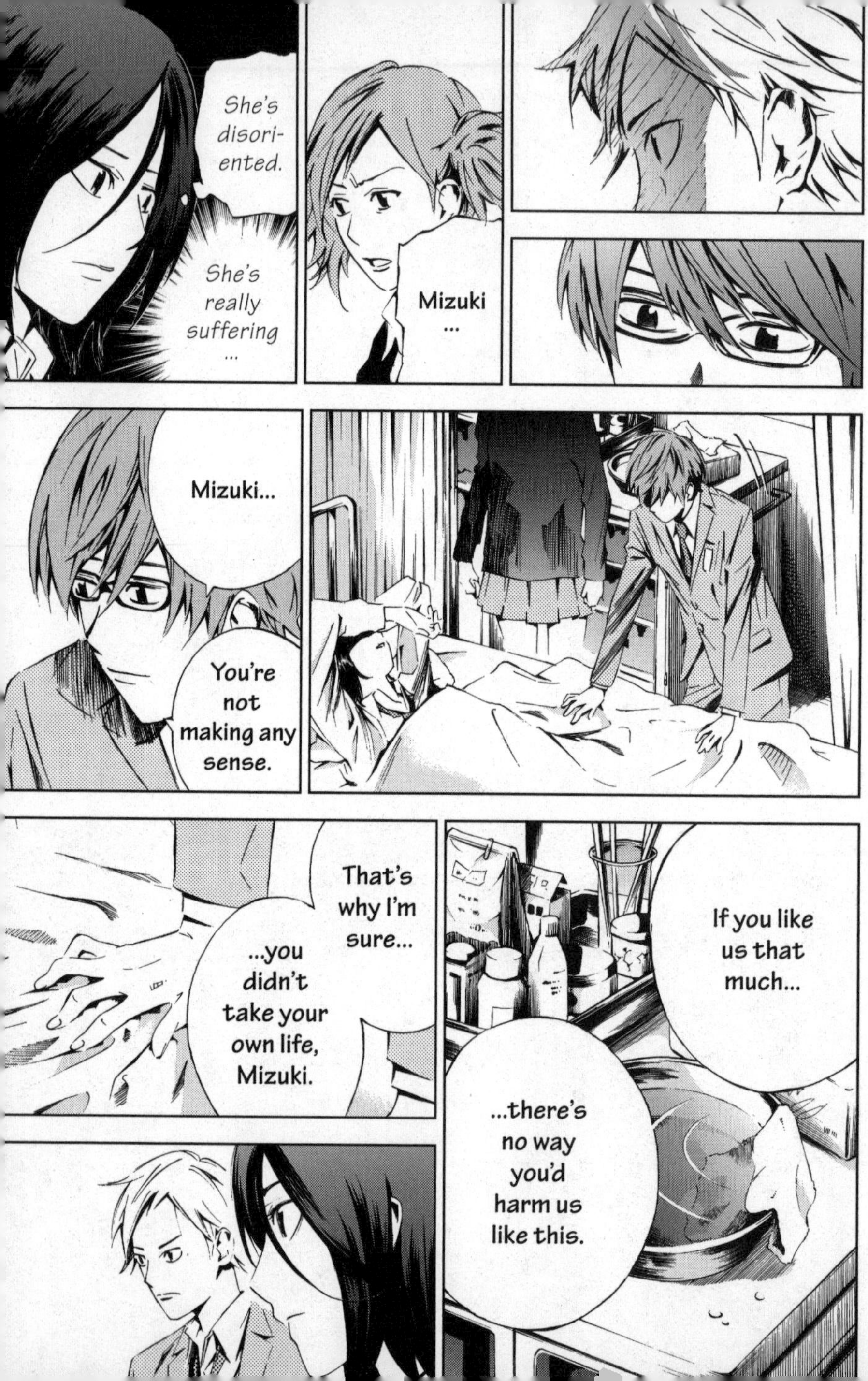
Mizuki ...
She's disori-ented.
She's really suffering ...
Mizuki...
You're not making any sense.
If you like us that much...
...there's no way you'd harm us like this.
That's why I'm sure...
...you didn't take your own life, Mizuki.

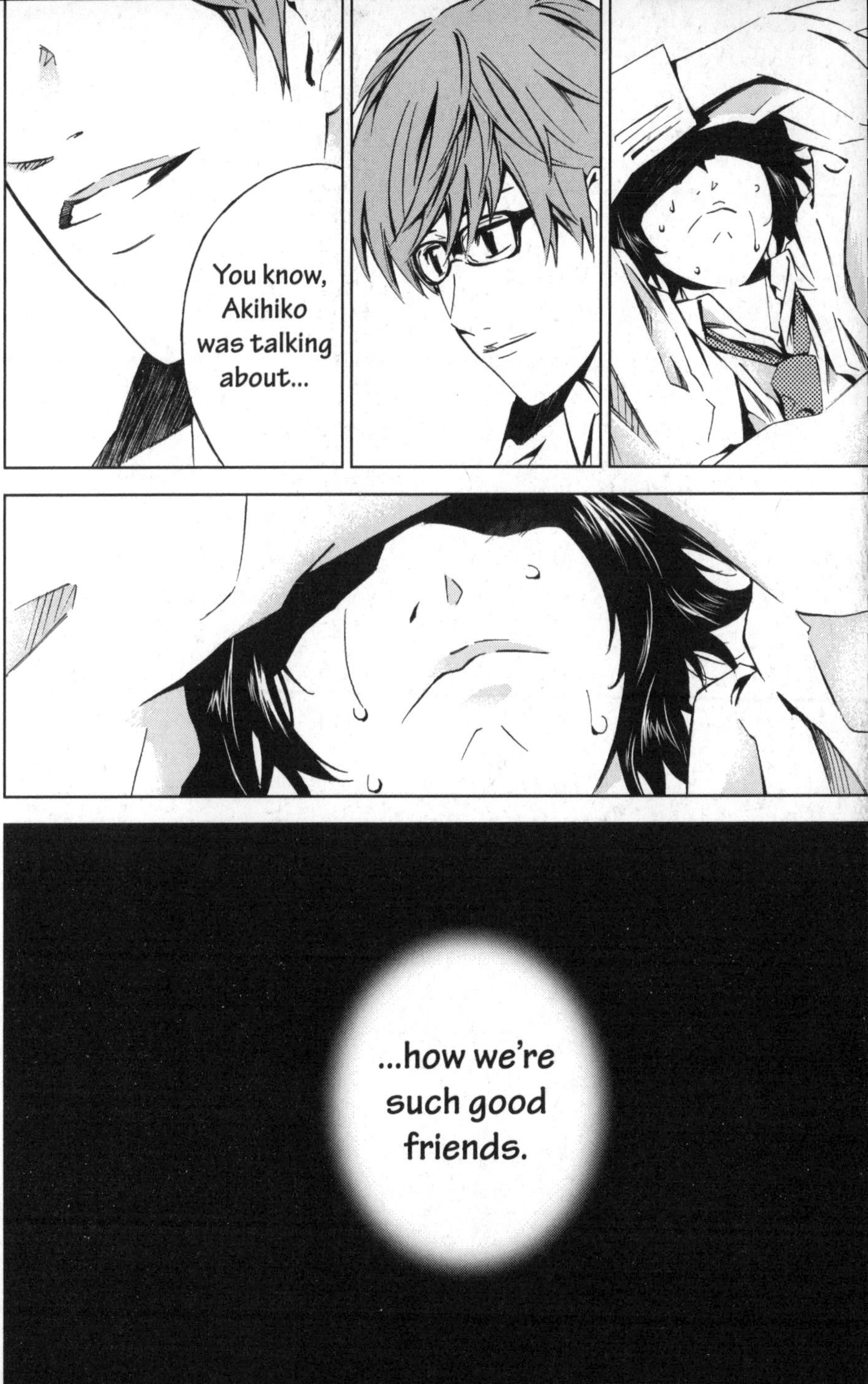
You know, Akihiko was talking about...
...how we're such good friends.

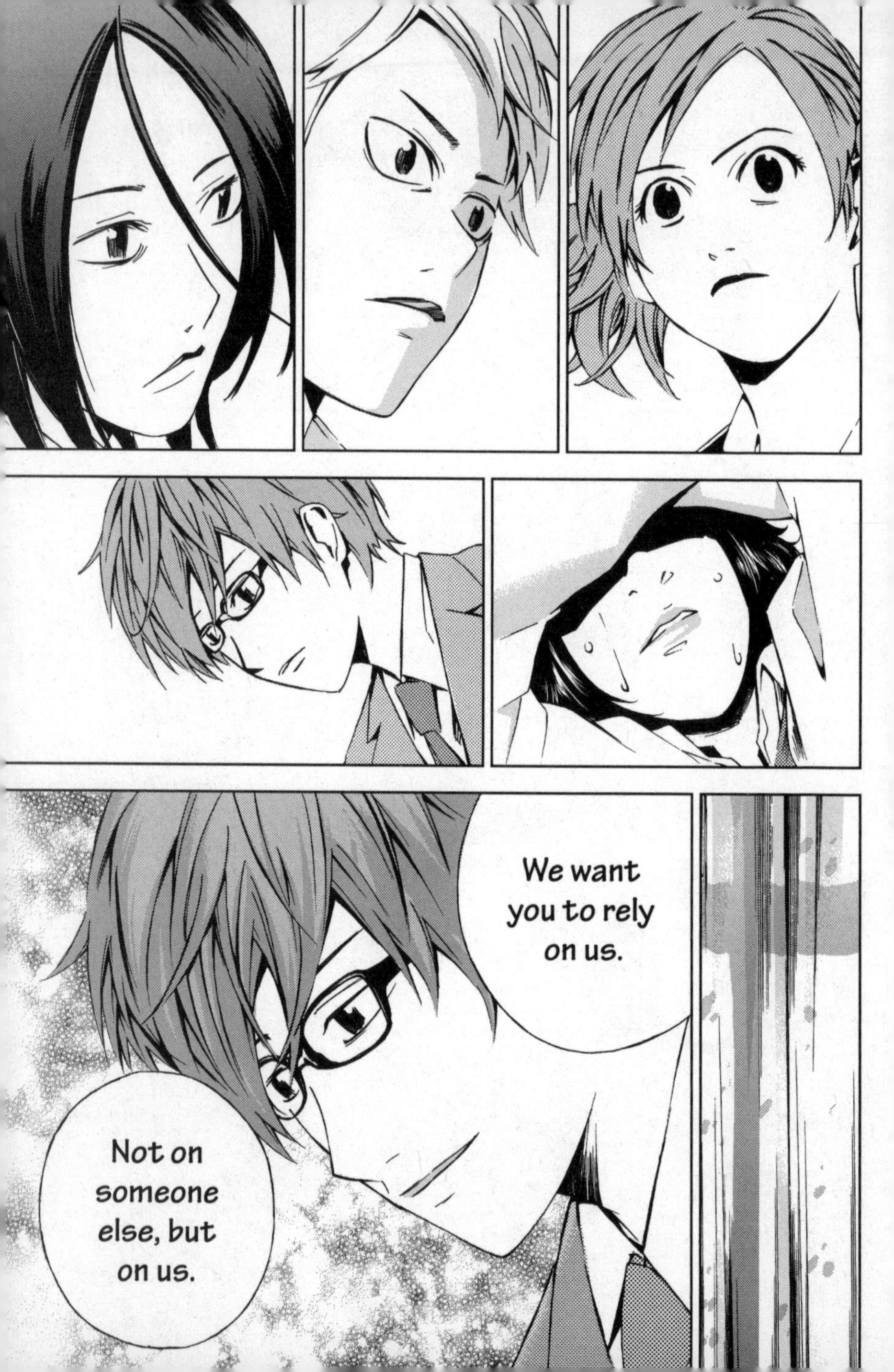
We want you to rely on us.
Not on someone else, but on us.

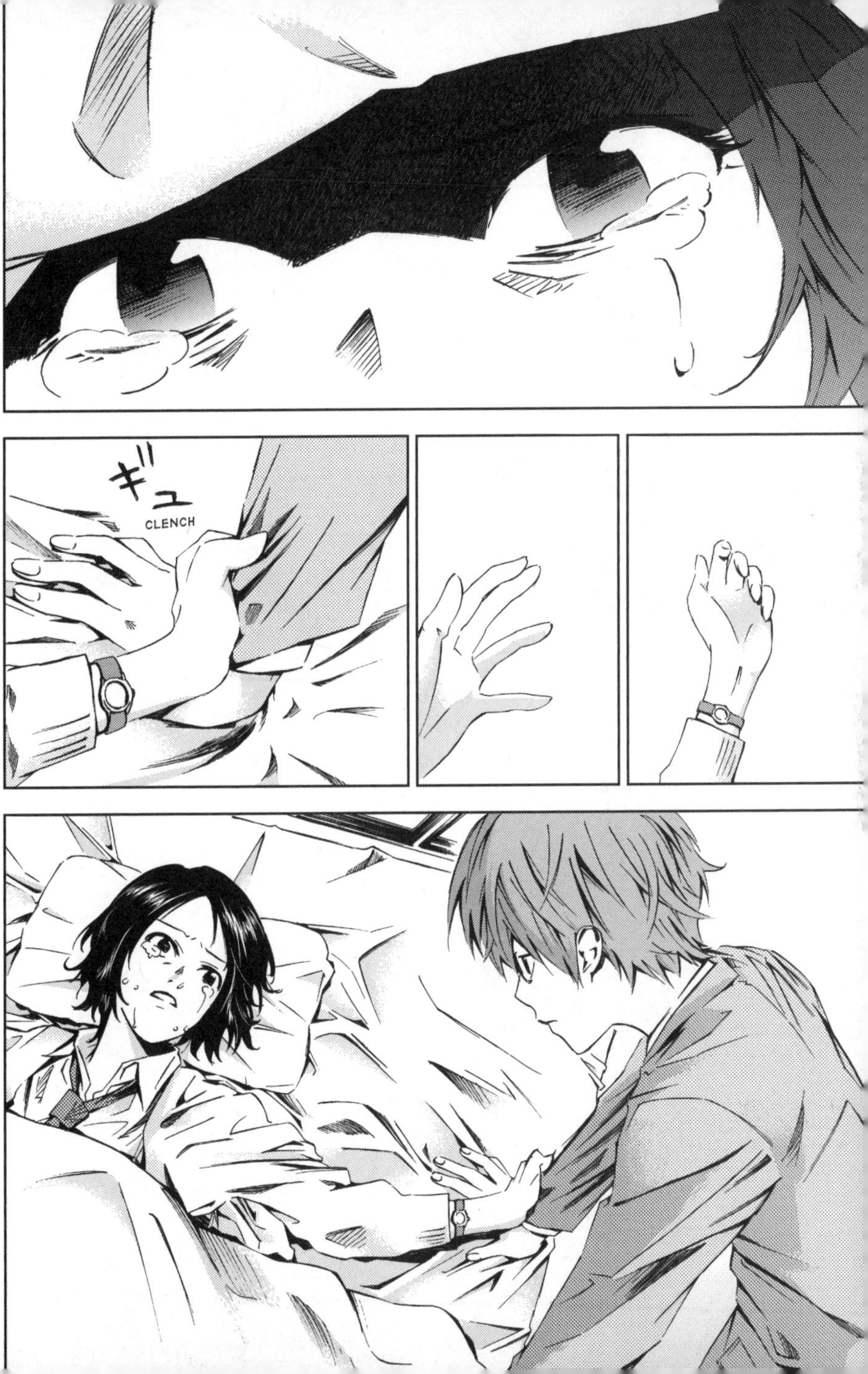
ギュ
CLENCH

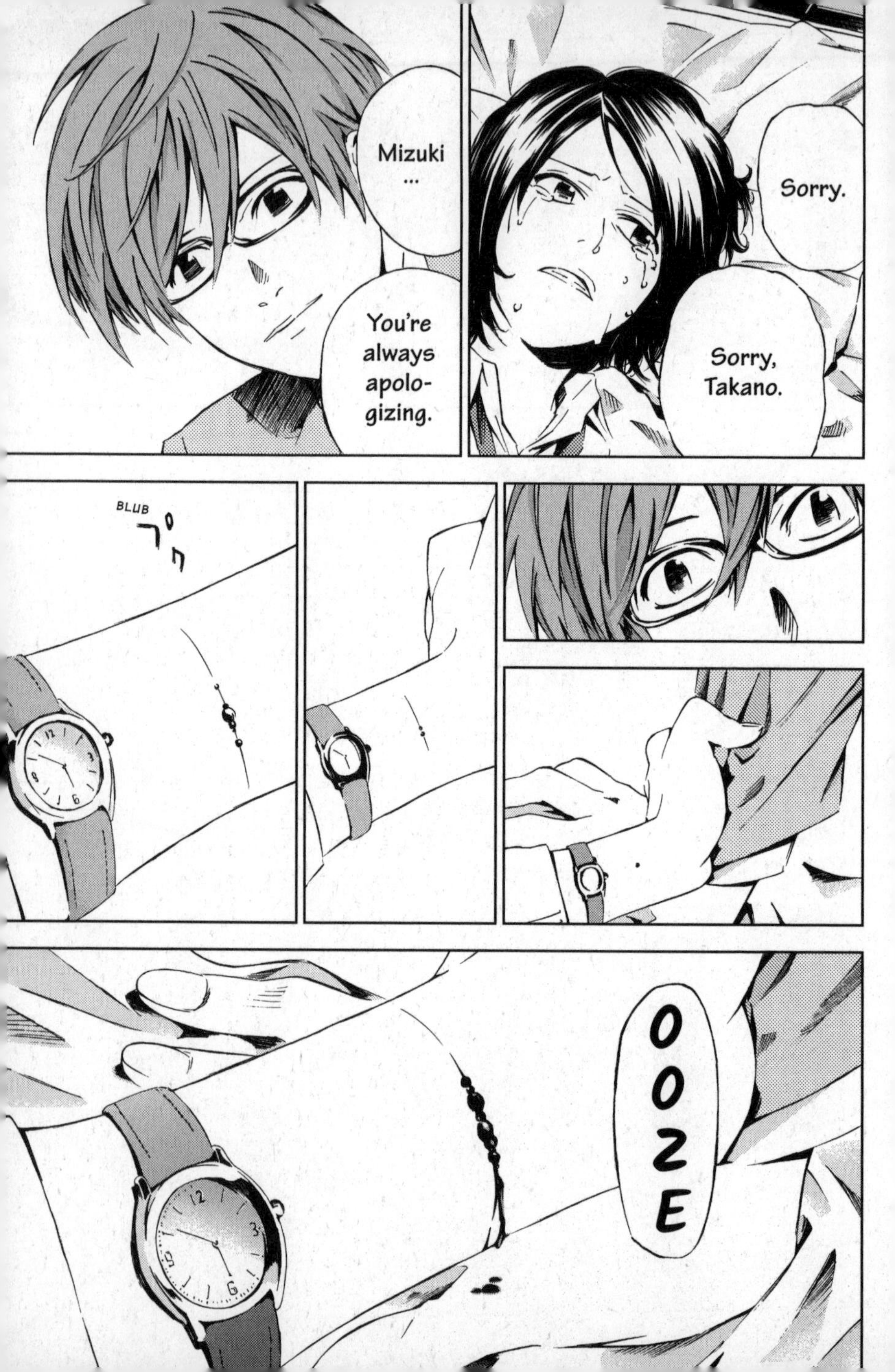
Sorry.
Sorry, Takano.
Mizuki ...
You're always apolo-gizing.
BLUB
OOZE

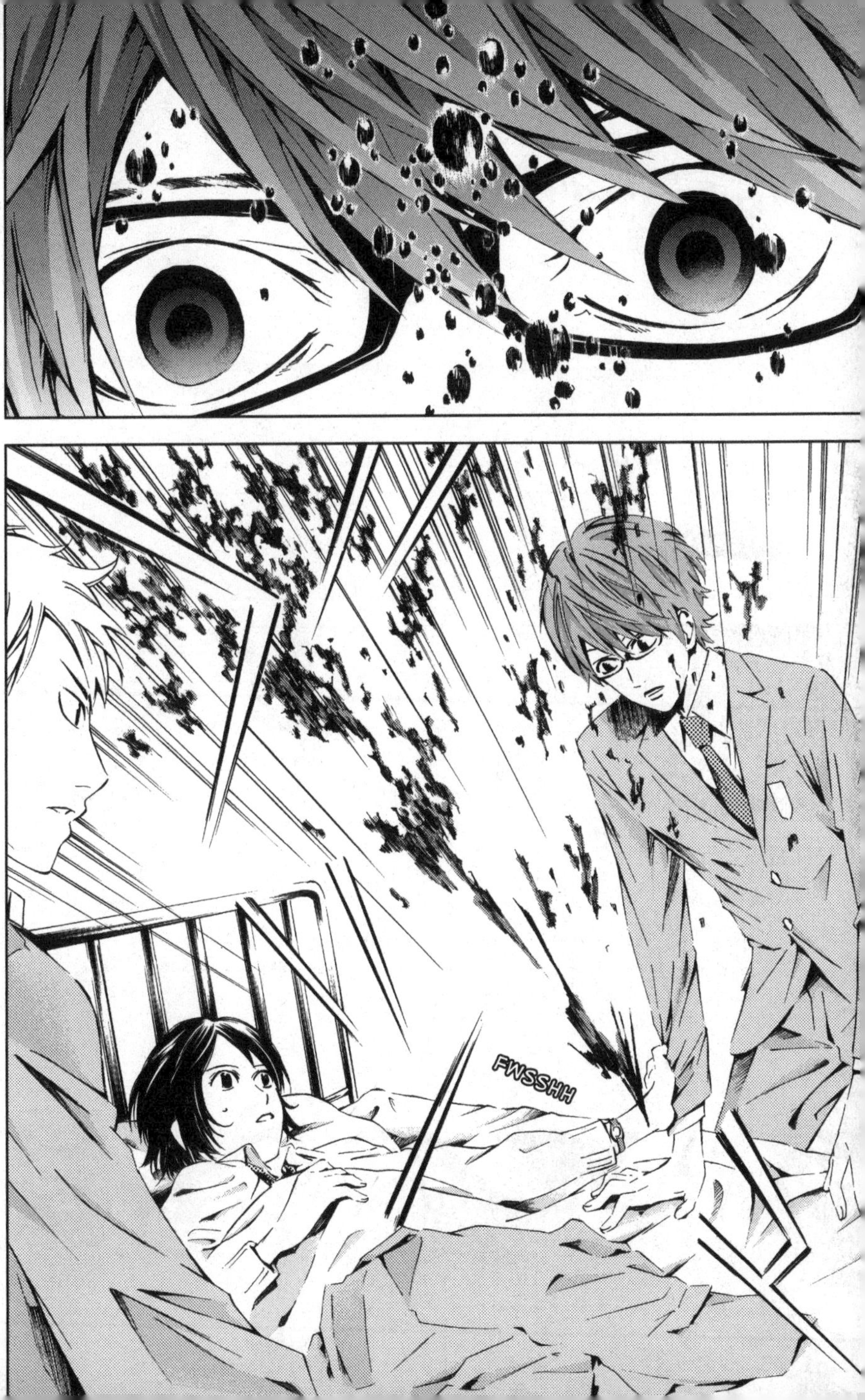
FWSSHH

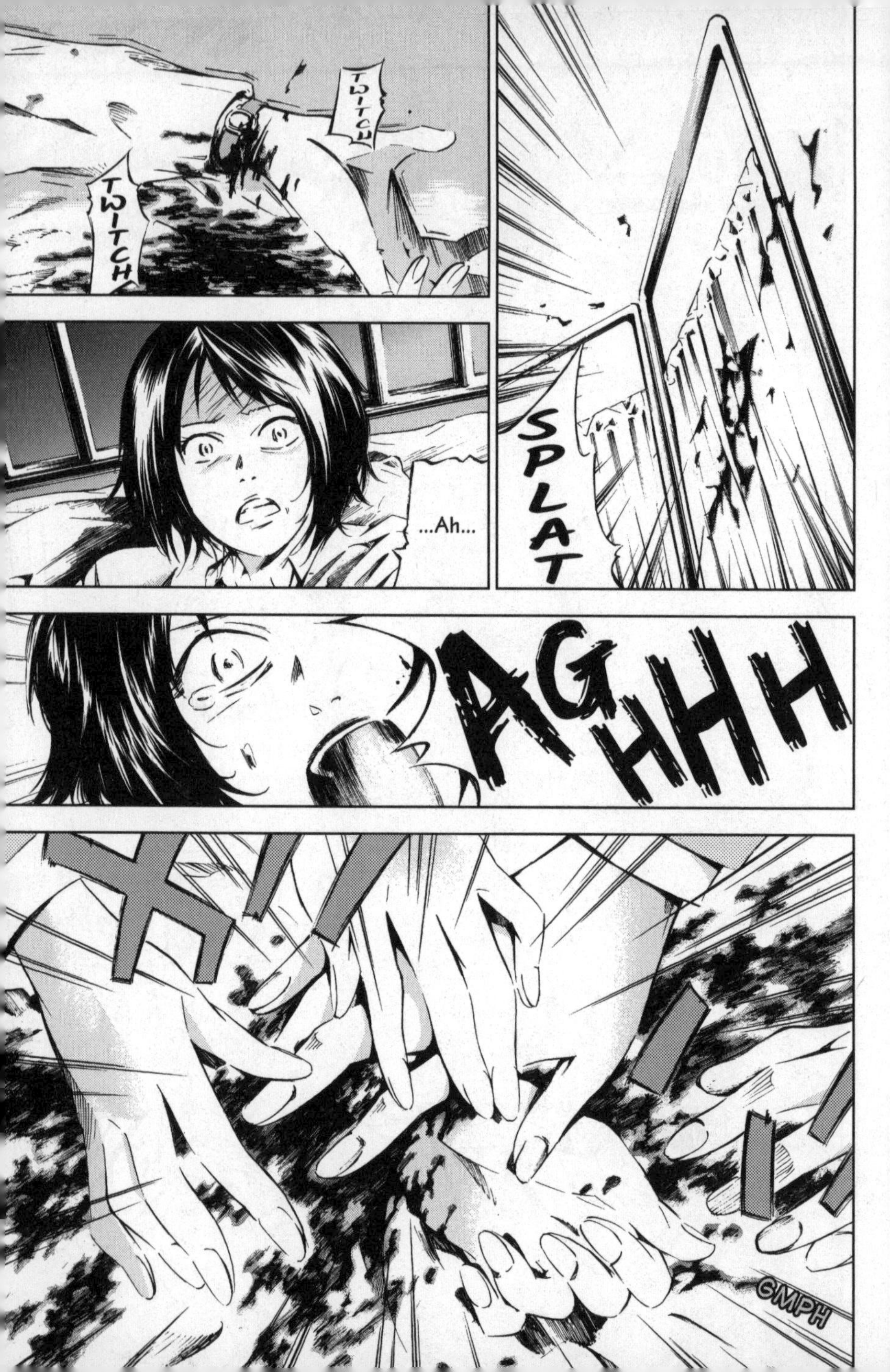
SPLAT
TWITCH
TWITCH
...Ah...
AGHHH
GMPH

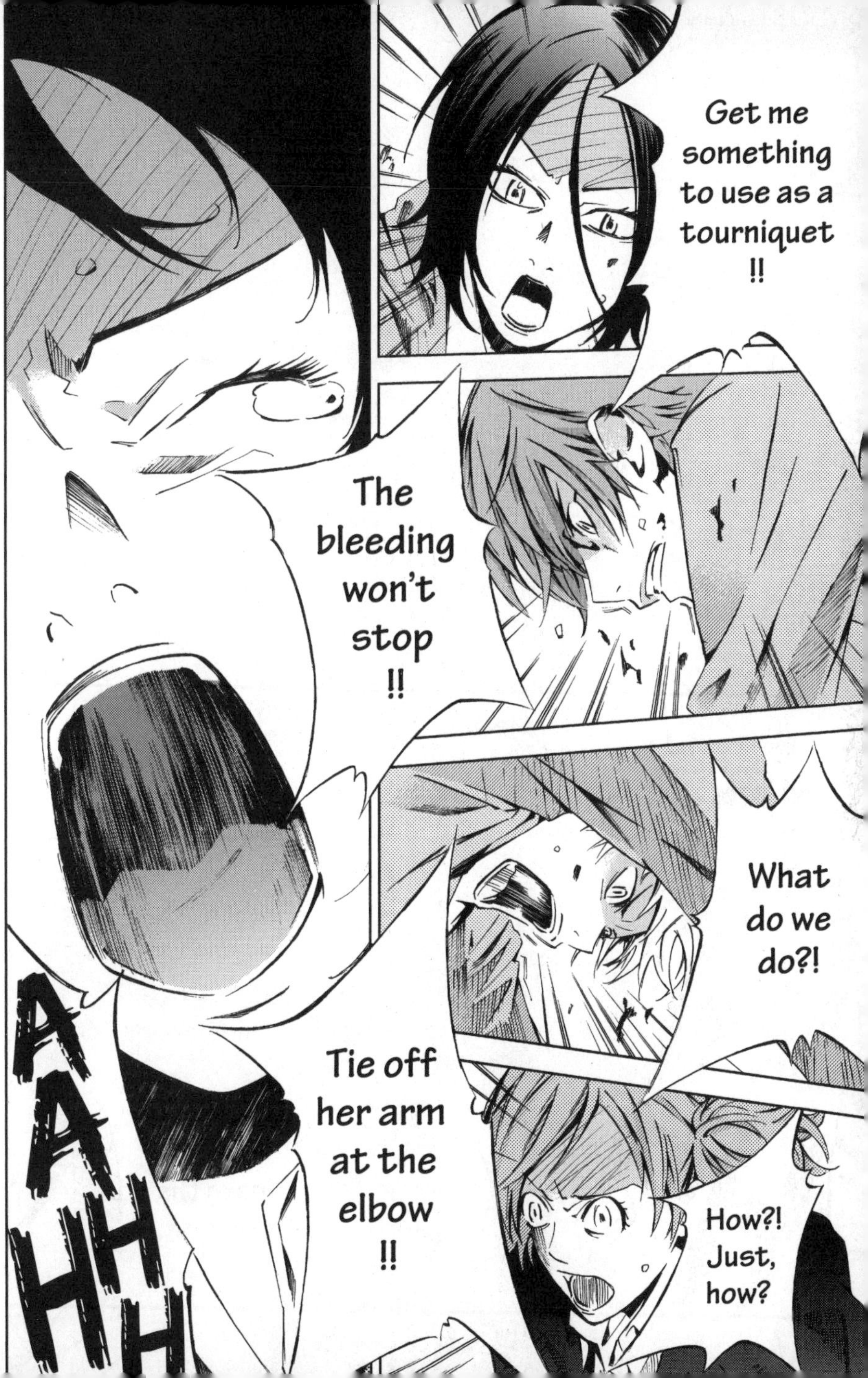
Get me something to use as a tourniquet!!
The bleeding won't stop!!
What do we do?!
Tie off her arm at the elbow!!
How?! Just, how?
AAHHHH

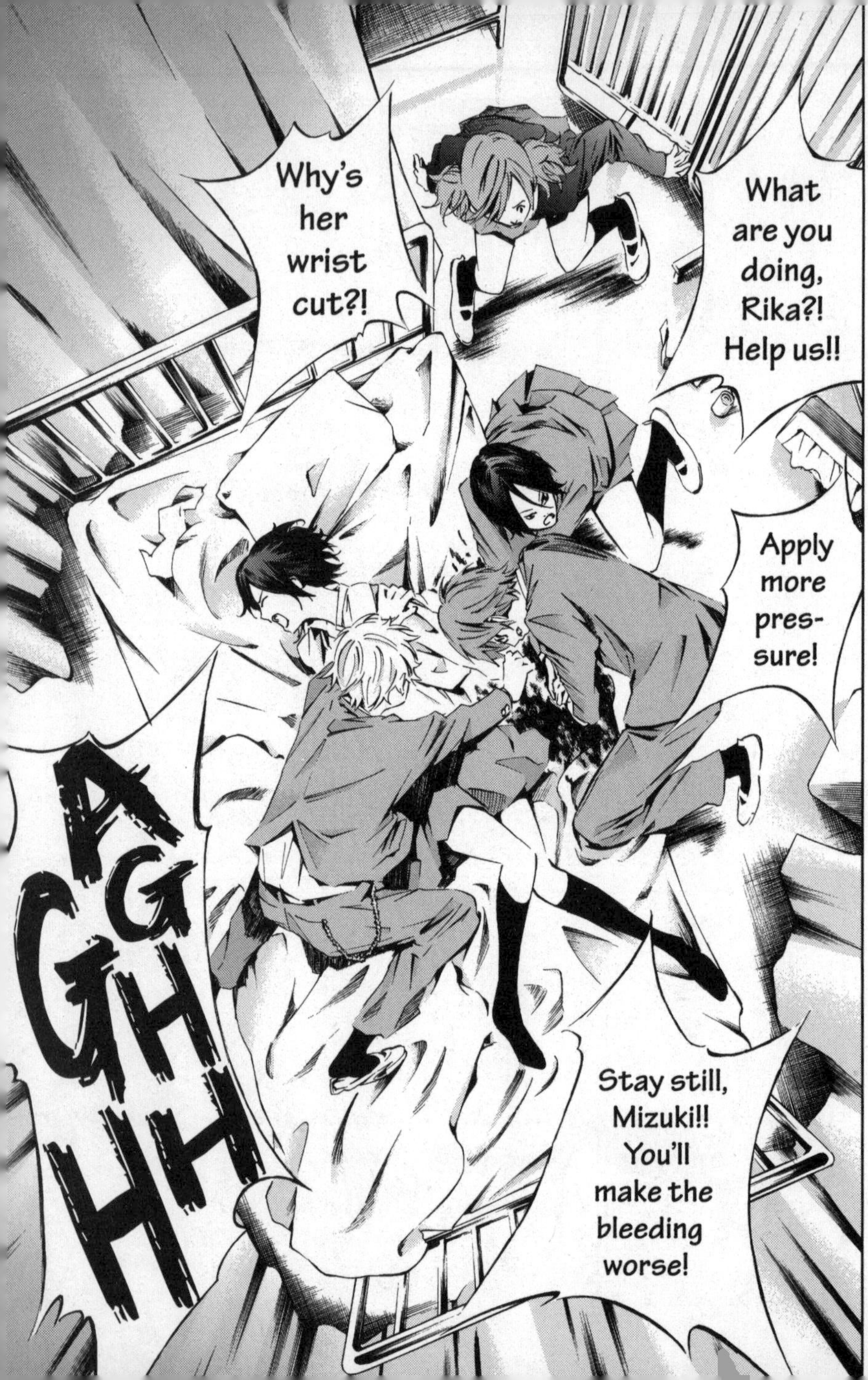
What are you doing, Rika?! Help us!!
Why's her wrist cut?!
Apply more pressure!
Stay still, Mizuki!! You'll make the bleeding worse!
AGGHHH

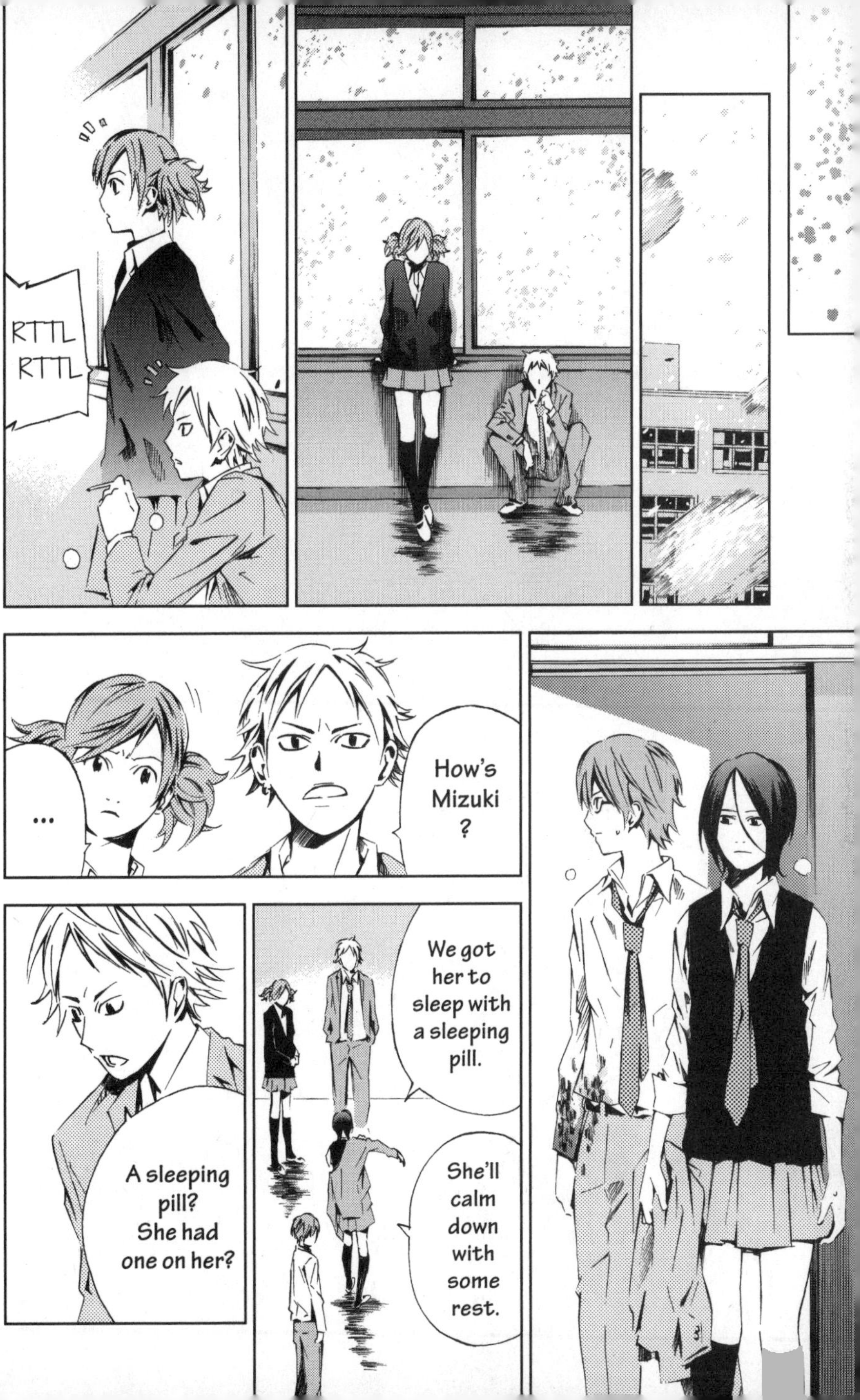
RTTL RTTL
How's Mizuki?
...
We got her to sleep with a sleeping pill.
She'll calm down with some rest.
A sleeping pill? She had one on her?

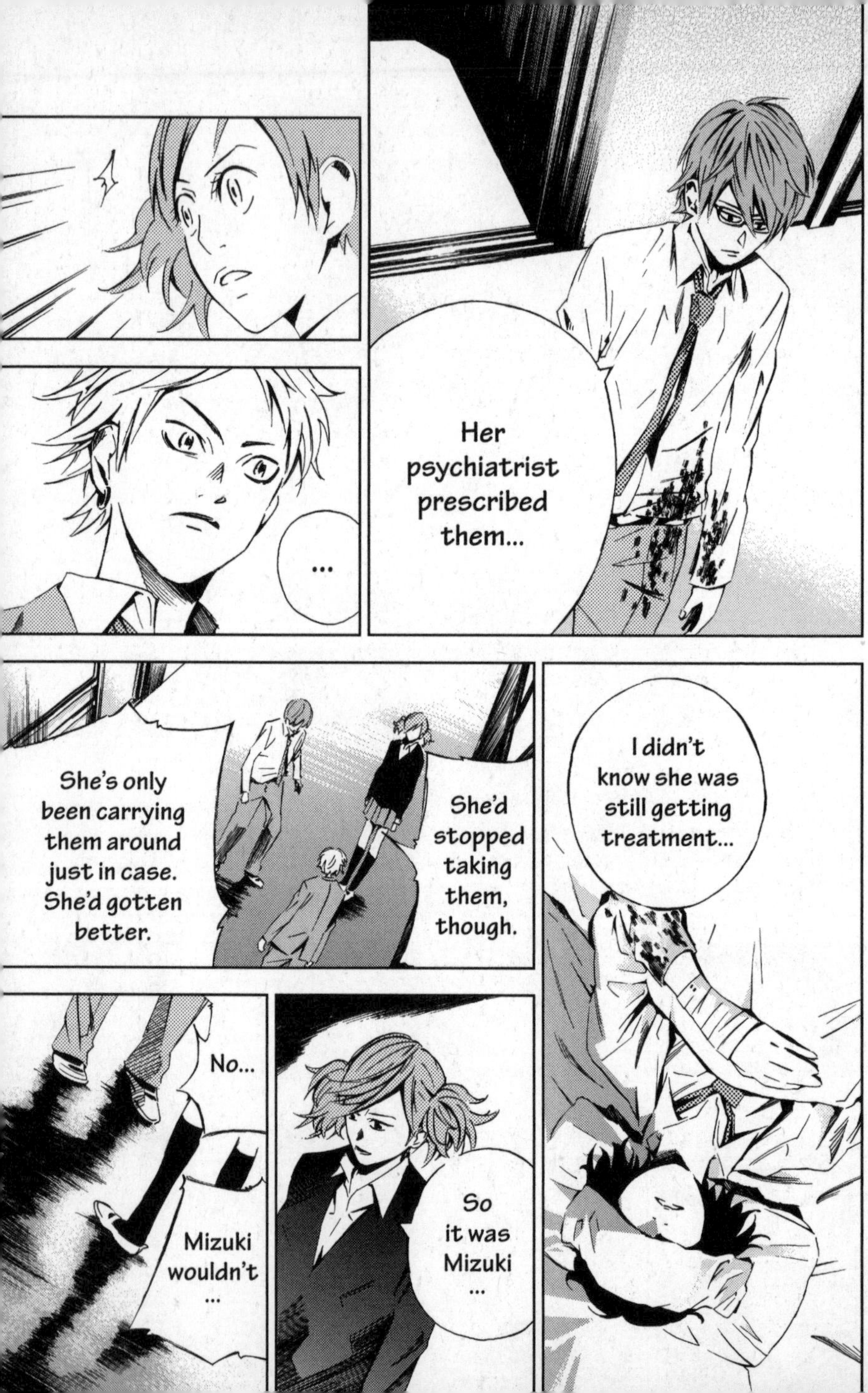
Her psychiatrist prescribed them...
...
I didn't know she was still getting treatment...
She'd stopped taking them, though.
She's only been carrying them around just in case. She'd gotten better.
So it was Mizuki ...
No...
Mizuki wouldn't ...

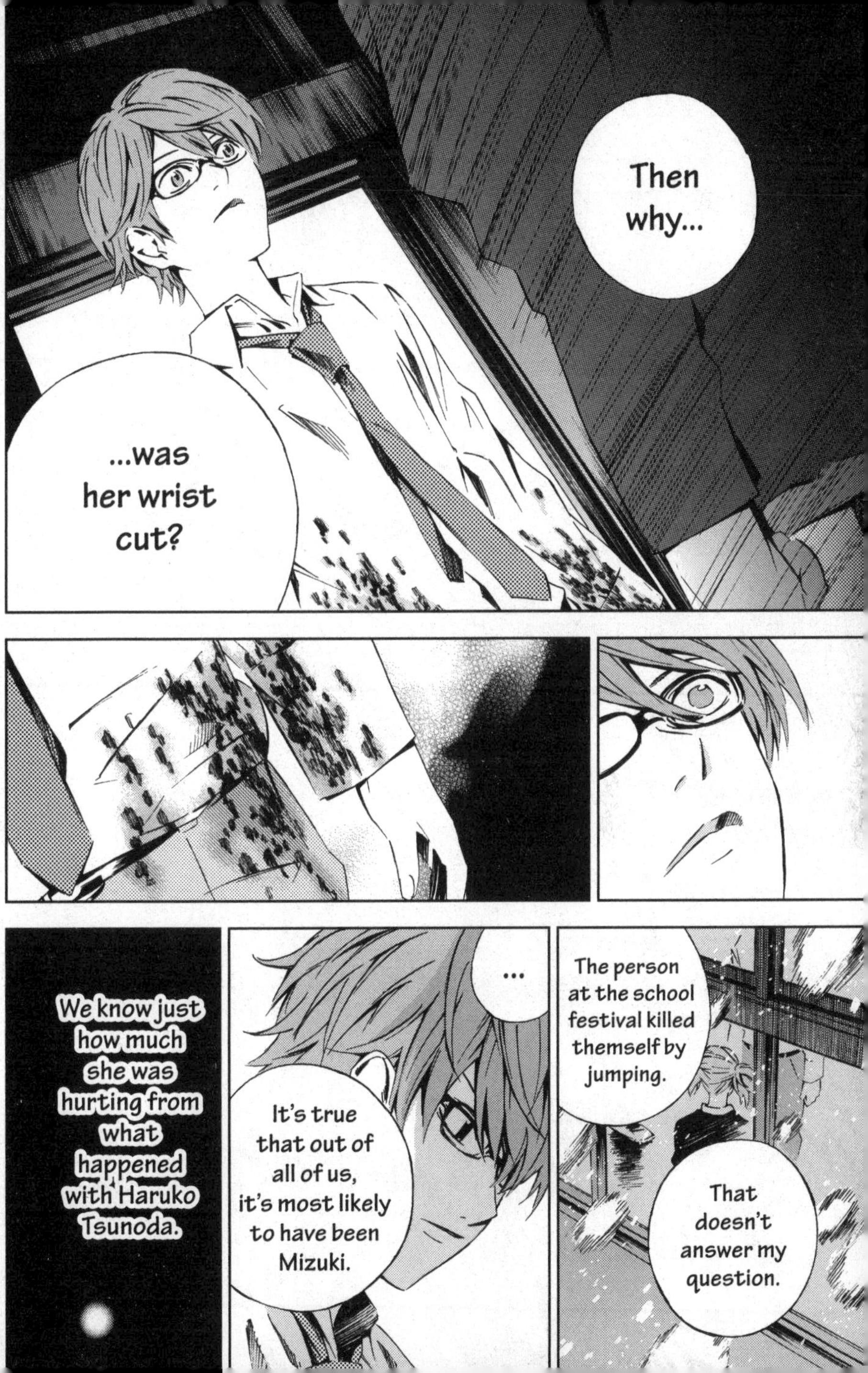
Then why...
...was her wrist cut?
The person at the school festival killed themself by jumping.
That doesn't answer my question.
...
It's true that out of all of us, it's most likely to have been Mizuki.
We know just how much she was hurting from what happened with Haruko Tsunoda.

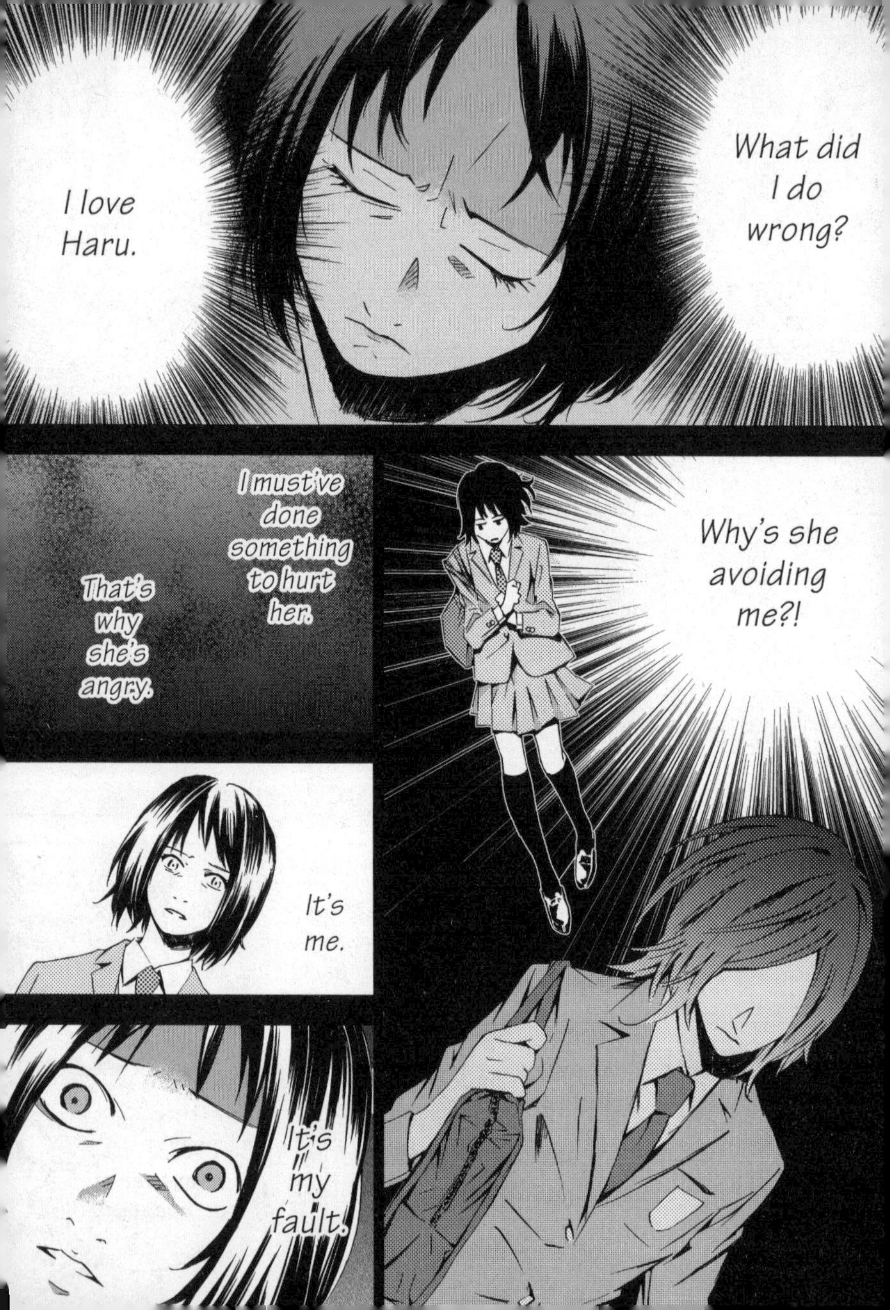
What did I do wrong?
I love Haru.
Why's she avoiding me?!
I must've done something to hurt her.
That's why she's angry.
It's me.
It's my fault.

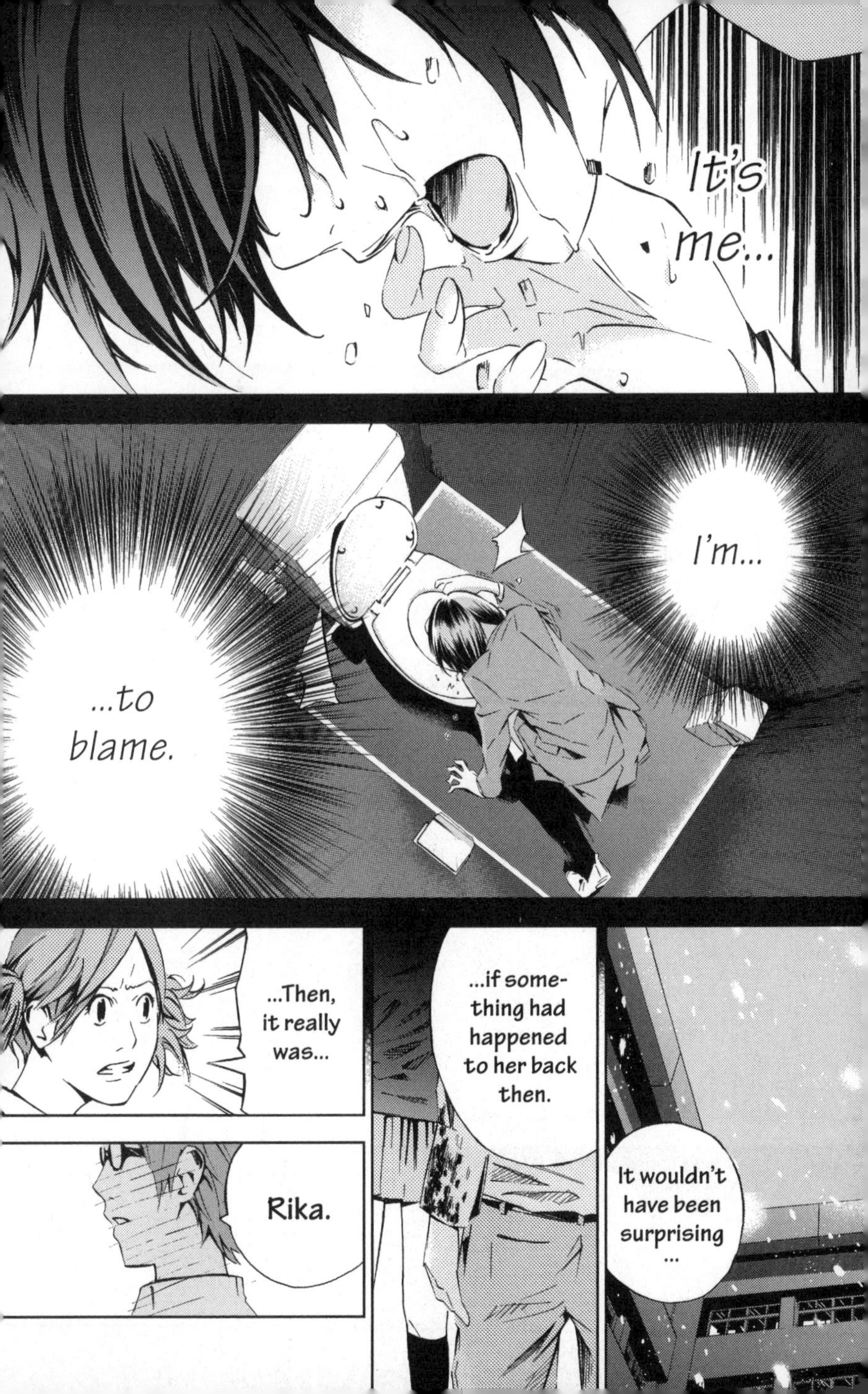
It's me...
I'm...
...to blame.
It wouldn't have been surprising ...
...if some-thing had happened to her back then.
...Then, it really was...
Rika.

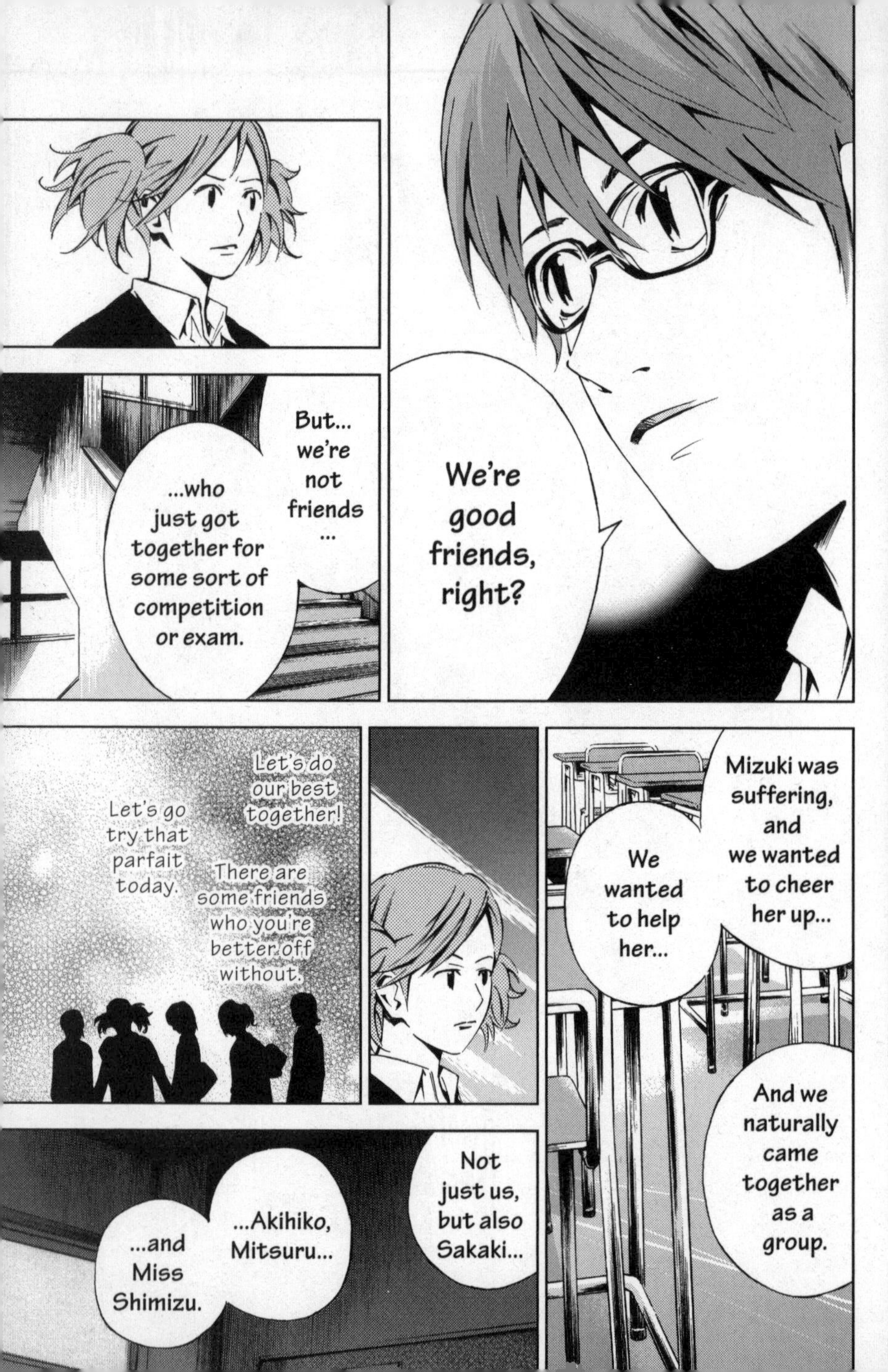
We're good friends, right?
But... we're not friends...
...who just got together for some sort of competition or exam.
Mizuki was suffering, and we wanted to cheer her up...
We wanted to help her...
And we naturally came together as a group.
Let's do our best together!
Let's go try that parfait today.
There are some friends who you're better off without.
Not just us, but also Sakaki...
...Akihiko, Mitsuru...
...and Miss Shimizu.

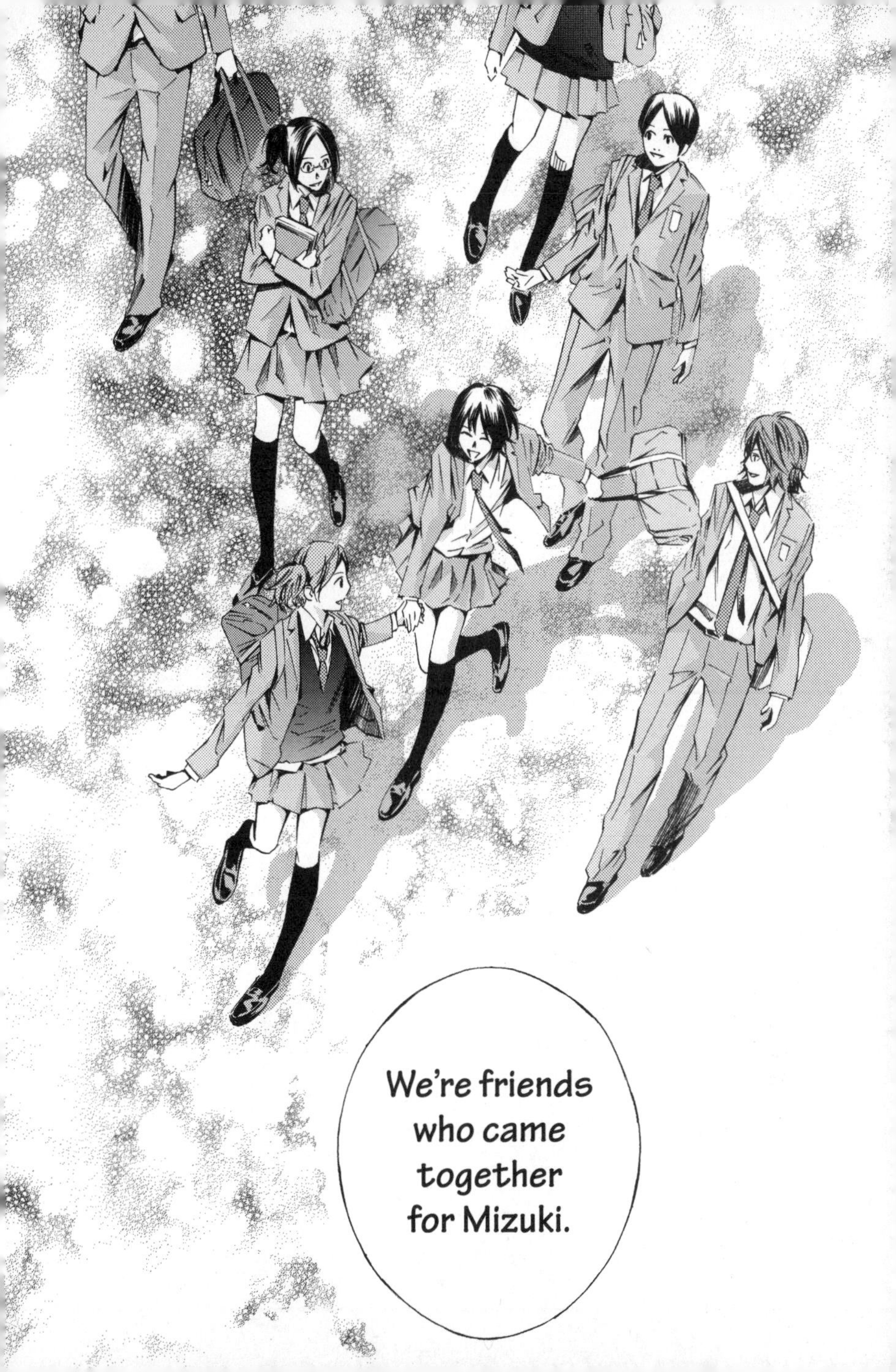
We're friends who came together for Mizuki.

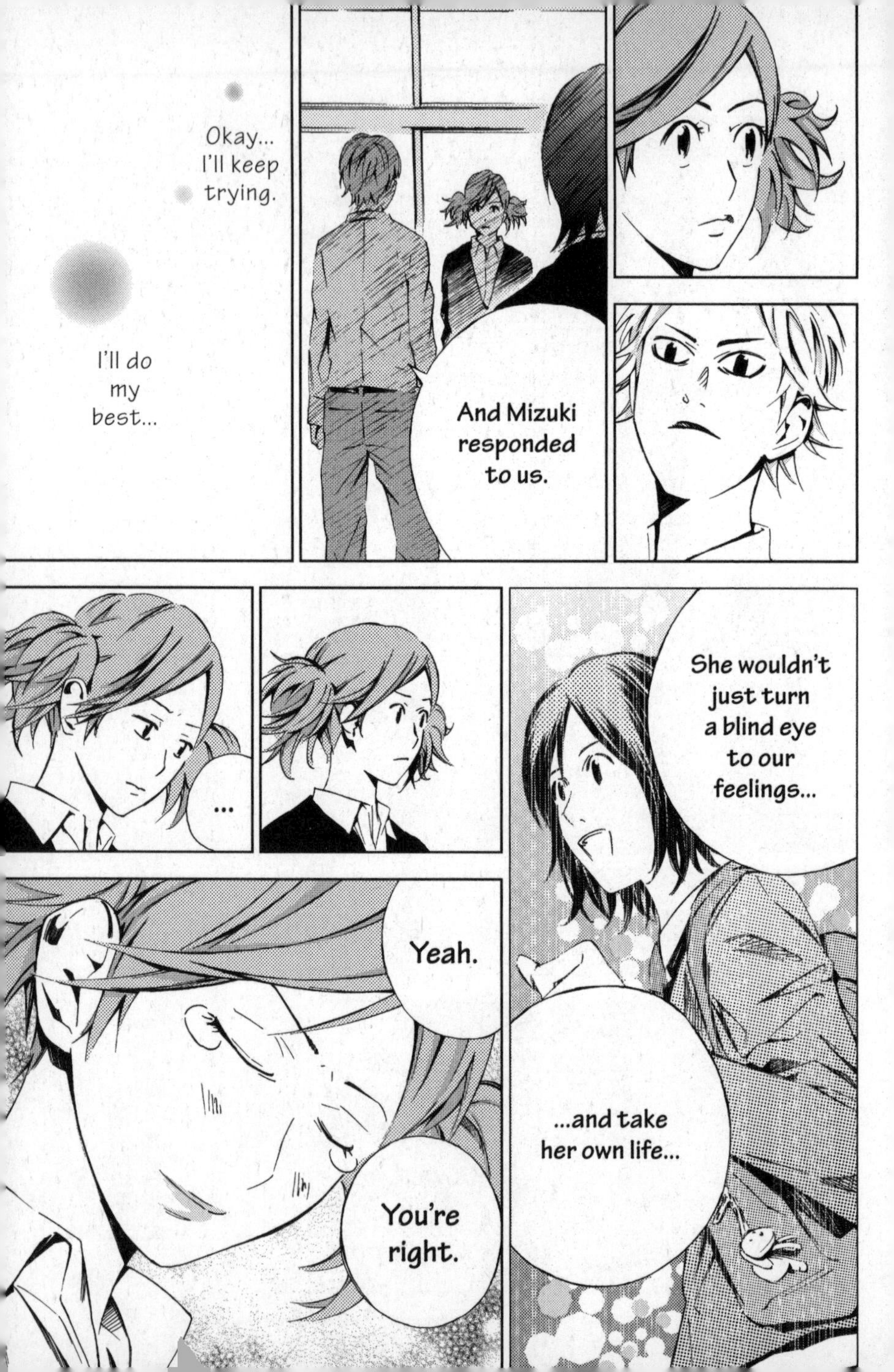
And Mizuki responded to us.
Okay... I'll keep trying.
I'll do my best...
She wouldn't just turn a blind eye to our feelings...
...and take her own life...
...
Yeah.
You're right.

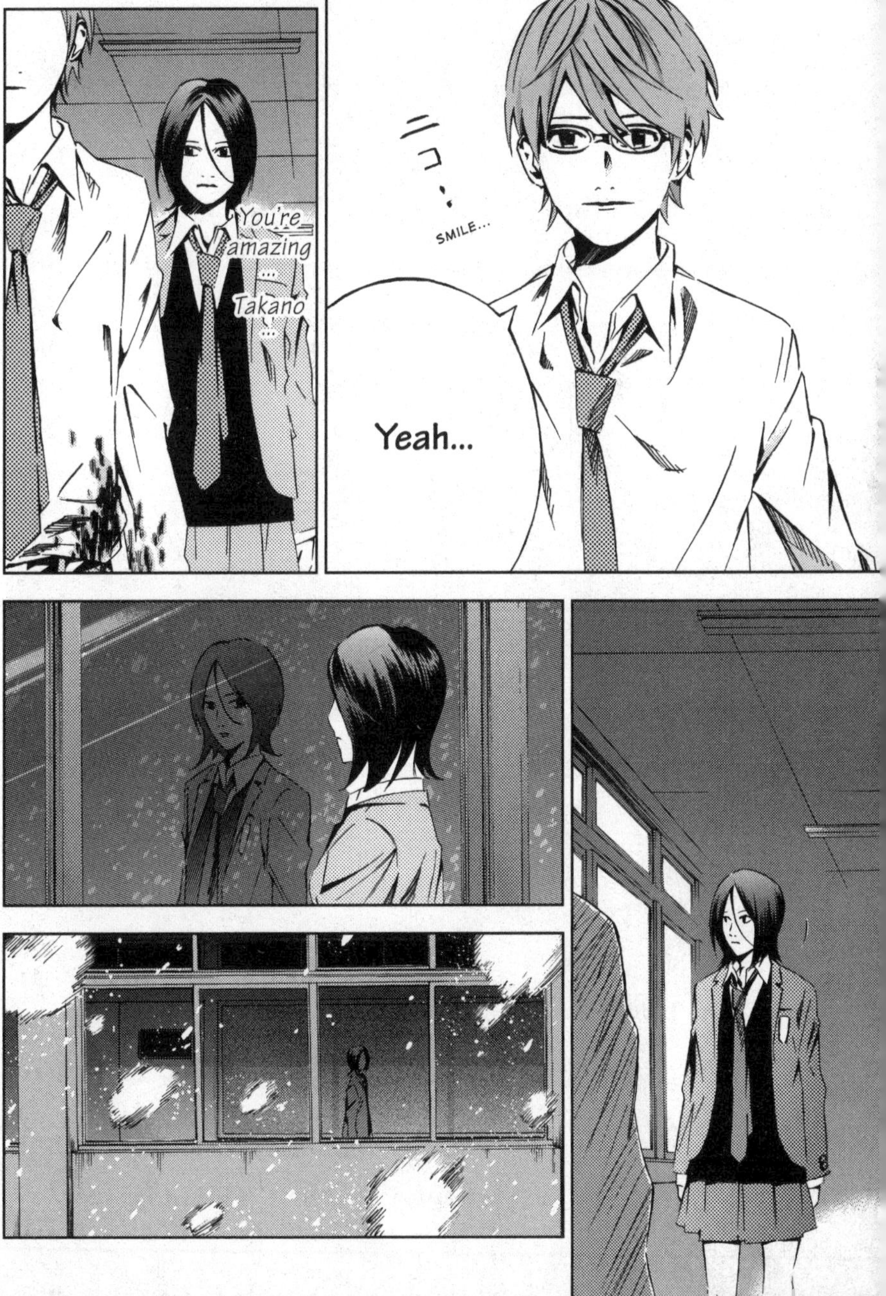
ニコ・・
SMILE...
Yeah...
You're amazing... Takano...

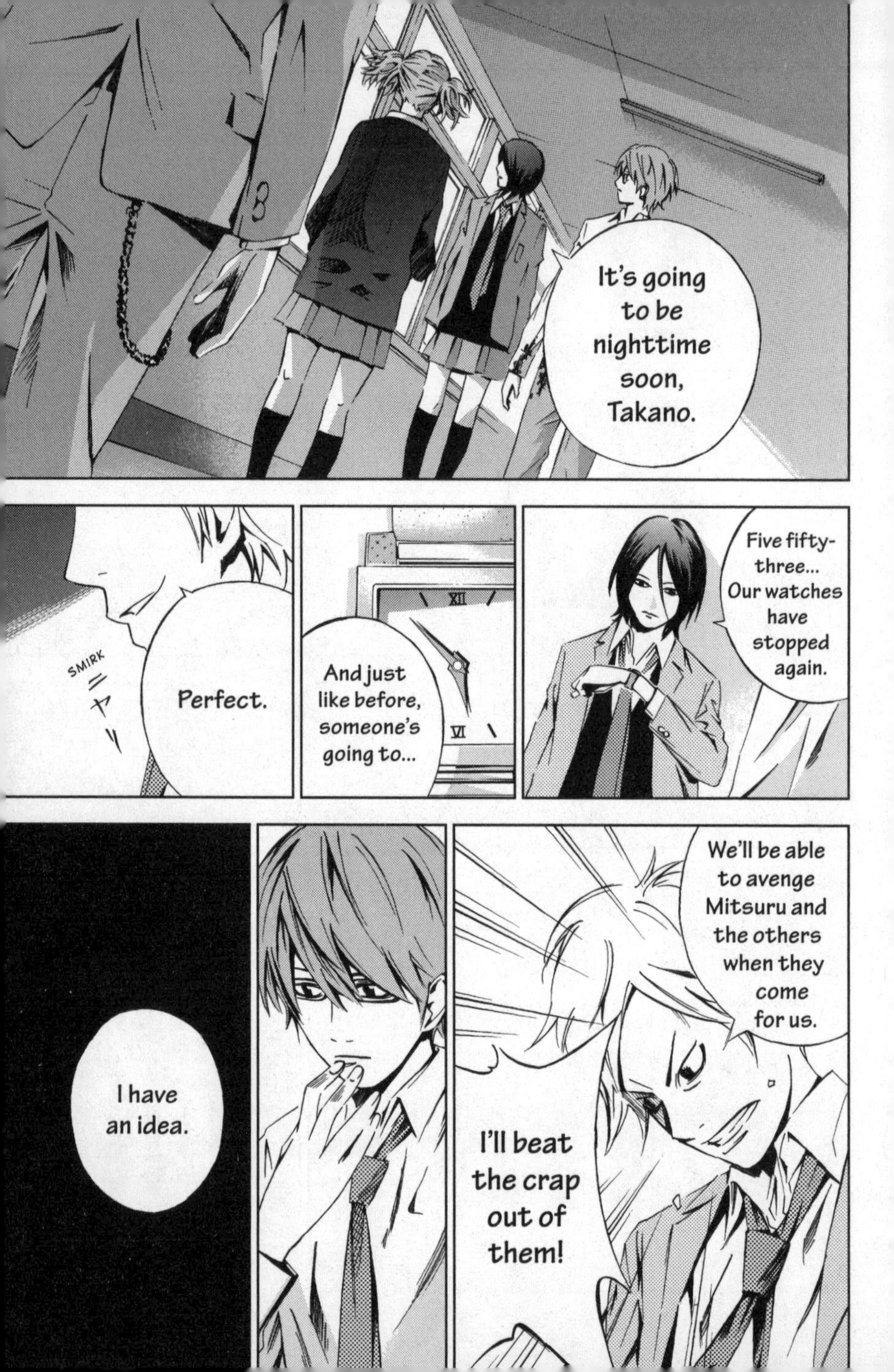
It's going to be nighttime soon, Takano.
Five fifty-three... Our watches have stopped again.
And just like before, someone's going to...
SMIRK
Perfect.
We'll be able to avenge Mitsuru and the others when they come for us.
I'll beat the crap out of them!
I have an idea.

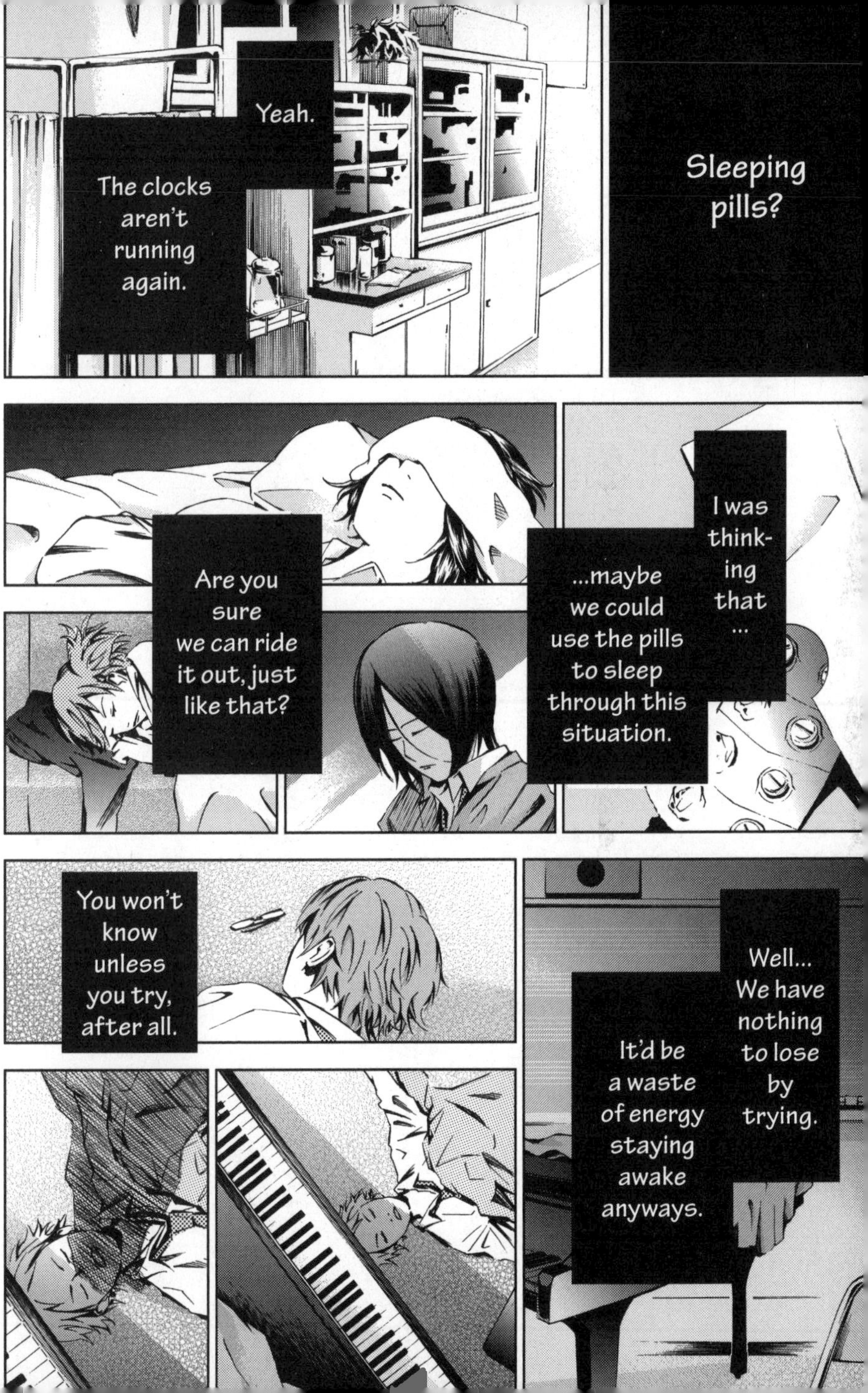
Sleeping pills?
Yeah.
The clocks aren't running again.
I was thinking that ...
...maybe we could use the pills to sleep through this situation.
Are you sure we can ride it out, just like that?
Well... We have nothing to lose by trying.
It'd be a waste of energy staying awake anyways.
You won't know unless you try, after all.

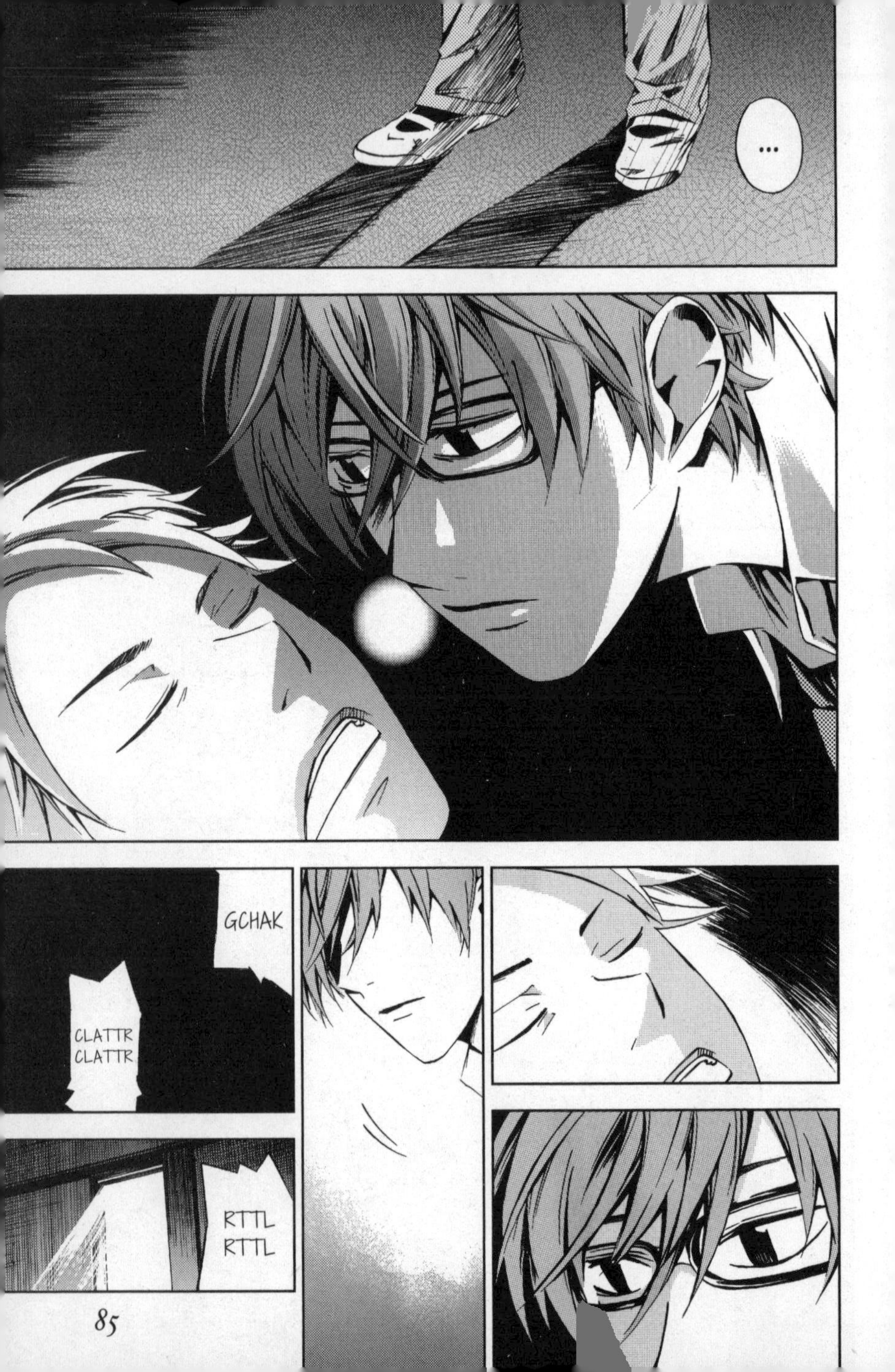
...
GCHAK
CLATTR
CLATTR
RTTL
RTTL

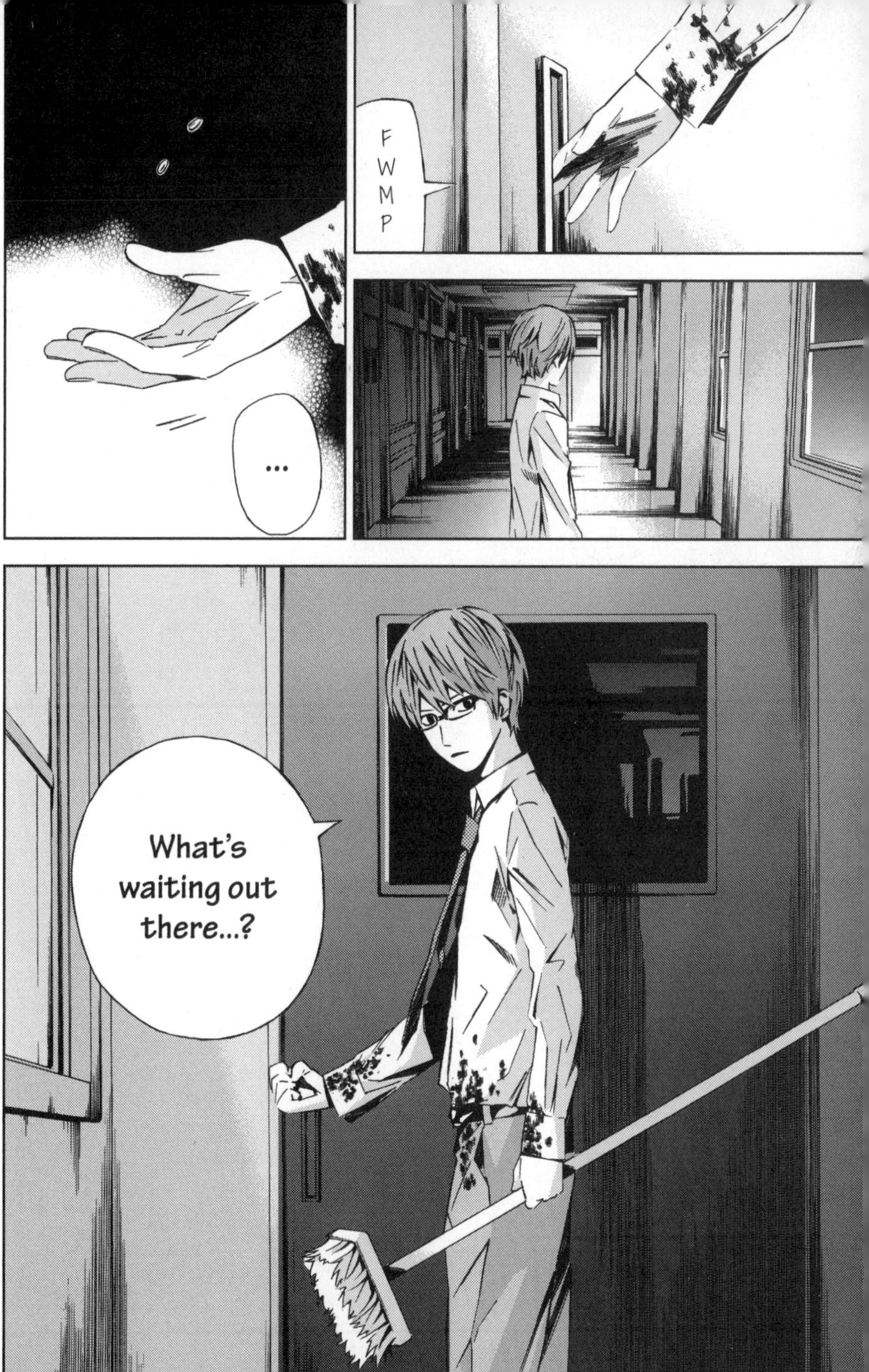
FWMP
...
What's waiting out there...?

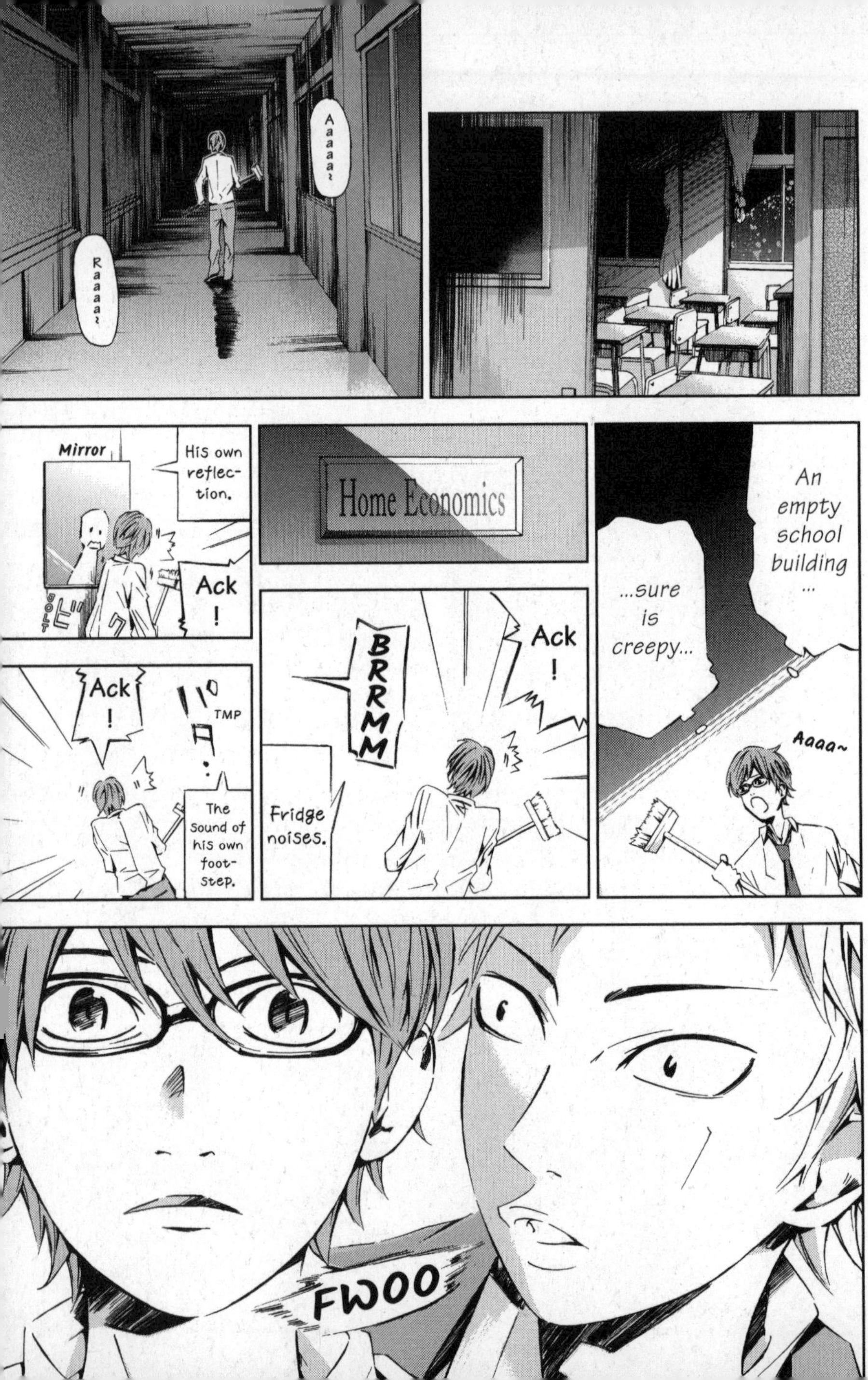

Aaaaa~
Raaaa~
An empty school building...
...sure is creepy...
Aaaa~
Home Economics
Ack!
BRRMM
Fridge noises.
Mirror
His own reflection.
Ack!
JOLT
Ack!
TMP
The sound of his own footstep.
FWOO

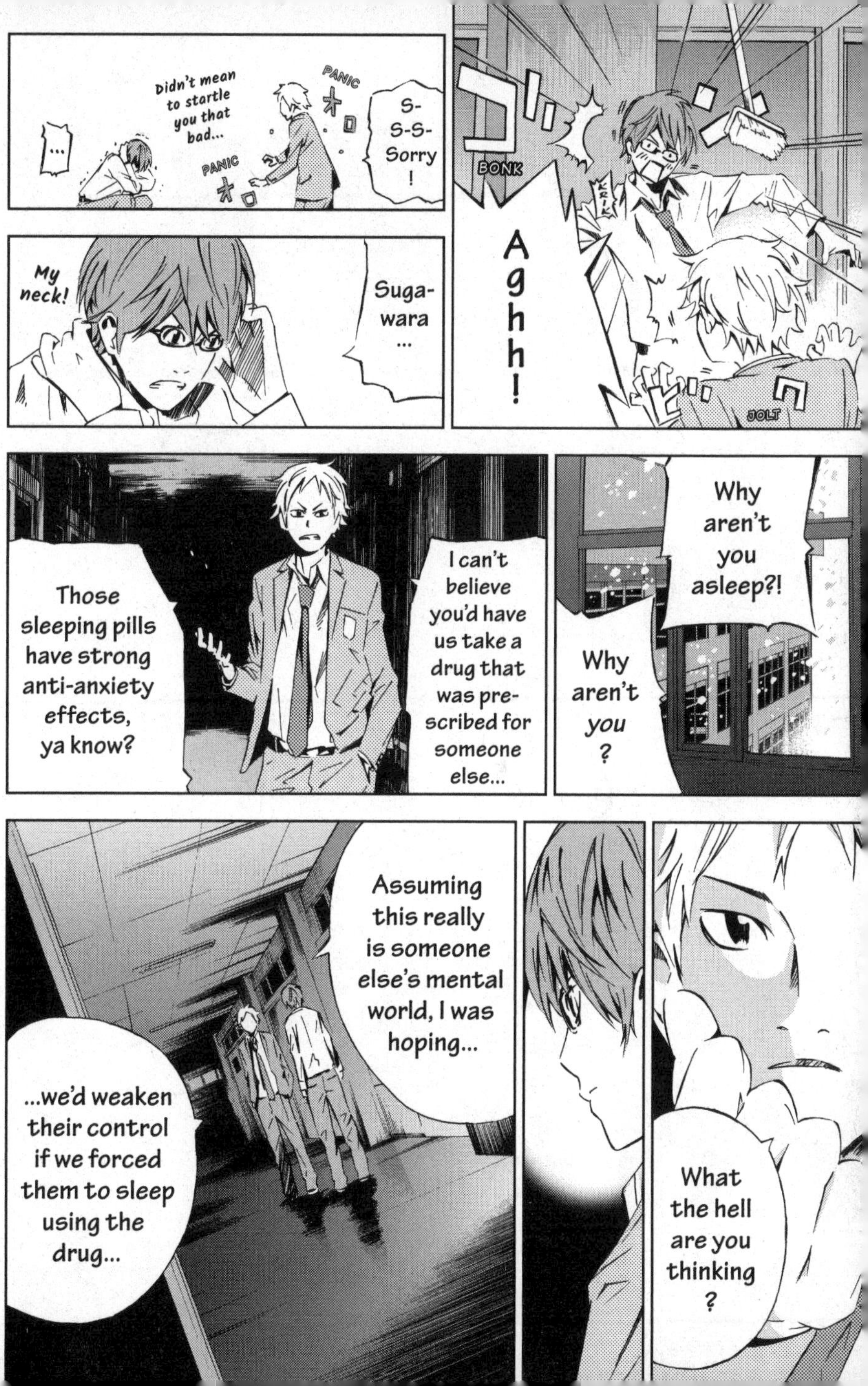
BONK
KRIK
Aghh!
JOLT
S-S-S-Sorry!
PANIC
PANIC
Didn't mean to startle you that bad...
...
Sugawara...
My neck!
Why aren't you asleep?!
Why aren't *you*?
I can't believe you'd have us take a drug that was prescribed for someone else...
Those sleeping pills have strong anti-anxiety effects, ya know?
What the hell are you thinking?
Assuming this really is someone else's mental world, I was hoping...
...we'd weaken their control if we forced them to sleep using the drug...

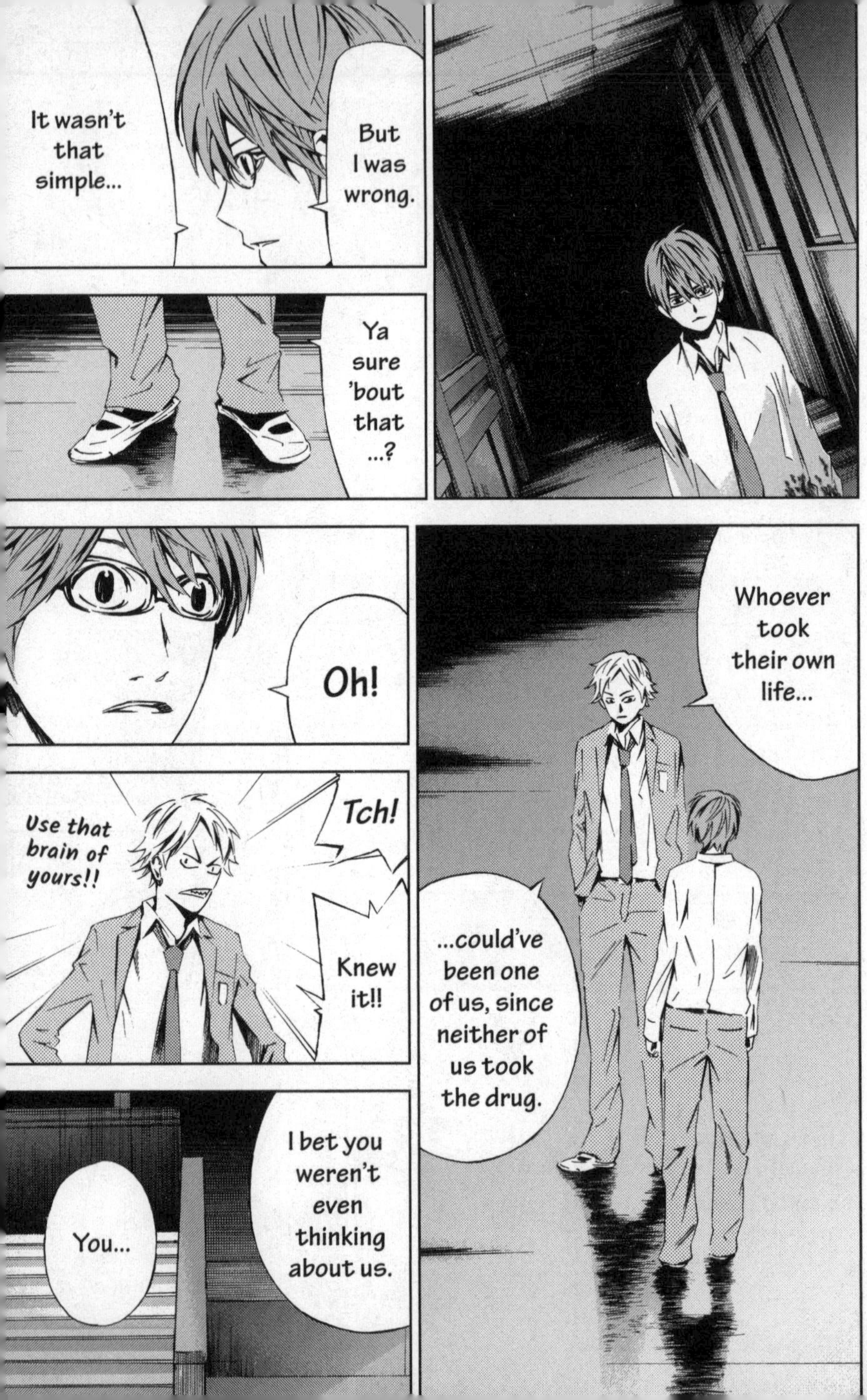

But I was wrong.
It wasn't that simple...
Ya sure 'bout that ...?
Whoever took their own life...
...could've been one of us, since neither of us took the drug.
Oh!
Tch!
Knew it!!
Use that brain of yours!!
I bet you weren't even thinking about us.
You...

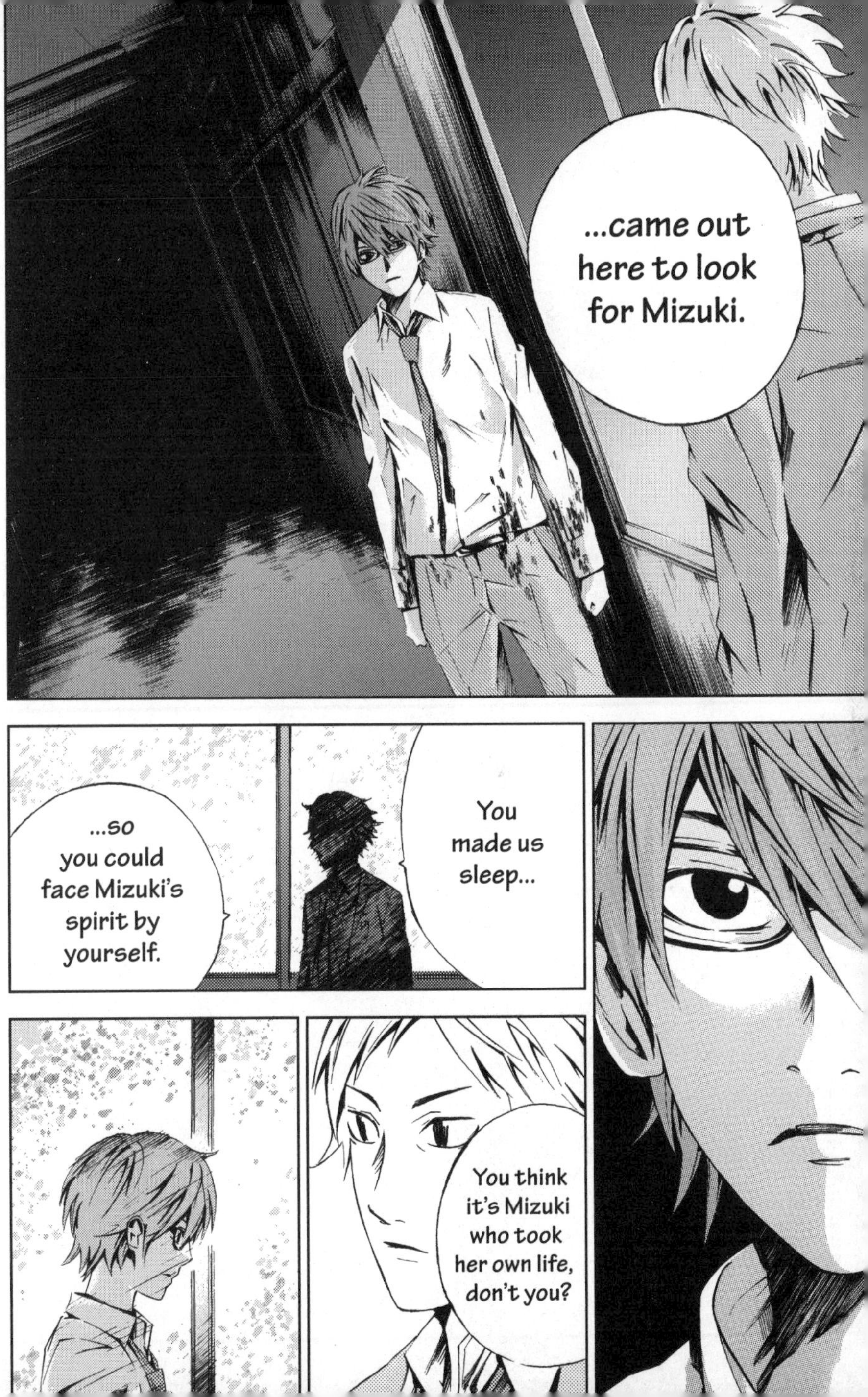
...came out here to look for Mizuki.
You made us sleep...
...so you could face Mizuki's spirit by yourself.
You think it's Mizuki who took her own life, don't you?

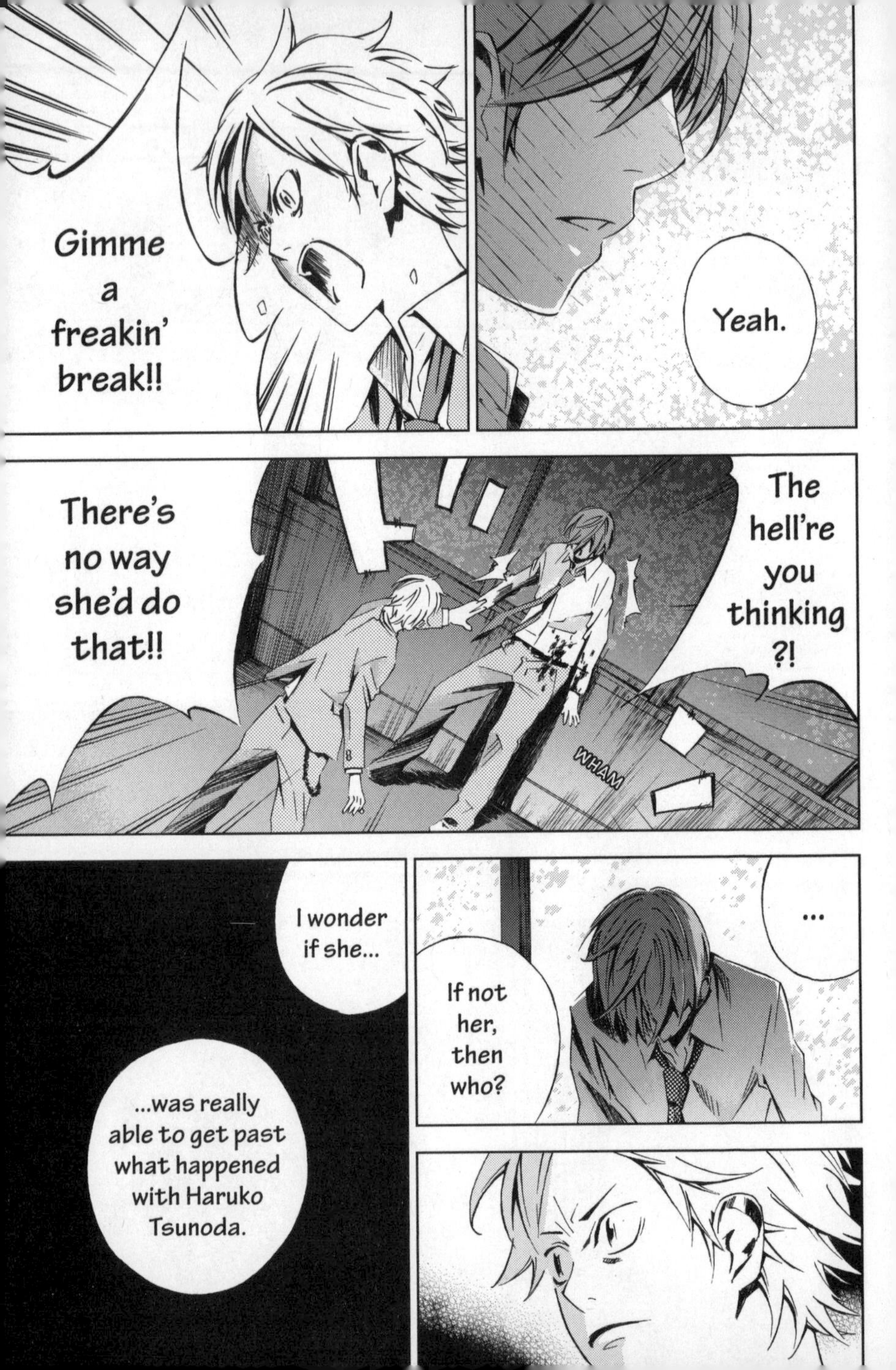
Yeah.
Gimme a freakin' break!!
The hell're you thinking?!
There's no way she'd do that!!
WHAM
...
If not her, then who?
I wonder if she...
...was really able to get past what happened with Haruko Tsunoda.

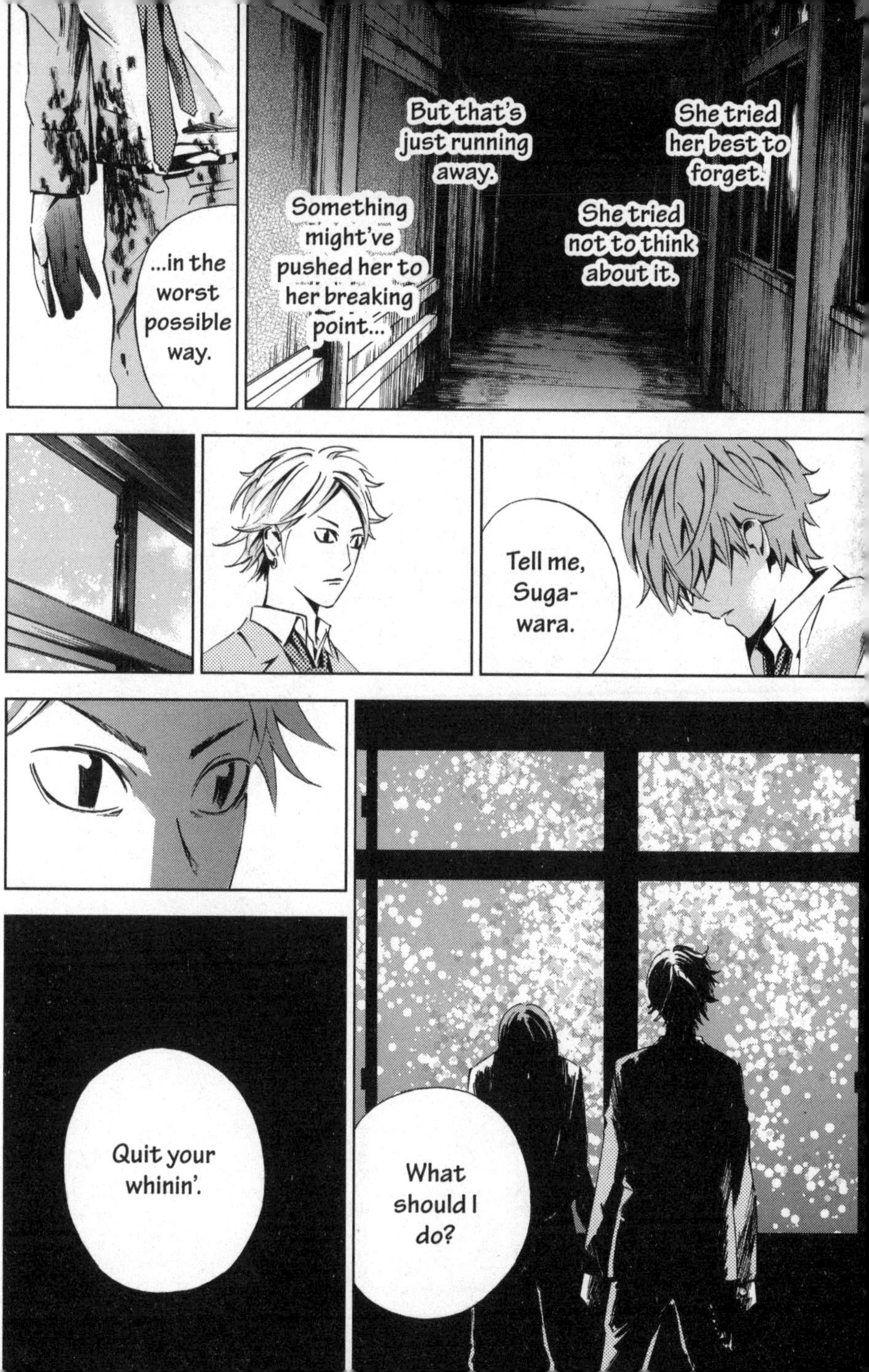

She tried her best to forget.
She tried not to think about it.
But that's just running away.
Something might've pushed her to her breaking point...
...in the worst possible way.
Tell me, Sugawara.
What should I do?
Quit your whinin'.

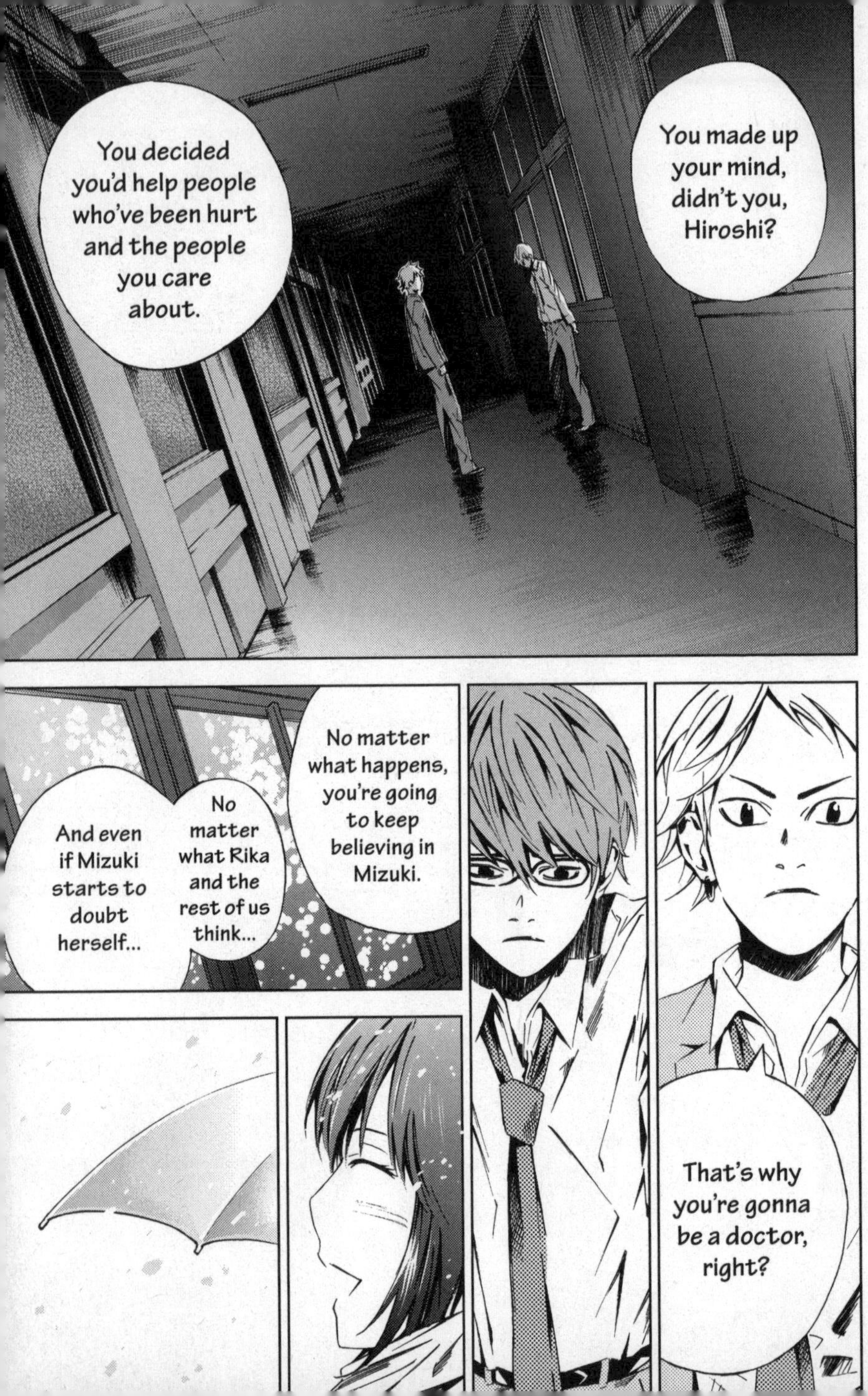
You made up your mind, didn't you, Hiroshi?
You decided you'd help people who've been hurt and the people you care about.
No matter what happens, you're going to keep believing in Mizuki.
No matter what Rika and the rest of us think...
And even if Mizuki starts to doubt herself...
That's why you're gonna be a doctor, right?

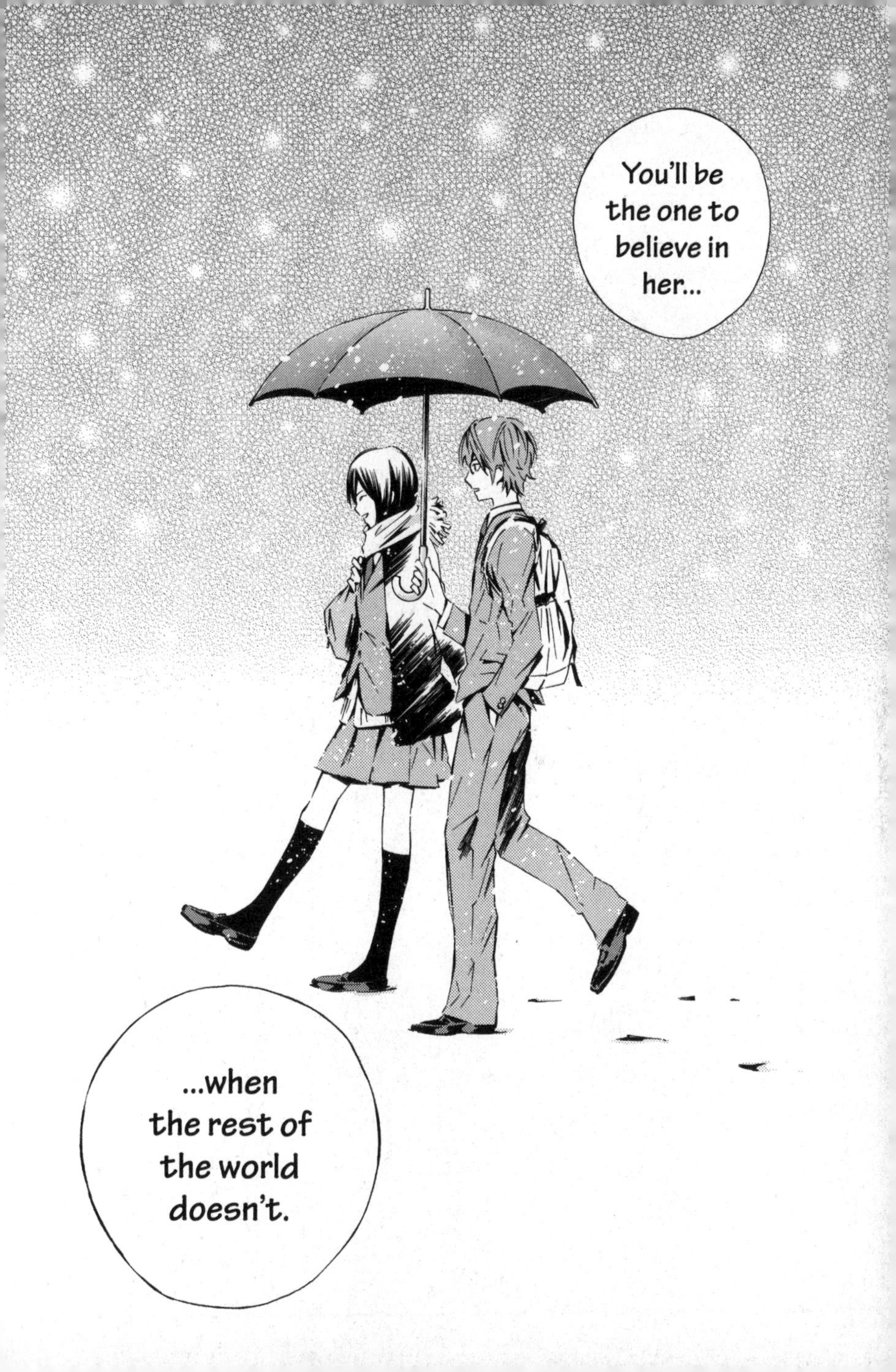
You'll be the one to believe in her...
...when the rest of the world doesn't.

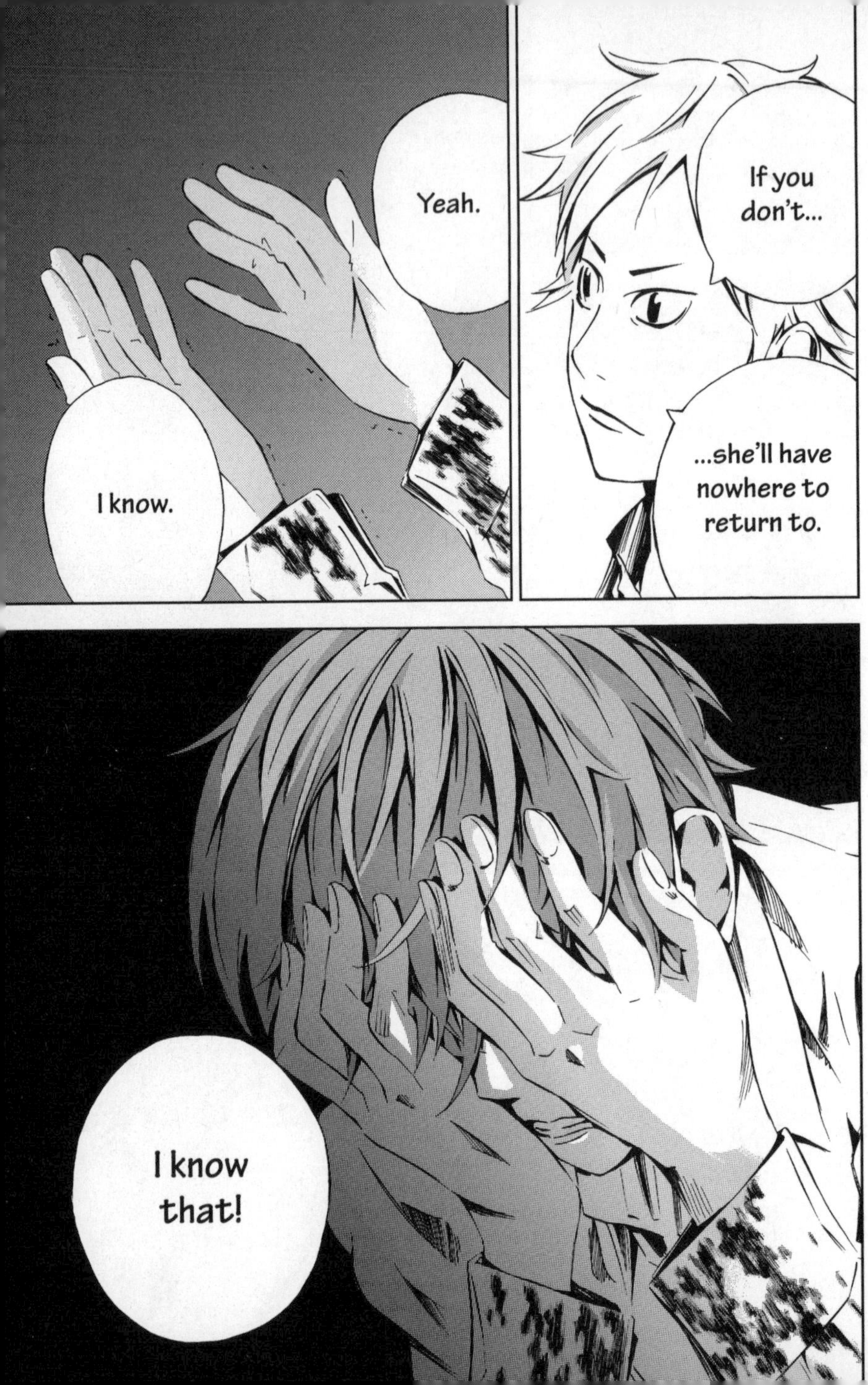
If you don't...
...she'll have nowhere to return to.
Yeah.
I know.
I know that!

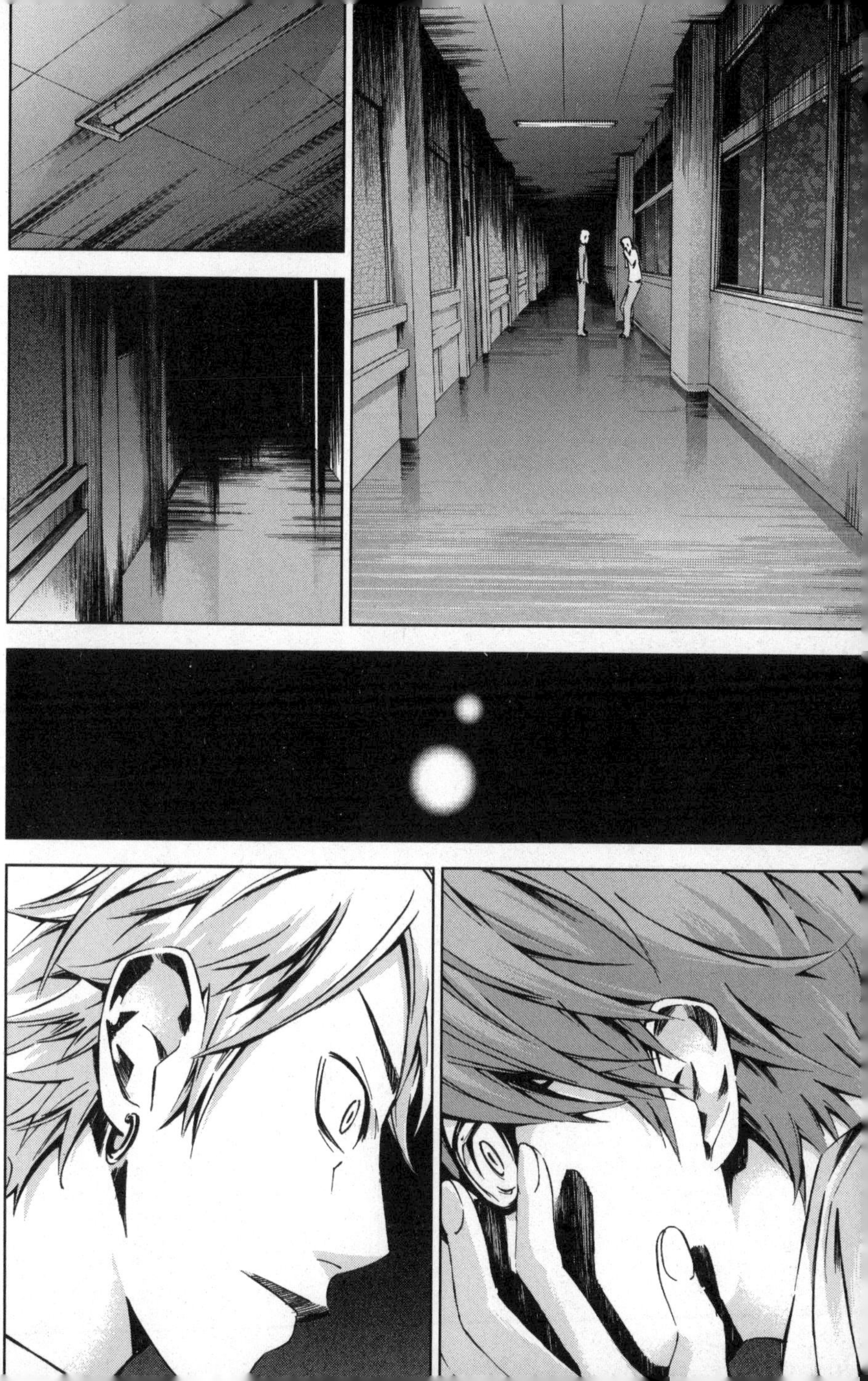

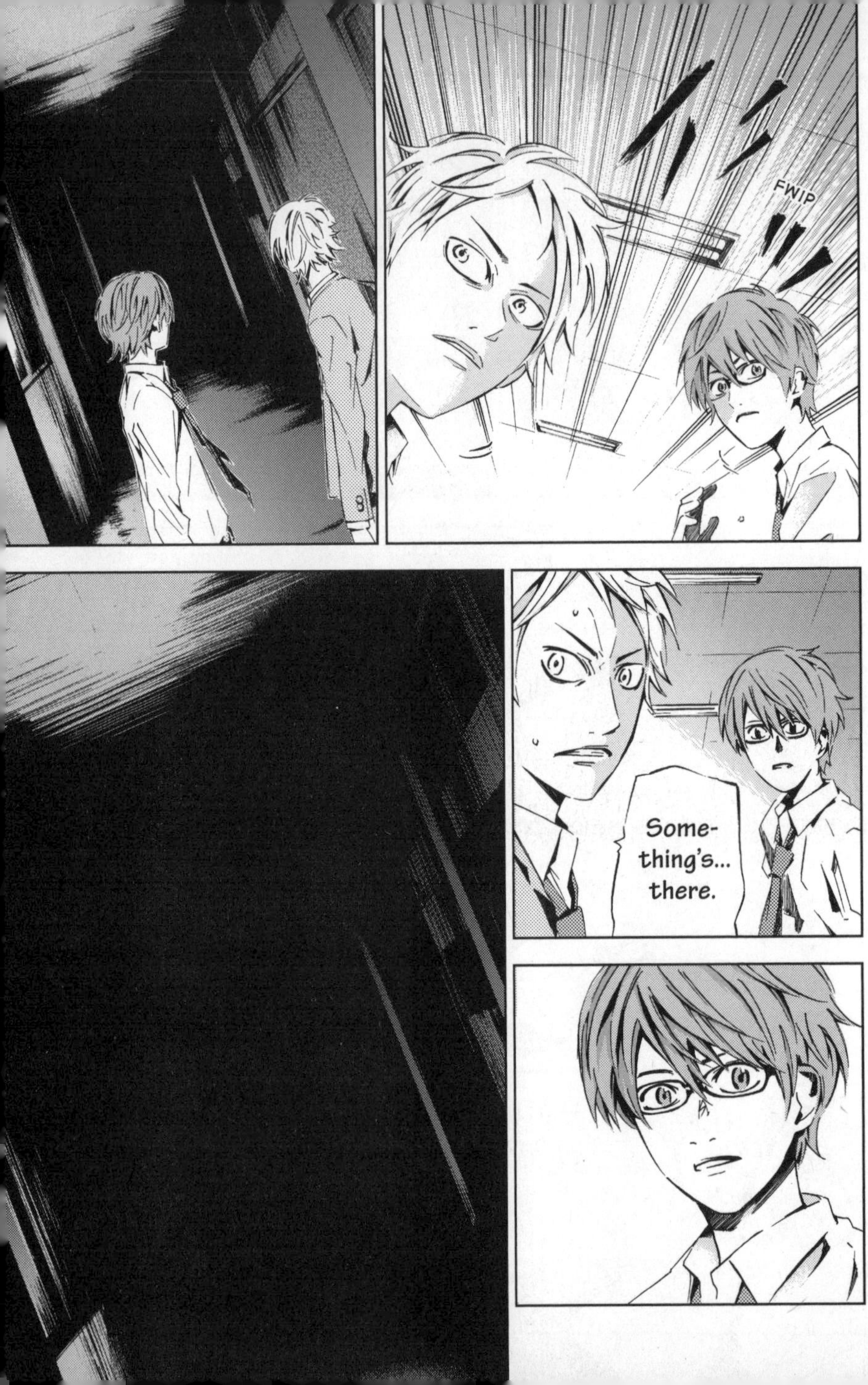
FWIP
Something's... there.

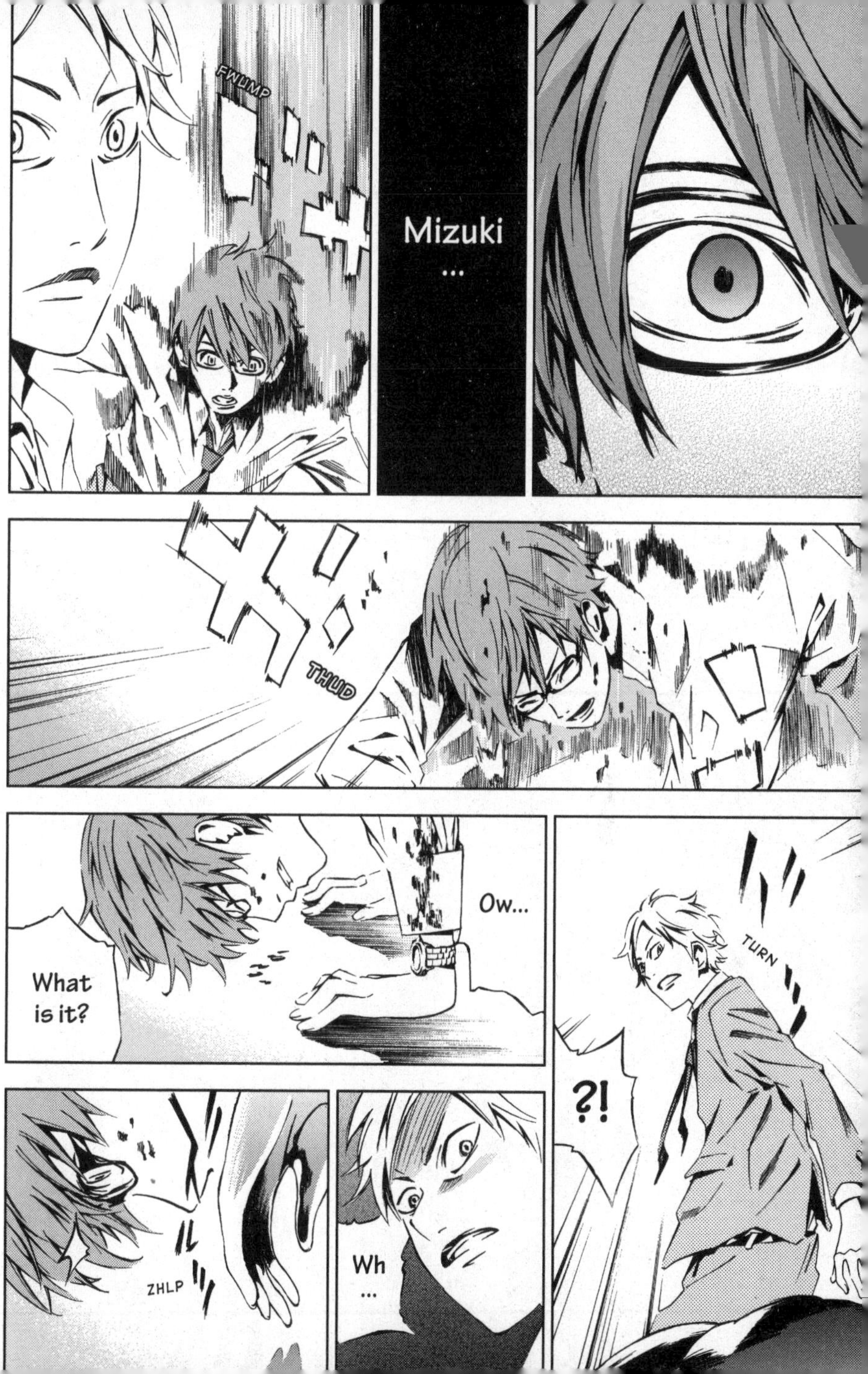
Mizuki
...
FWUMP
THUD
TURN
?!
Ow...
What
is it?
Wh
...
ZHLP

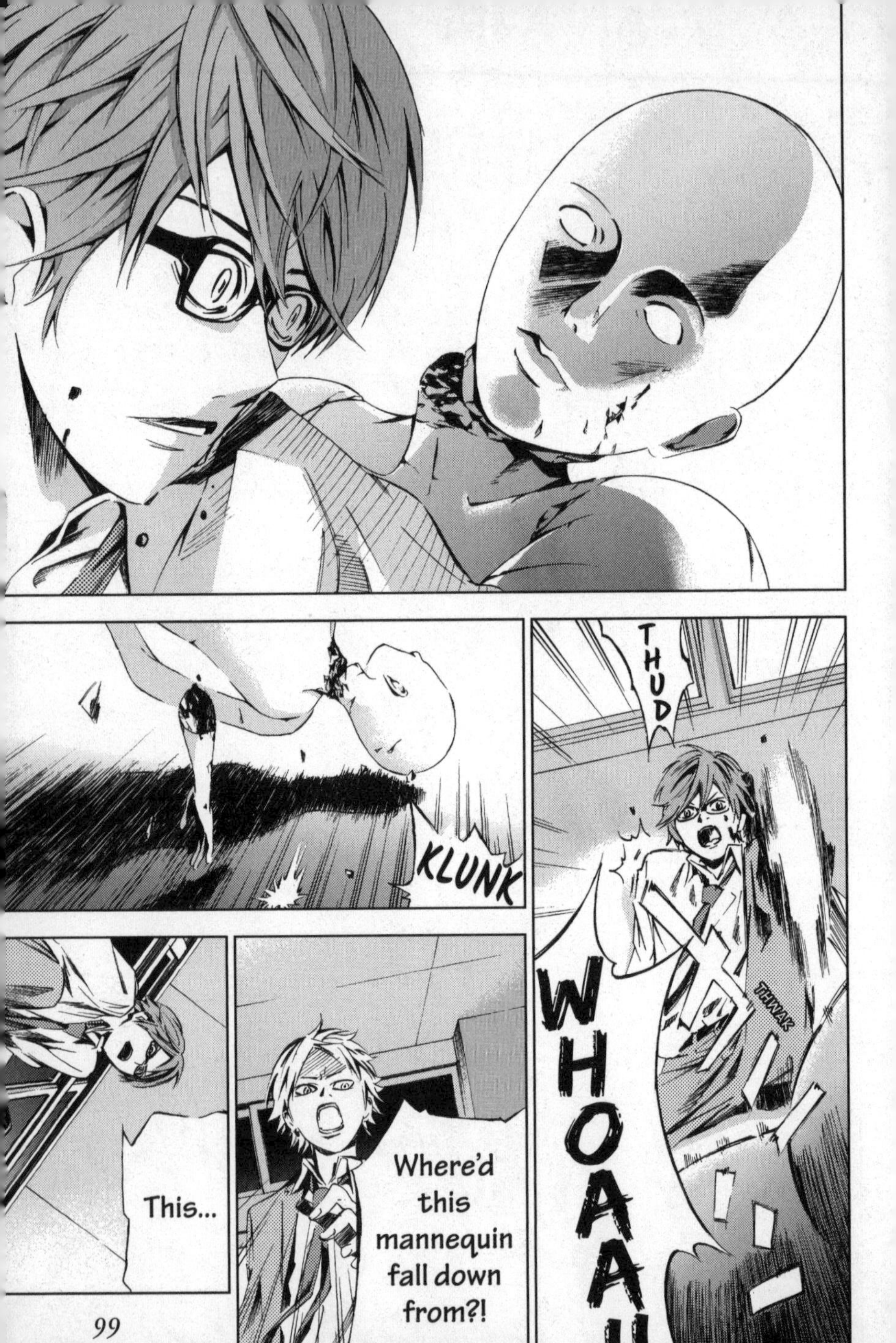
THUD
WHOAA!!
THWAK
KLUNK
Where'd this mannequin fall down from?!
This...

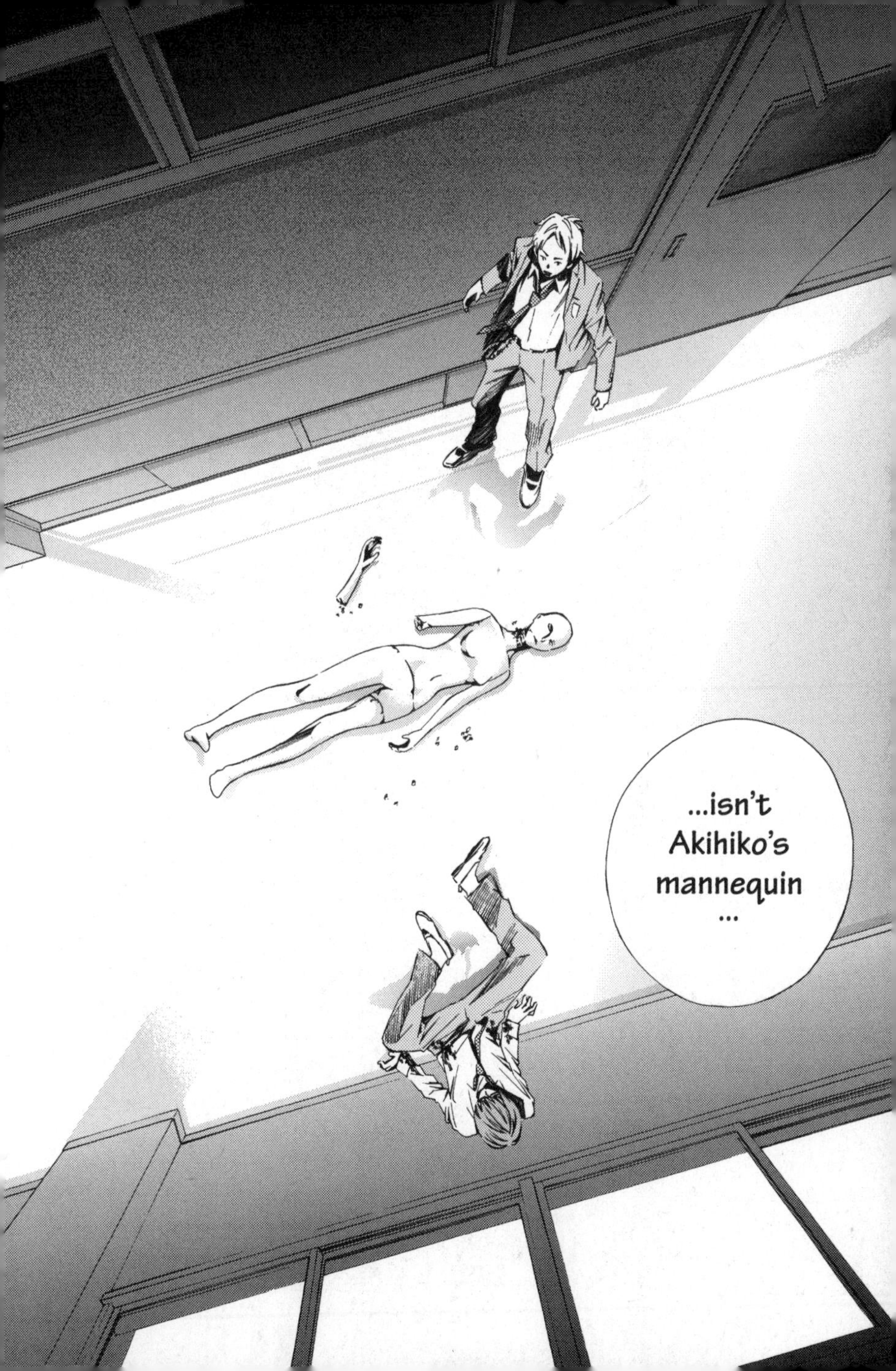
...isn't Akihiko's mannequin ...

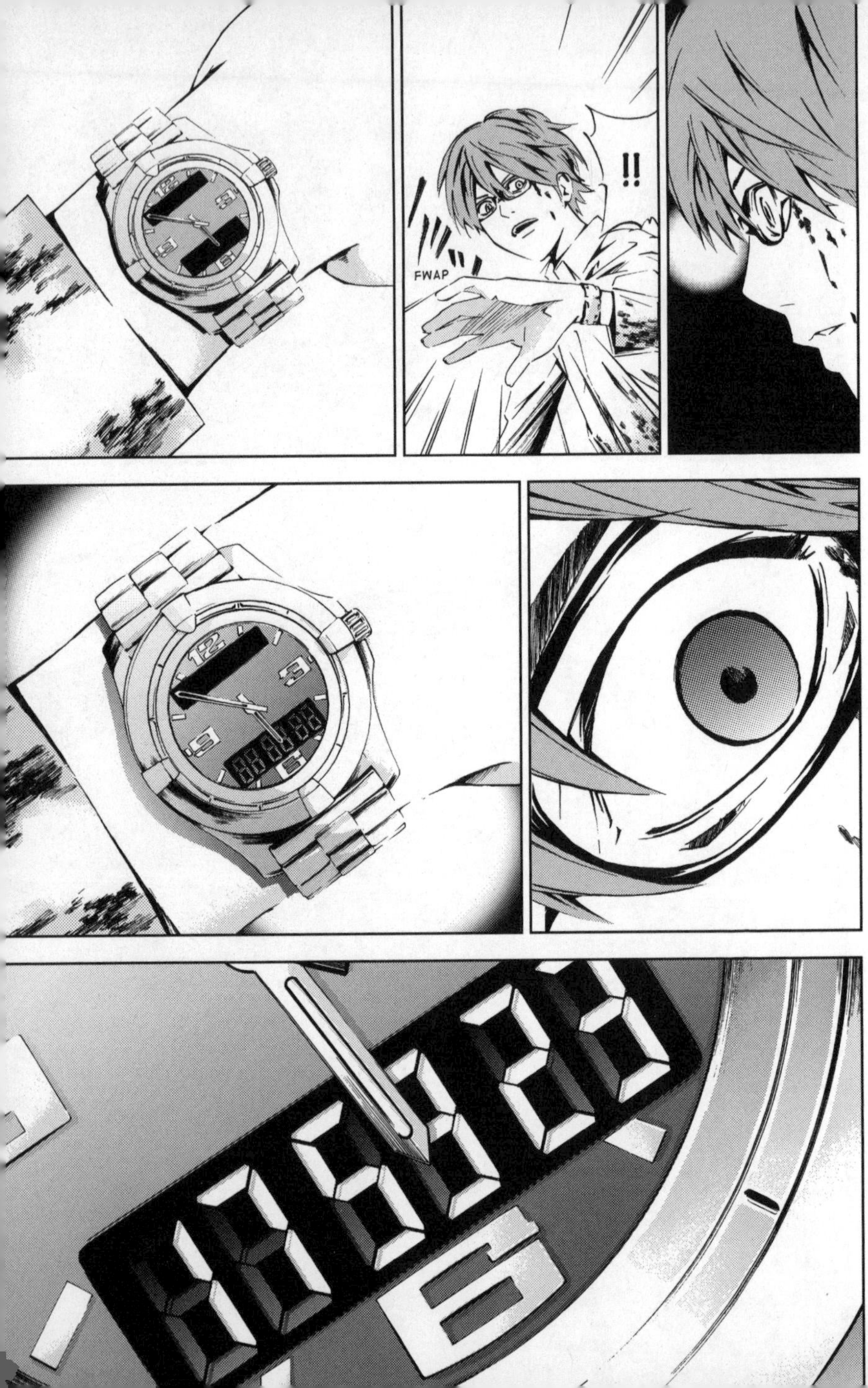
!!
FWAP

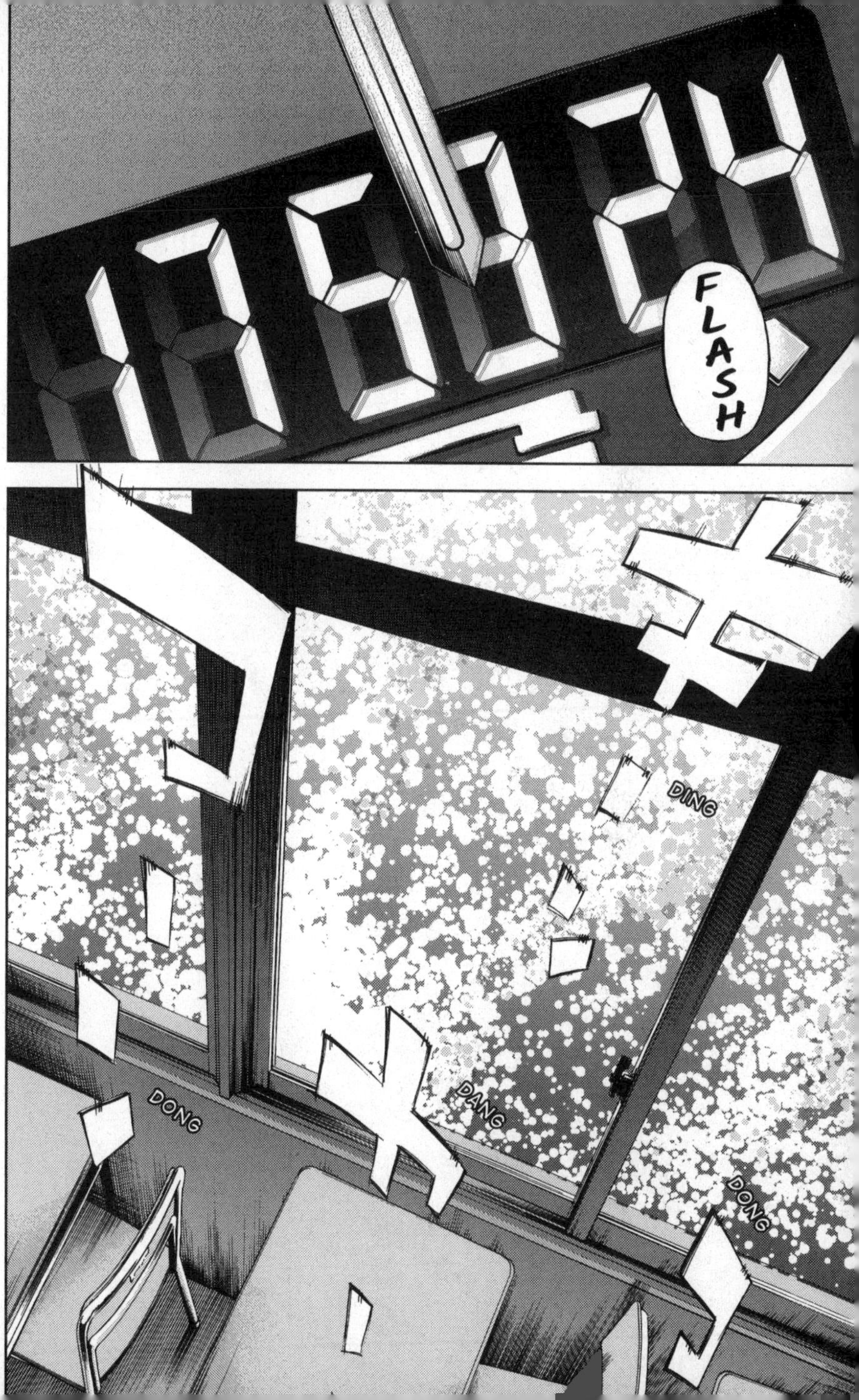
FLASH
DING
DONG
DANG
DONG

A School
Frozen
in Time

A School
Frozen
in Time

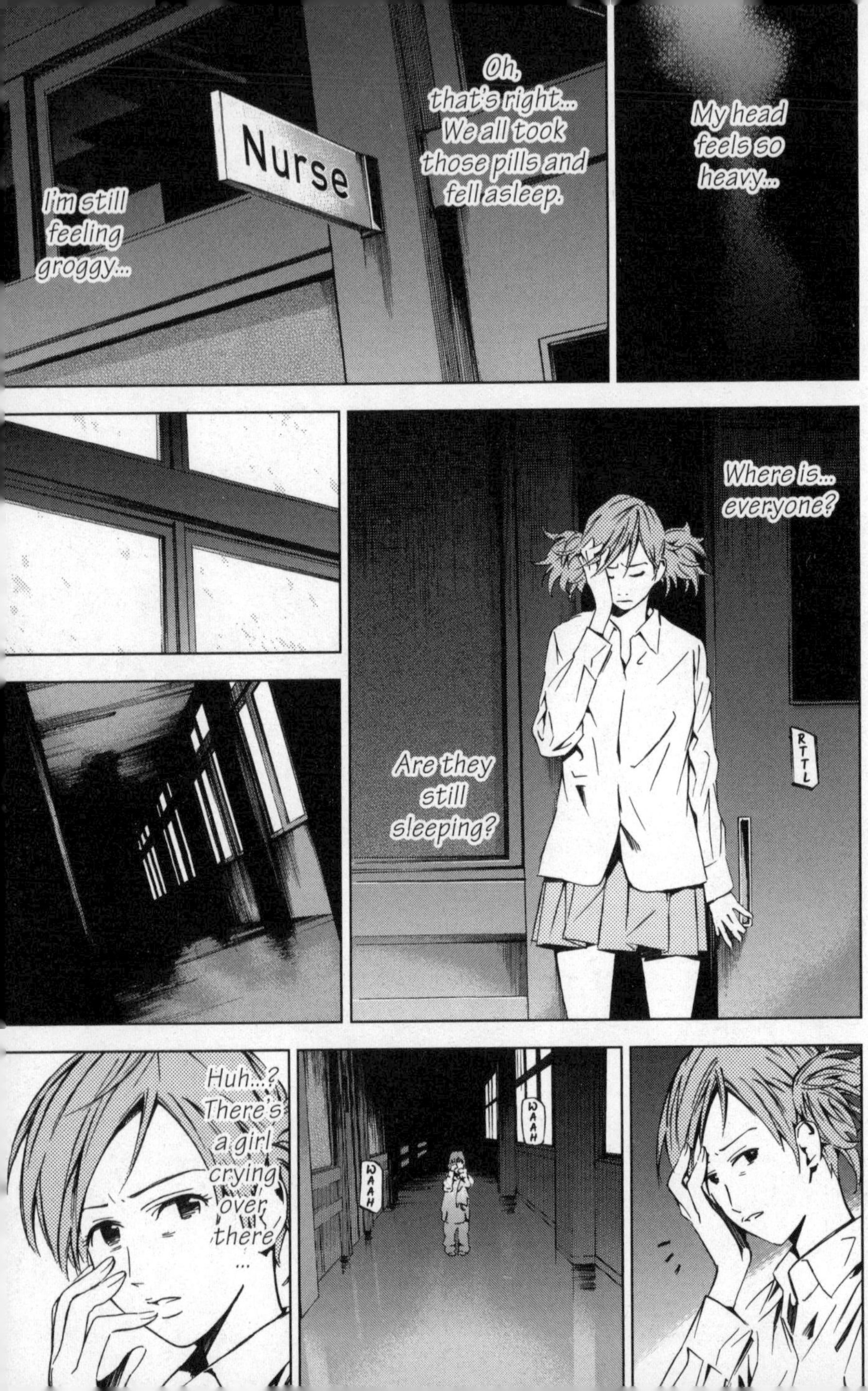
My head feels so heavy...
Oh, that's right... We all took those pills and fell asleep.
Nurse
I'm still feeling groggy...
Where is... everyone?
RTTL
Are they still sleeping?
WAAH
WAAH
Huh...? There's a girl crying over there...

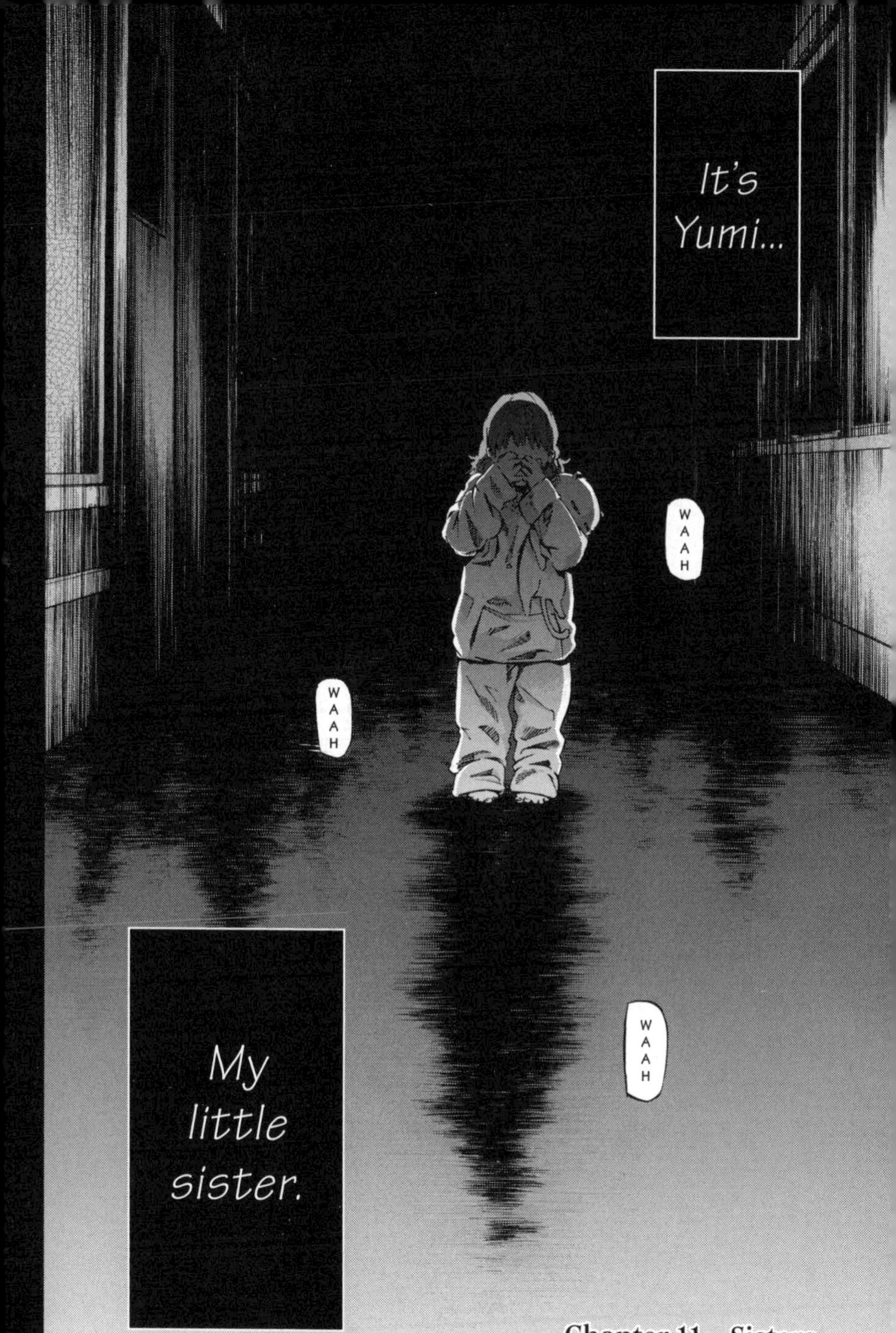
It's Yumi...
WAAH
WAAH
WAAH
My little sister.

Chapter 11 Sisters

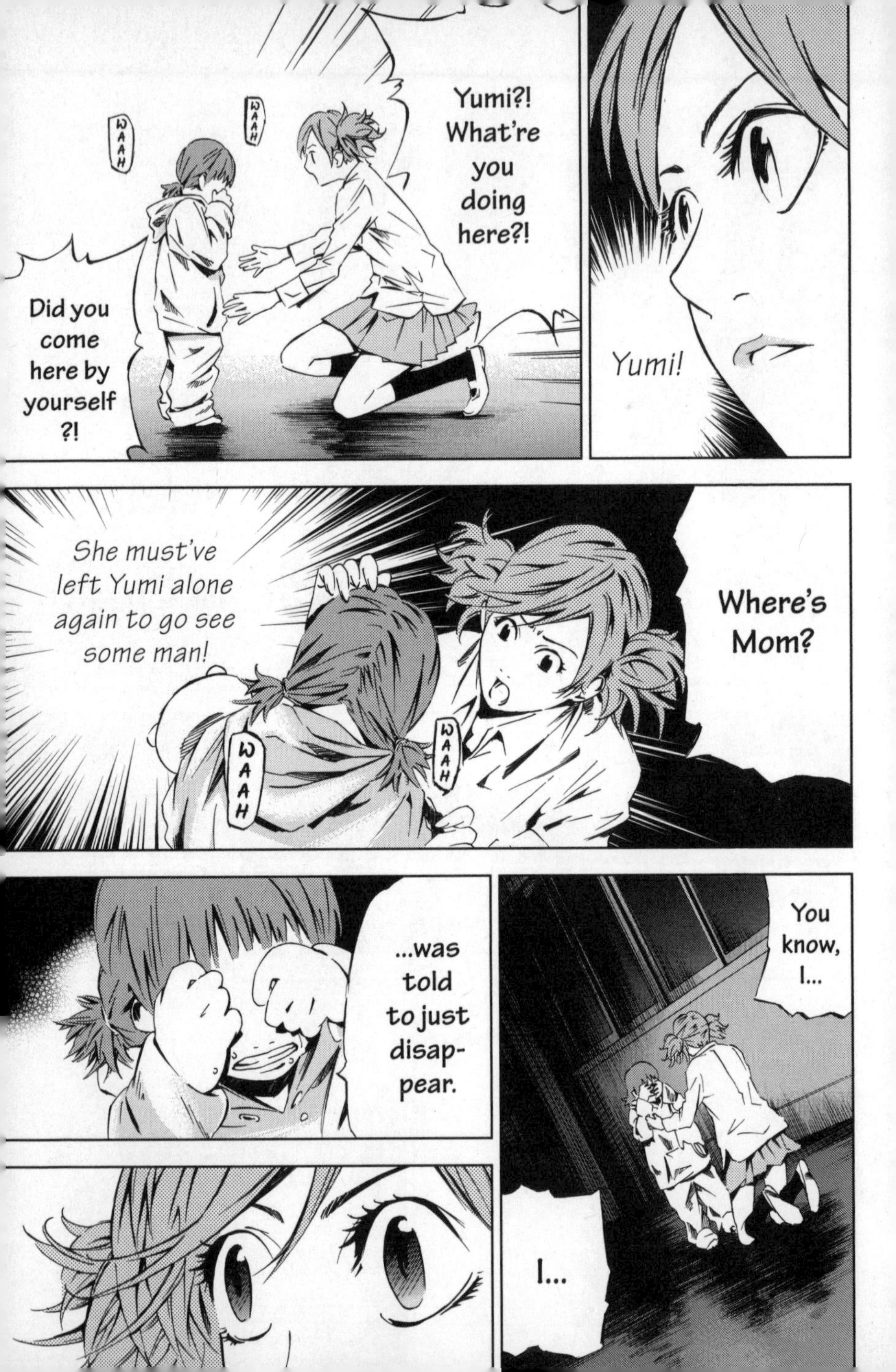

Yumi!
Yumi?! What're you doing here?!
WAAAH
WAAAH
Did you come here by yourself?!
Where's Mom?
She must've left Yumi alone again to go see some man!
WAAAH
WAAAH
You know, I...
...was told to just disap-pear.
I...

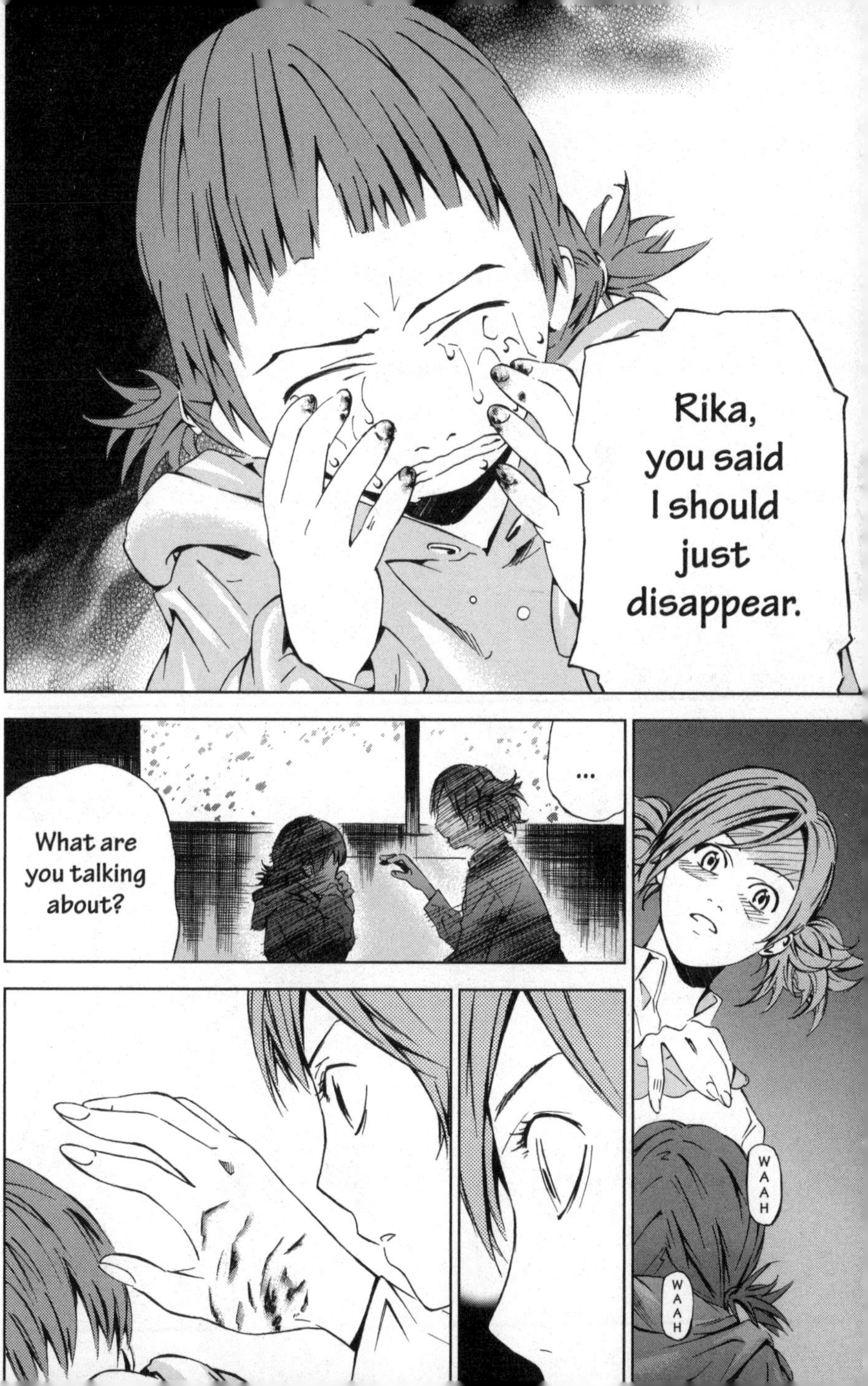
Rika, you said I should just disappear.
WAAH
WAAH
...
What are you talking about?

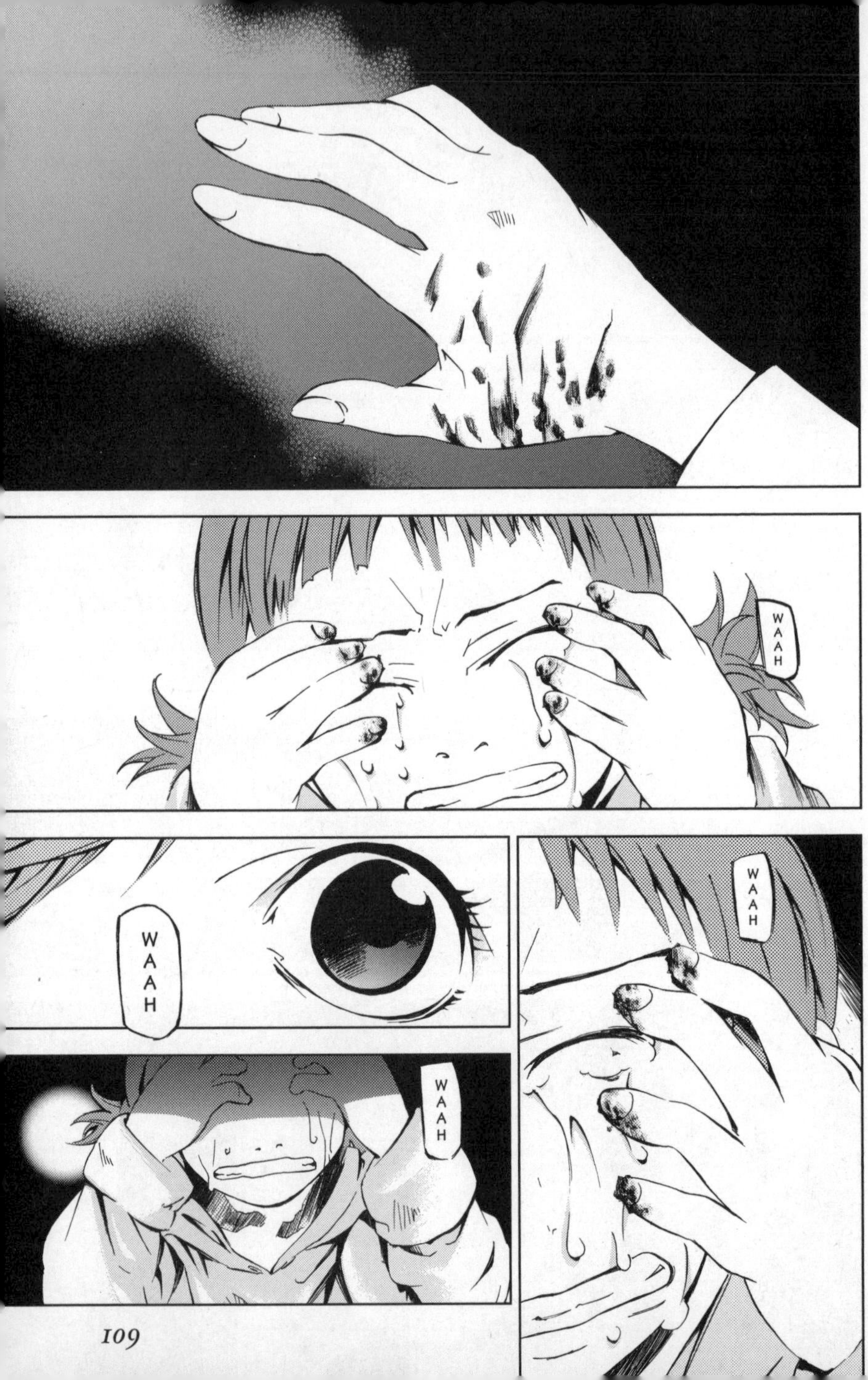
WAAH
WAAH
WAAH
WAAH

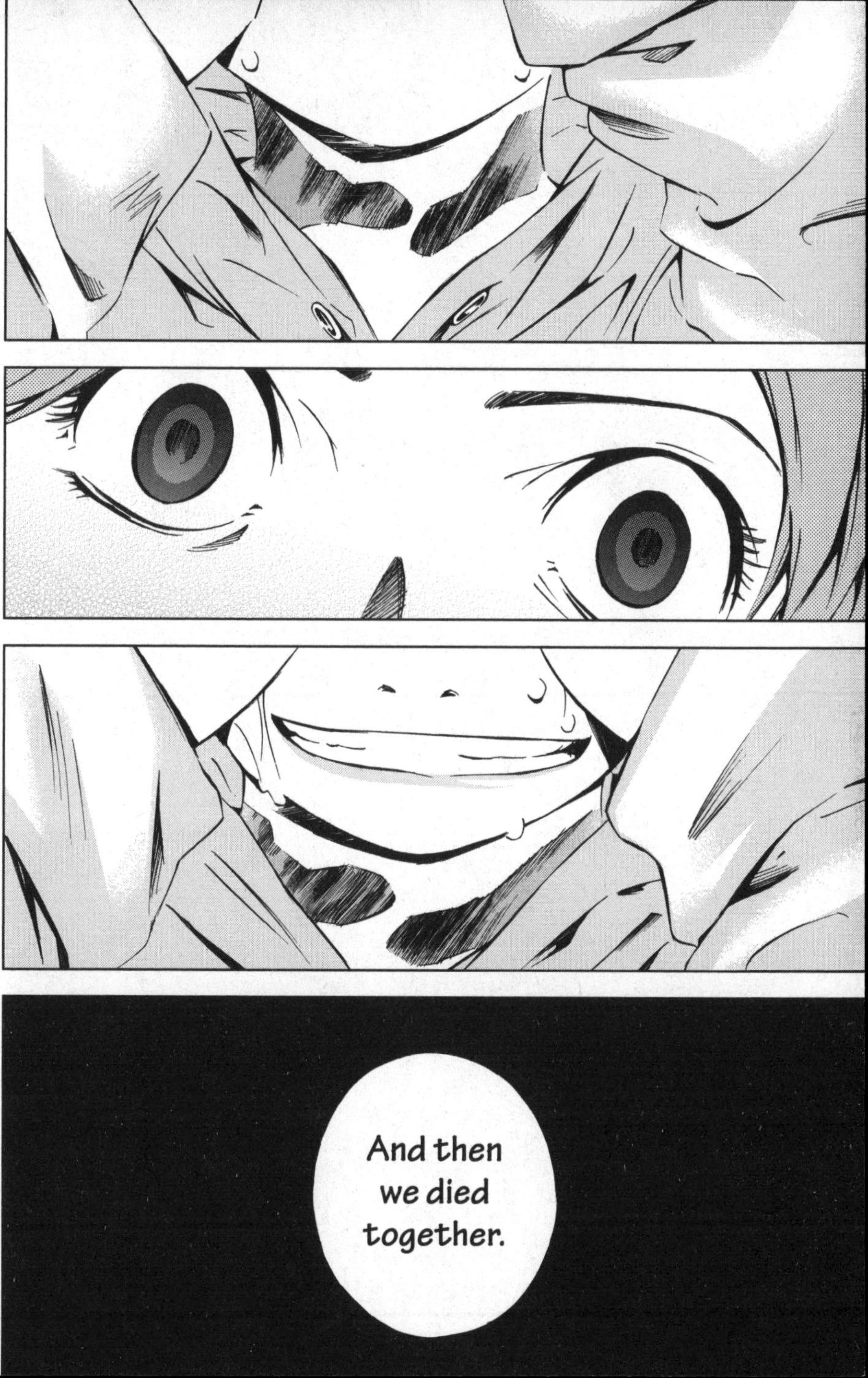
And then we died together.

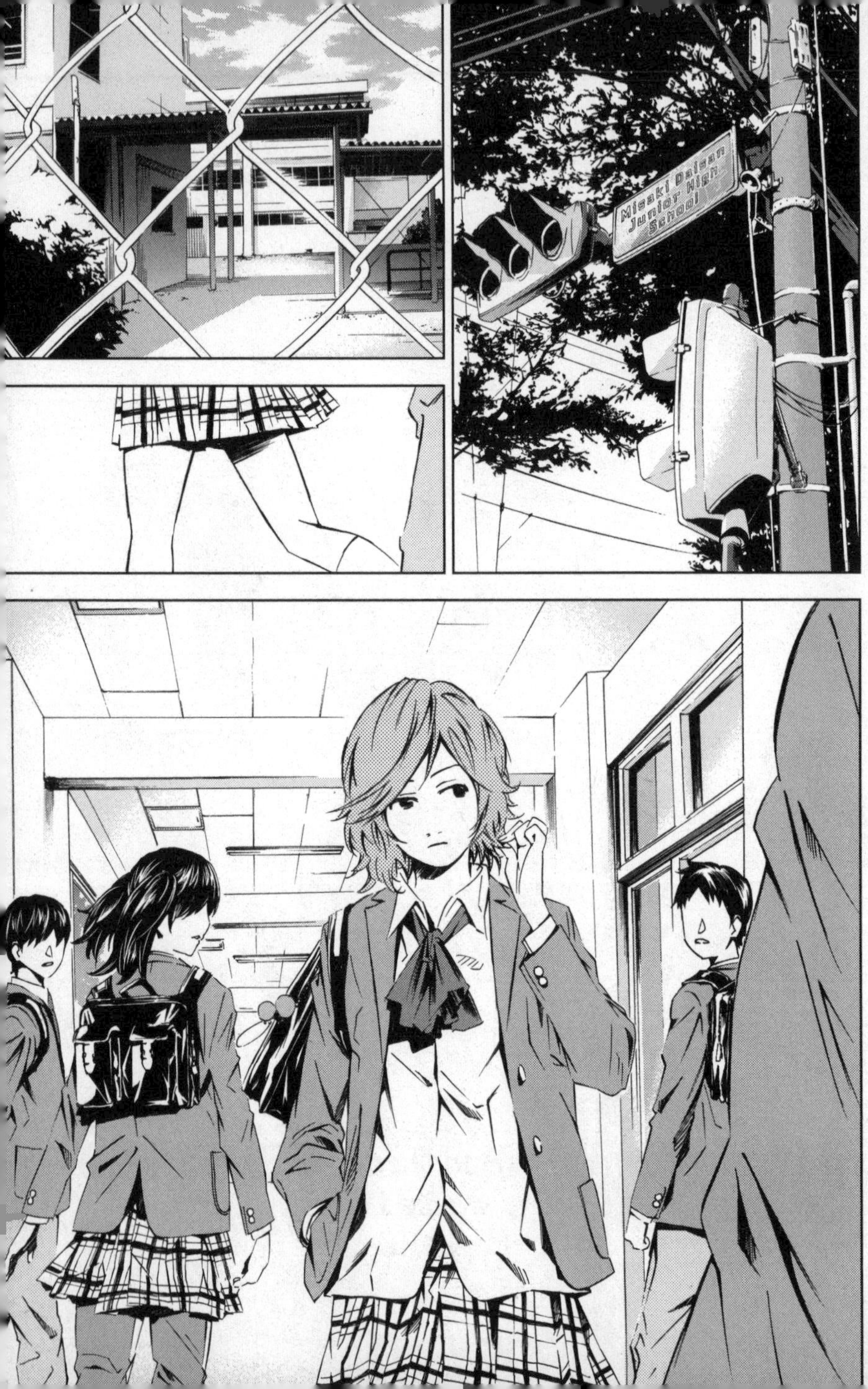
Misaki Daisan
Junior High
School

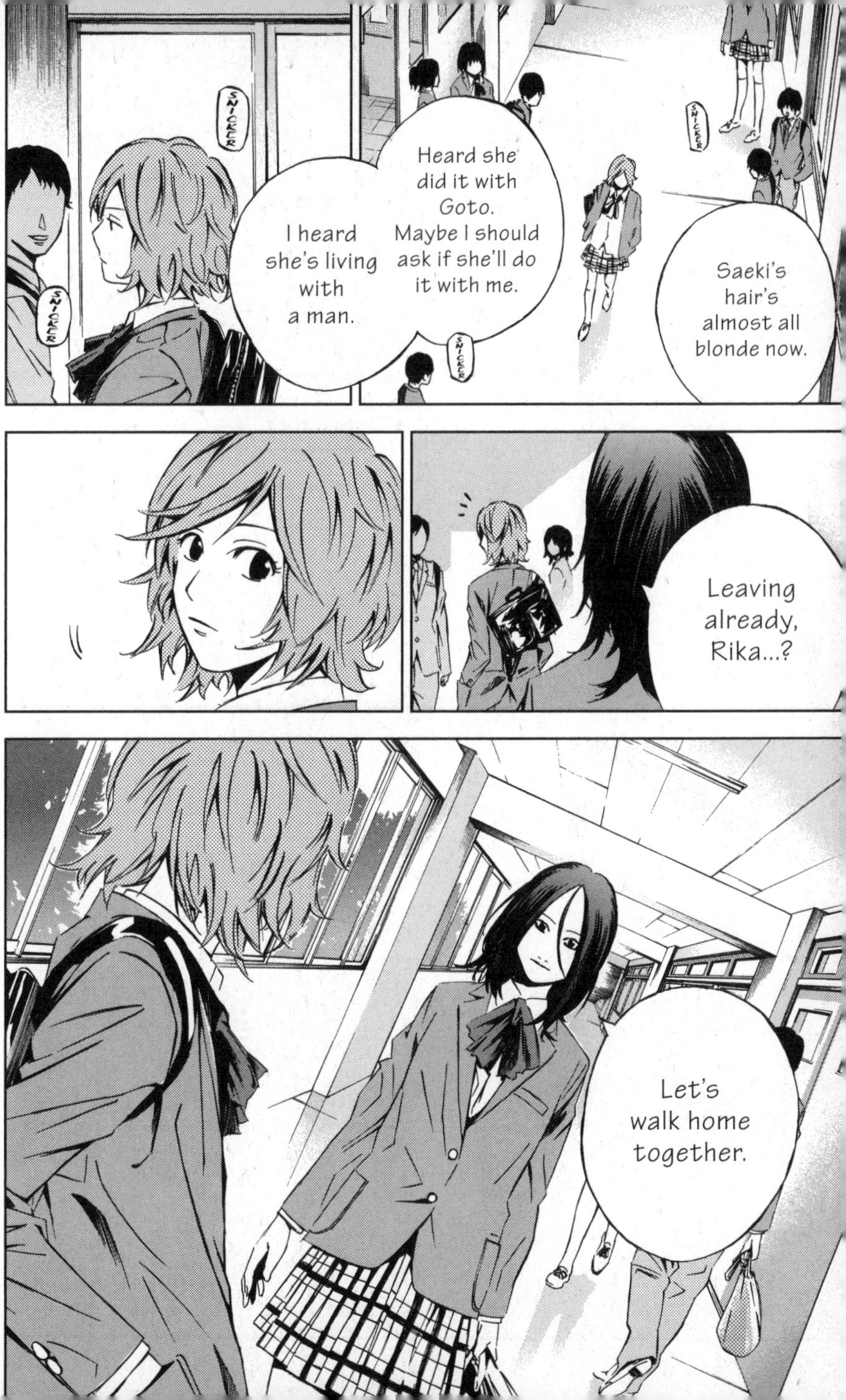
SNICKER
Saeki's hair's almost all blonde now.
Heard she did it with Goto. Maybe I should ask if she'll do it with me.
SNICKER
SNICKER
I heard she's living with a man.
SNICKER
Leaving already, Rika...?
Let's walk home together.

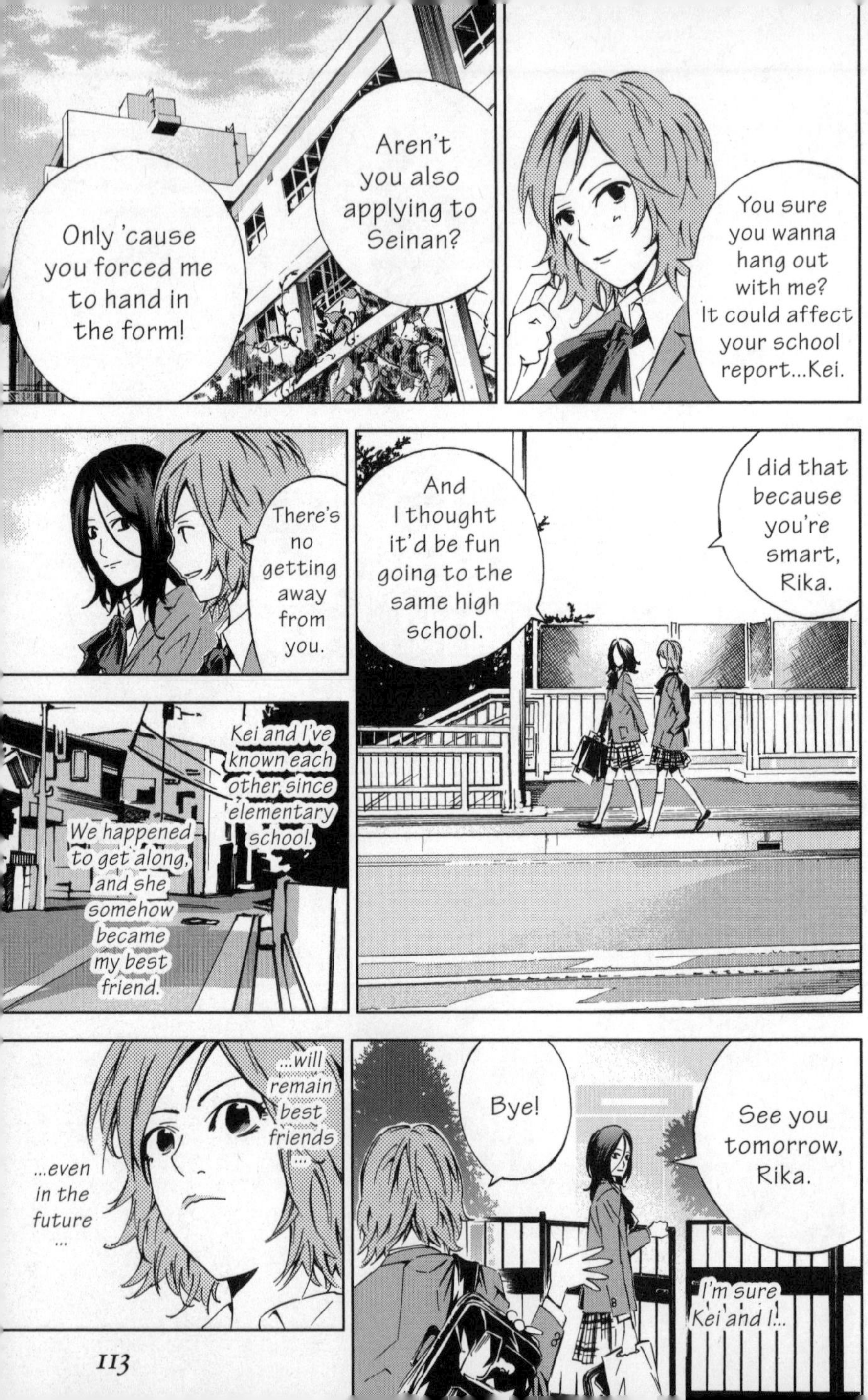
You sure you wanna hang out with me? It could affect your school report...Kei.
Aren't you also applying to Seinan?
Only 'cause you forced me to hand in the form!
I did that because you're smart, Rika.
And I thought it'd be fun going to the same high school.
There's no getting away from you.
Kei and I've known each other since elementary school.
We happened to get along, and she somehow became my best friend.
See you tomorrow, Rika.
Bye!
I'm sure Kei and I...
...will remain best friends...
...even in the future...

But...
I don't
want to
be around
her.

Being
with
Kei...

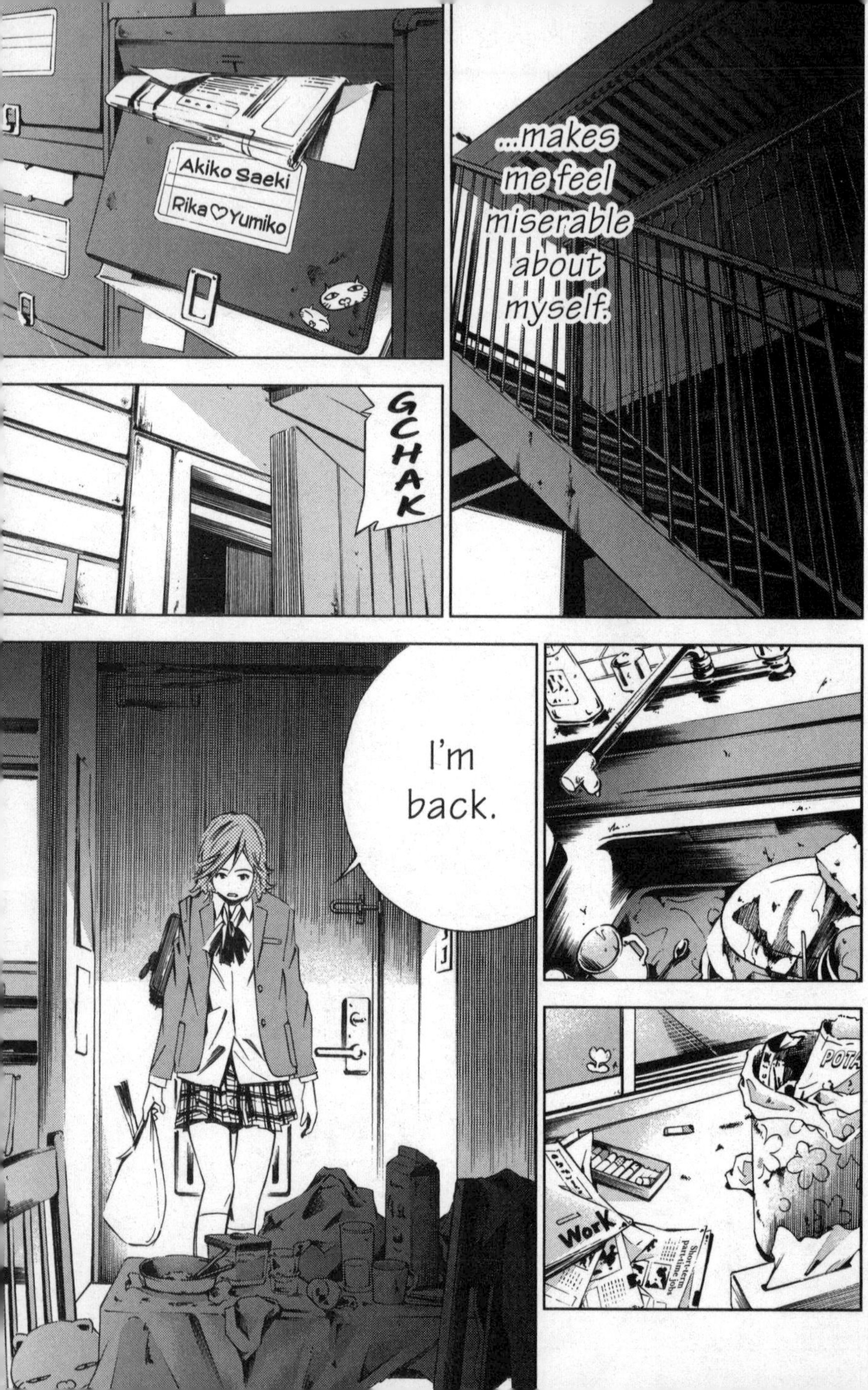

...makes me feel miserable about myself.
Akiko Saeki
Rika♡Yumiko
GCHAK
POTA
WorK
Short-term part-time jobs
I'm back.

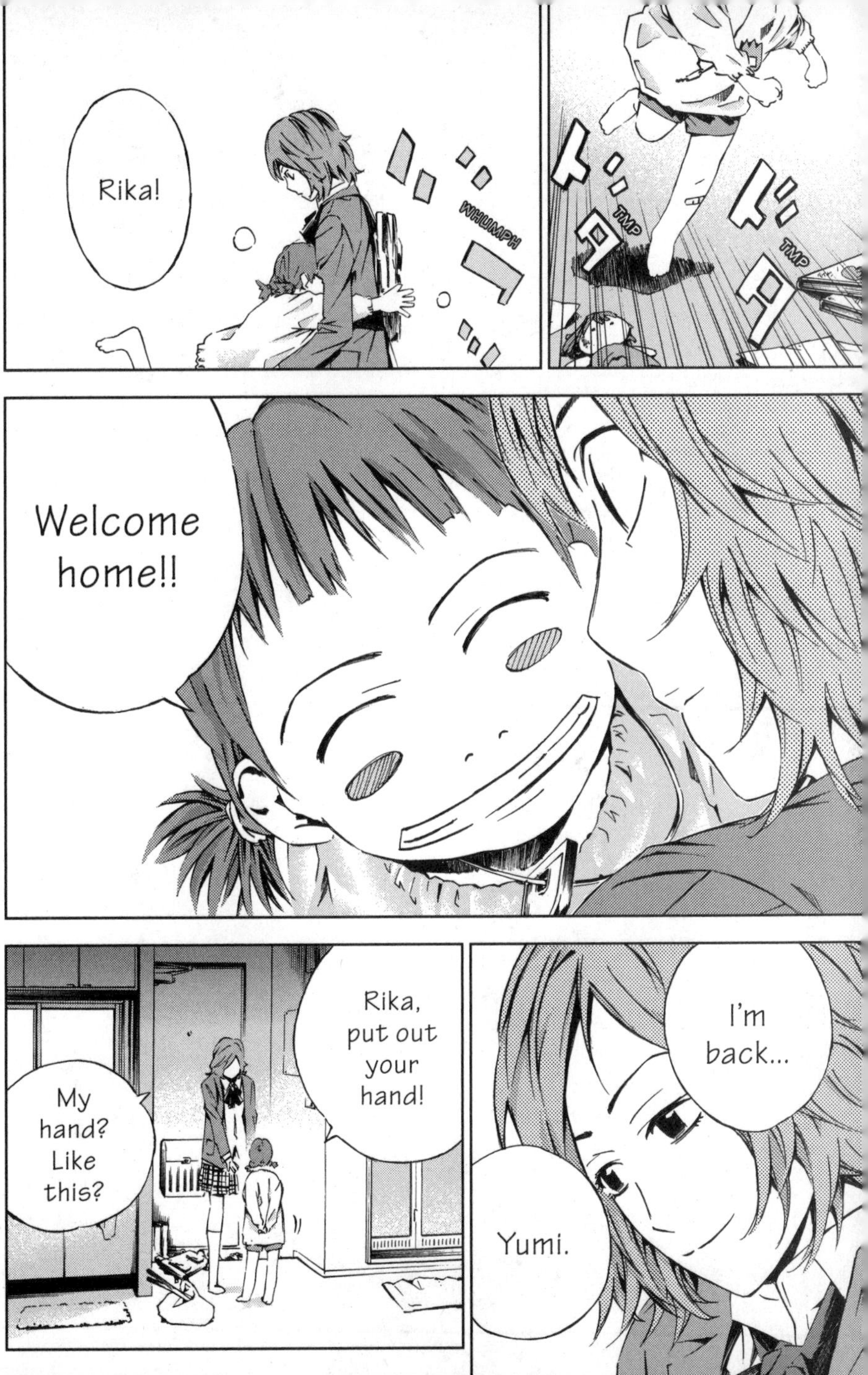
TMP
TMP
WHUMPH
Rika!
Welcome home!!
I'm back...
Yumi.
Rika, put out your hand!
My hand? Like this?

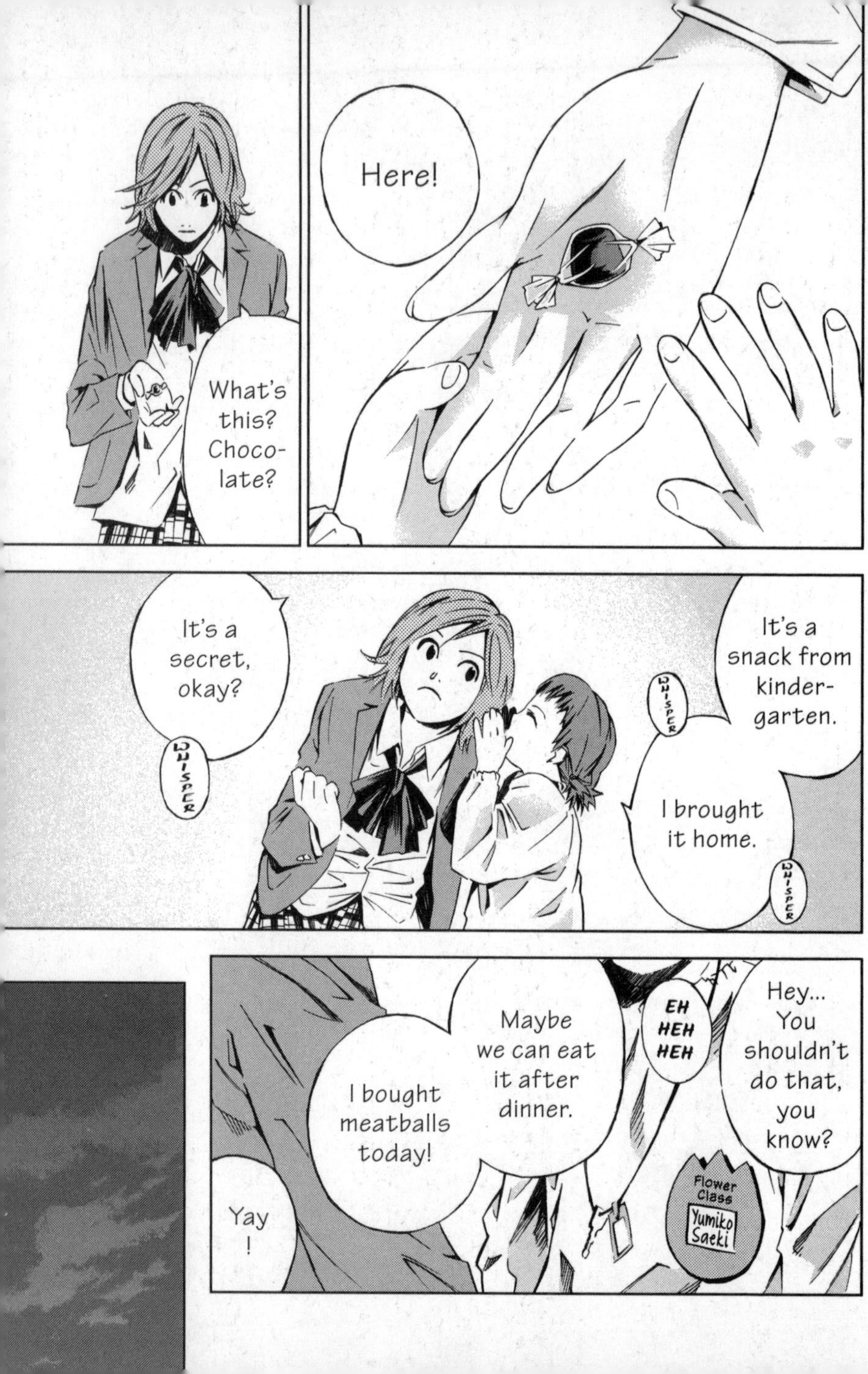
Here!
What's this? Chocolate?
It's a snack from kindergarten.
WHISPER
I brought it home.
WHISPER
It's a secret, okay?
WHISPER
Hey... You shouldn't do that, you know?
EH HEH HEH
Maybe we can eat it after dinner.
I bought meatballs today!
Yay!
Flower Class
Yumiko Saeki

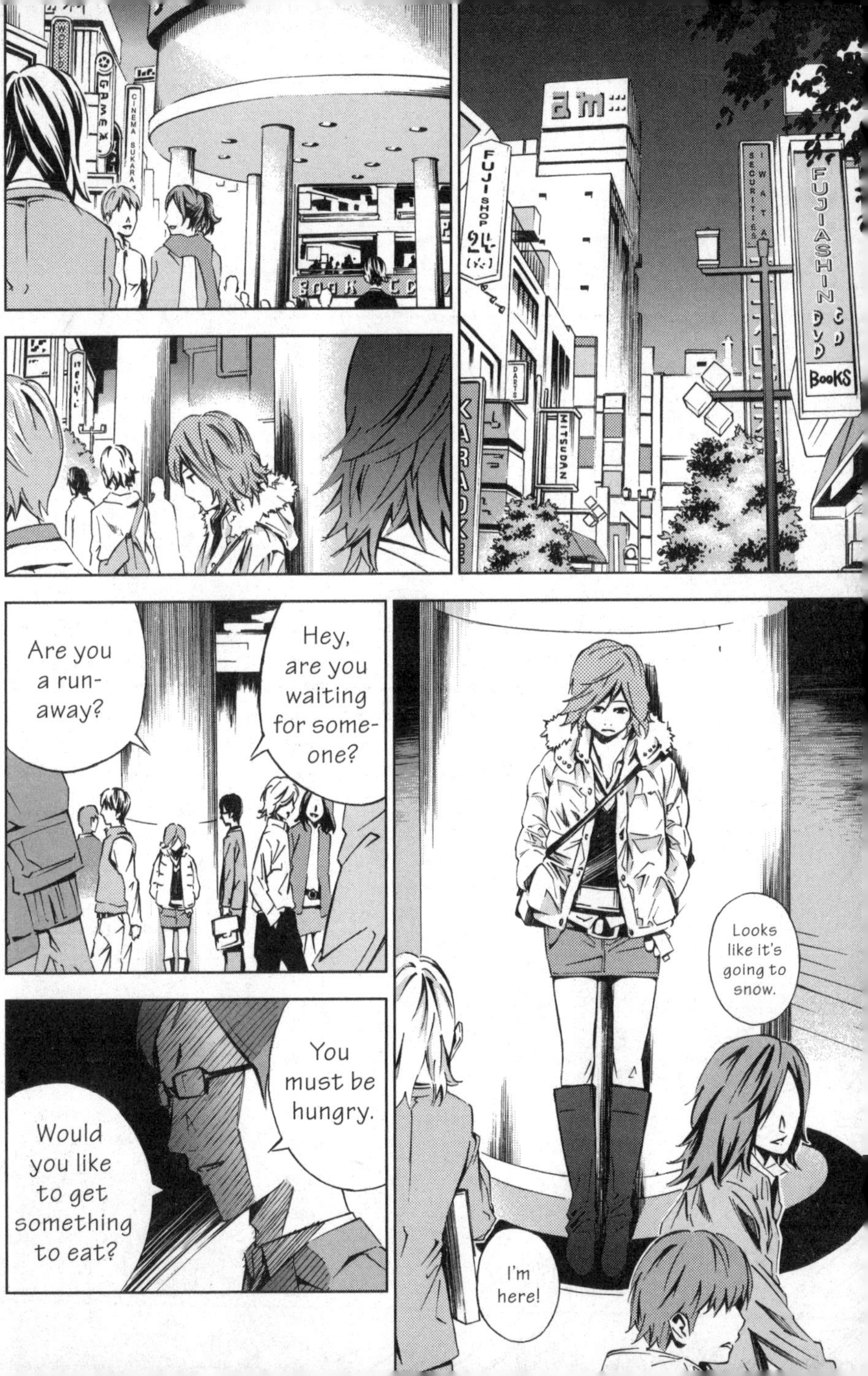
FUJI SHOP
FUJIASHIN
CD DVD
BOOKS
IWATA SECURITIES
DARTS
MITSUDAN
CINEMA SUKARA
GAMEX
Looks like it's going to snow.
I'm here!
Hey, are you waiting for some-one?
Are you a run-away?
You must be hungry.
Would you like to get something to eat?

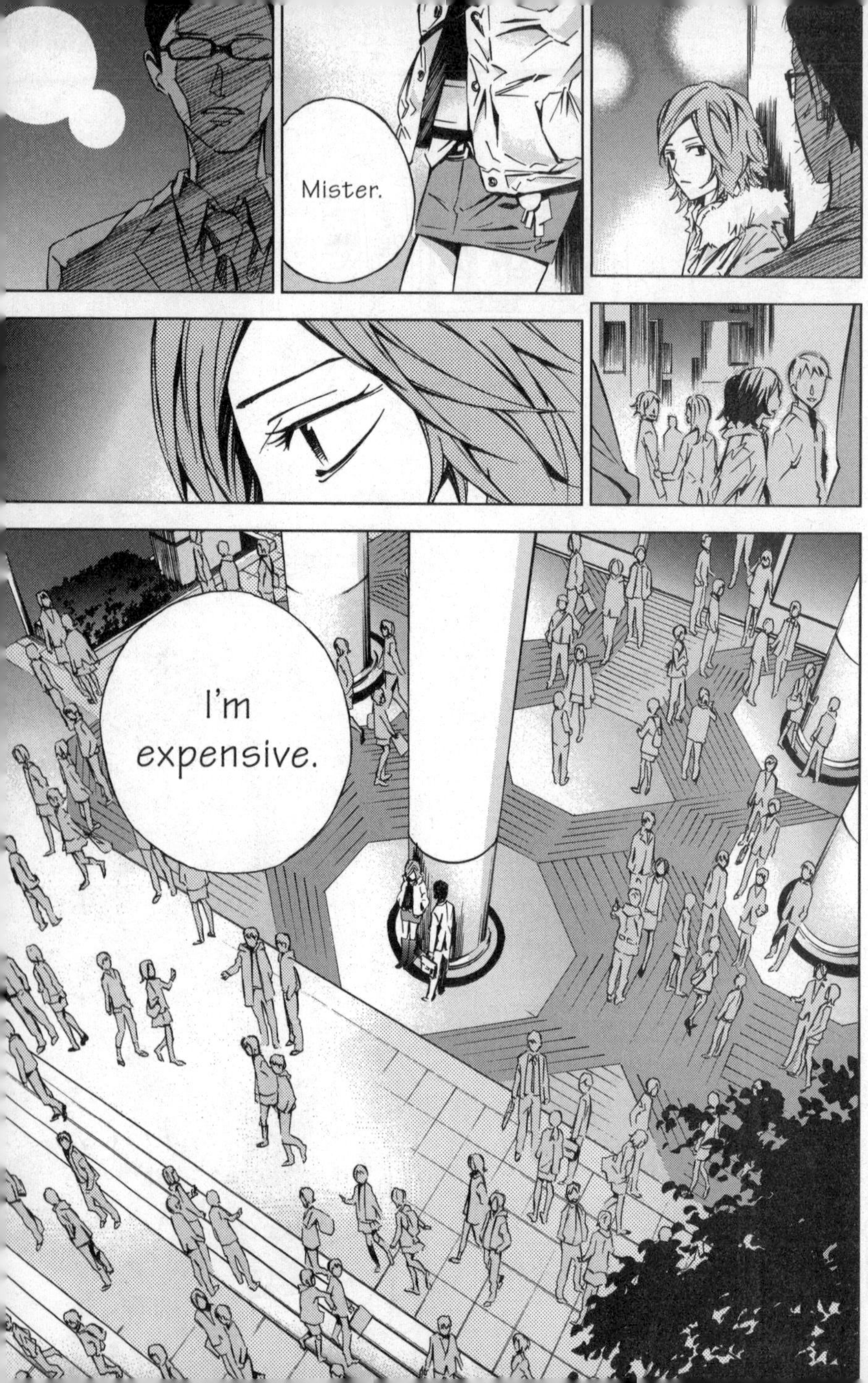
Mister.
I'm expensive.

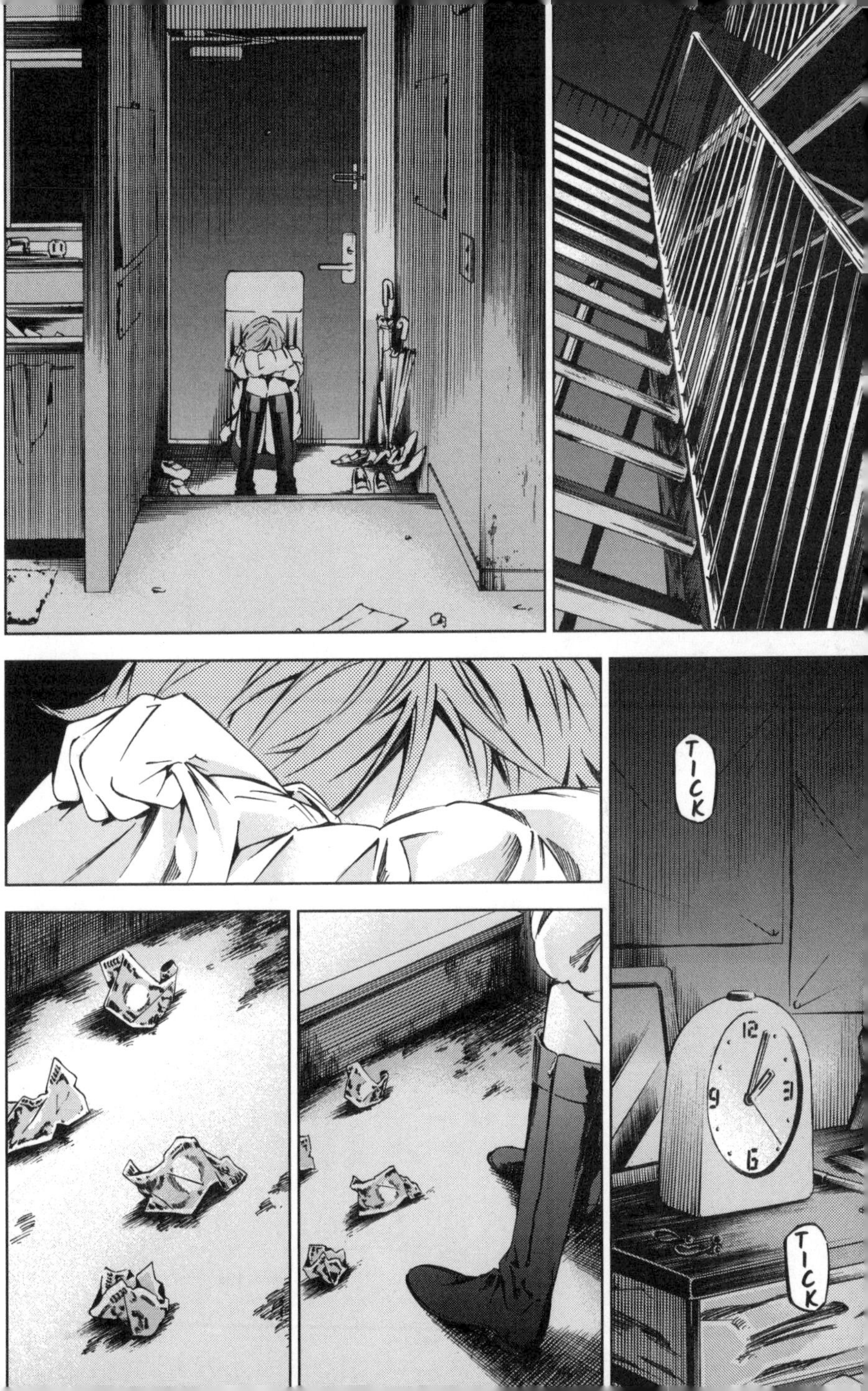
TICK
TICK

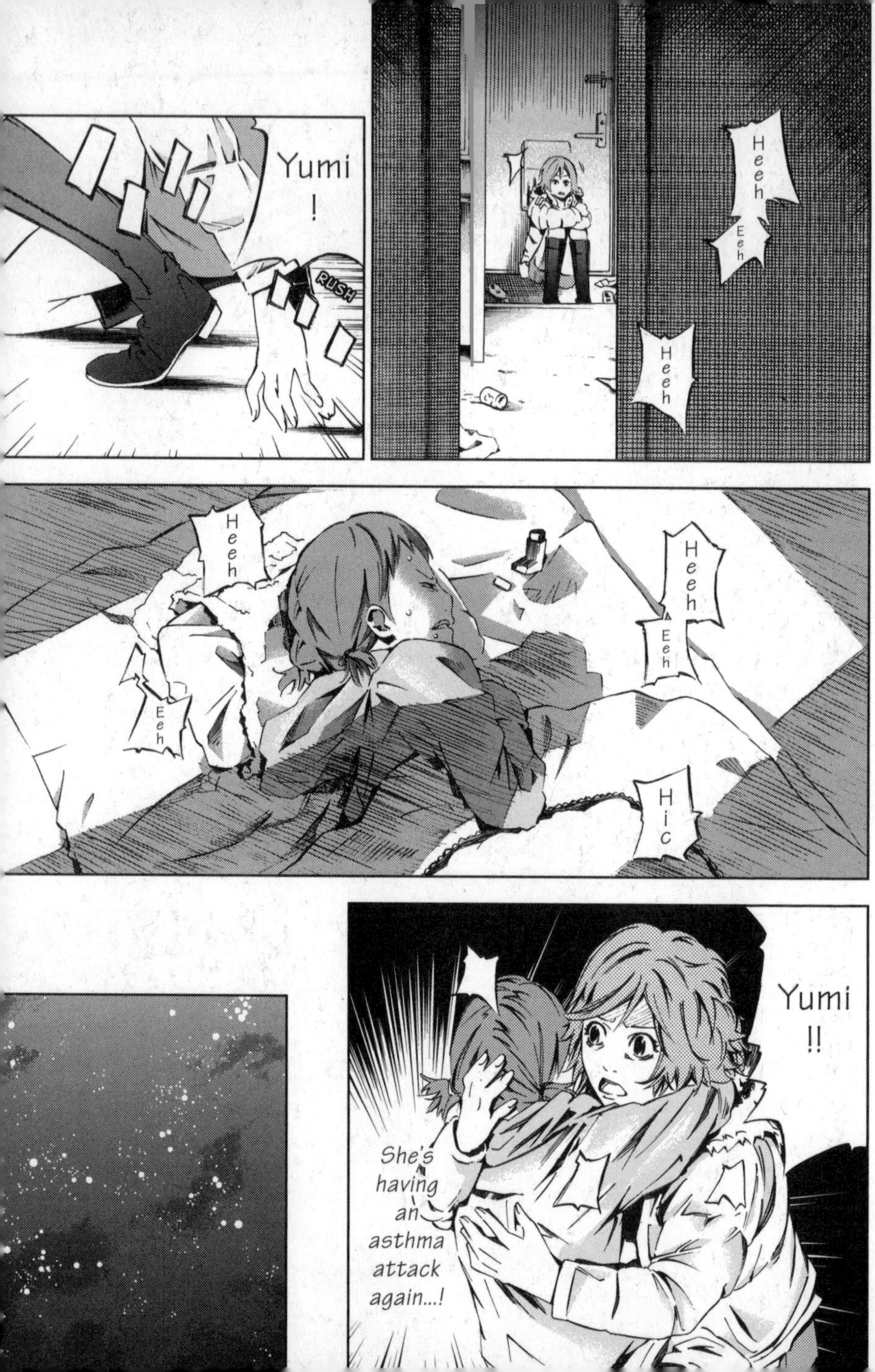
Heeh
Eeh
Heeh
Yumi
!
RUSH
Heeh
Eeh
Hic
Heeh
Eeh
Yumi
!!
She's having an asthma attack again...!

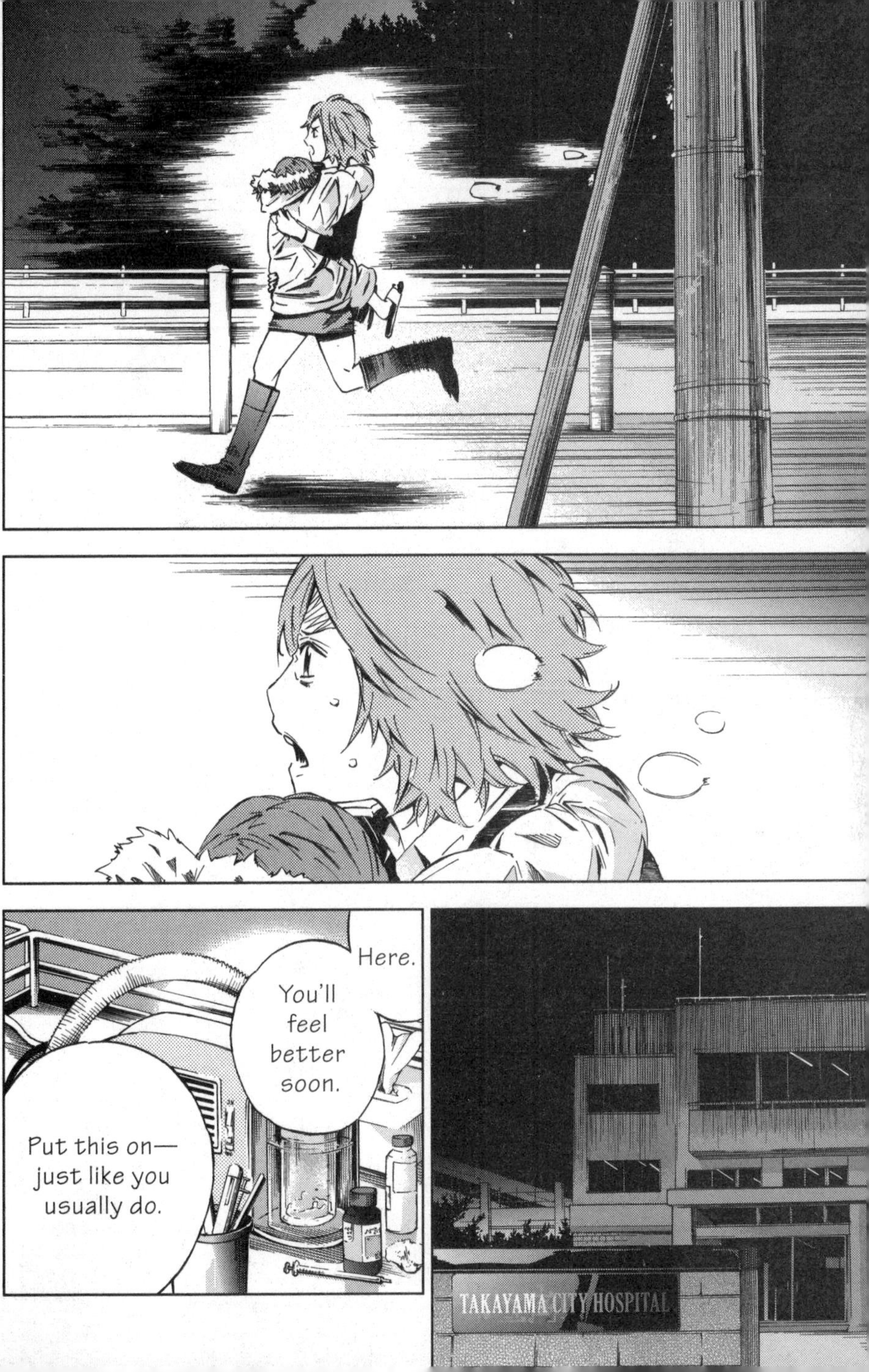
TAKAYAMA CITY HOSPITAL
Here.
You'll feel better soon.
Put this on— just like you usually do.

Miss Saeki, please make sure she takes her medicine...

...so you don't have to bring her in at night.

Take deep, slow breaths.

FWOO

FWOO

CASHIER

Sorry, she's been taking her medicine...

But the new prescription doesn't seem to be helping...

Let's try increasing the dosage then.

Is it okay if I come back later to pay the medical bill?

Oh... I'm sorry. I forgot to put cash in.

Flower!

Flower!

03:12

"Flor!"
"Flor!"

It's "flor" in Spanish!

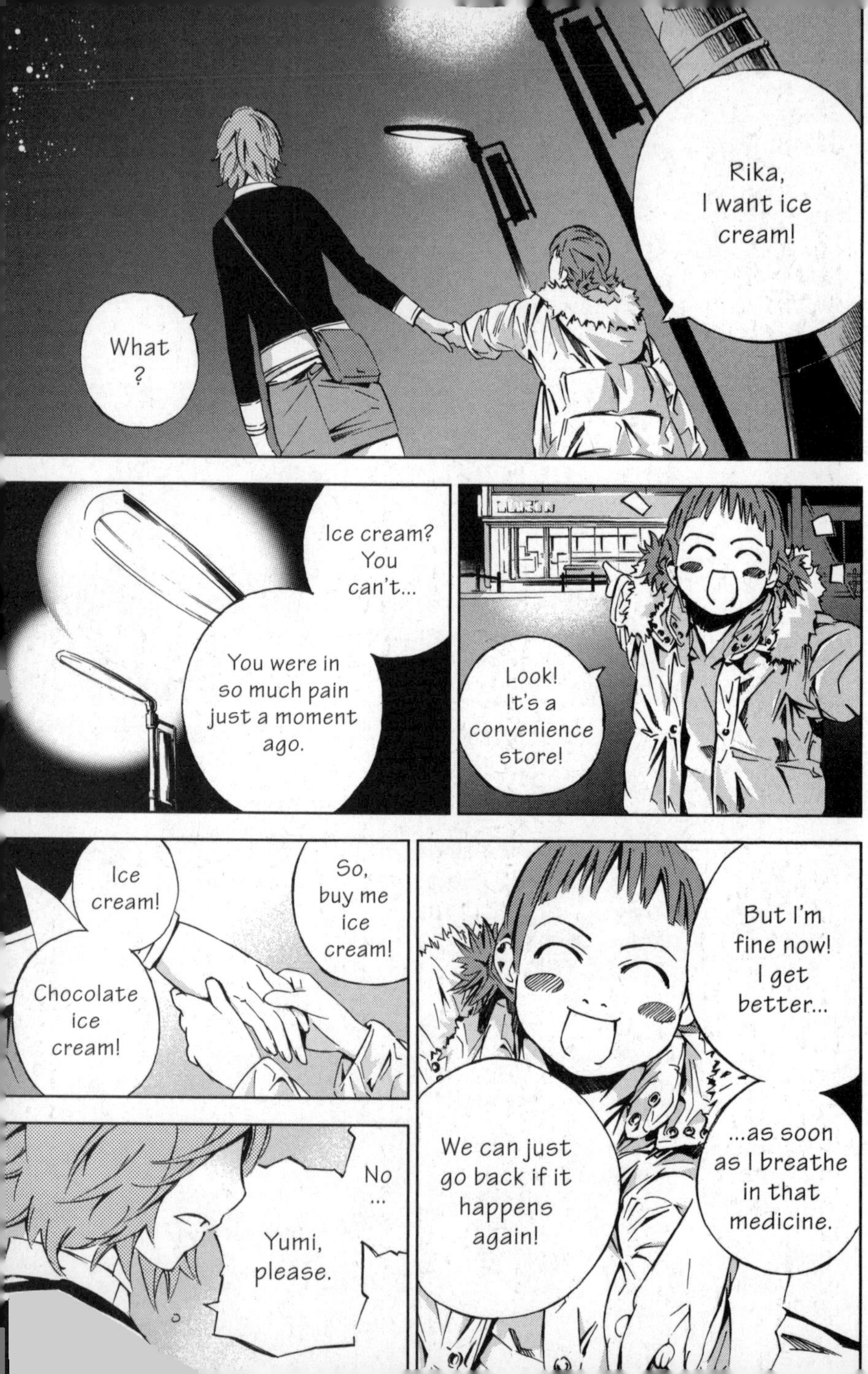
Rika, I want ice cream!
What?
Look! It's a convenience store!
Ice cream? You can't...
You were in so much pain just a moment ago.
But I'm fine now! I get better...
...as soon as I breathe in that medicine.
We can just go back if it happens again!
So, buy me ice cream!
Ice cream!
Chocolate ice cream!
No...
Yumi, please.

Please.

Stop being so selfish.

Why does this always happen to me...?

So, don't cry...

I'm sorry...

I'm sorry... I'll be a good girl.

Why...?

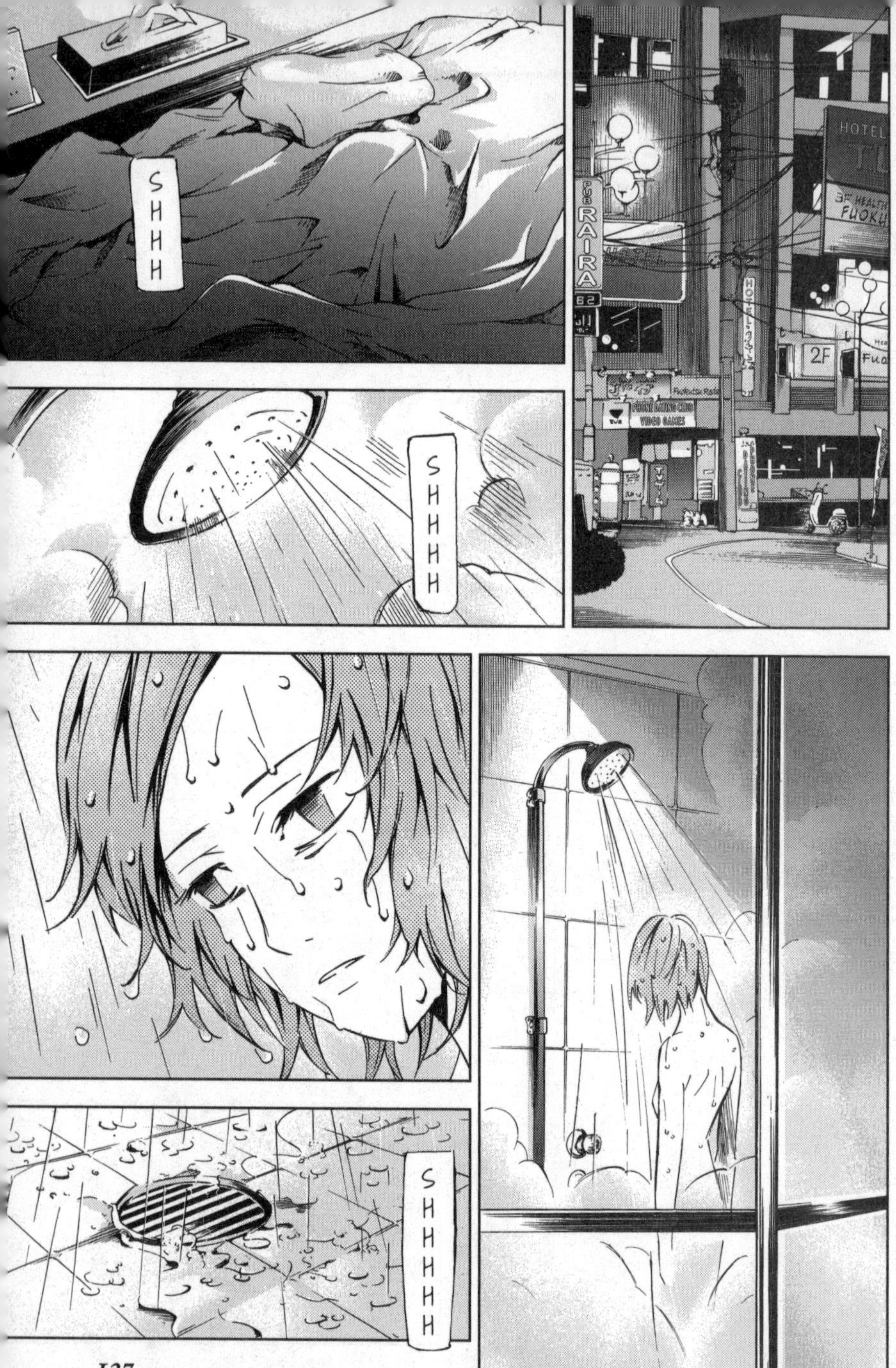
HOTEL
PUB RAIRA
B2
HOTEL
2F
PHONE DATING CLUB
VIDEO GAMES
SHHH
SHHHH
SHHHHH

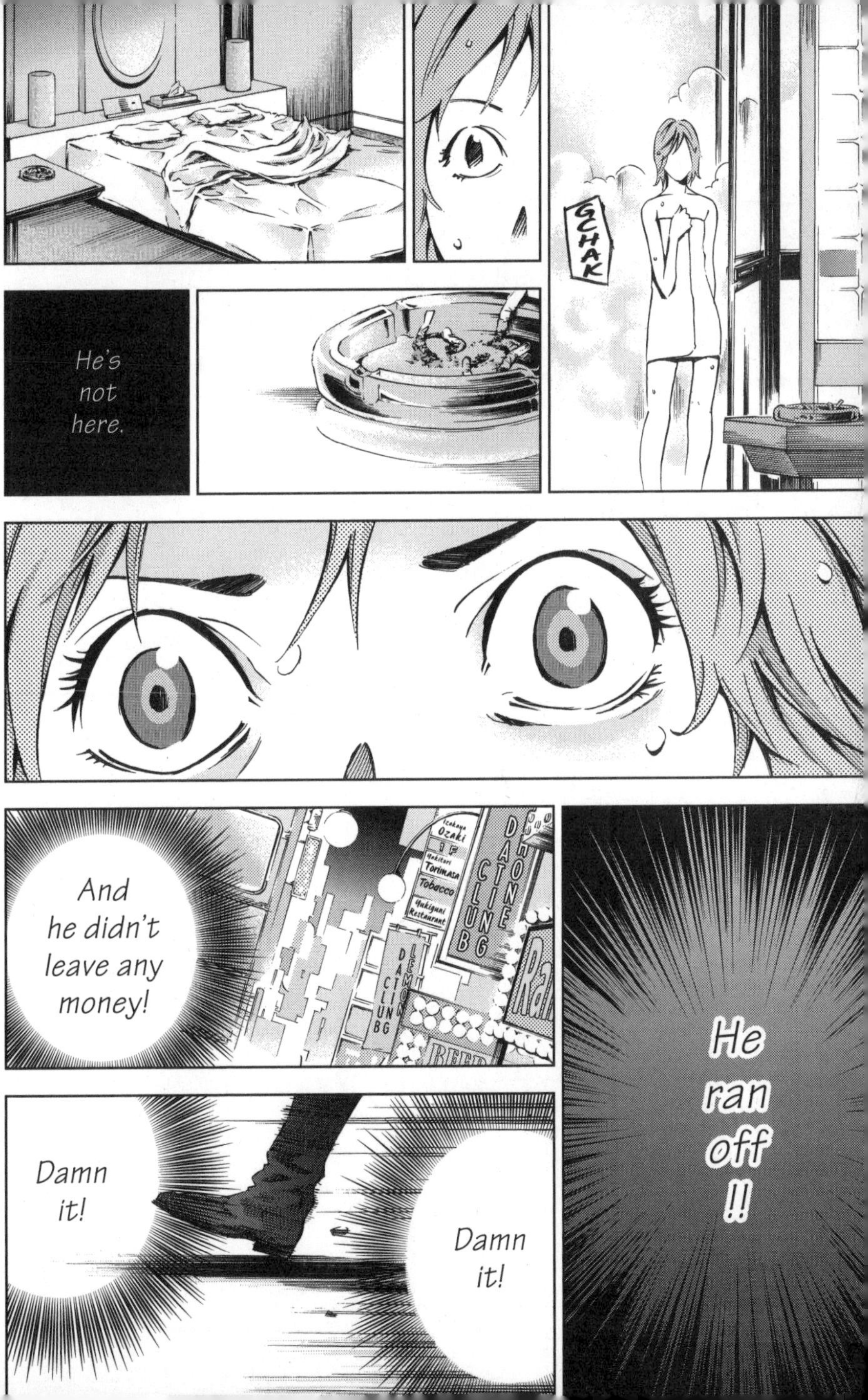
GCHAK
He's not here.
He ran off!!
And he didn't leave any money!
Ozaki
1F
Torimasa
Tobacco
Restaurant
BEER
Damn it!
Damn it!

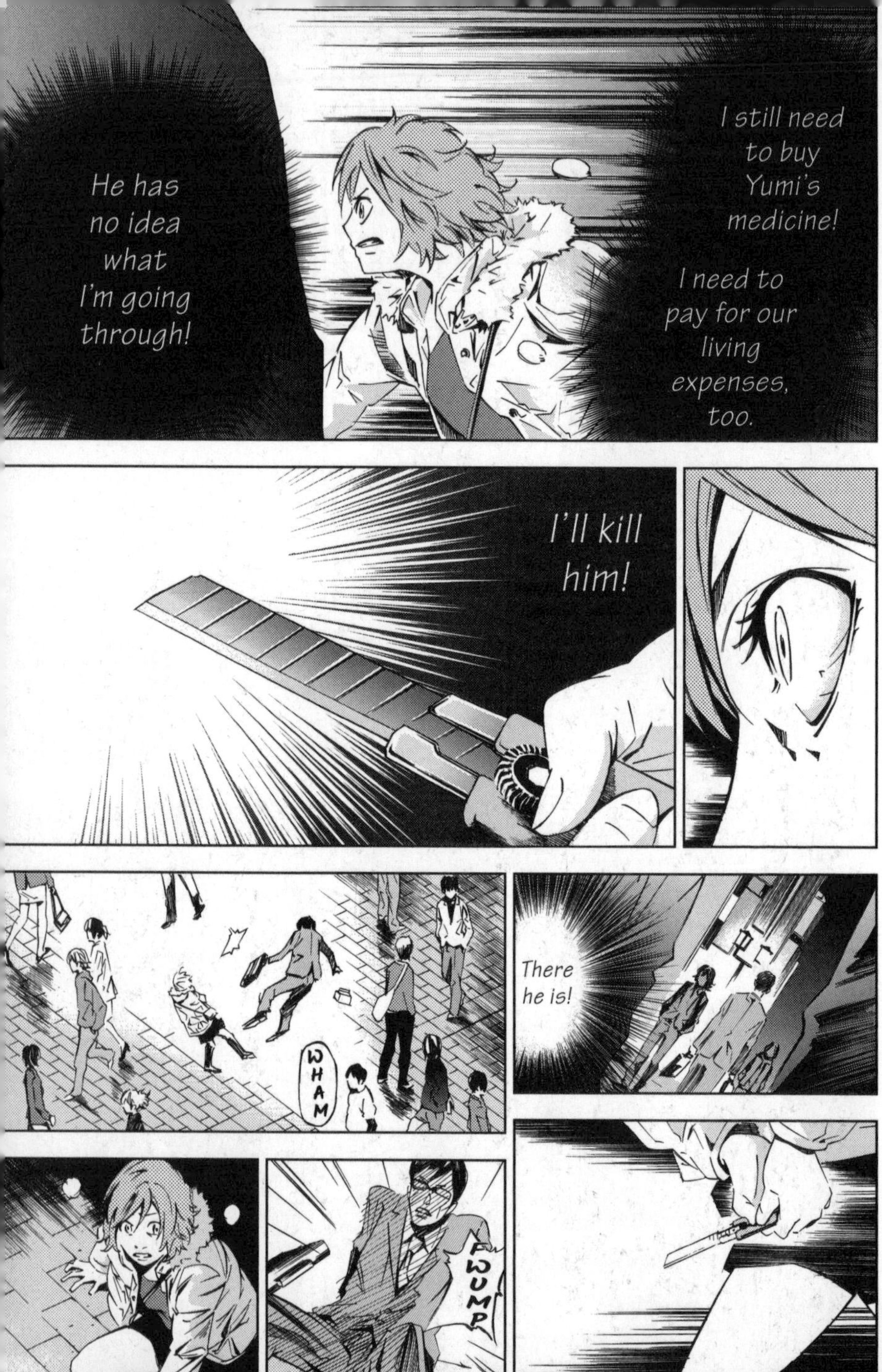
I still need to buy Yumi's medicine!
I need to pay for our living expenses, too.
He has no idea what I'm going through!
I'll kill him!
There he is!
WHAM
FWUMP

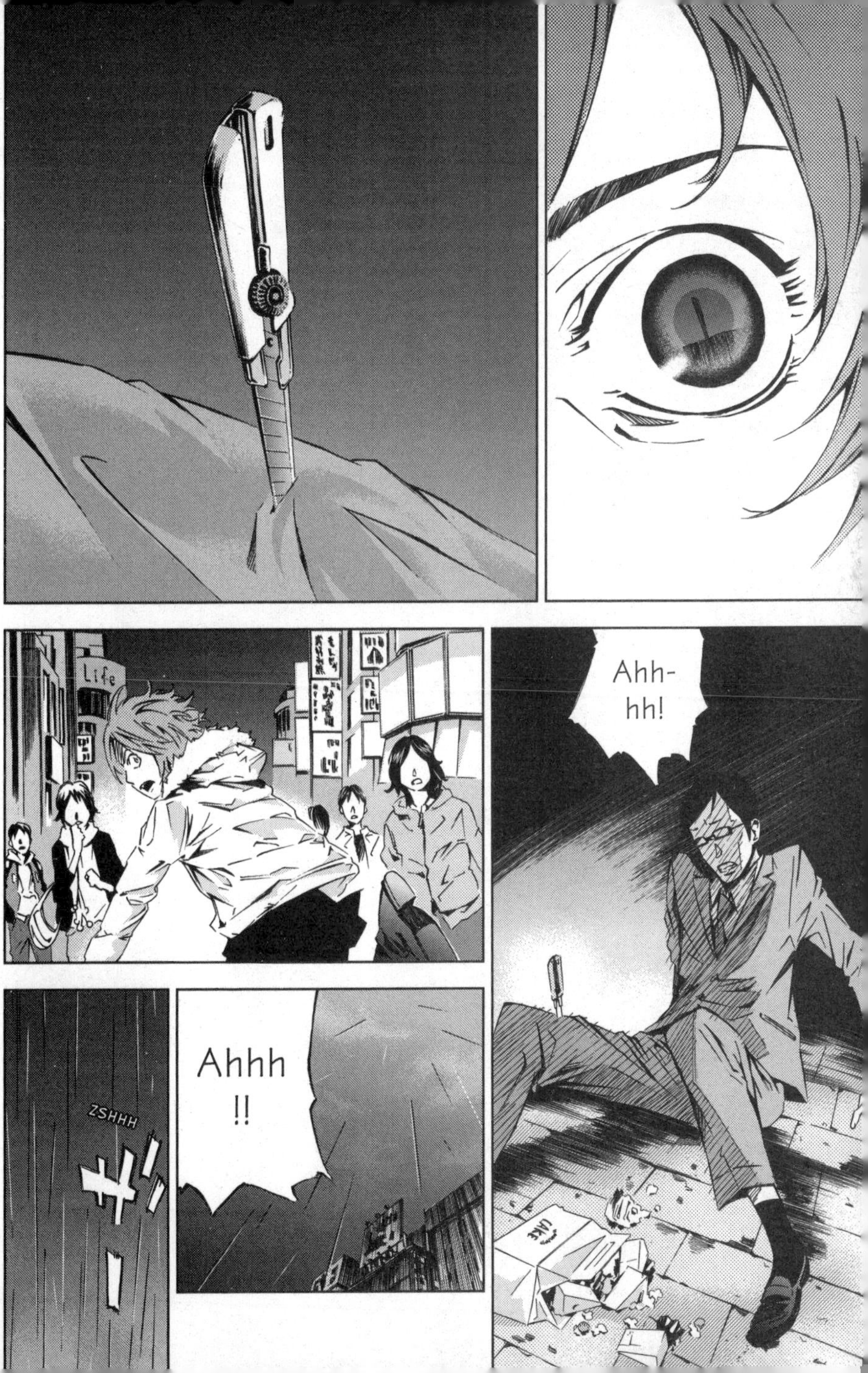

Ahh-
hh!
CAKE
Life
Ahhh
!!
ZSHHH

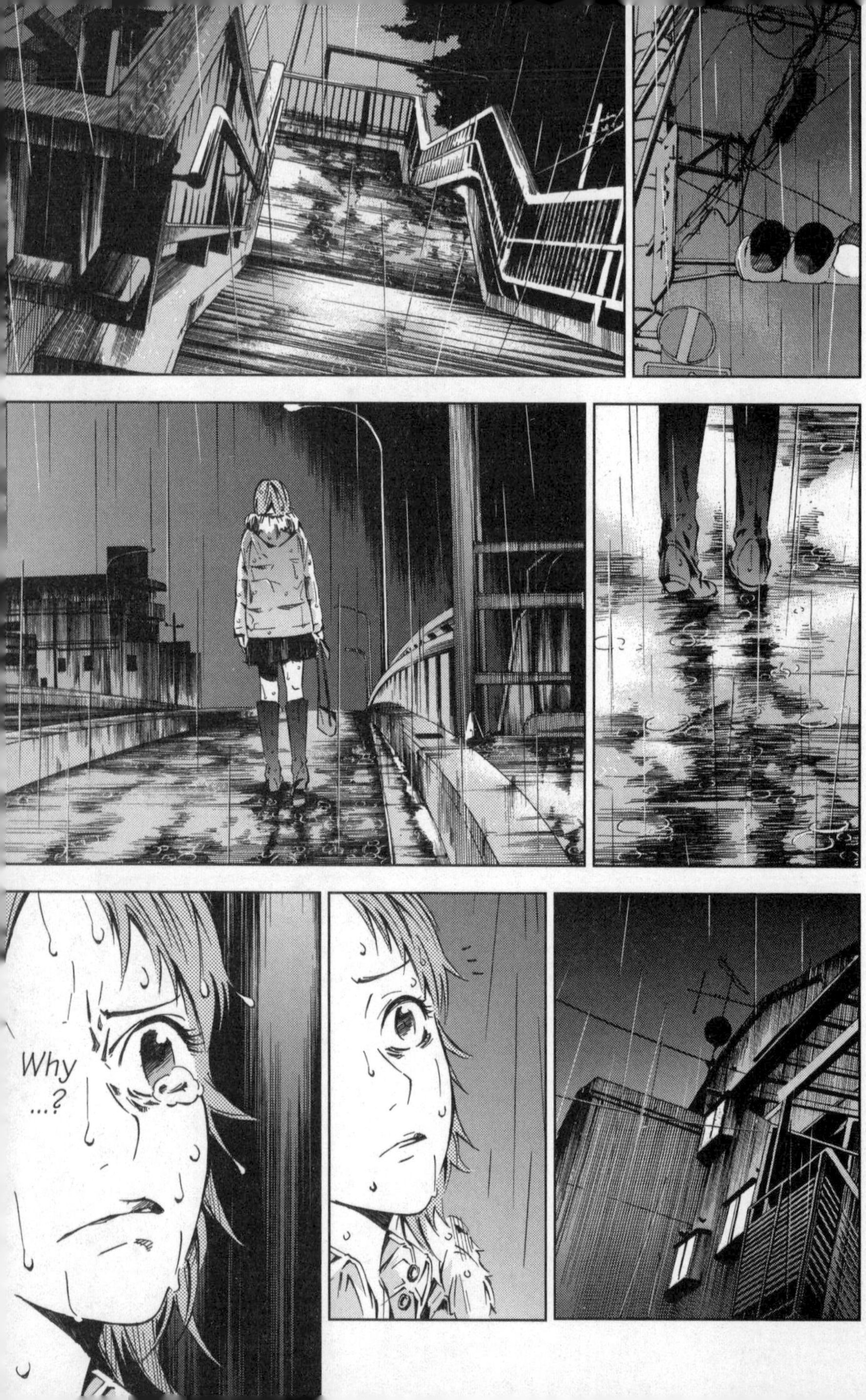
Why ...?

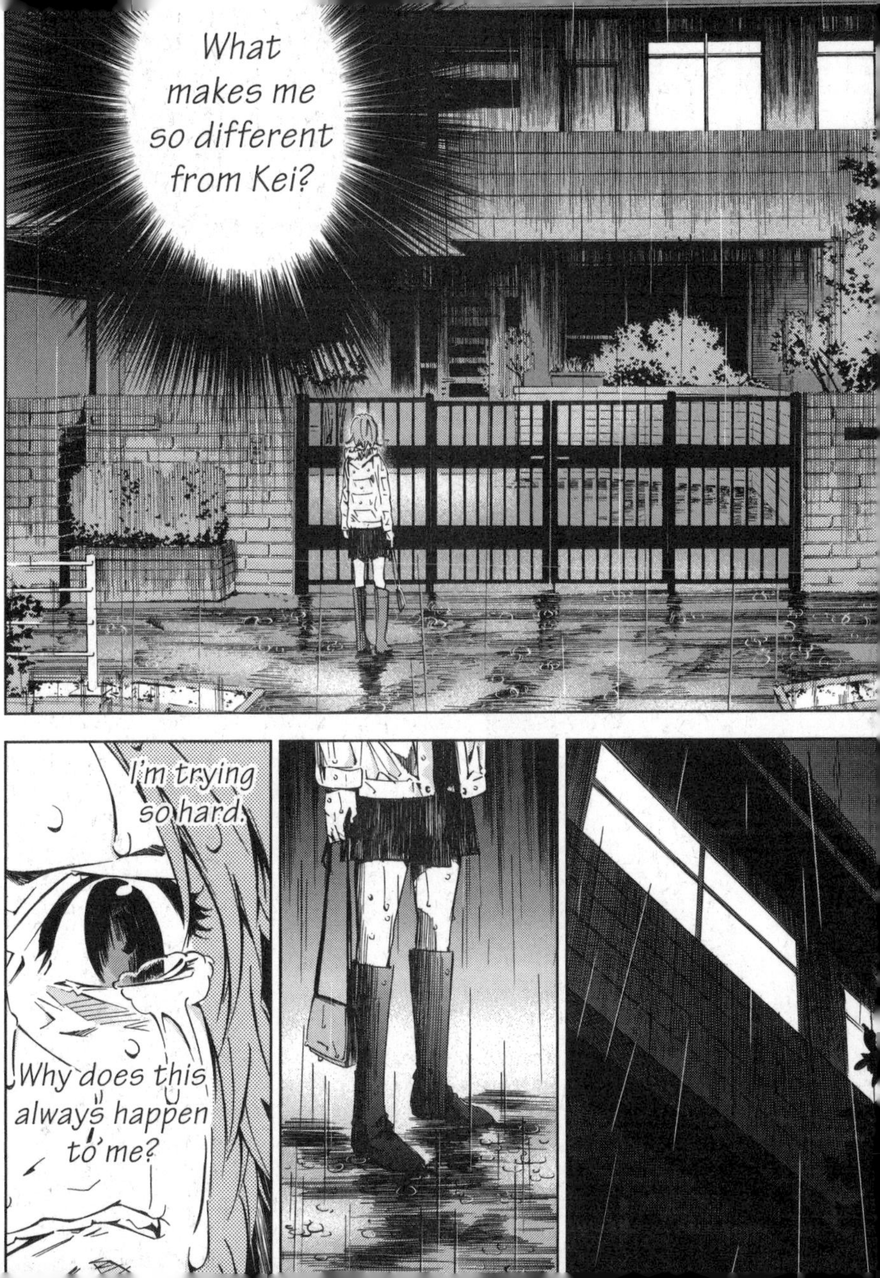
What makes me so different from Kei?
I'm trying so hard.
Why does this always happen to me?

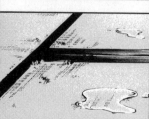

I've...

...had
enough...

I'd rather
die...

I hate
this...

If
my life's
going
to keep
being like
this...

I can't...
keep doing
this...

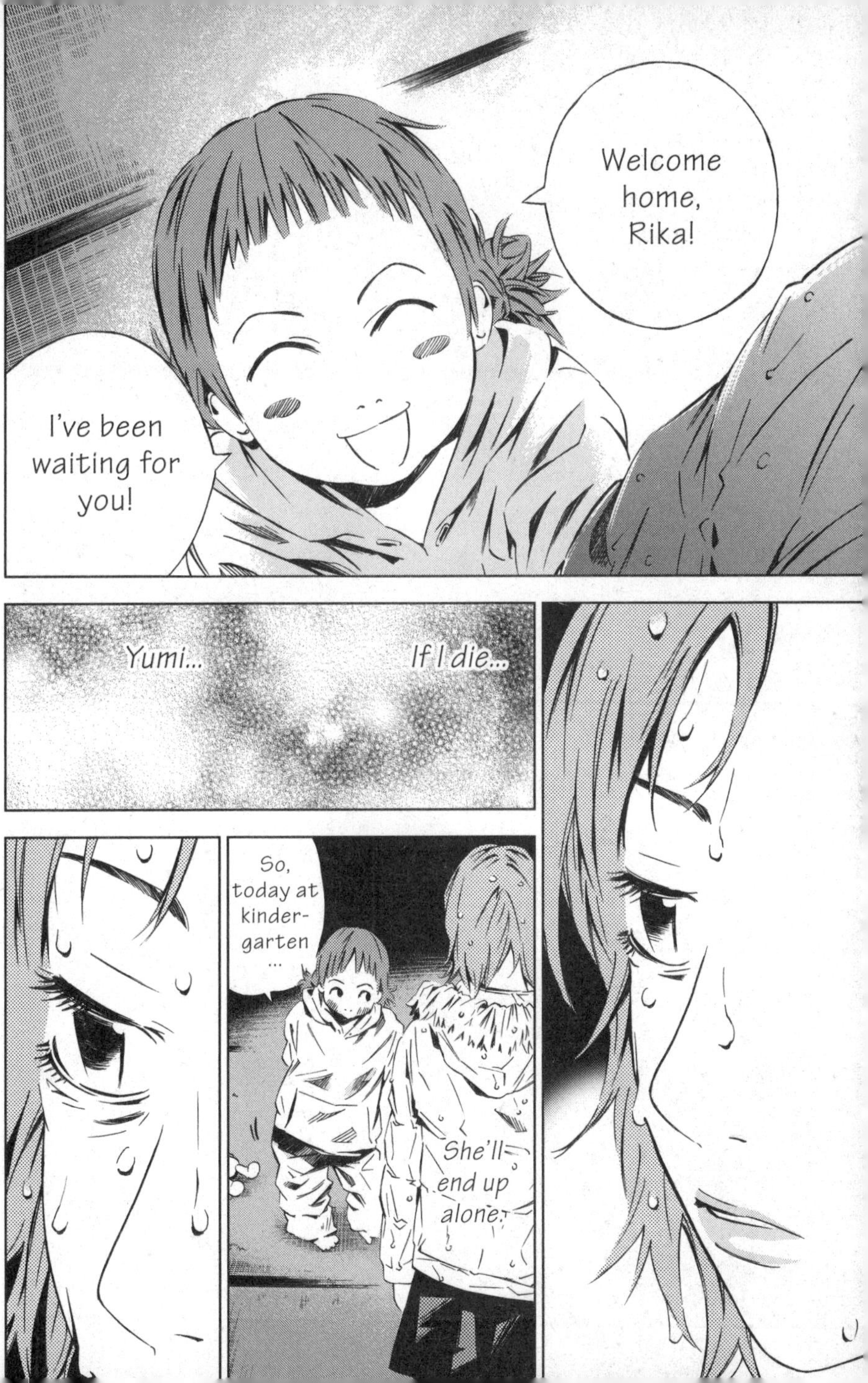
Welcome home, Rika!
I've been waiting for you!
If I die...
Yumi...
So, today at kinder-garten ...
She'll end up alone.

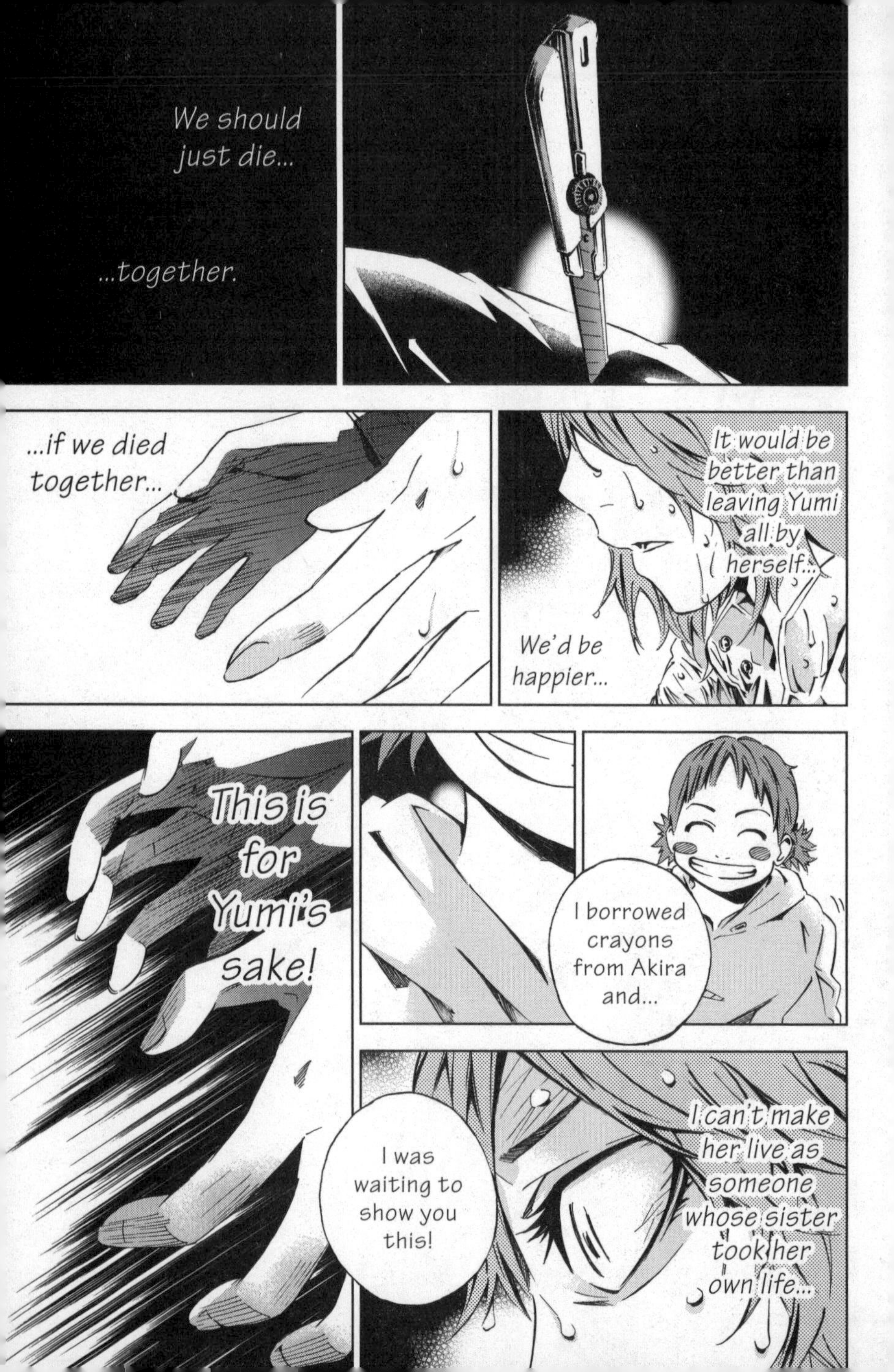
We should just die...
...together.
It would be better than leaving Yumi all by herself...
We'd be happier...
...if we died together...
I borrowed crayons from Akira and...
I can't make her live as someone whose sister took her own life...
I was waiting to show you this!
This is for Yumi's sake!

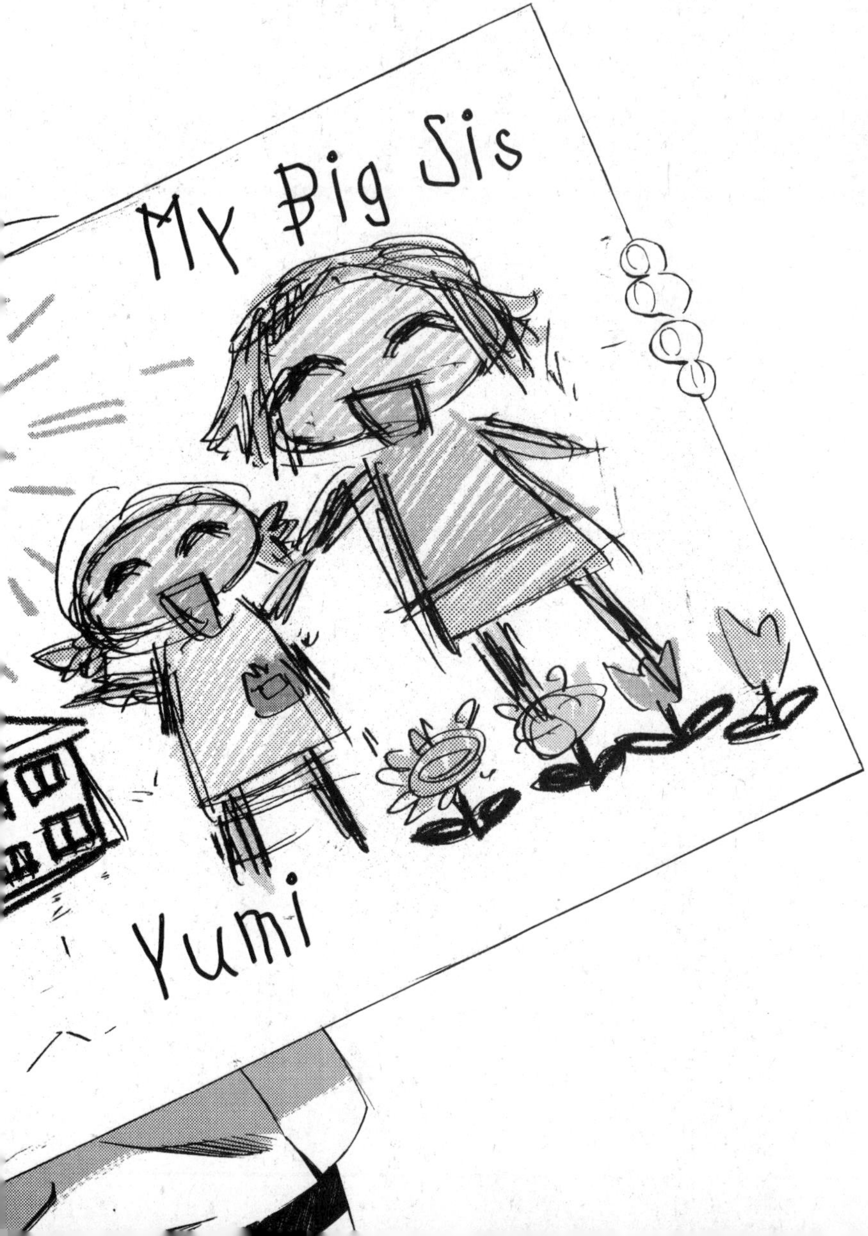

My Big Sis
Yumi

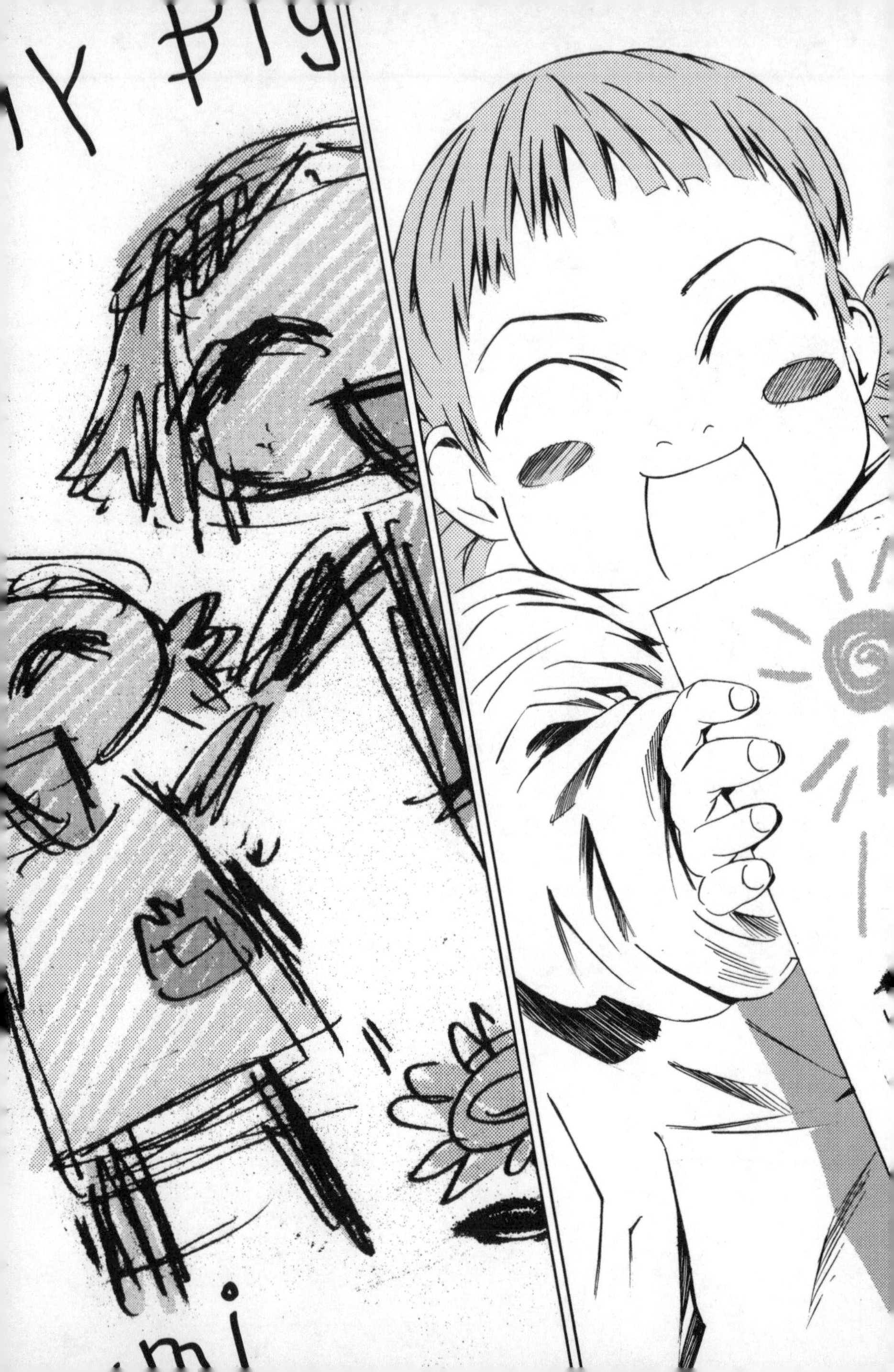
ly Big
mi

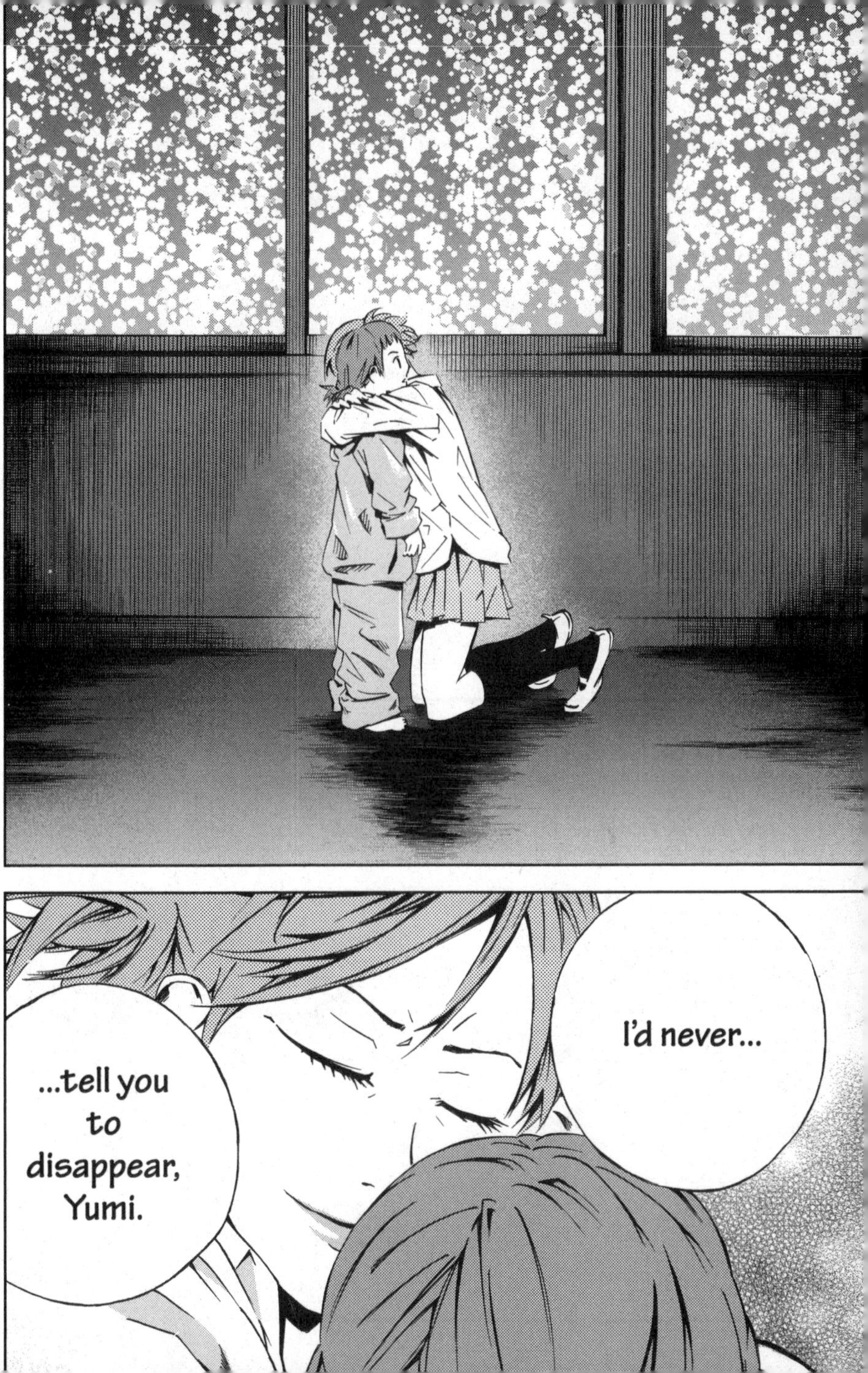
I'd never...
...tell you to disappear, Yumi.

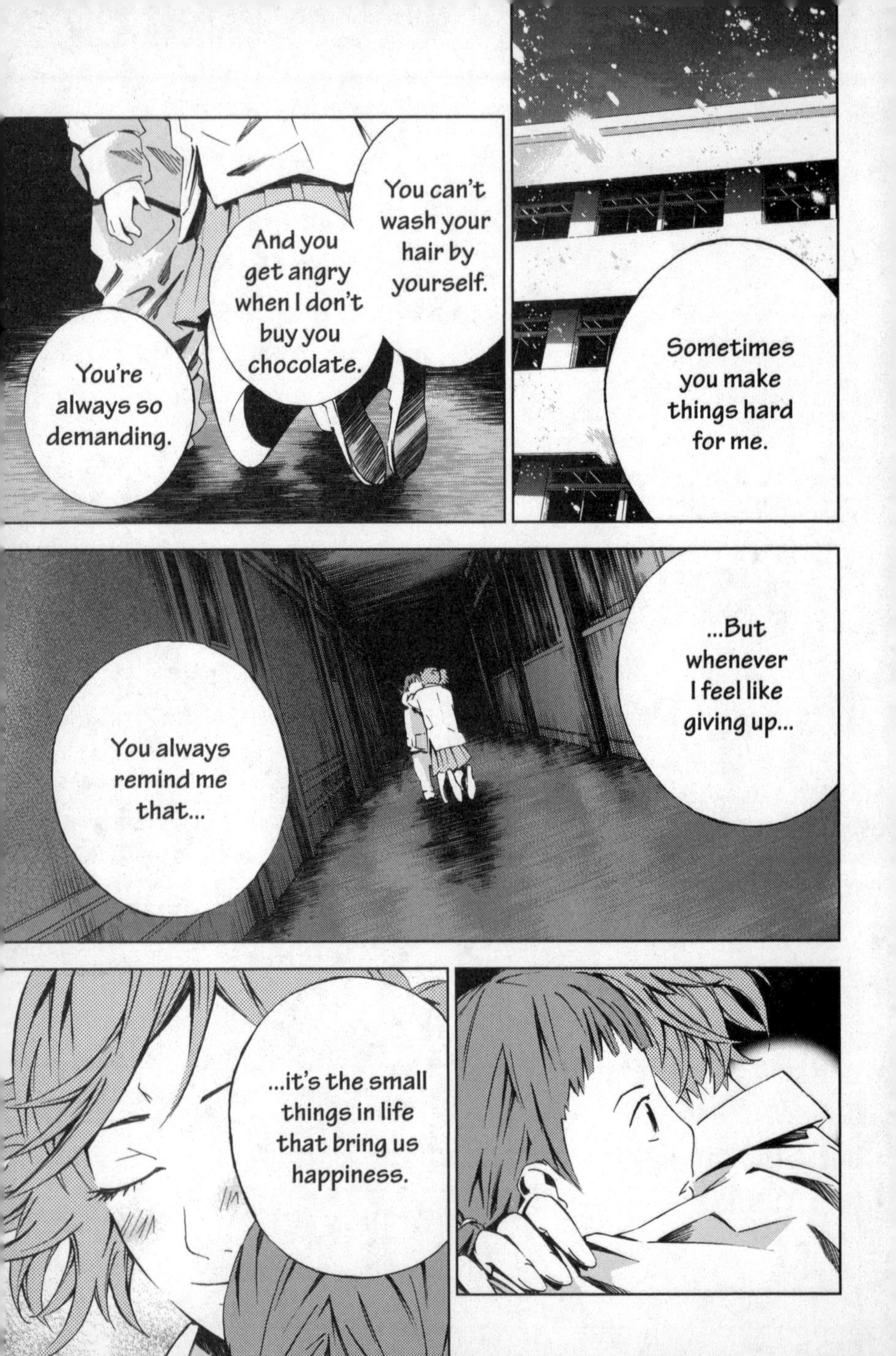
Sometimes you make things hard for me.
You can't wash your hair by yourself.
And you get angry when I don't buy you chocolate.
You're always so demanding.
...But whenever I feel like giving up...
You always remind me that...
...it's the small things in life that bring us happiness.

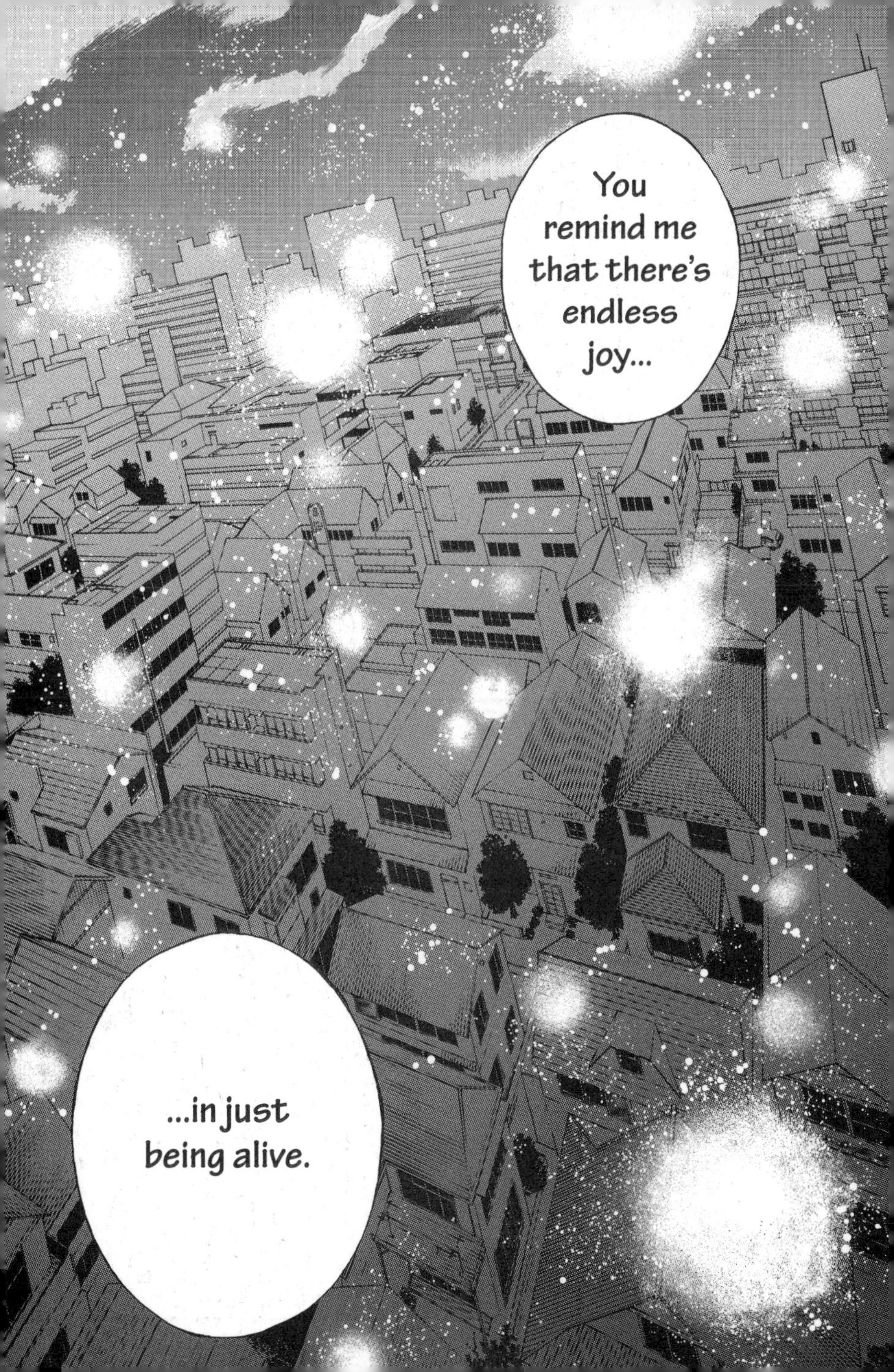
You remind me that there's endless joy...
...in just being alive.

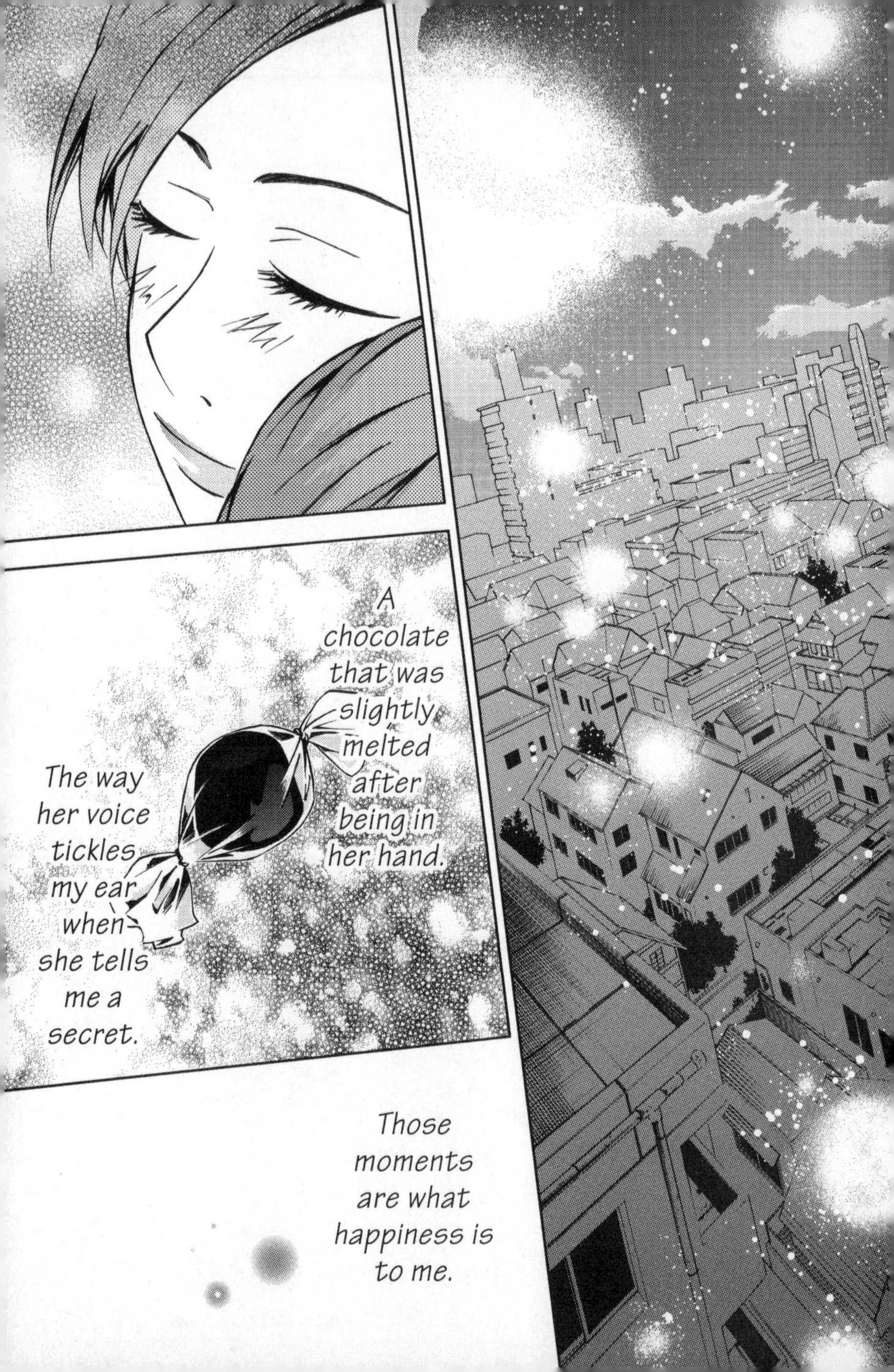
A chocolate that was slightly melted after being in her hand.
The way her voice tickles my ear when she tells me a secret.
Those moments are what happiness is to me.

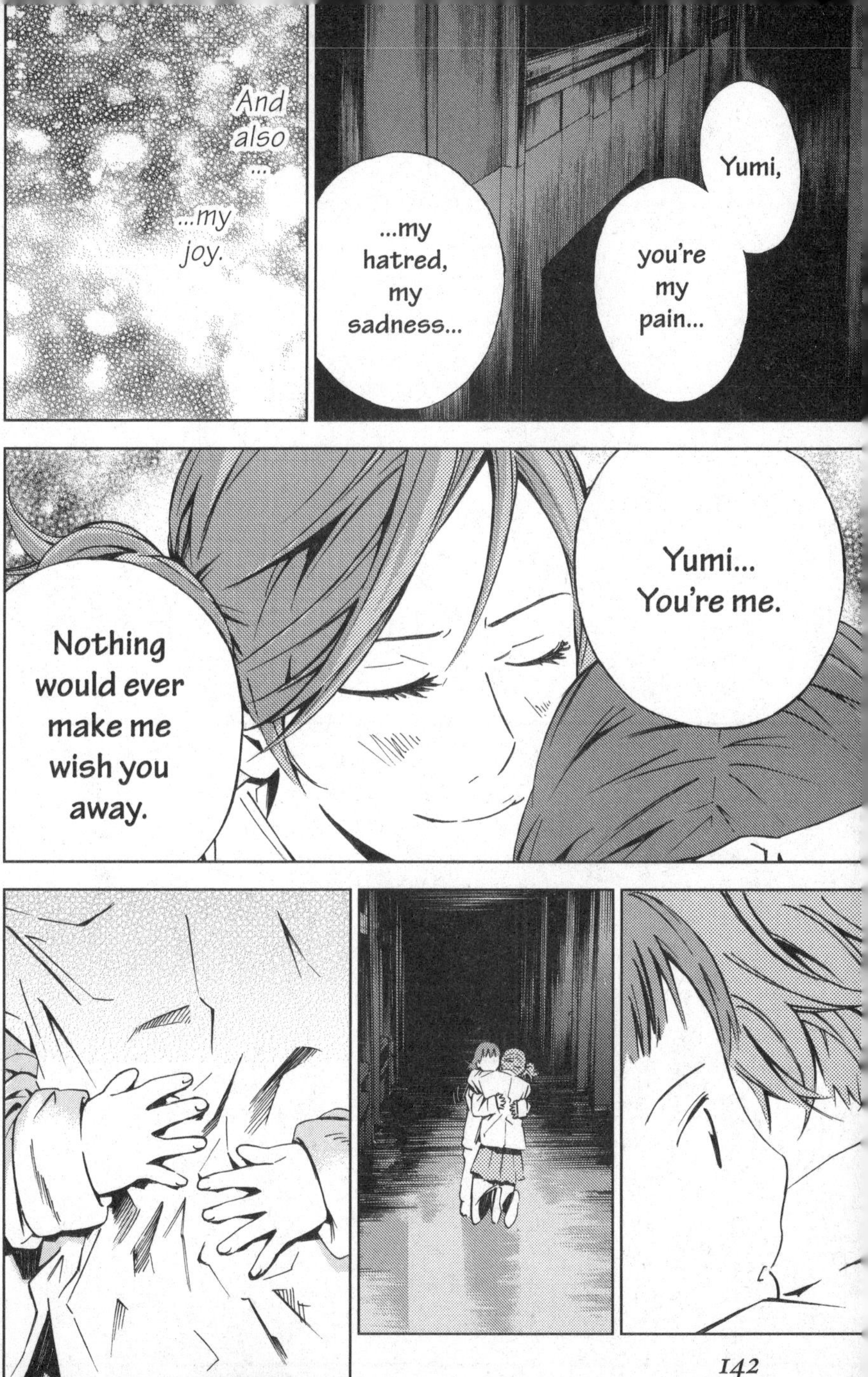

Yumi,
you're my pain...
...my hatred, my sadness...
And also ...
...my joy.
Yumi... You're me.
Nothing would ever make me wish you away.

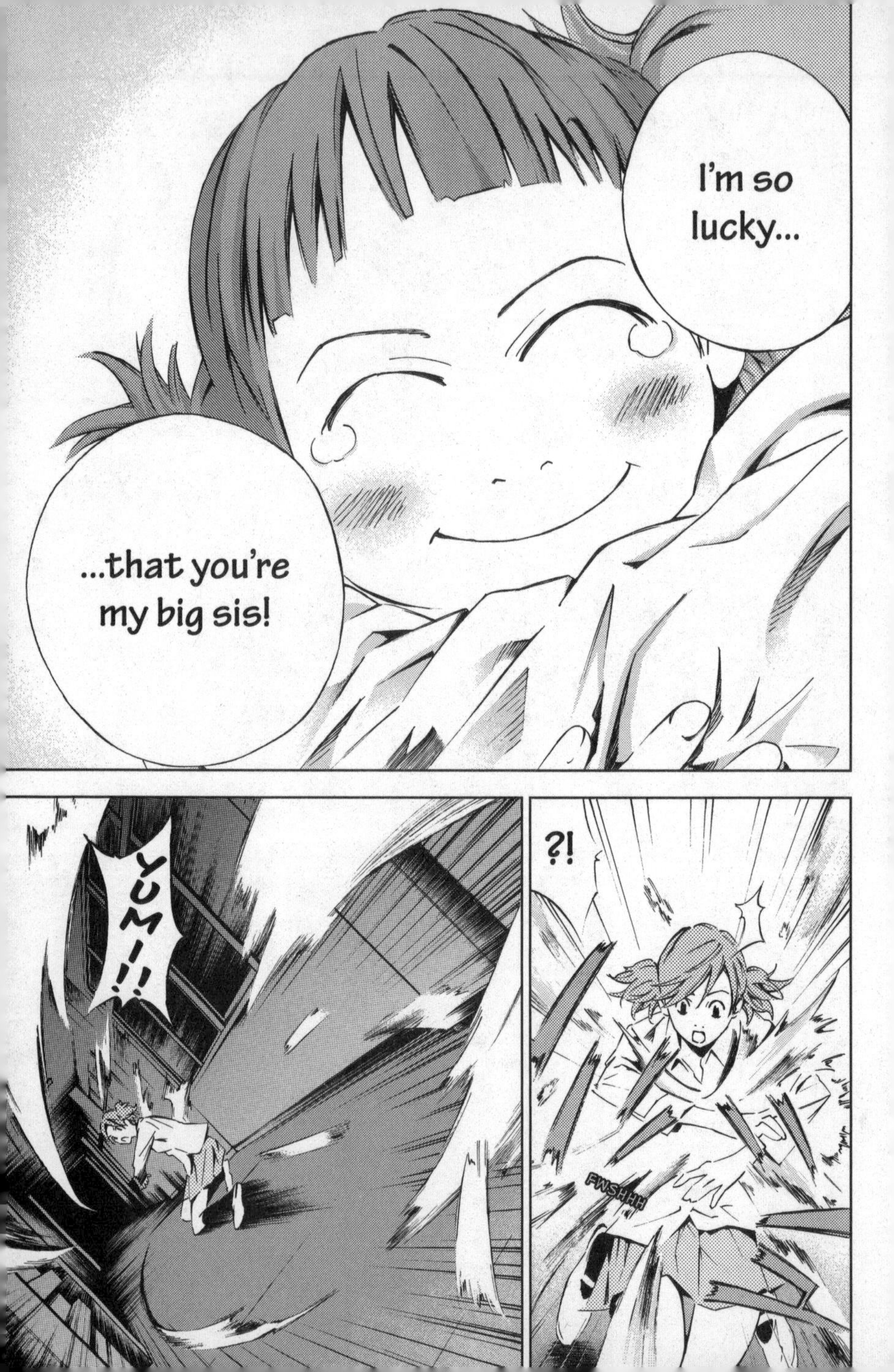
I'm so lucky...
...that you're my big sis!
?!
FWSHHH
YUMI!!!

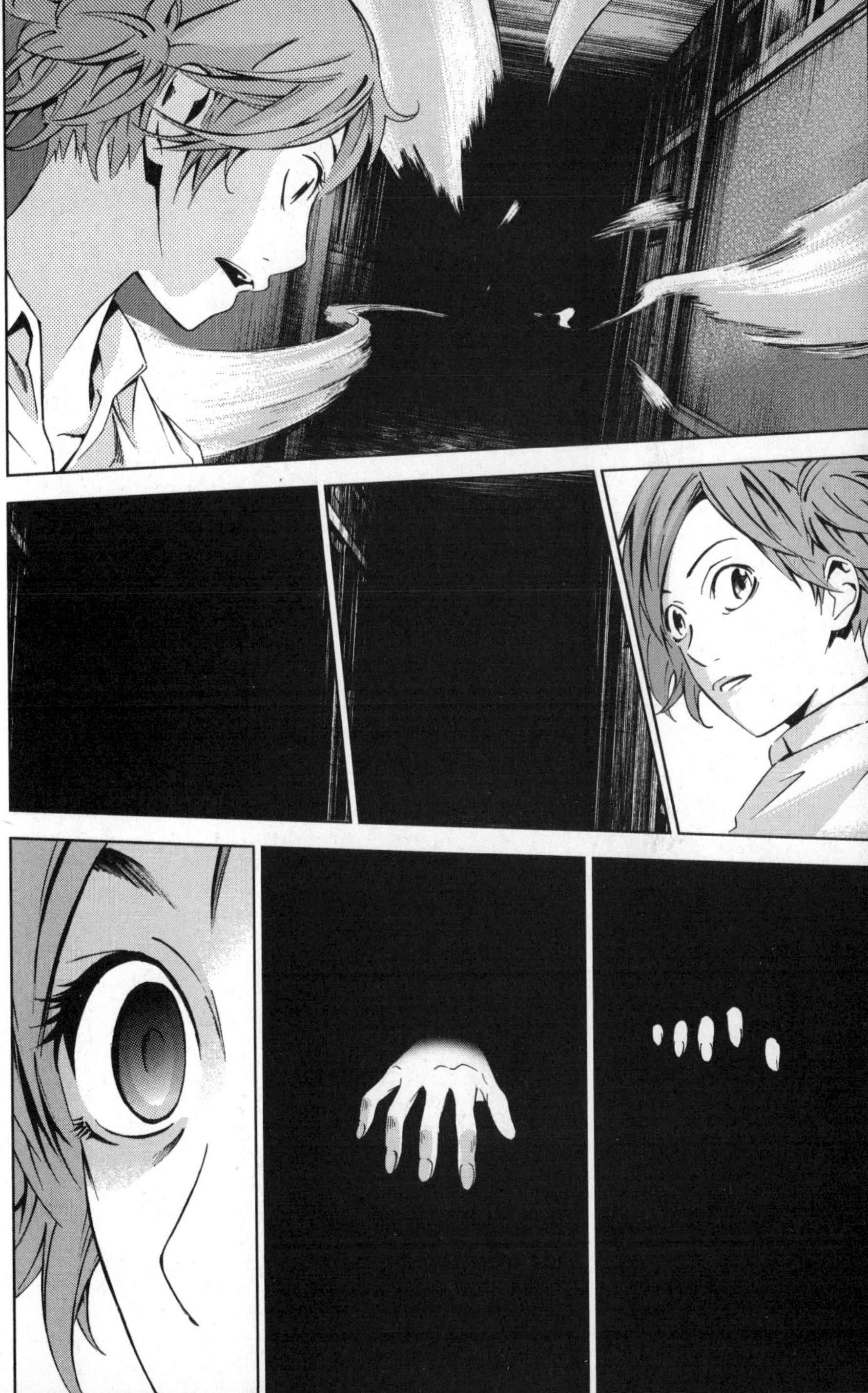

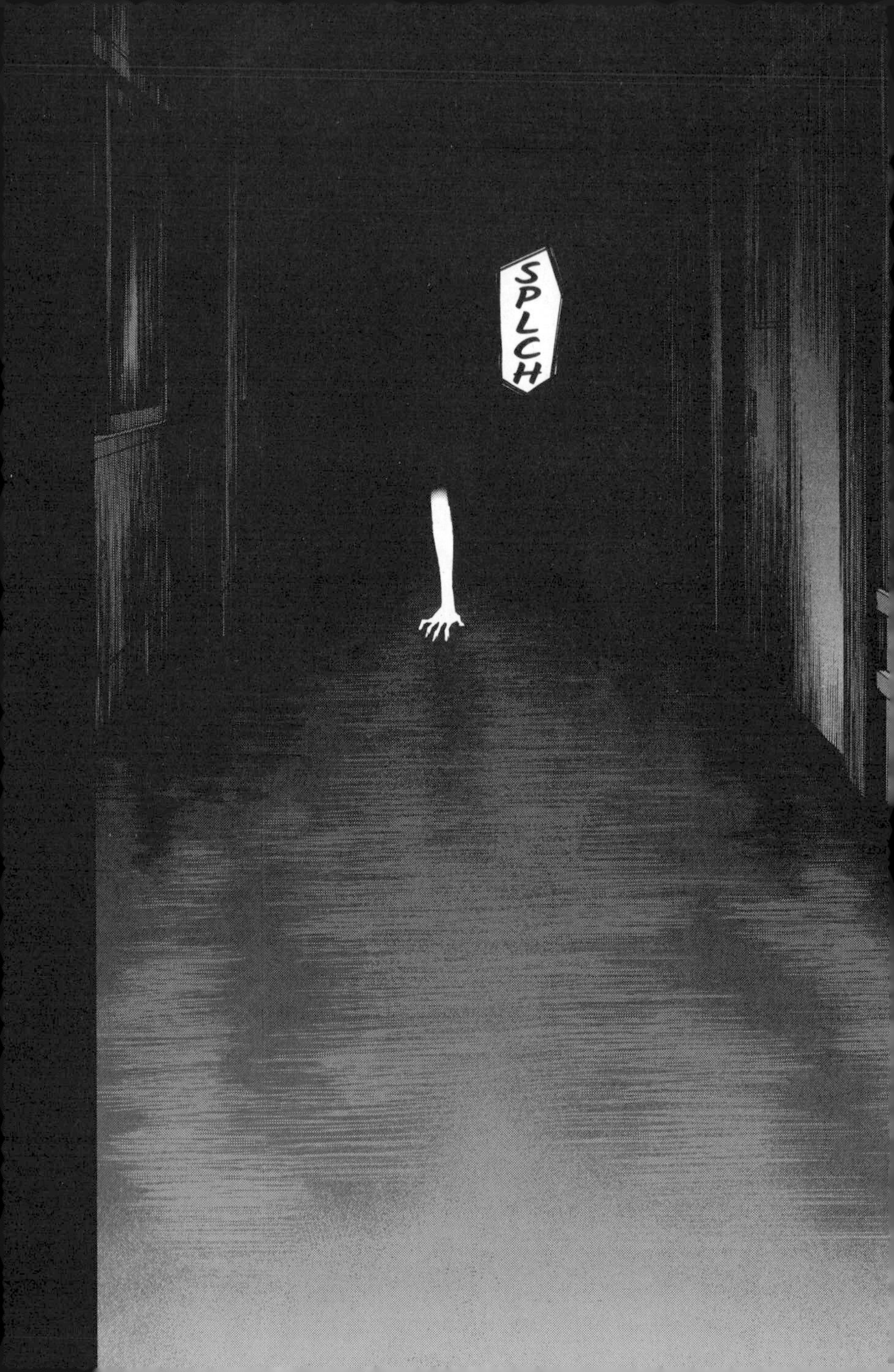
SPLCH

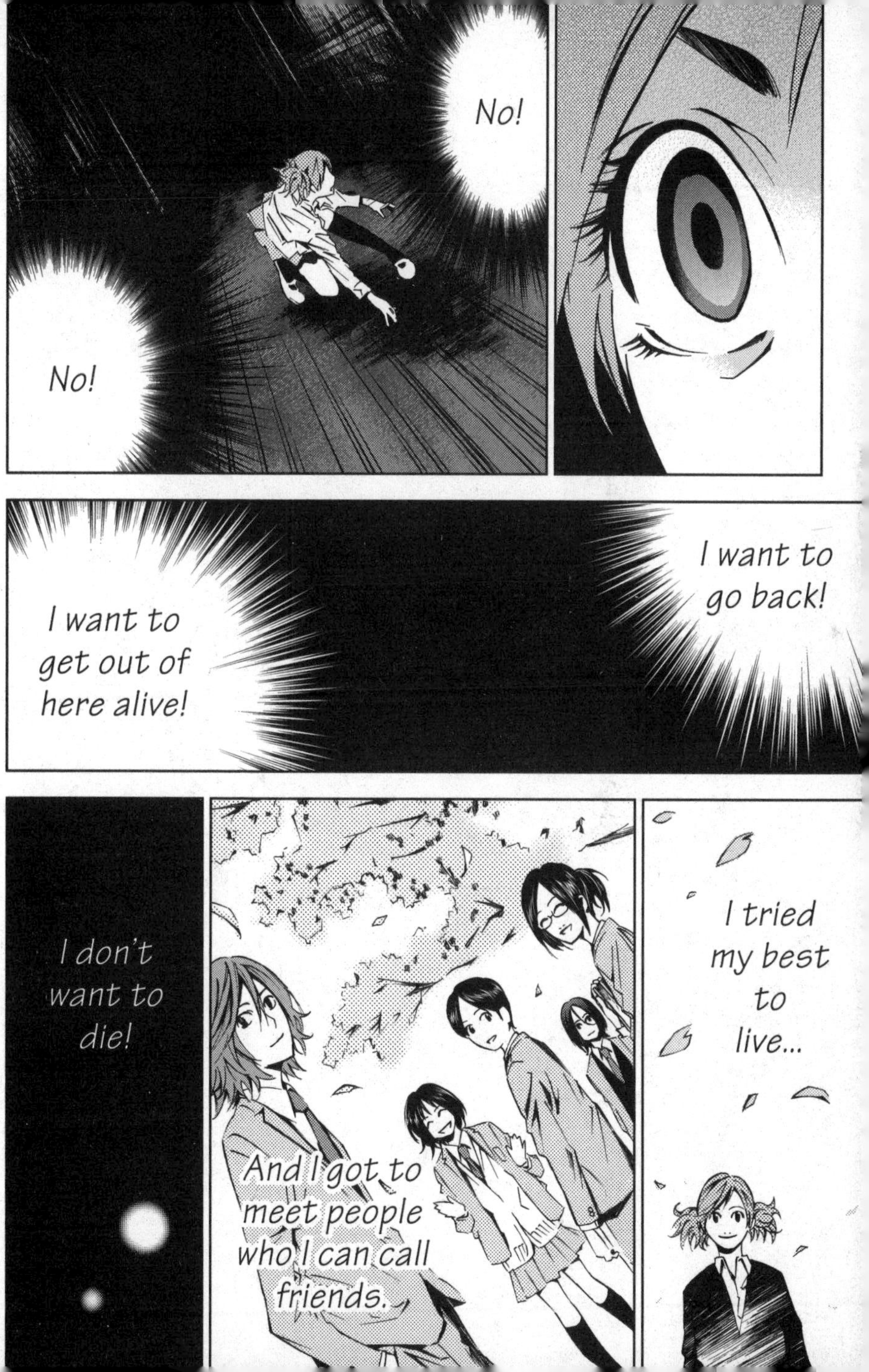
No!
No!
I want to go back!
I want to get out of here alive!
I tried my best to live...
And I got to meet people who I can call friends.
I don't want to die!

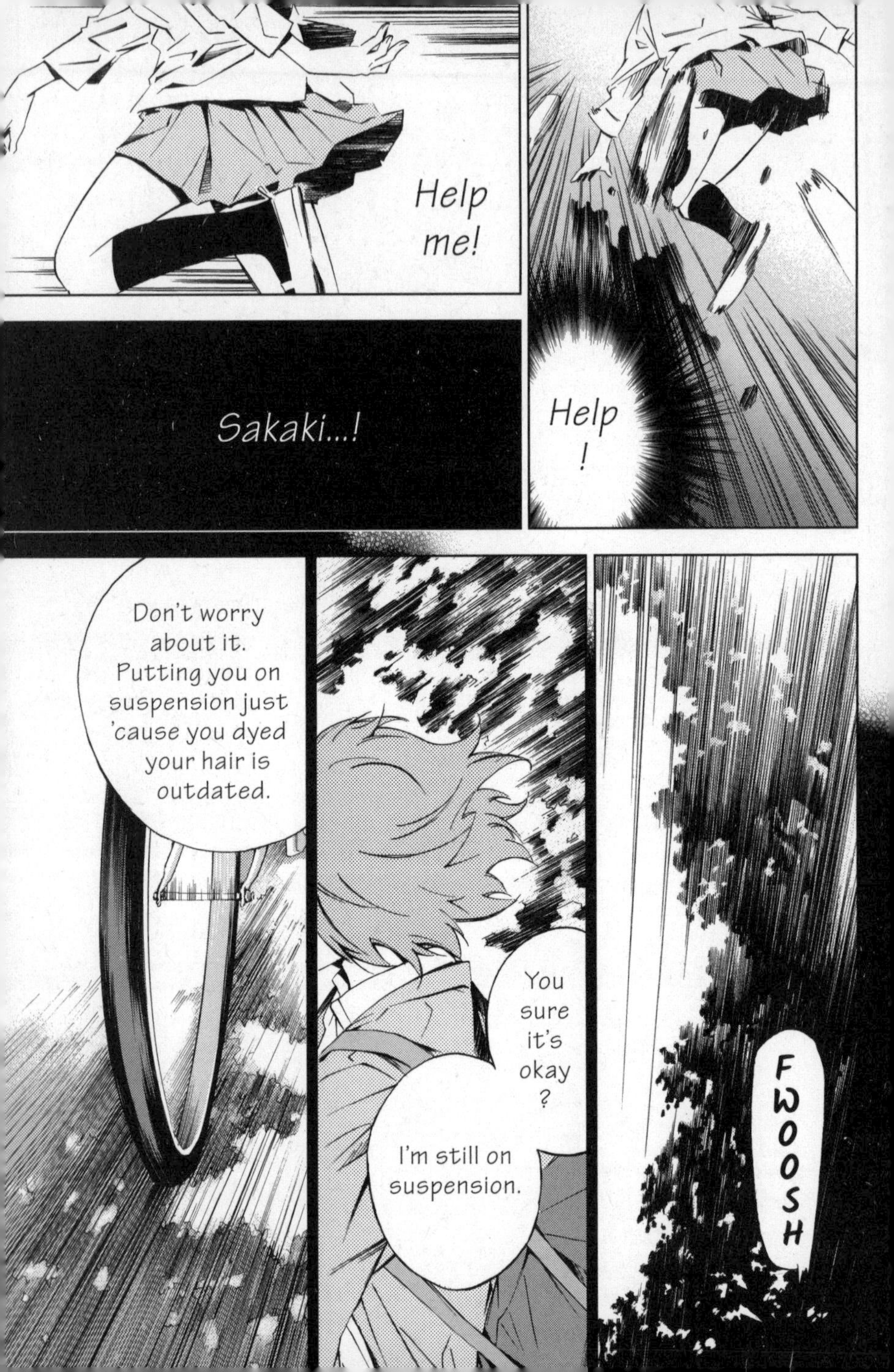
Help!
Help me!
Sakaki...!
FWOOSH
You sure it's okay?
I'm still on suspension.
Don't worry about it. Putting you on suspension just 'cause you dyed your hair is outdated.

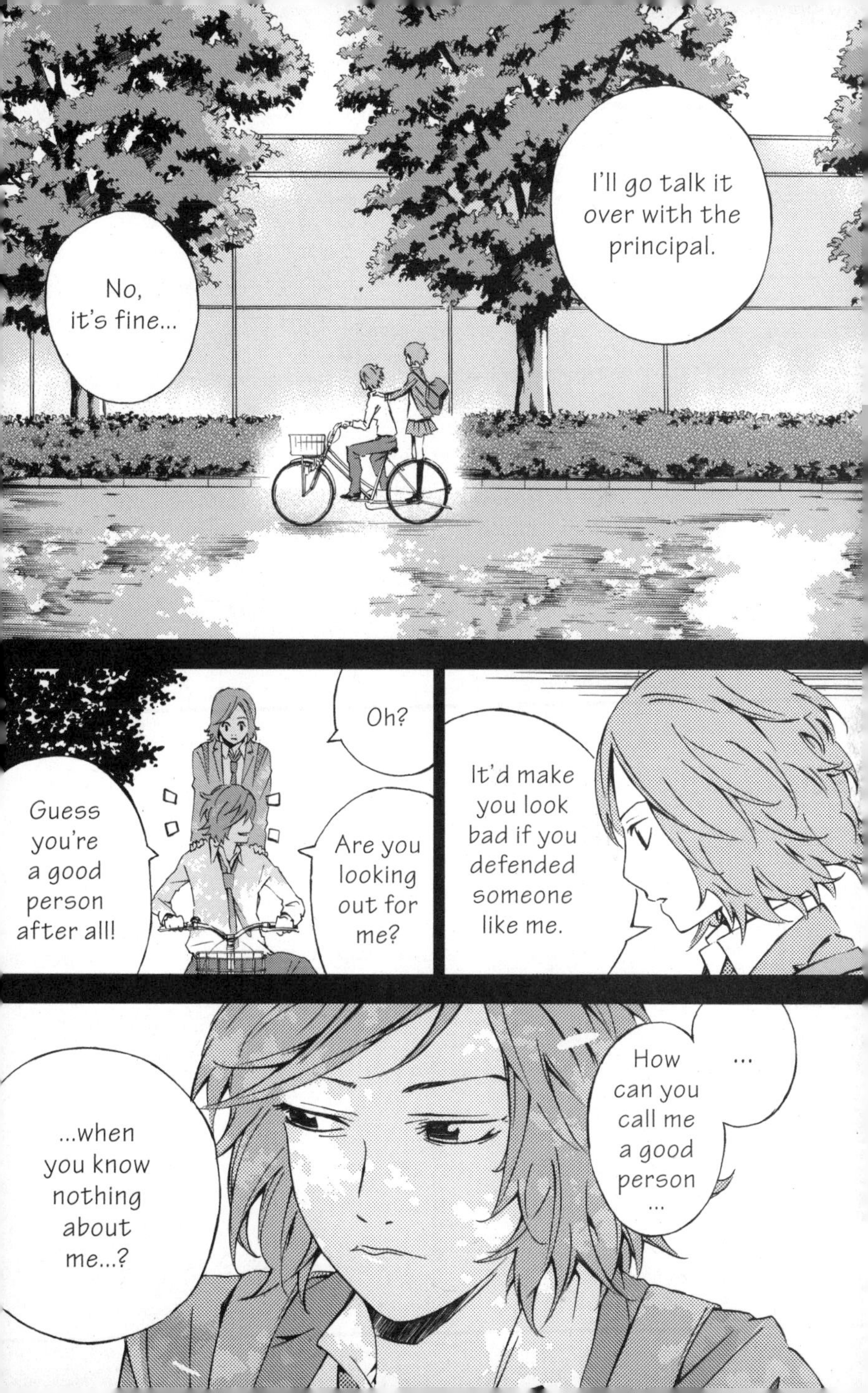
I'll go talk it over with the principal.
No, it's fine...
It'd make you look bad if you defended someone like me.
Oh?
Are you looking out for me?
Guess you're a good person after all!
...
How can you call me a good person ...
...when you know nothing about me...?

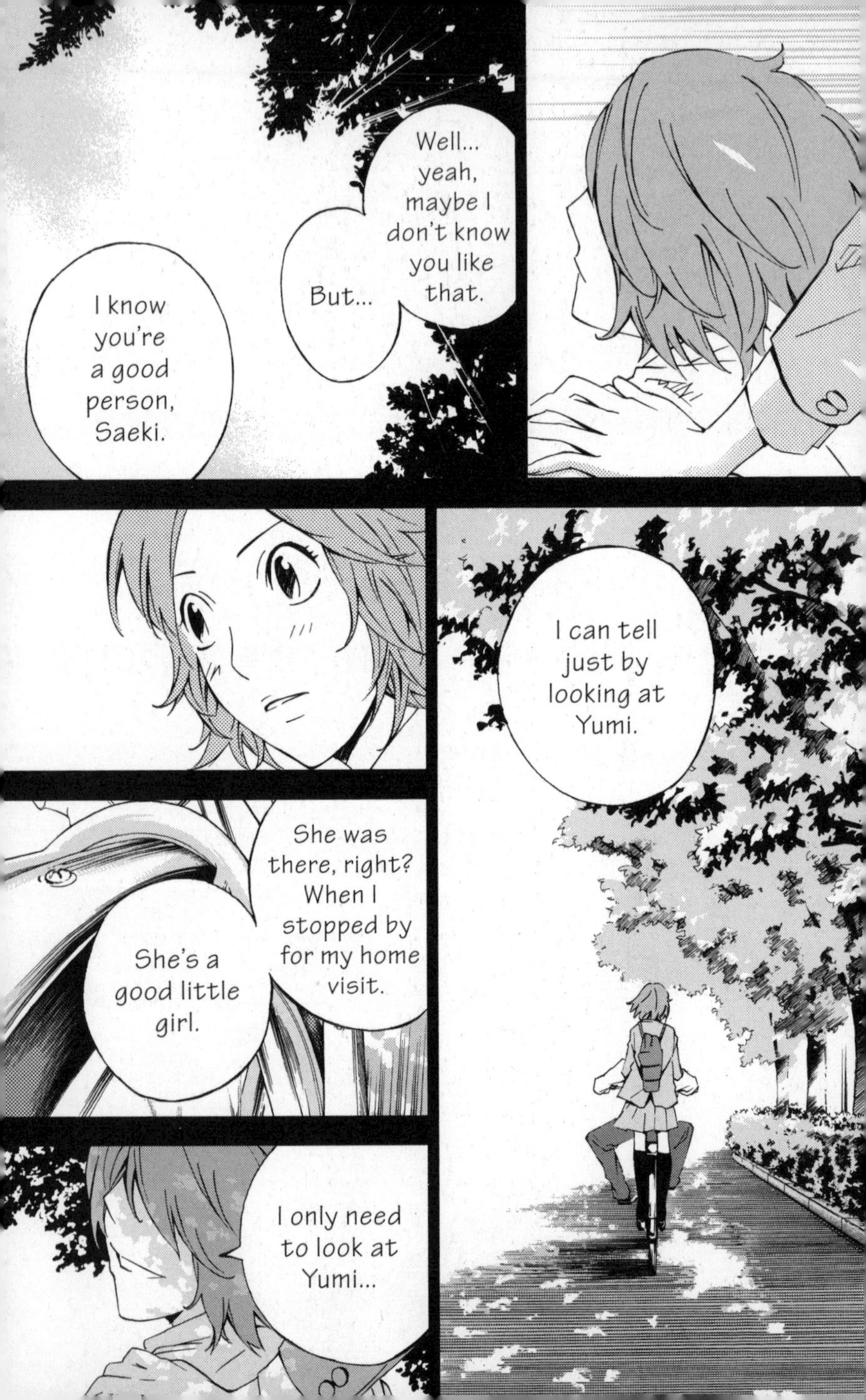
Well... yeah, maybe I don't know you like that.
But...
I know you're a good person, Saeki.
I can tell just by looking at Yumi.
She was there, right? When I stopped by for my home visit.
She's a good little girl.
I only need to look at Yumi...

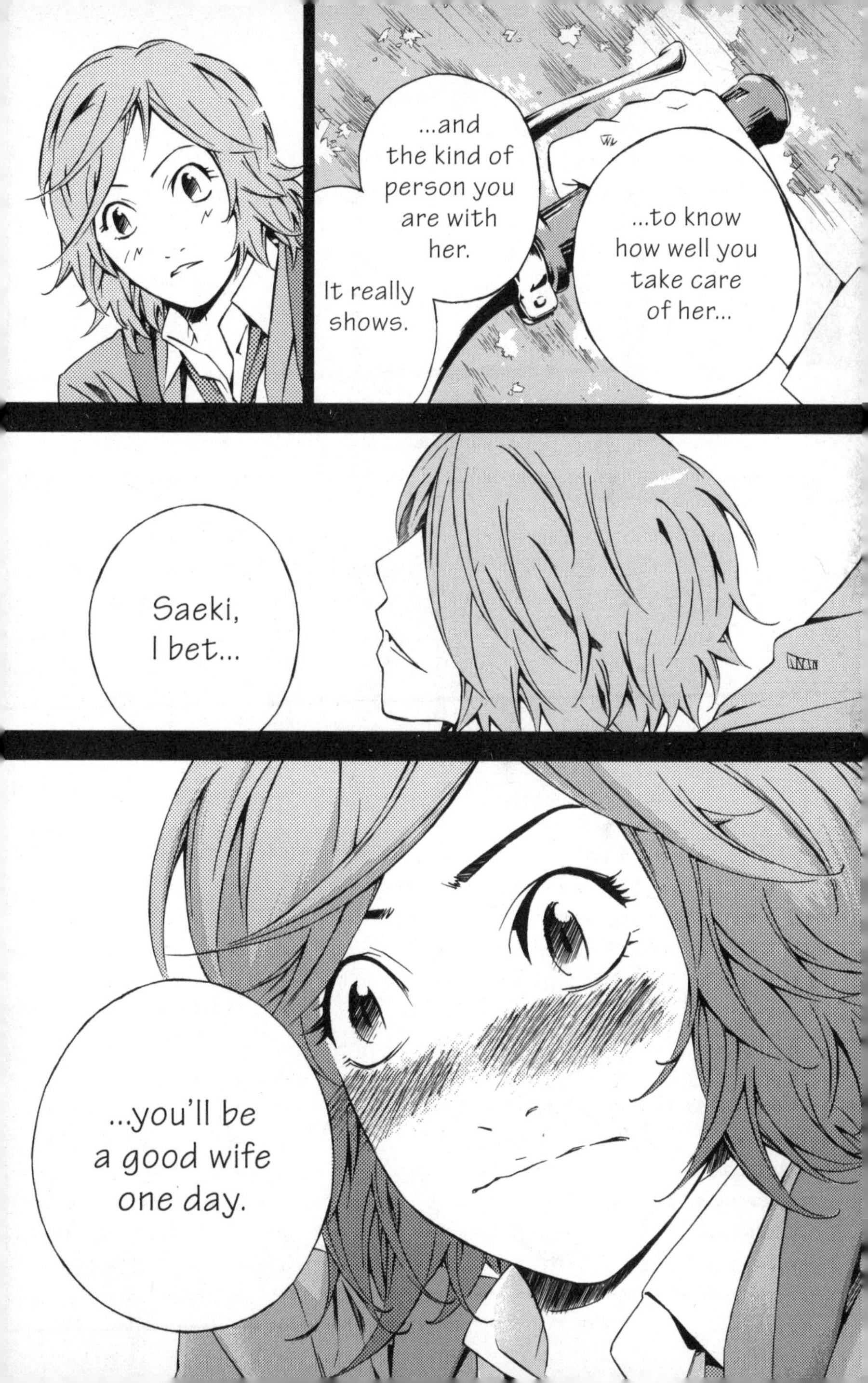
...to know how well you take care of her...
...and the kind of person you are with her.
It really shows.
Saeki, I bet...
...you'll be a good wife one day.

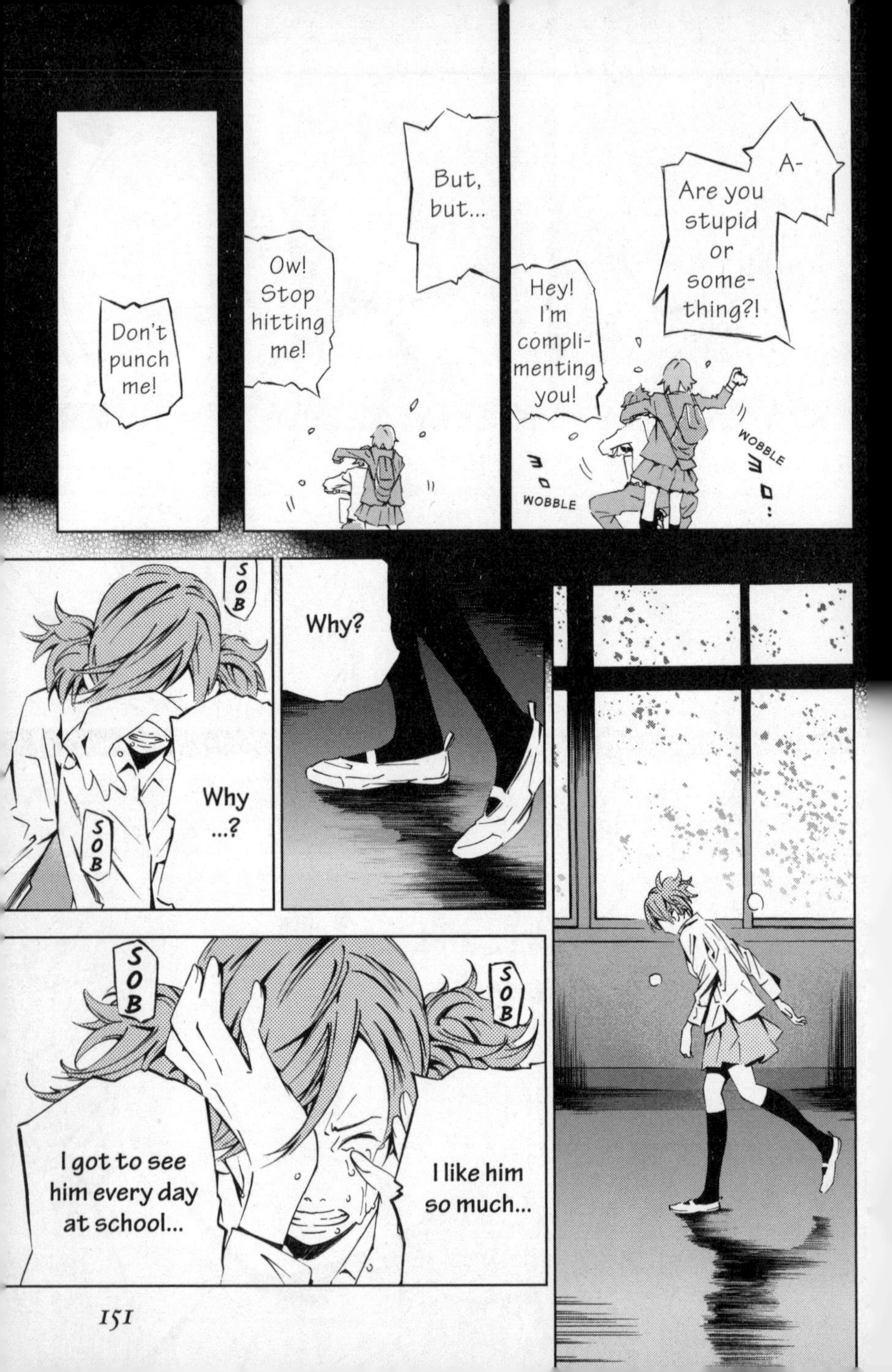
A-
Are you stupid or something?!
Hey! I'm compli-menting you!
WOBBLE
WOBBLE
But, but...
Ow! Stop hitting me!
Don't punch me!
Why?
SOB
Why ...?
SOB
SOB
SOB
I like him so much...
I got to see him every day at school...

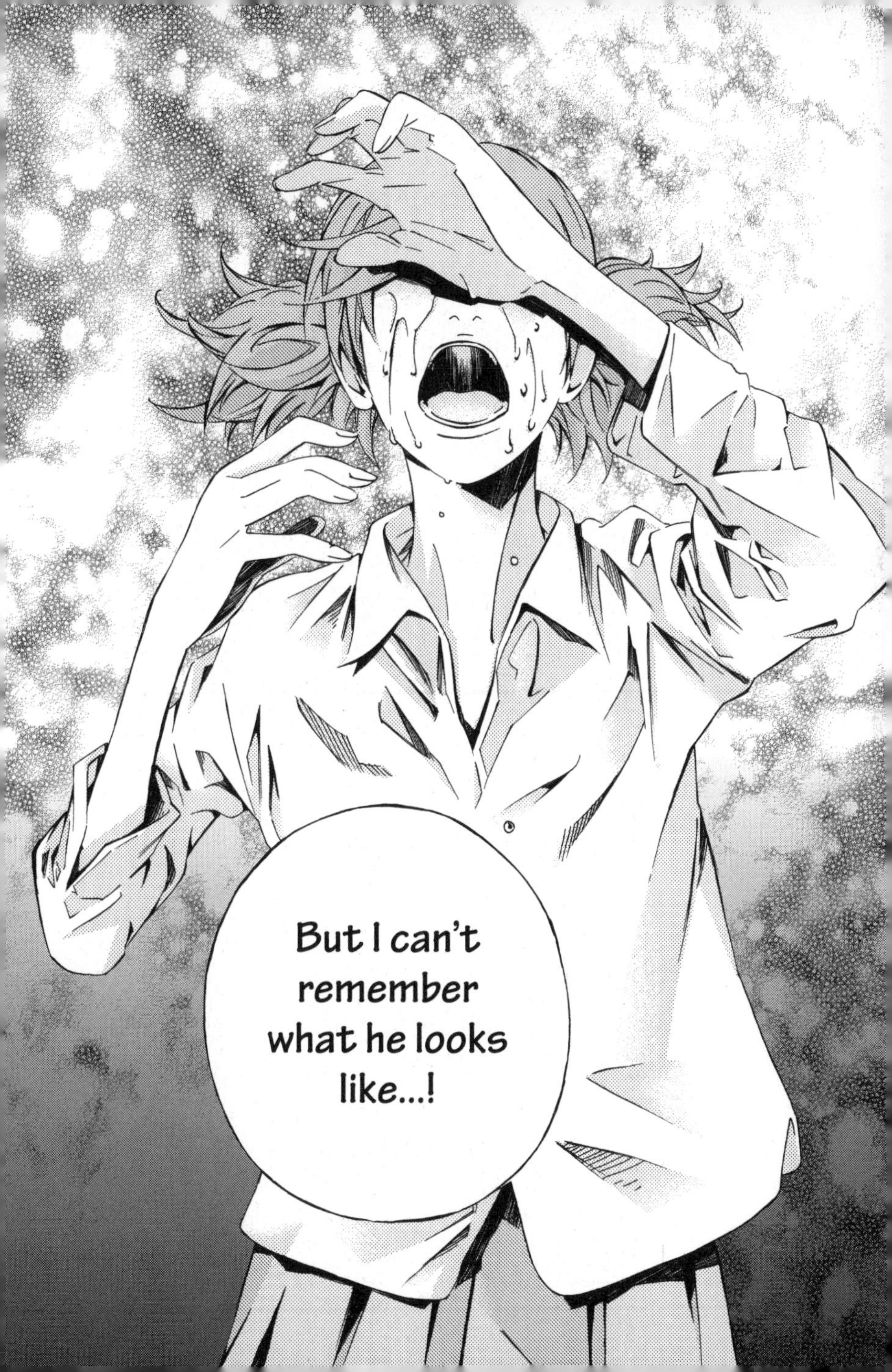
But I can't remember what he looks like...!

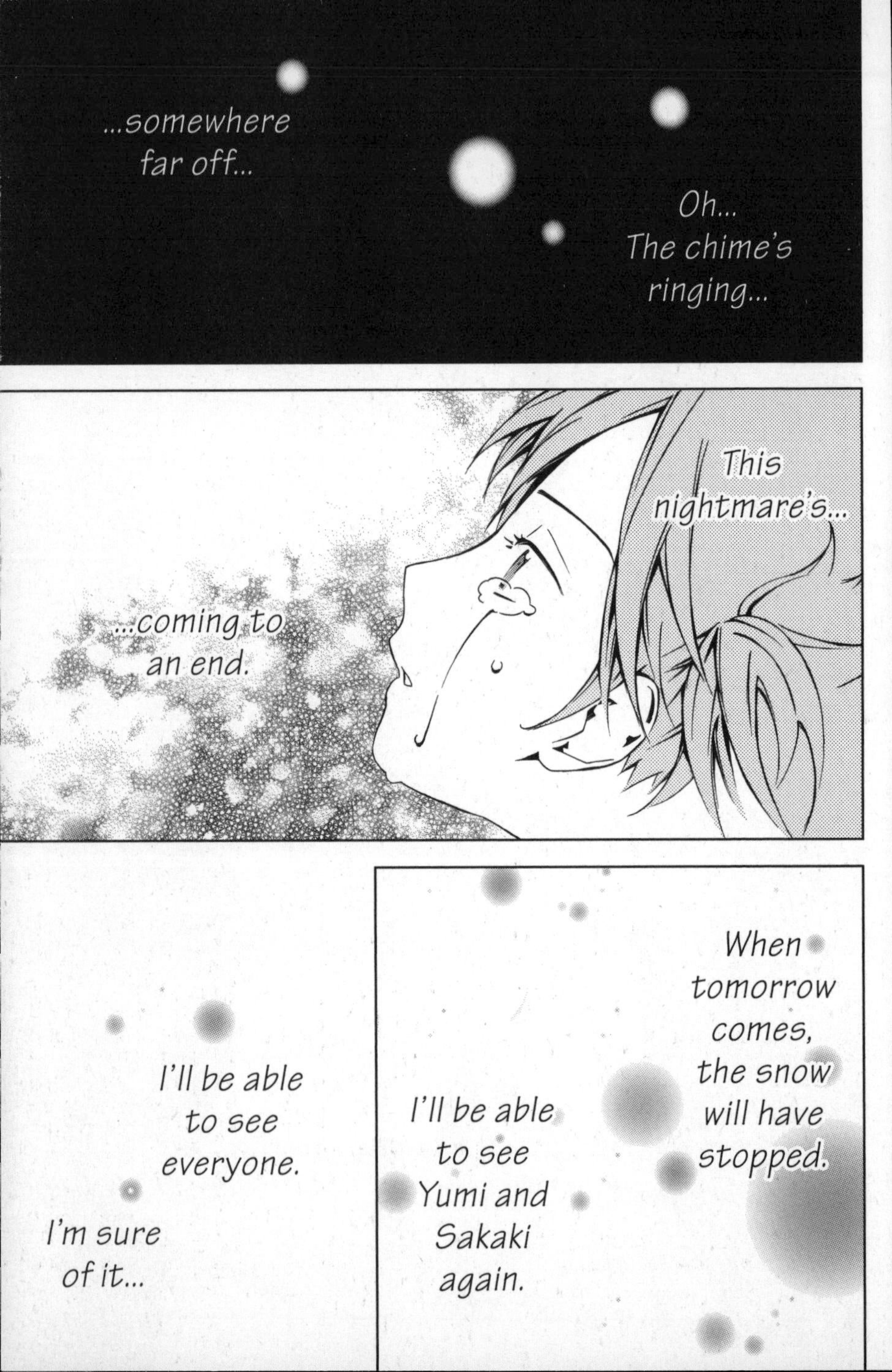
...somewhere far off...
Oh... The chime's ringing...
This nightmare's...
...coming to an end.
When tomorrow comes, the snow will have stopped.
I'll be able to see Yumi and Sakaki again.
I'll be able to see everyone.
I'm sure of it...

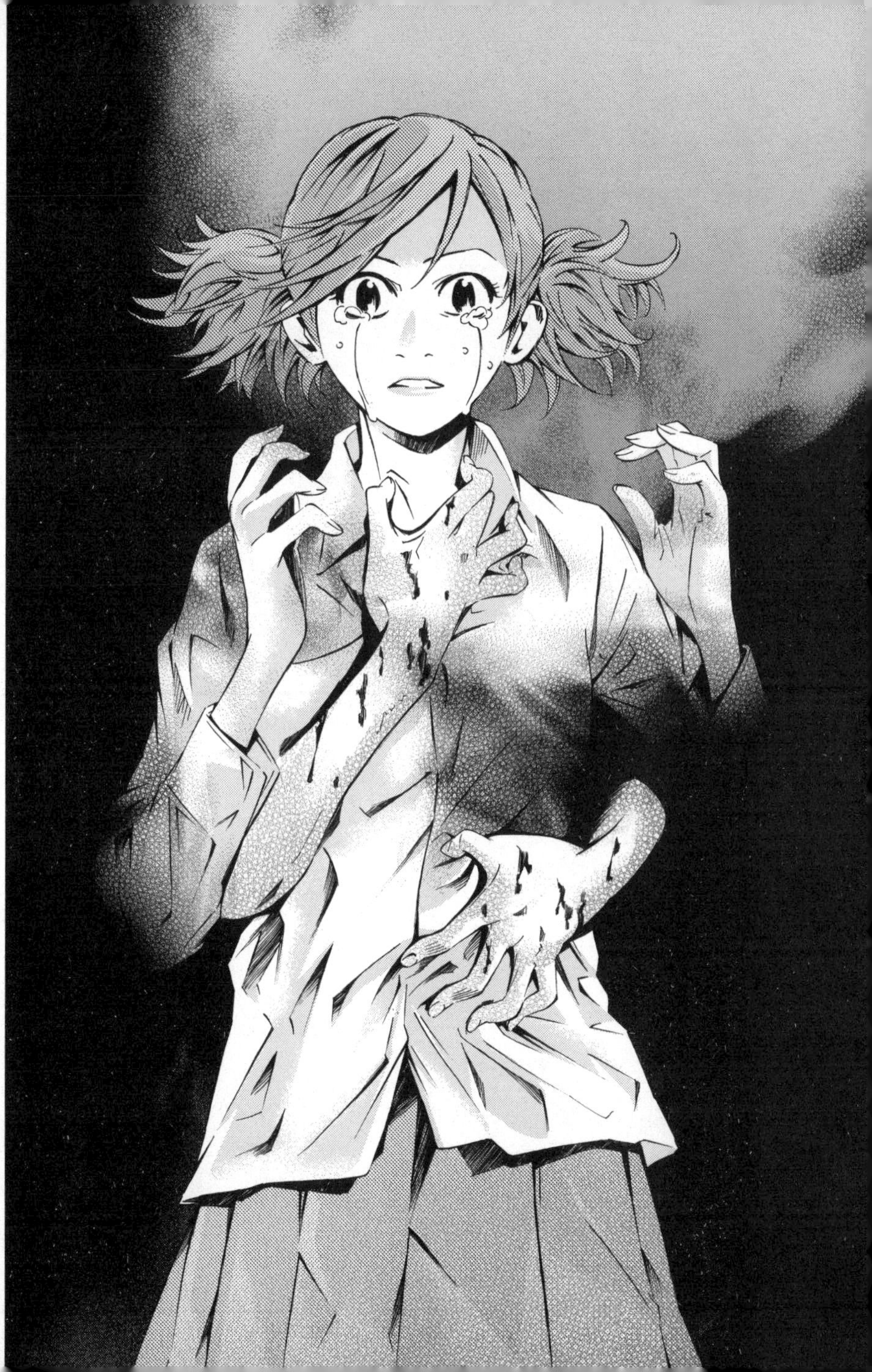

A School Frozen in Time

A School
Frozen
in Time

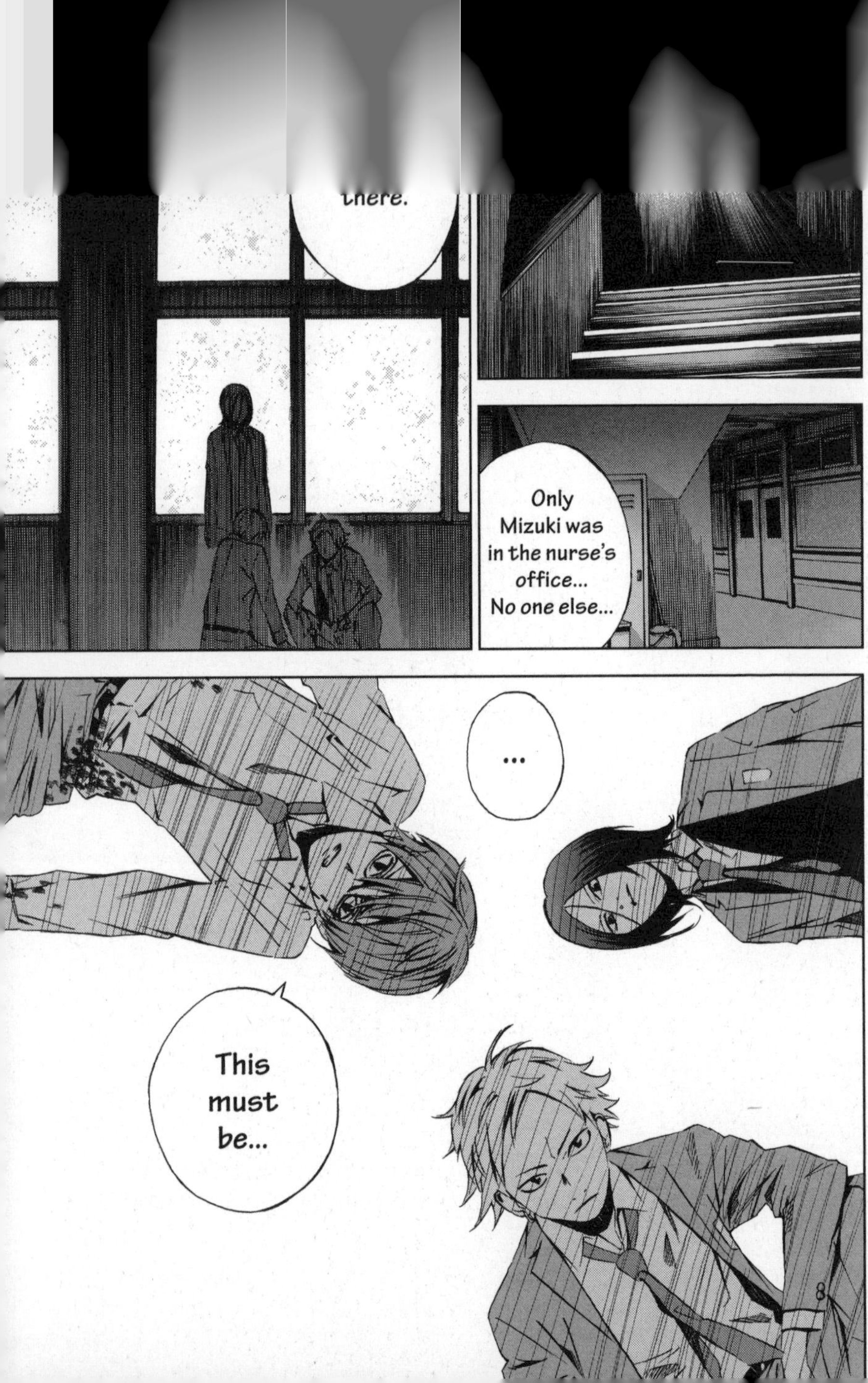
Only Mizuki was in the nurse's office... No one else...
there.
...
This must be...

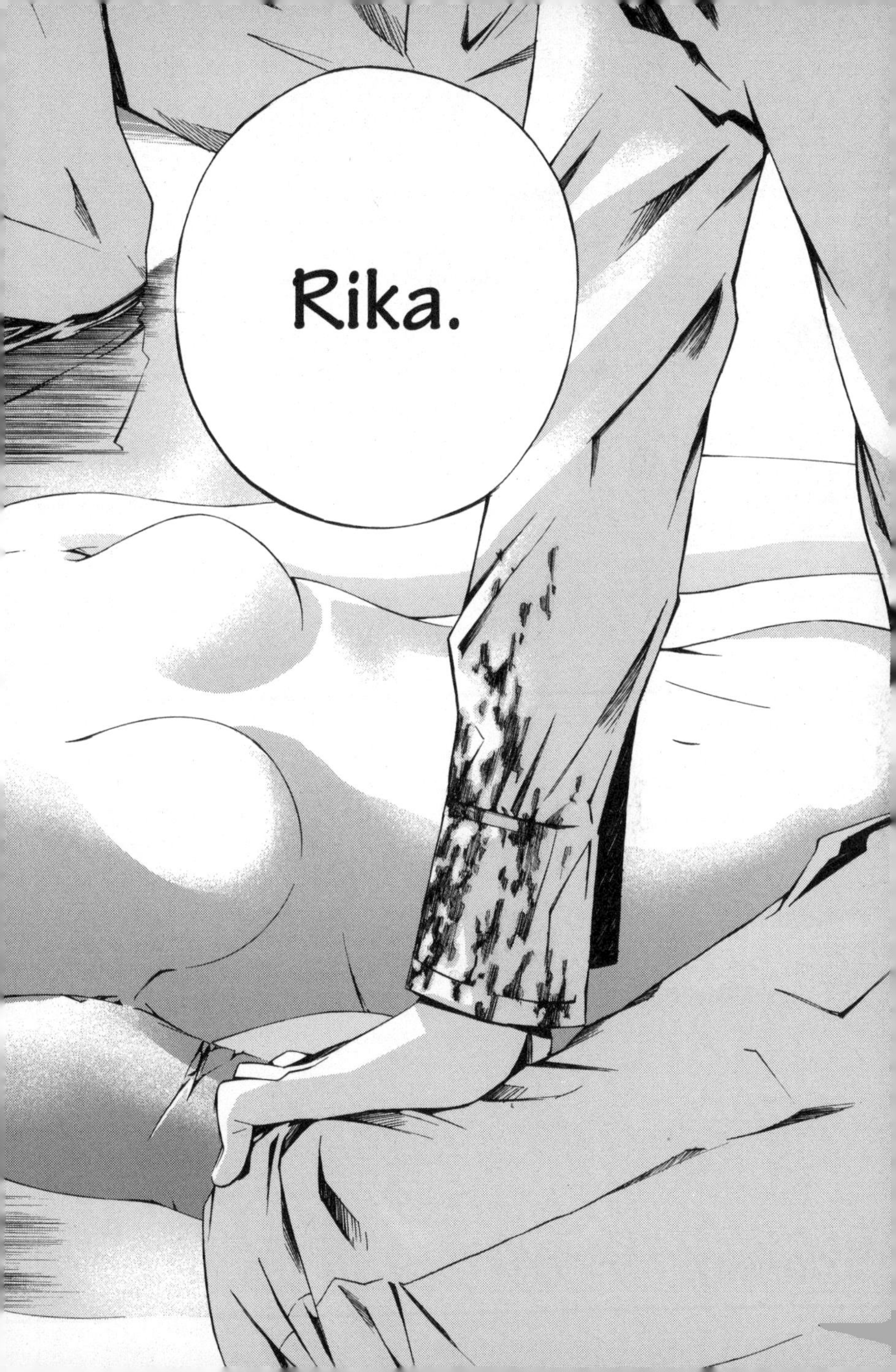
Rika.

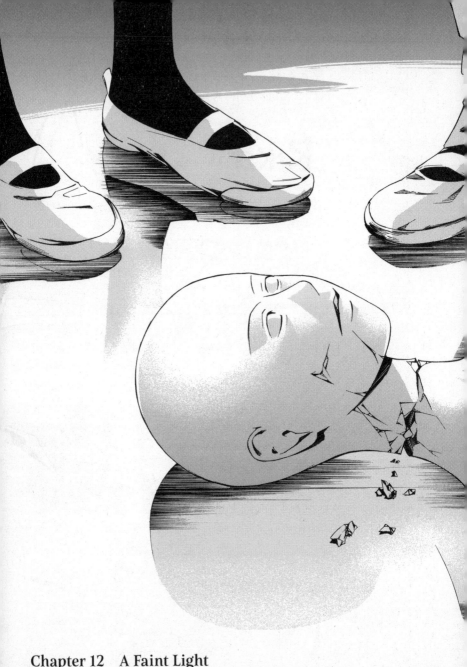

Chapter 12   A Faint Light

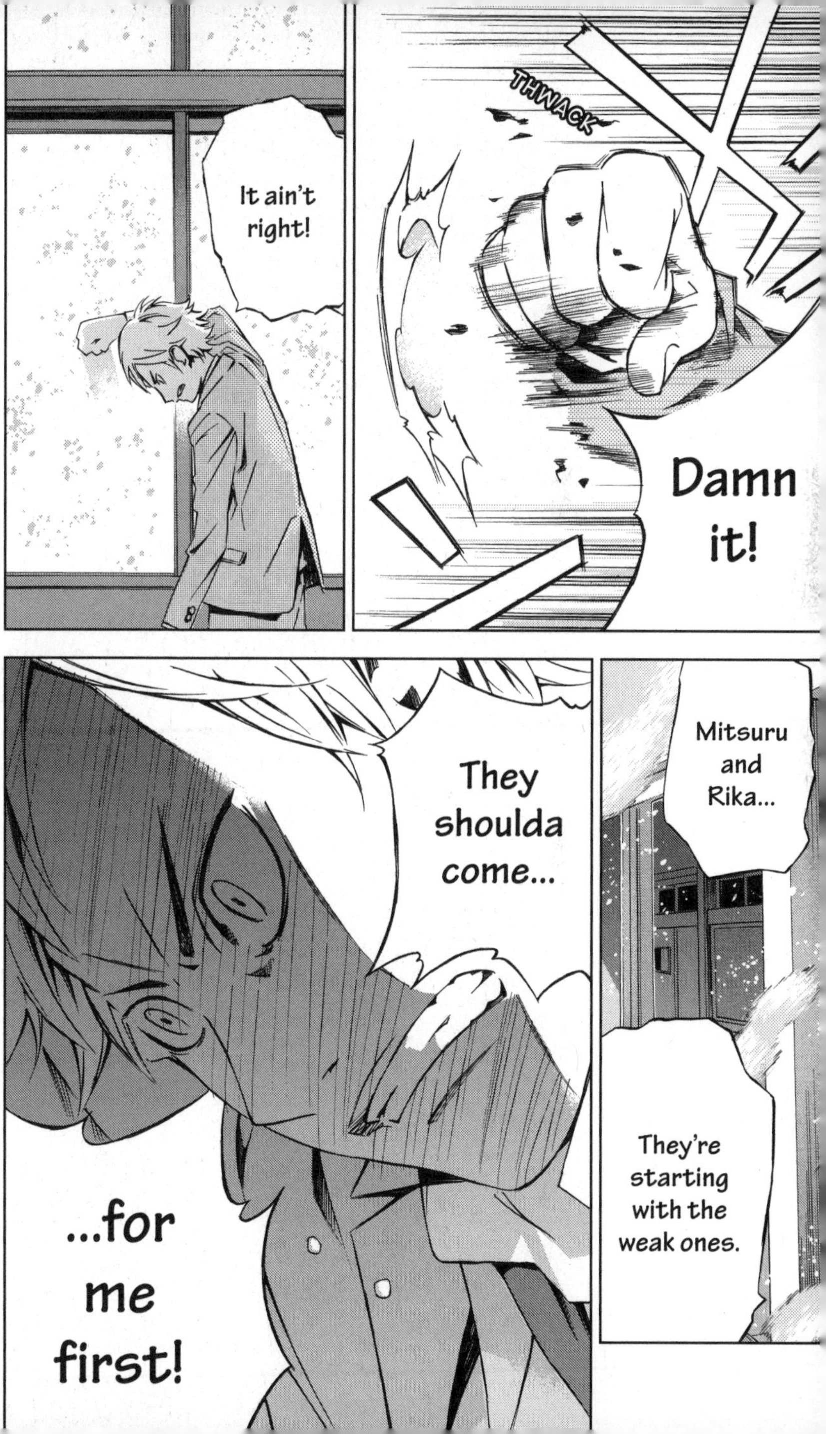
THWACK
Damn it!
It ain't right!
Mitsuru and Rika...
They're starting with the weak ones.
They shoulda come...
...for me first!

I'd beat the hell out of them!

RUSTLE

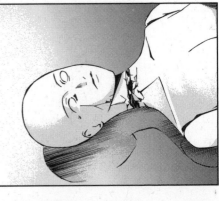

Kei!

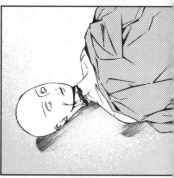

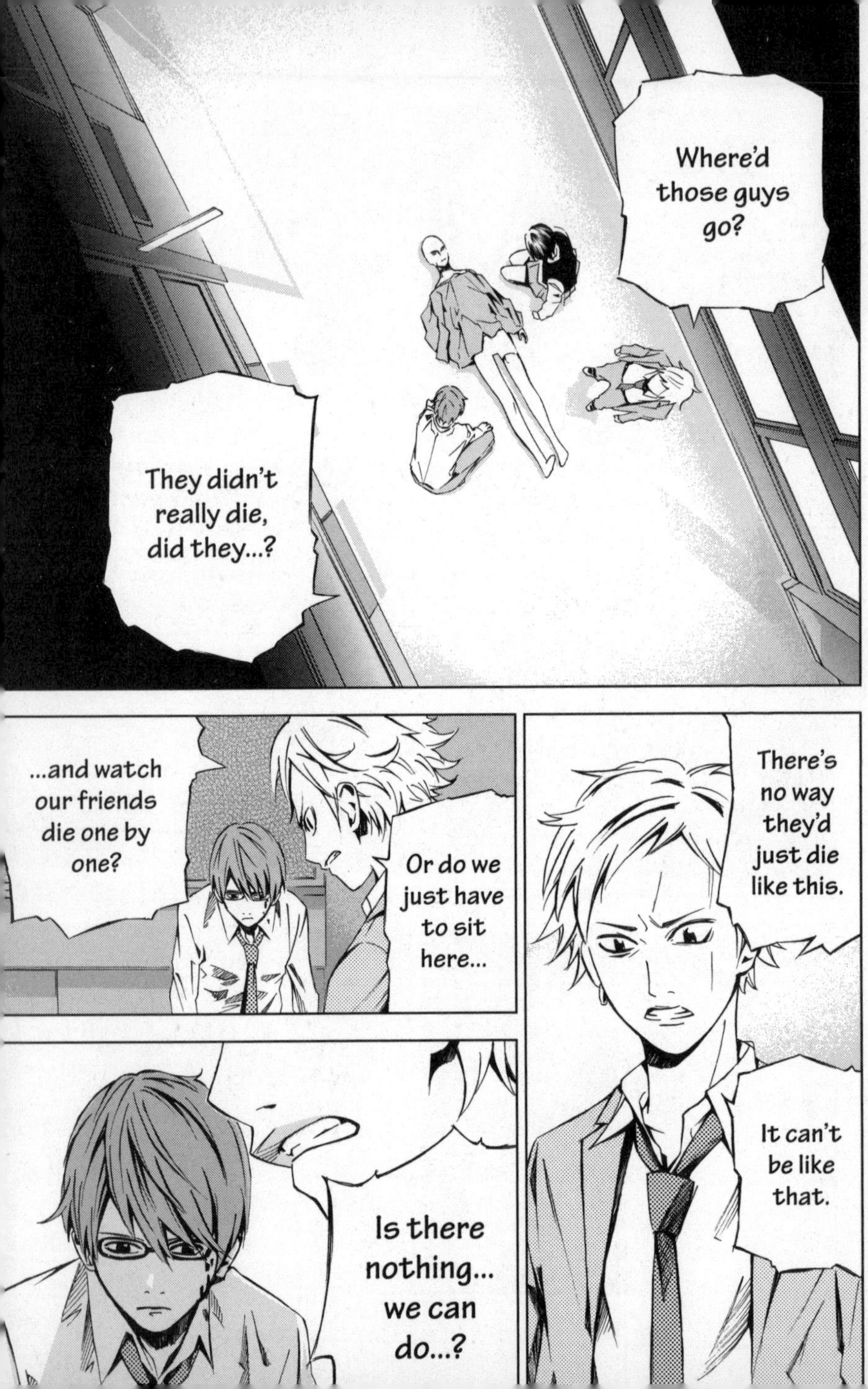
Where'd those guys go?
They didn't really die, did they...?
There's no way they'd just die like this.
It can't be like that.
Or do we just have to sit here...
...and watch our friends die one by one?
Is there nothing... we can do...?

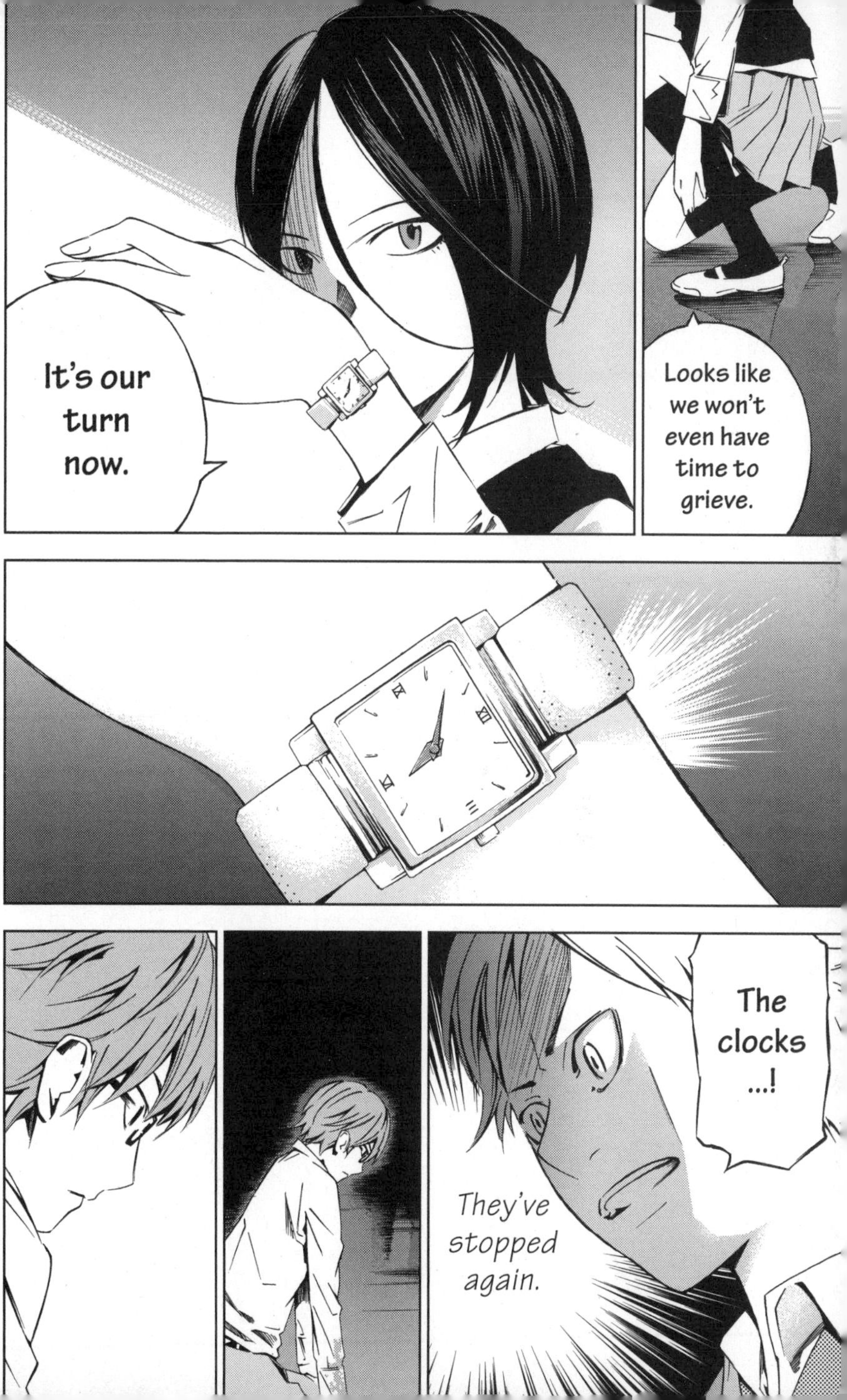
Looks like we won't even have time to grieve.
It's our turn now.
The clocks ...!
They've stopped again.

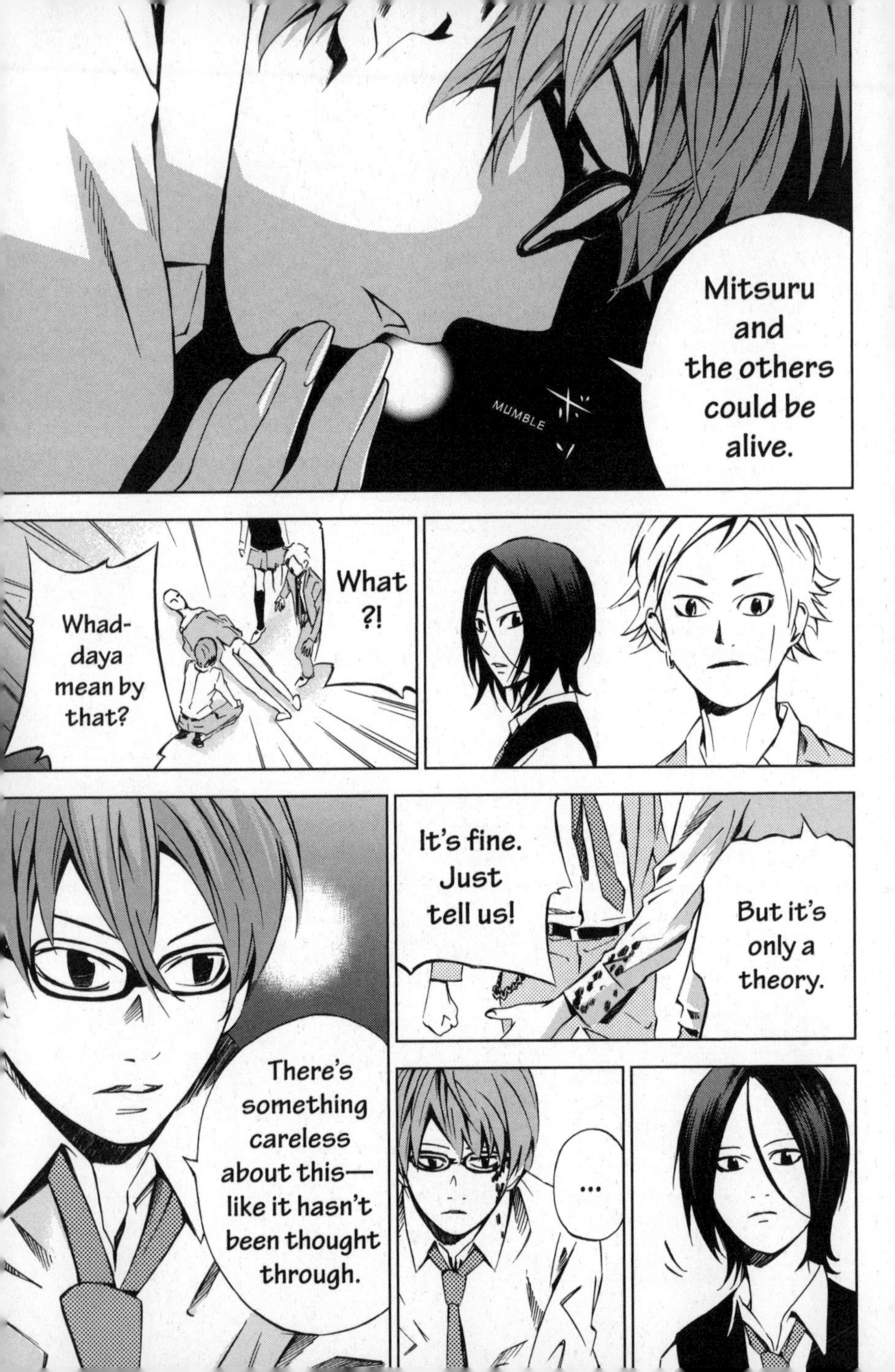
Mitsuru and the others could be alive.
MUMBLE
What ?!
Whad-daya mean by that?
But it's only a theory.
It's fine. Just tell us!
...
There's something careless about this—like it hasn't been thought through.

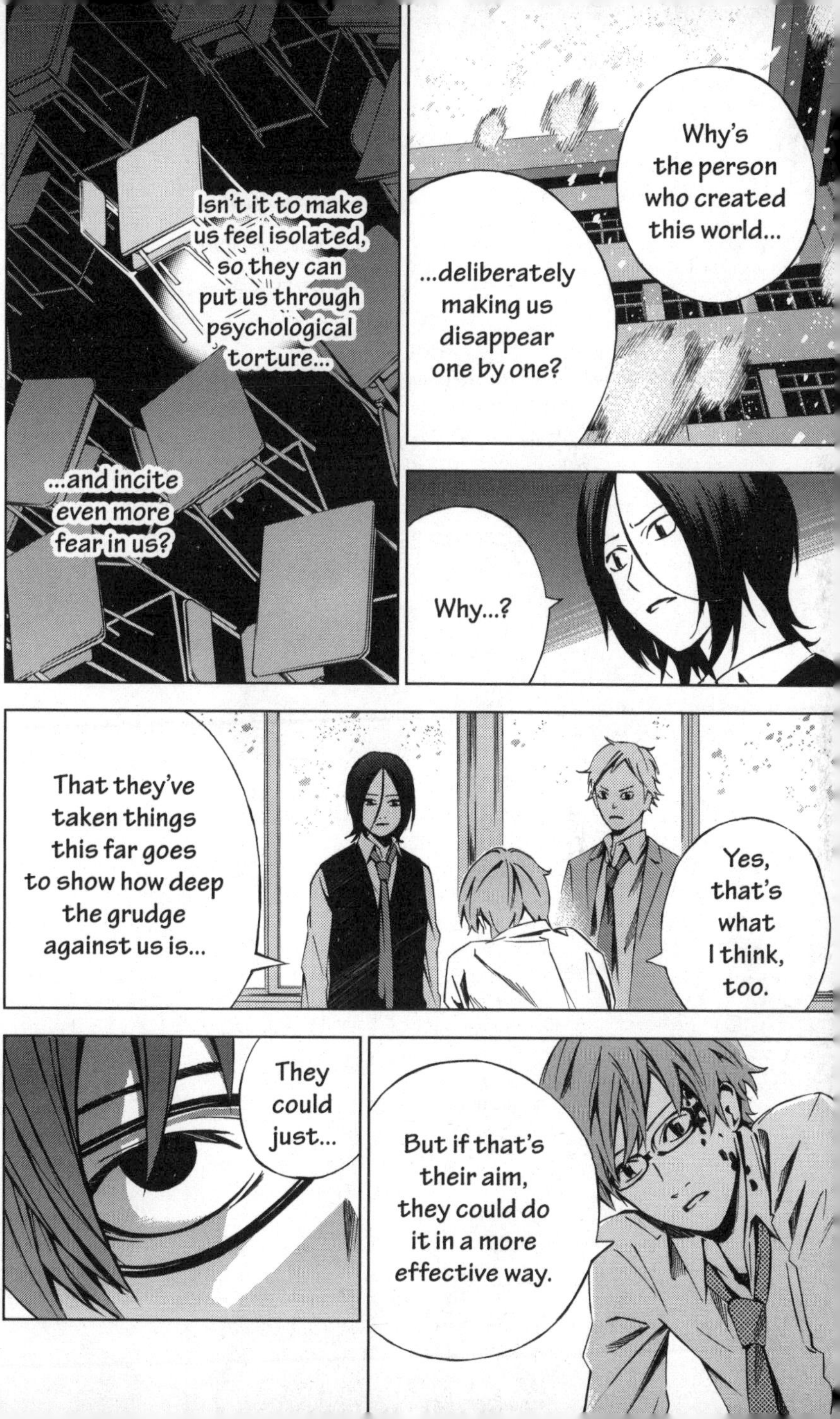
Why's the person who created this world...
...deliberately making us disappear one by one?
Why...?
Isn't it to make us feel isolated, so they can put us through psychological torture...
...and incite even more fear in us?
Yes, that's what I think, too.
That they've taken things this far goes to show how deep the grudge against us is...
But if that's their aim, they could do it in a more effective way.
They could just...

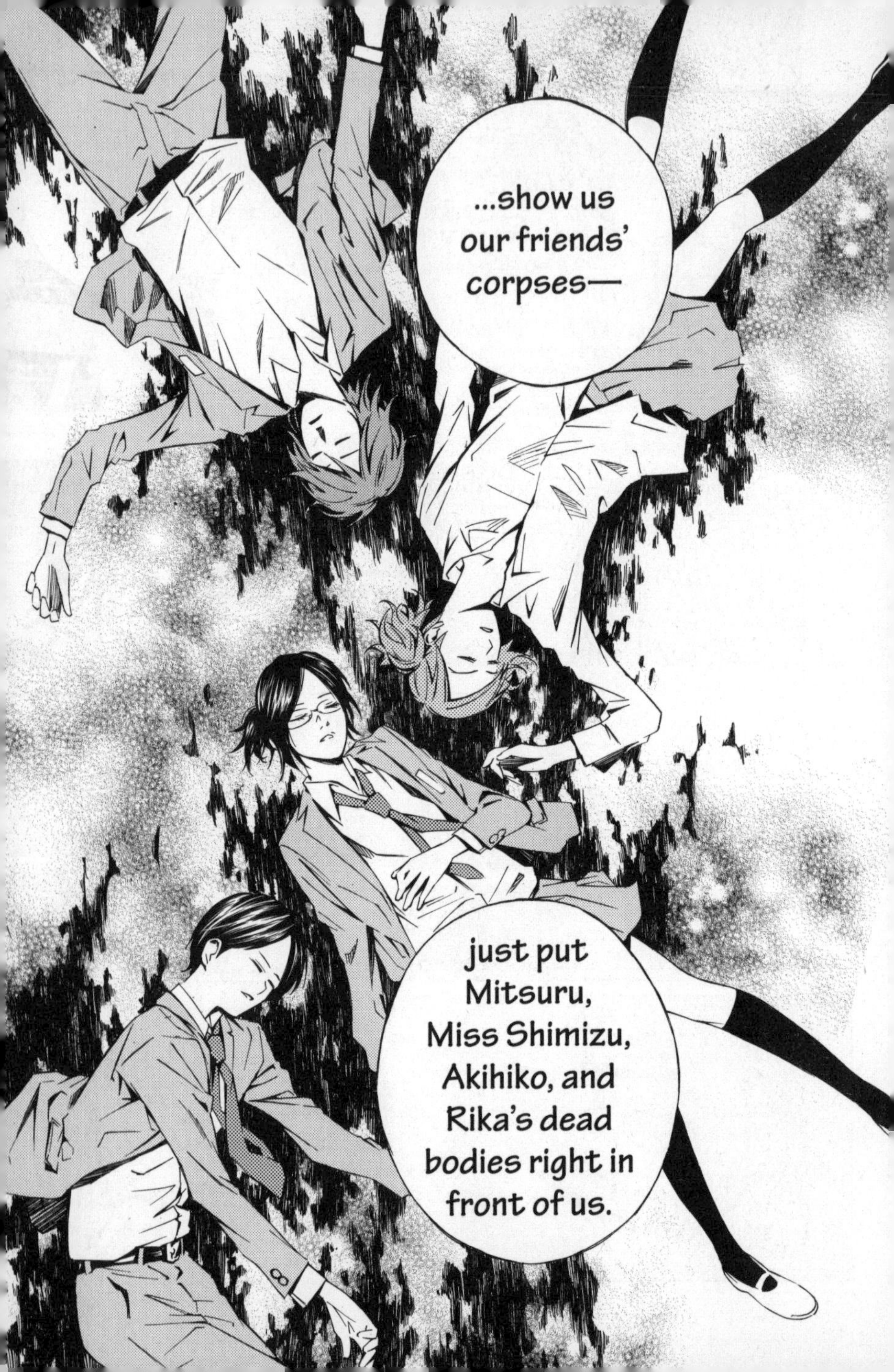
...show us our friends' corpses—
just put Mitsuru, Miss Shimizu, Akihiko, and Rika's dead bodies right in front of us.

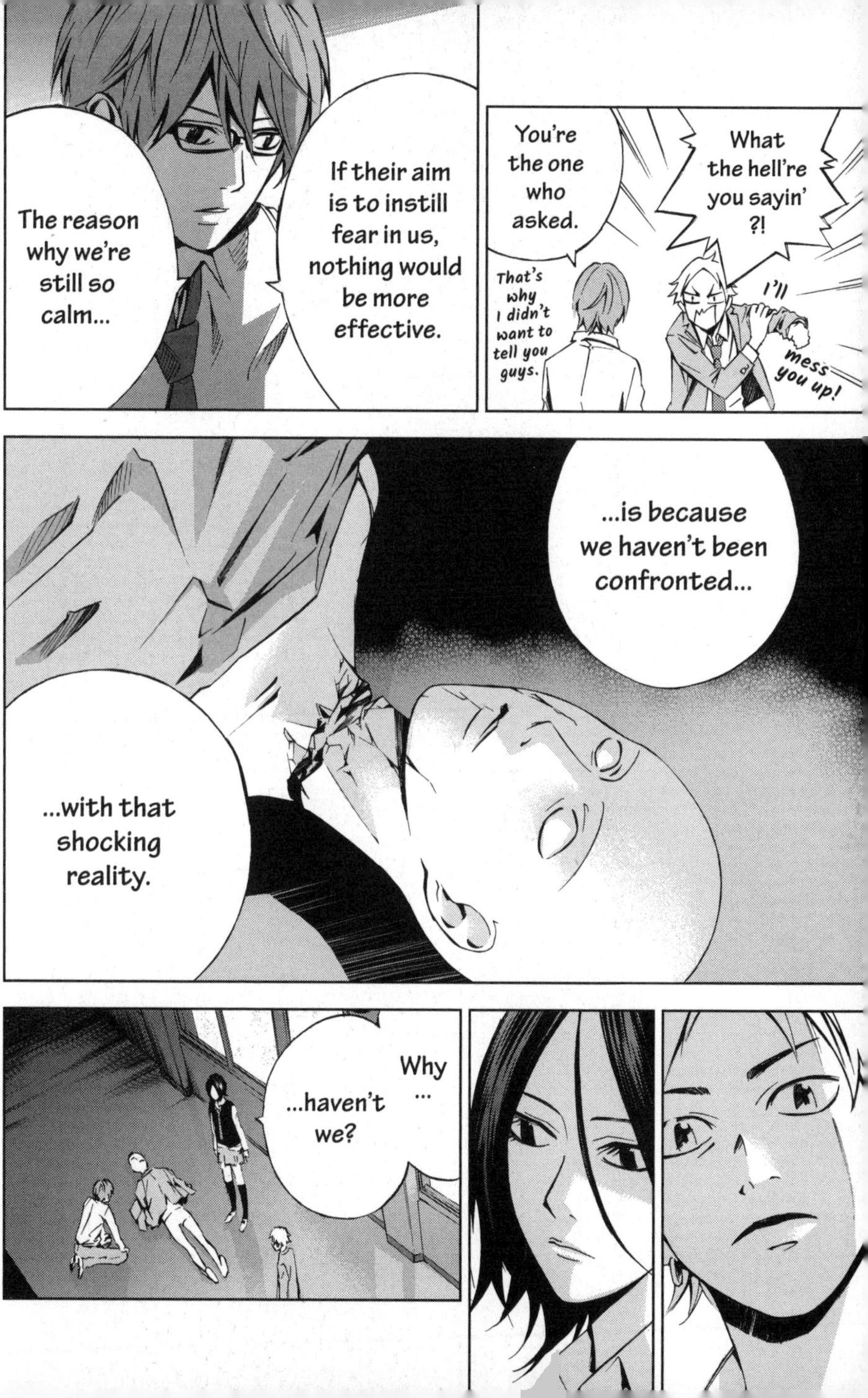
What the hell're you sayin'?!
You're the one who asked.
I'll mess you up!
That's why I didn't want to tell you guys.
If their aim is to instill fear in us, nothing would be more effective.
The reason why we're still so calm...
...is because we haven't been confronted...
...with that shocking reality.
Why...
...haven't we?

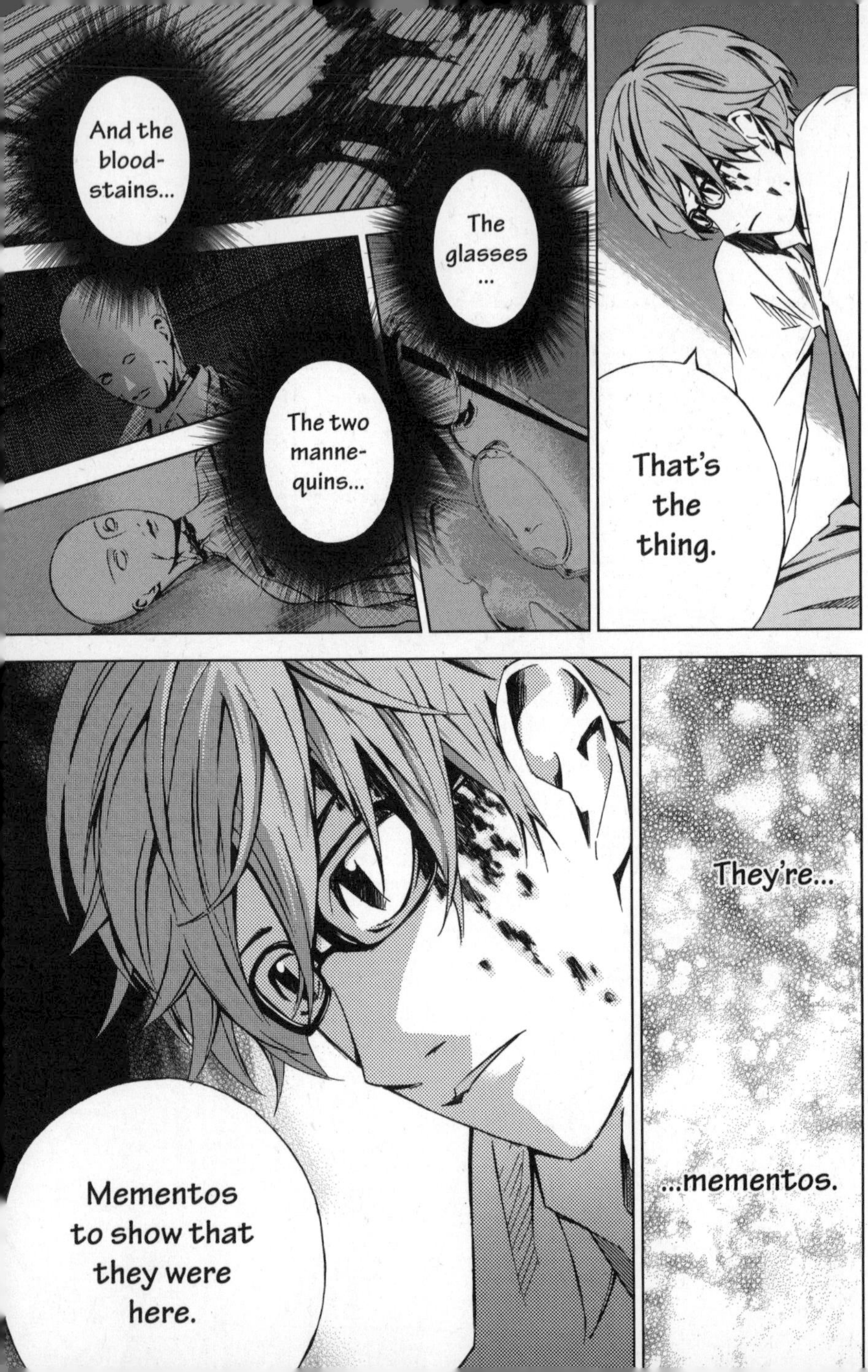
That's the thing.
And the blood-stains...
The glasses...
The two manne-quins...
They're...
...mementos.
Mementos to show that they were here.

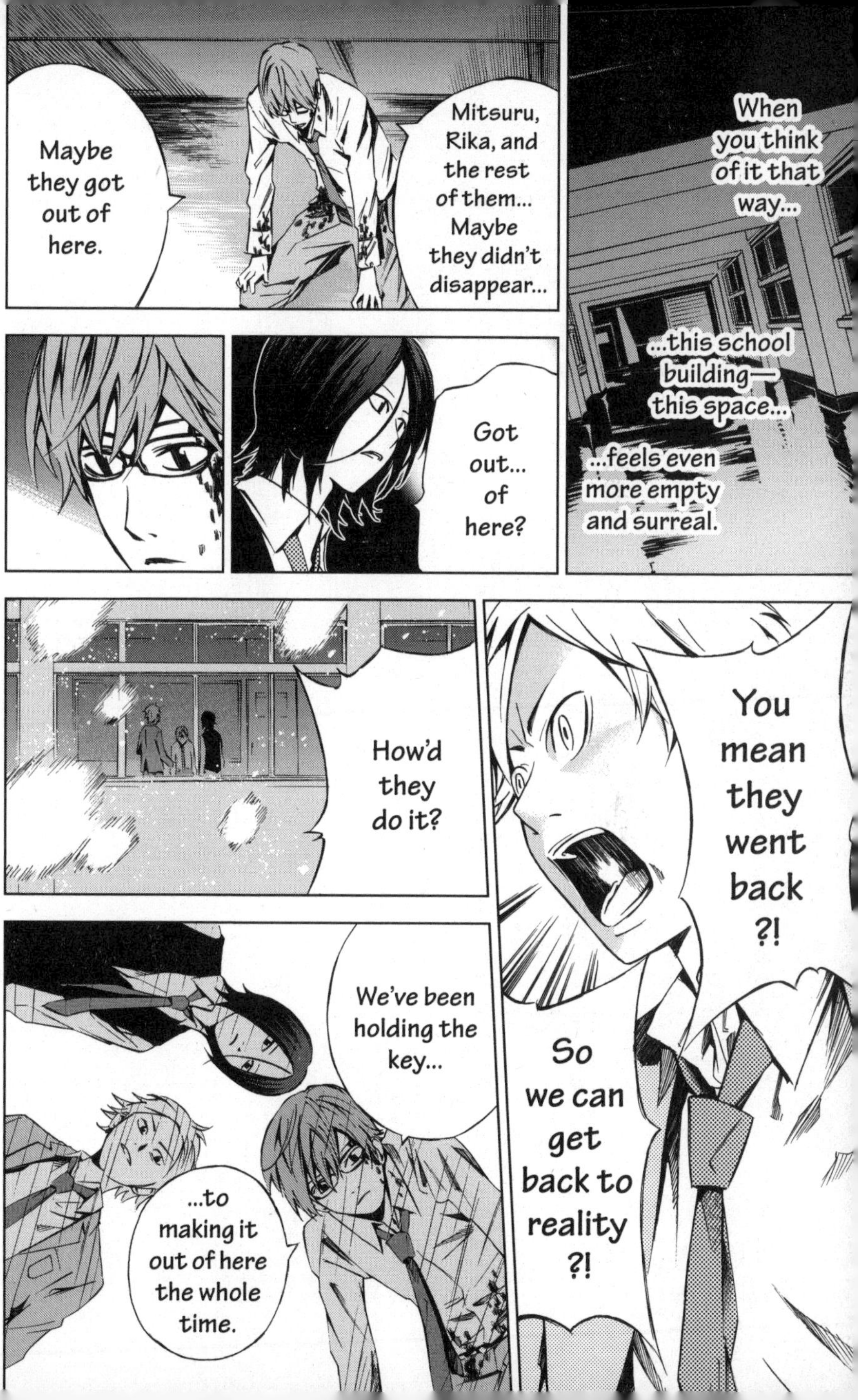
When you think of it that way...
...this school building—this space...
...feels even more empty and surreal.
Mitsuru, Rika, and the rest of them... Maybe they didn't disappear...
Maybe they got out of here.
Got out... of here?
You mean they went back?!
So we can get back to reality?!
How'd they do it?
We've been holding the key...
...to making it out of here the whole time.

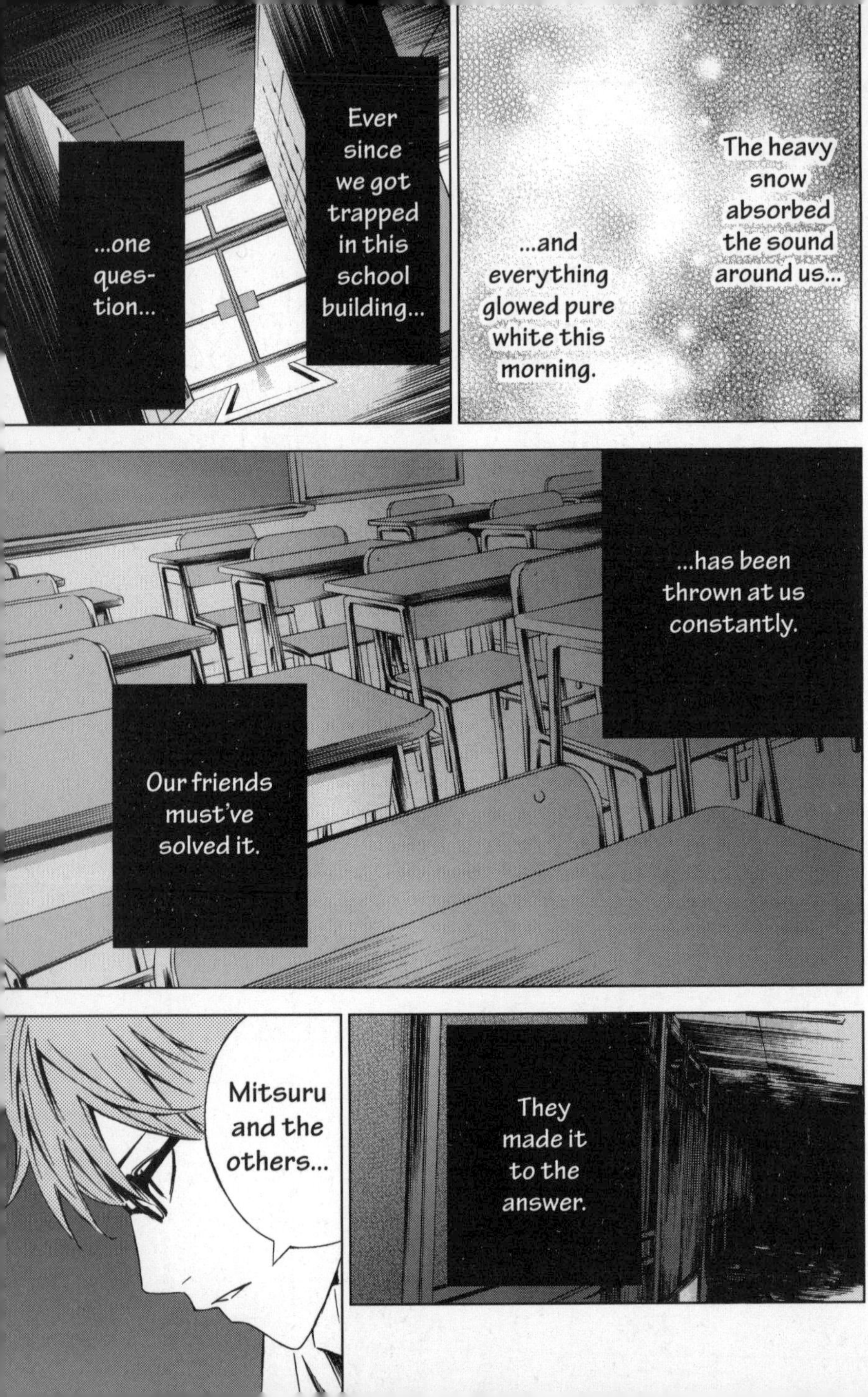
The heavy snow absorbed the sound around us...
...and everything glowed pure white this morning.
Ever since we got trapped in this school building...
...one question...
...has been thrown at us constantly.
Our friends must've solved it.
They made it to the answer.
Mitsuru and the others...

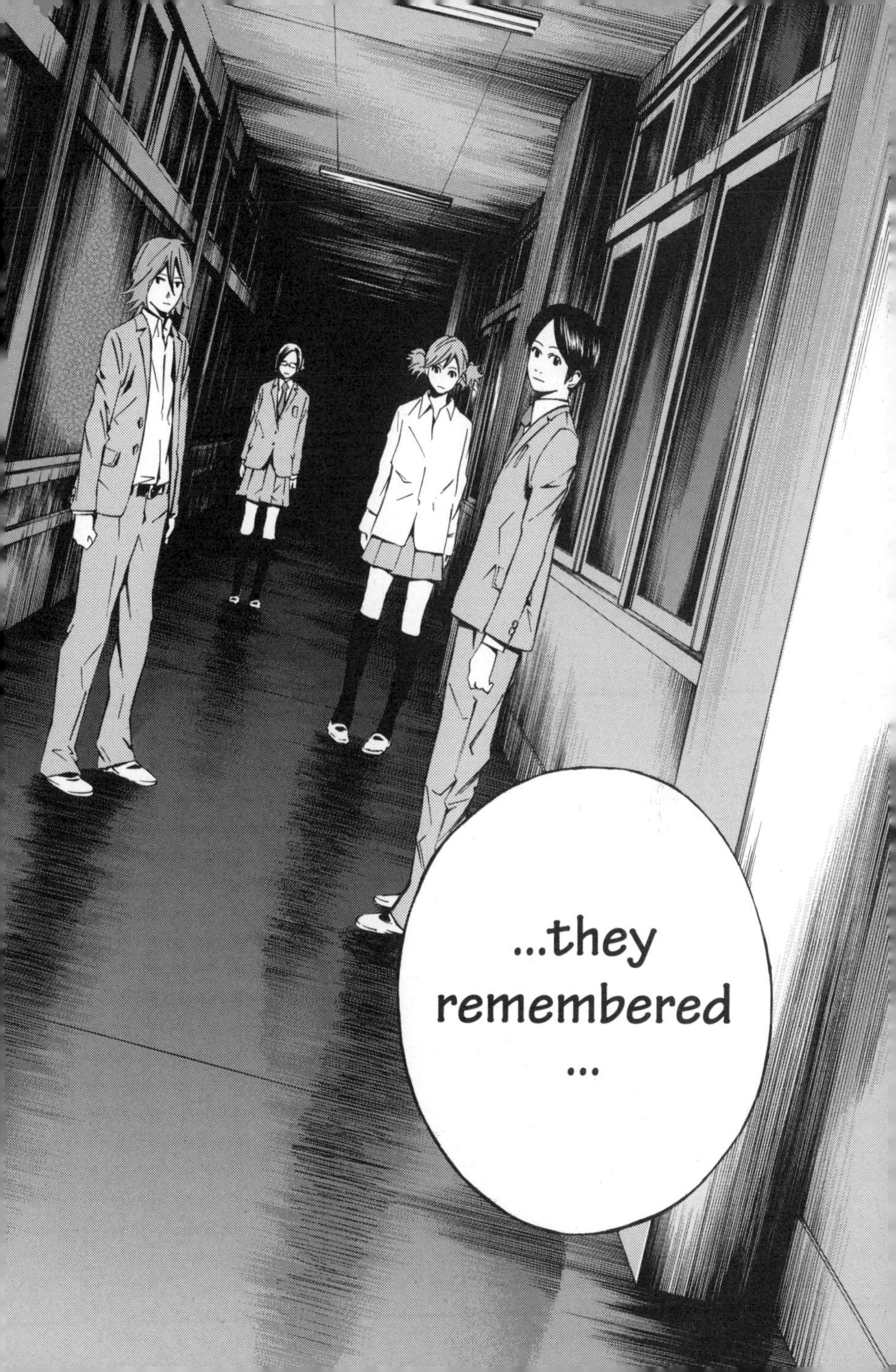
...they remembered ...

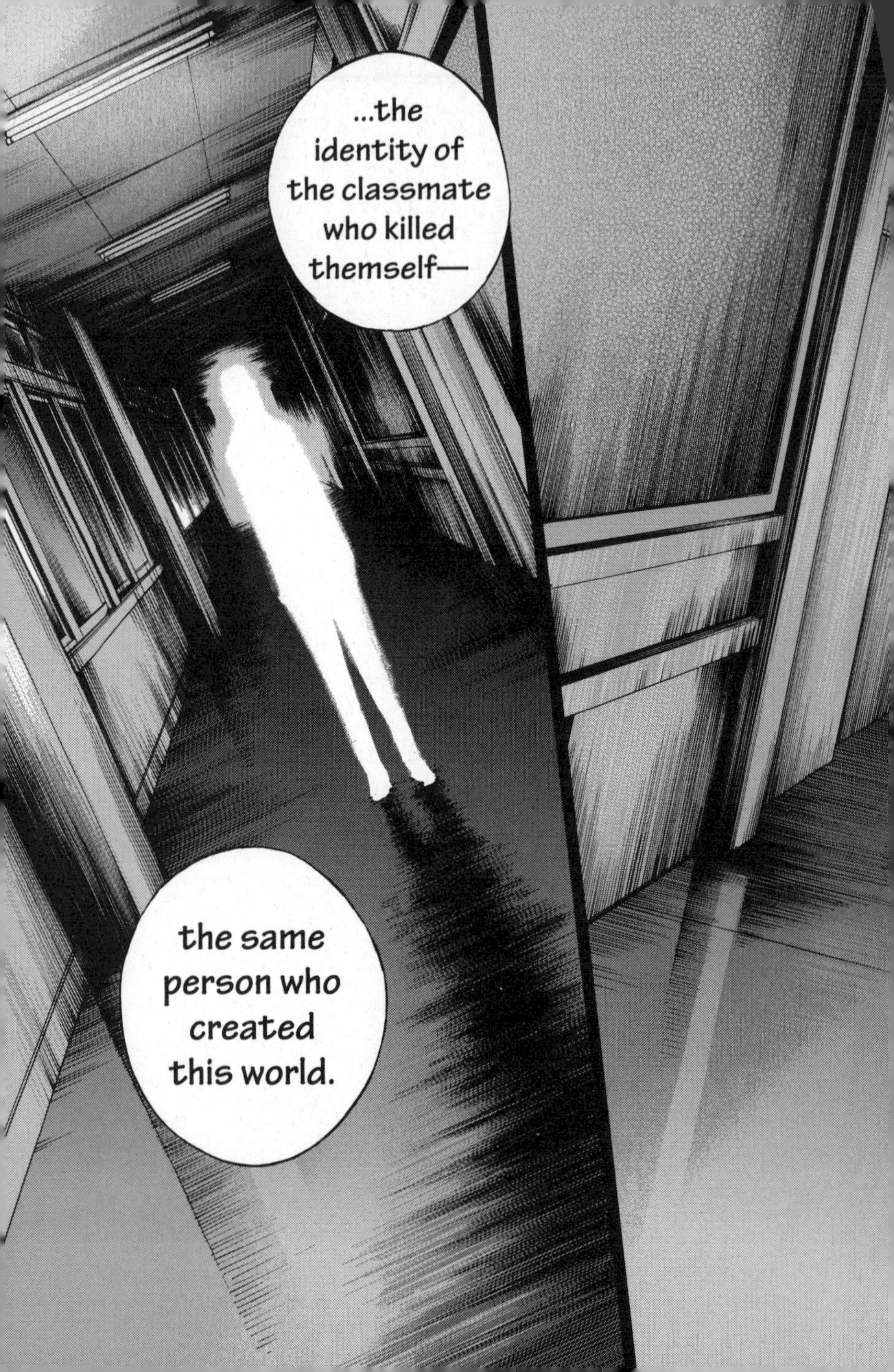
...the identity of the classmate who killed themself—
the same person who created this world.

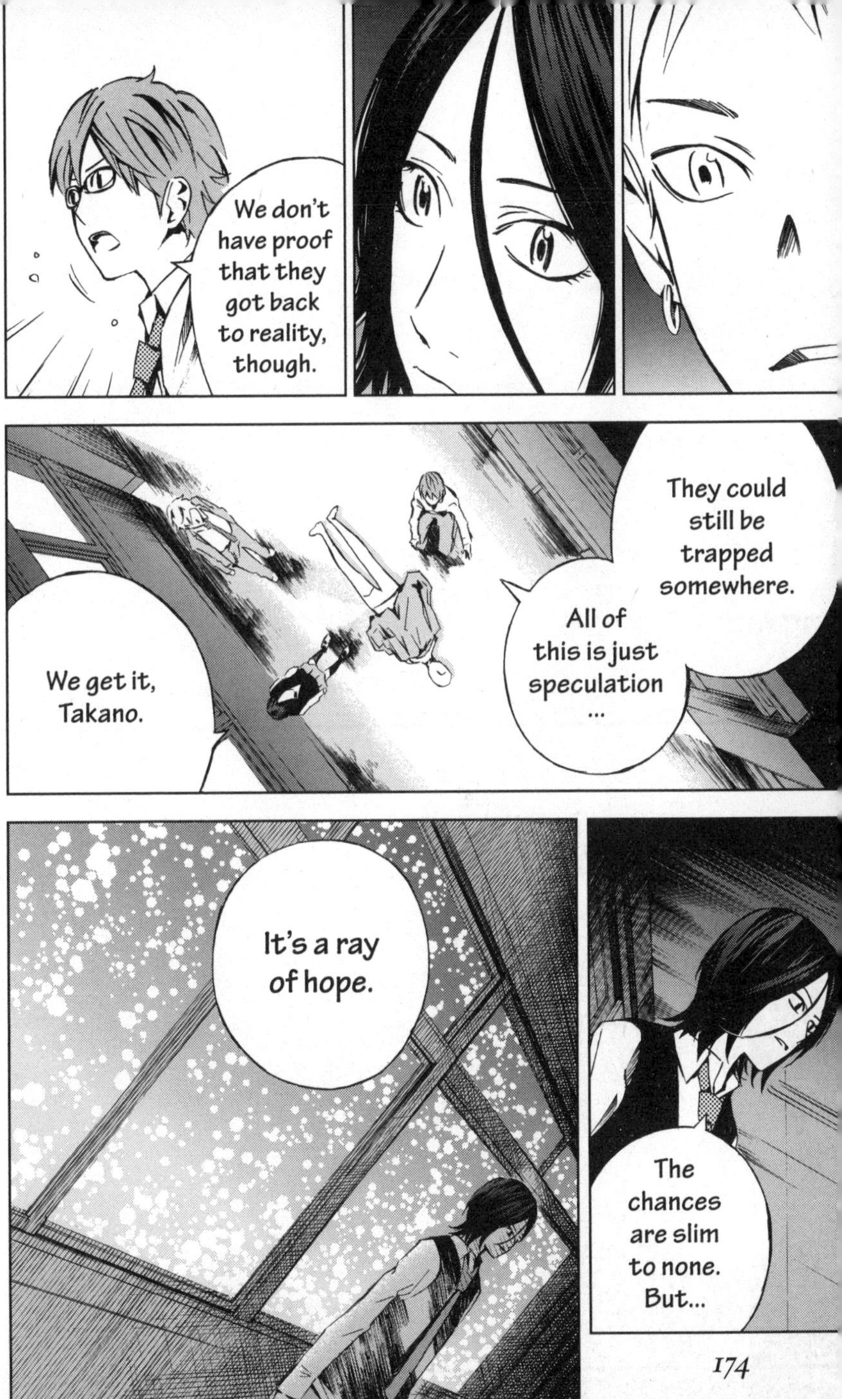
We don't have proof that they got back to reality, though.
They could still be trapped somewhere.
All of this is just speculation ...
We get it, Takano.
The chances are slim to none. But...
It's a ray of hope.

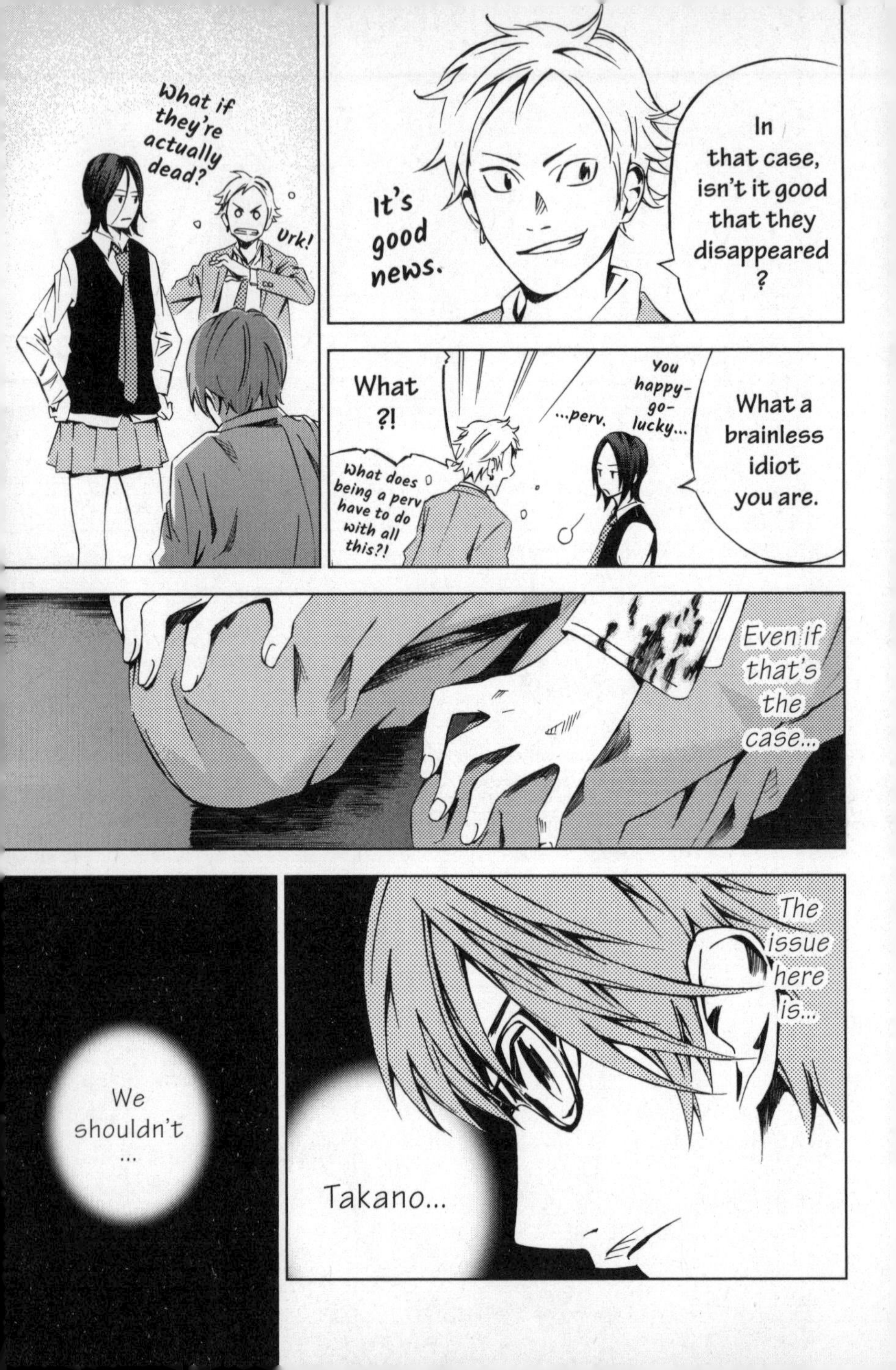
In that case, isn't it good that they disappeared?
It's good news.
What a brainless idiot you are.
You happy-go-lucky...
...perv.
What?!
What does being a perv have to do with all this?!
What if they're actually dead?
Urk!
Even if that's the case...
The issue here is...
Takano...
We shouldn't ...

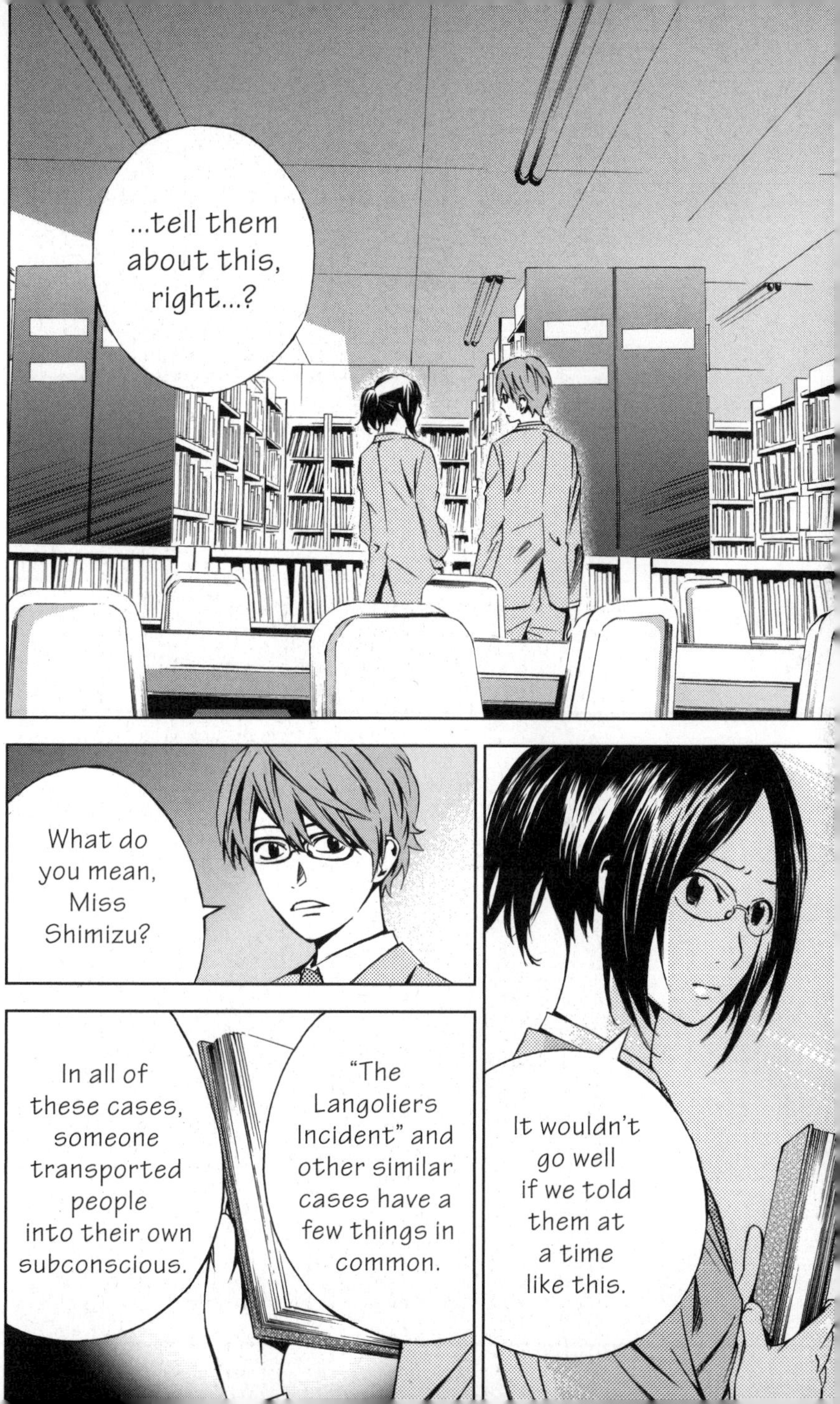
...tell them about this, right...?
It wouldn't go well if we told them at a time like this.
What do you mean, Miss Shimizu?
"The Langoliers Incident" and other similar cases have a few things in common.
In all of these cases, someone transported people into their own subconscious.

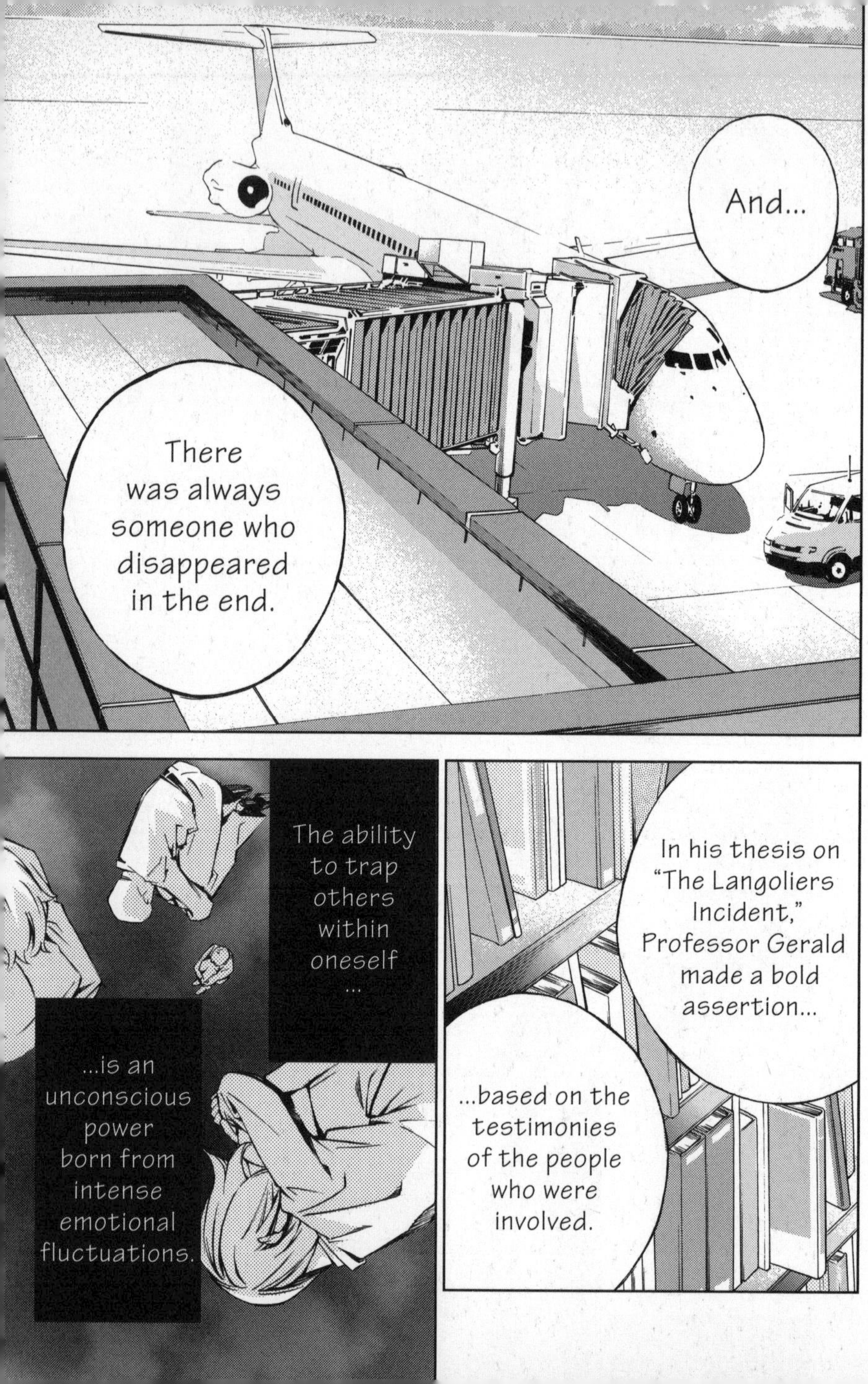
And...
There was always someone who disappeared in the end.
In his thesis on "The Langoliers Incident," Professor Gerald made a bold assertion...
...based on the testimonies of the people who were involved.
The ability to trap others within oneself ...
...is an unconscious power born from intense emotional fluctuations.

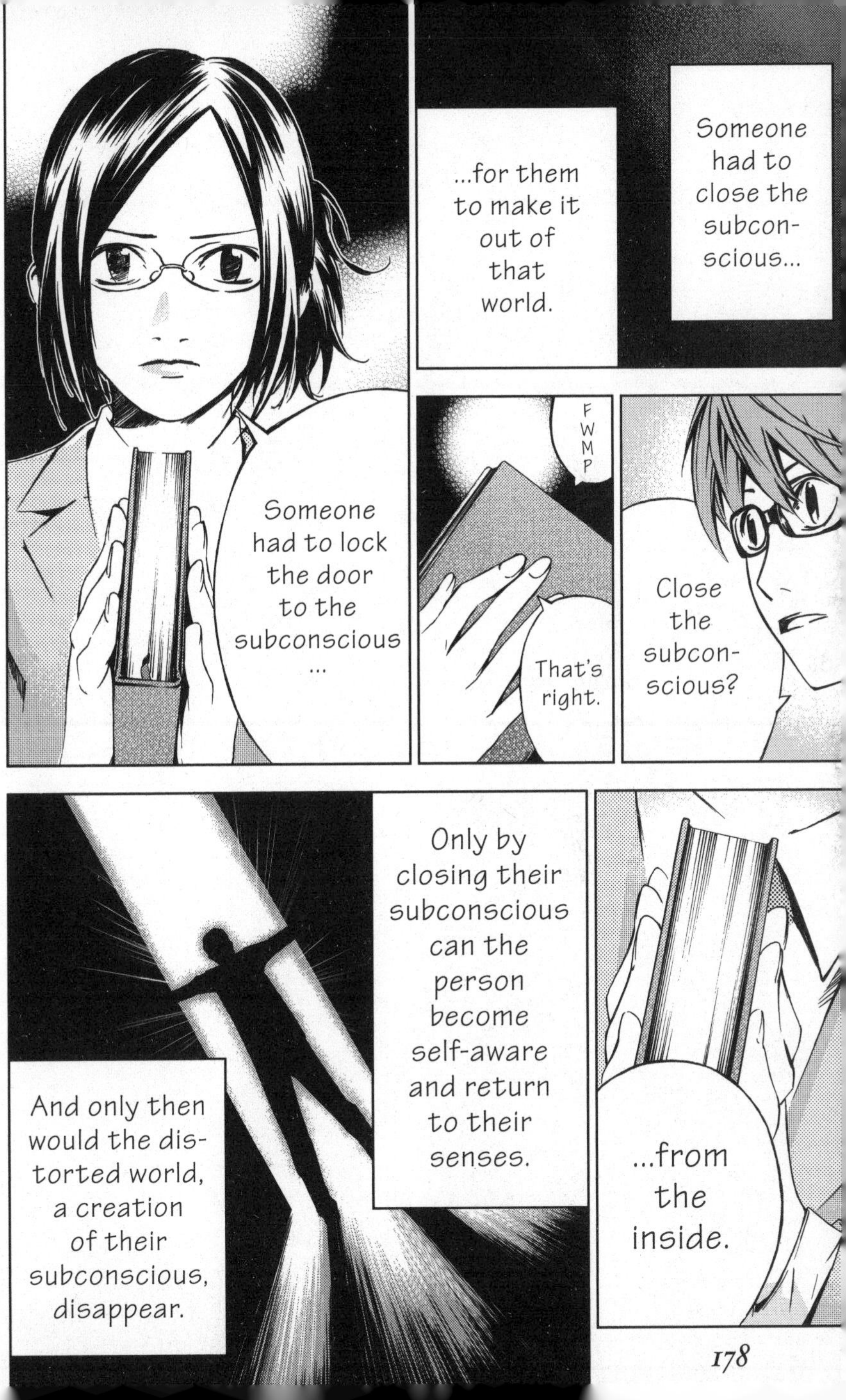
Someone had to close the subconscious...
...for them to make it out of that world.
Close the subconscious?
FWMP
That's right.
Someone had to lock the door to the subconscious...
...from the inside.
Only by closing their subconscious can the person become self-aware and return to their senses.
And only then would the distorted world, a creation of their subconscious, disappear.

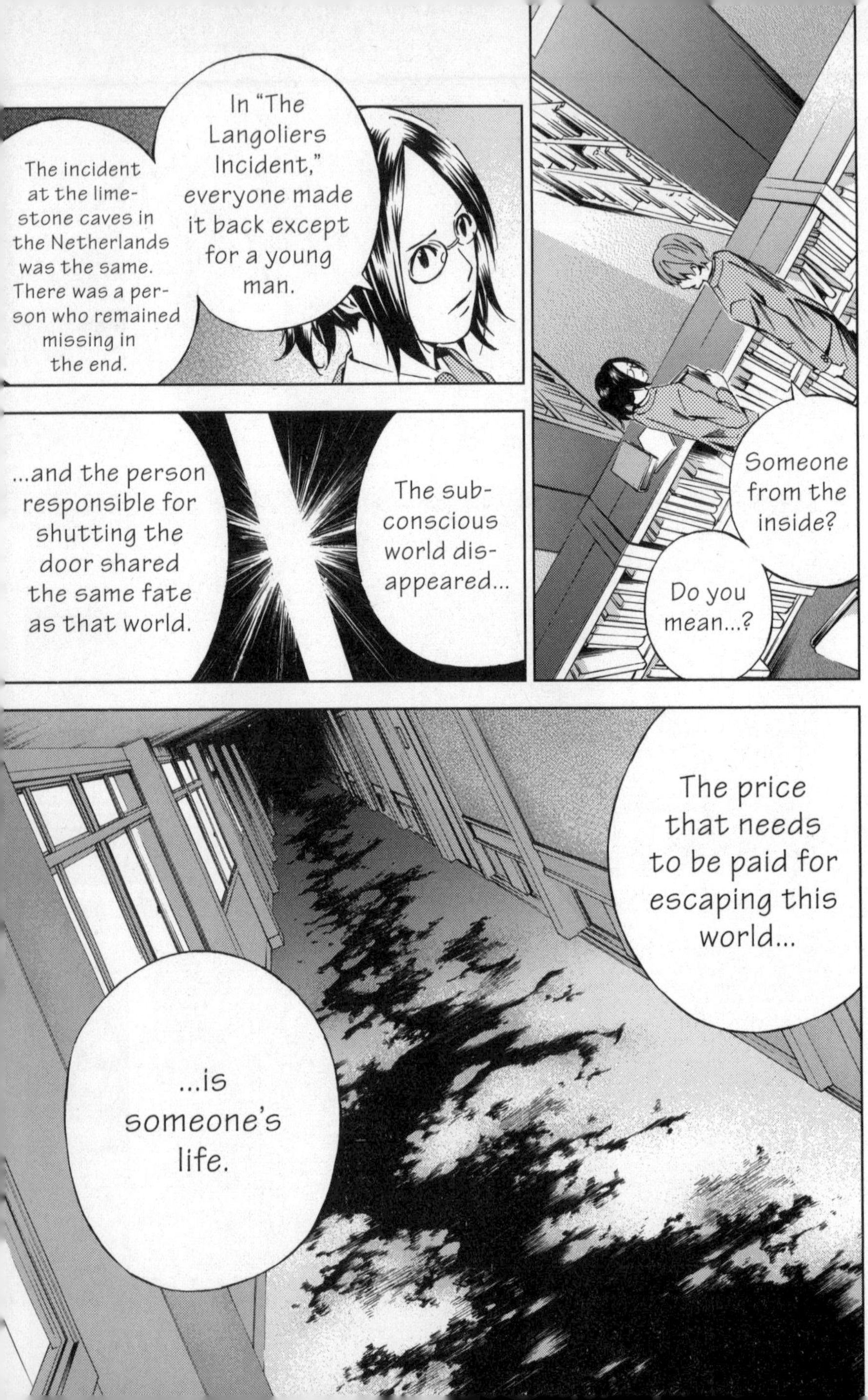
Someone from the inside?
Do you mean...?
In "The Langoliers Incident," everyone made it back except for a young man.
The incident at the limestone caves in the Netherlands was the same. There was a person who remained missing in the end.
The subconscious world disappeared...
...and the person responsible for shutting the door shared the same fate as that world.
The price that needs to be paid for escaping this world...
...is someone's life.

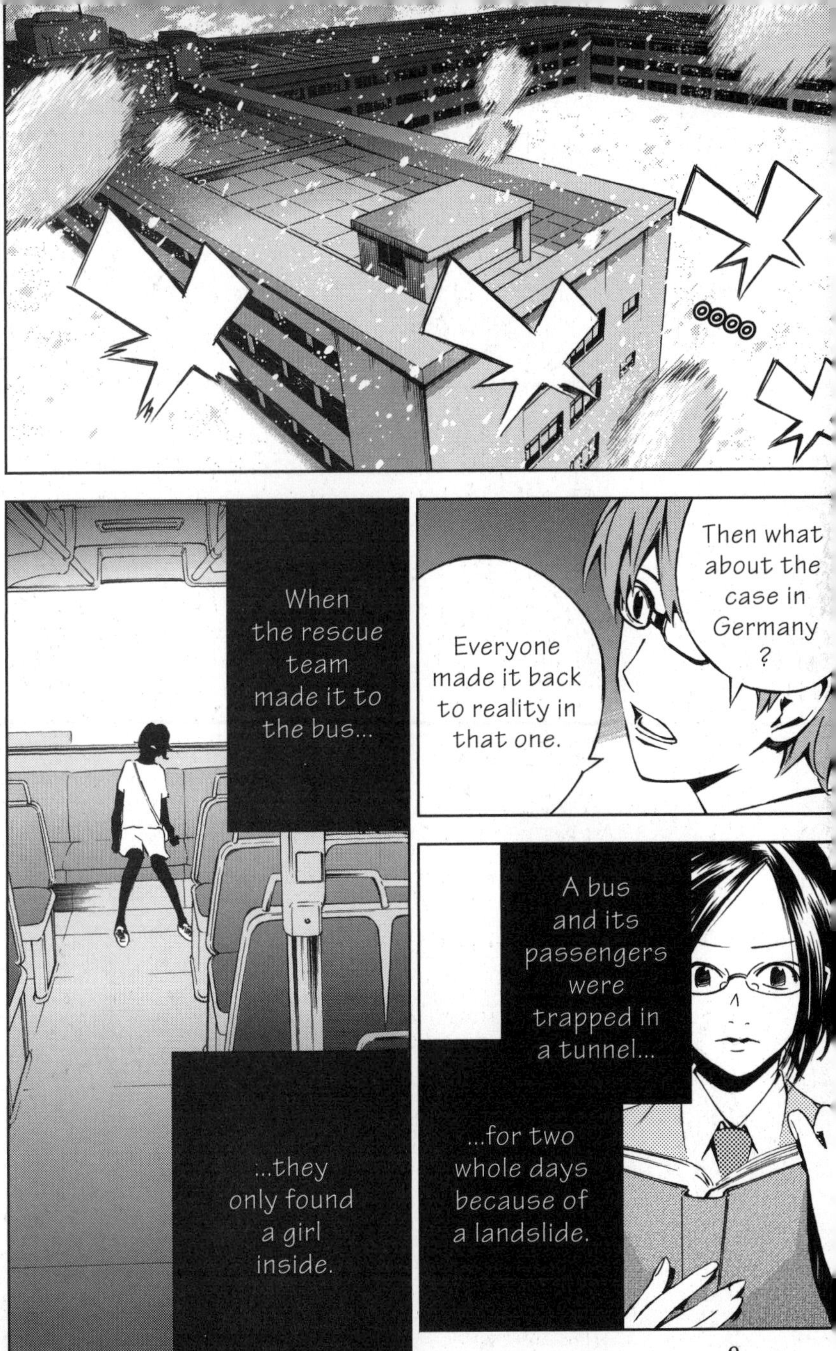
Then what about the case in Germany?
Everyone made it back to reality in that one.
A bus and its passengers were trapped in a tunnel...
...for two whole days because of a landslide.
When the rescue team made it to the bus...
...they only found a girl inside.

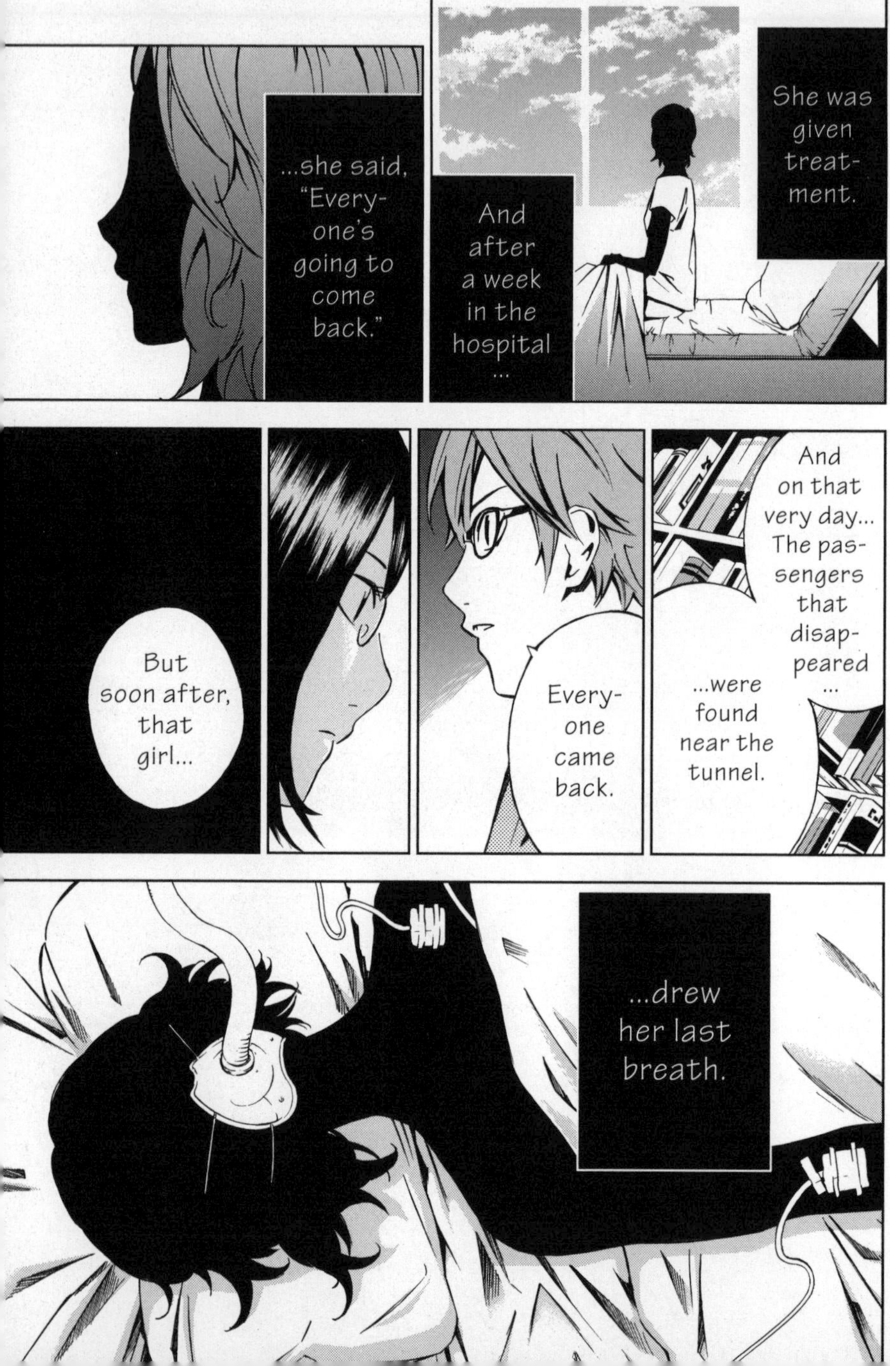
She was given treatment.
And after a week in the hospital...
...she said, "Everyone's going to come back."
And on that very day... The passengers that disappeared...
...were found near the tunnel.
Everyone came back.
But soon after, that girl...
...drew her last breath.

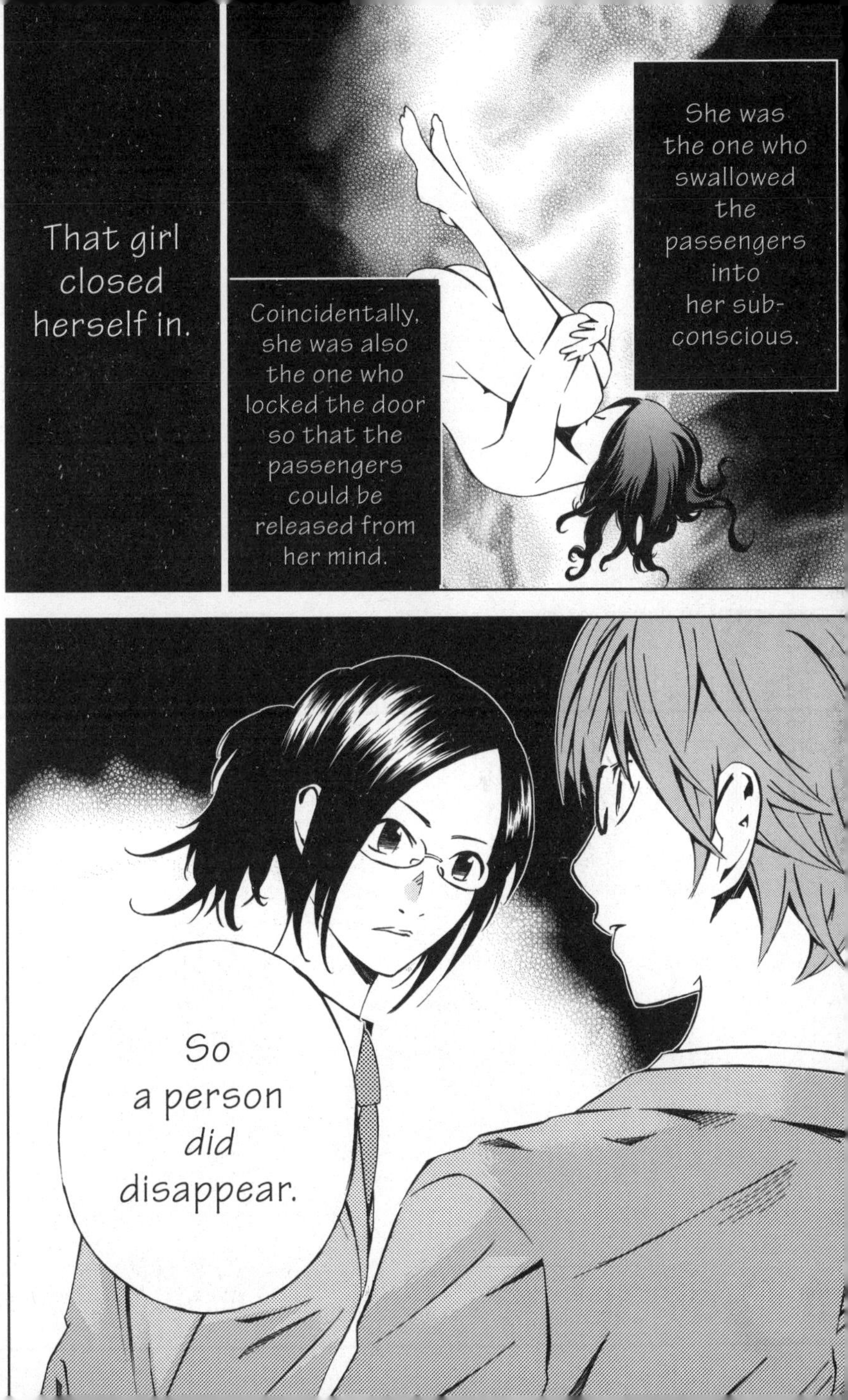
She was the one who swallowed the passengers into her sub-conscious.
Coincidentally, she was also the one who locked the door so that the passengers could be released from her mind.
That girl closed herself in.
So a person *did* disappear.

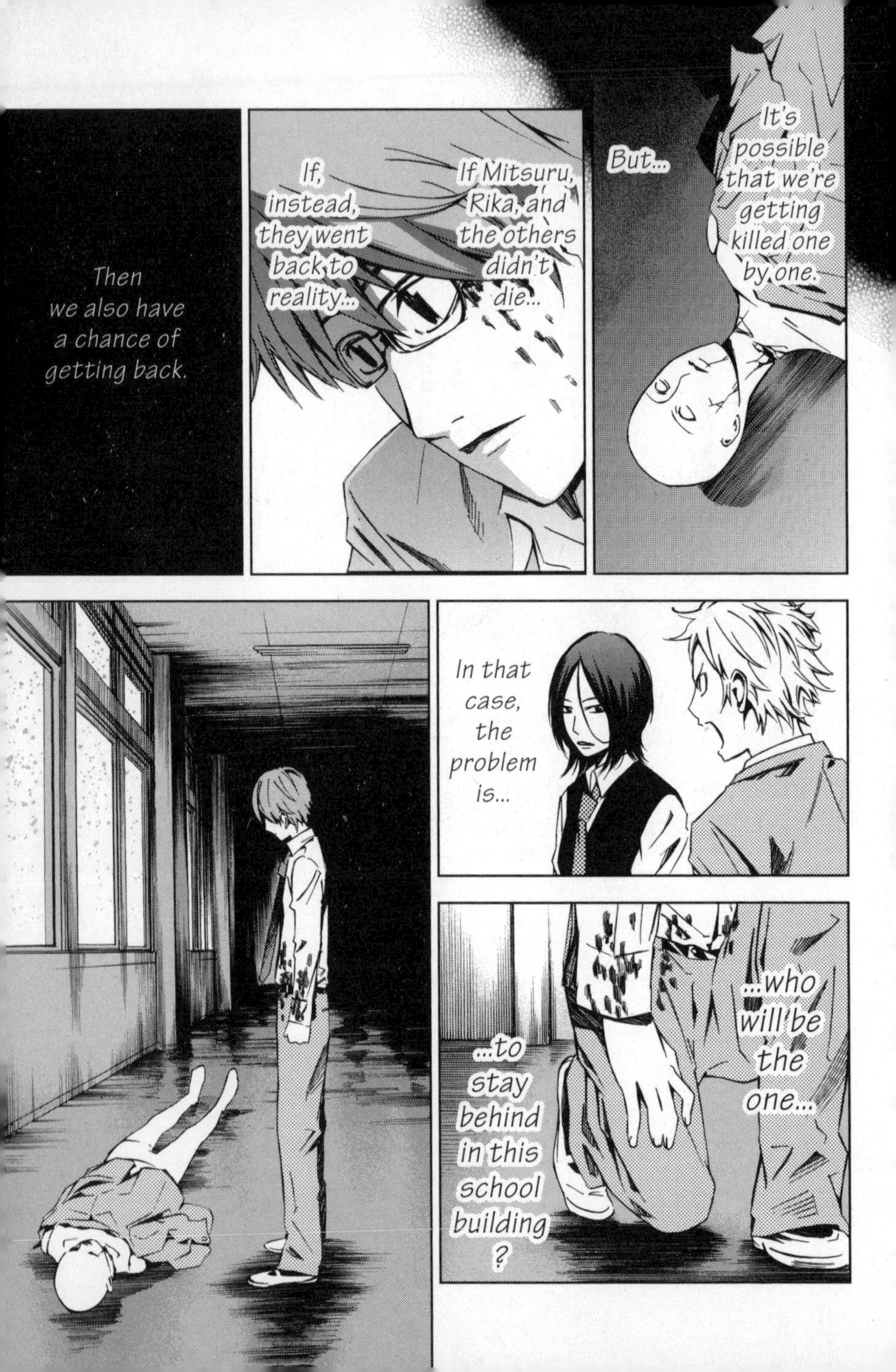
It's possible that we're getting killed one by one.
But...
If Mitsuru, Rika, and the others didn't die...
If, instead, they went back to reality...
Then we also have a chance of getting back.
In that case, the problem is...
...who will be the one...
...to stay behind in this school building?

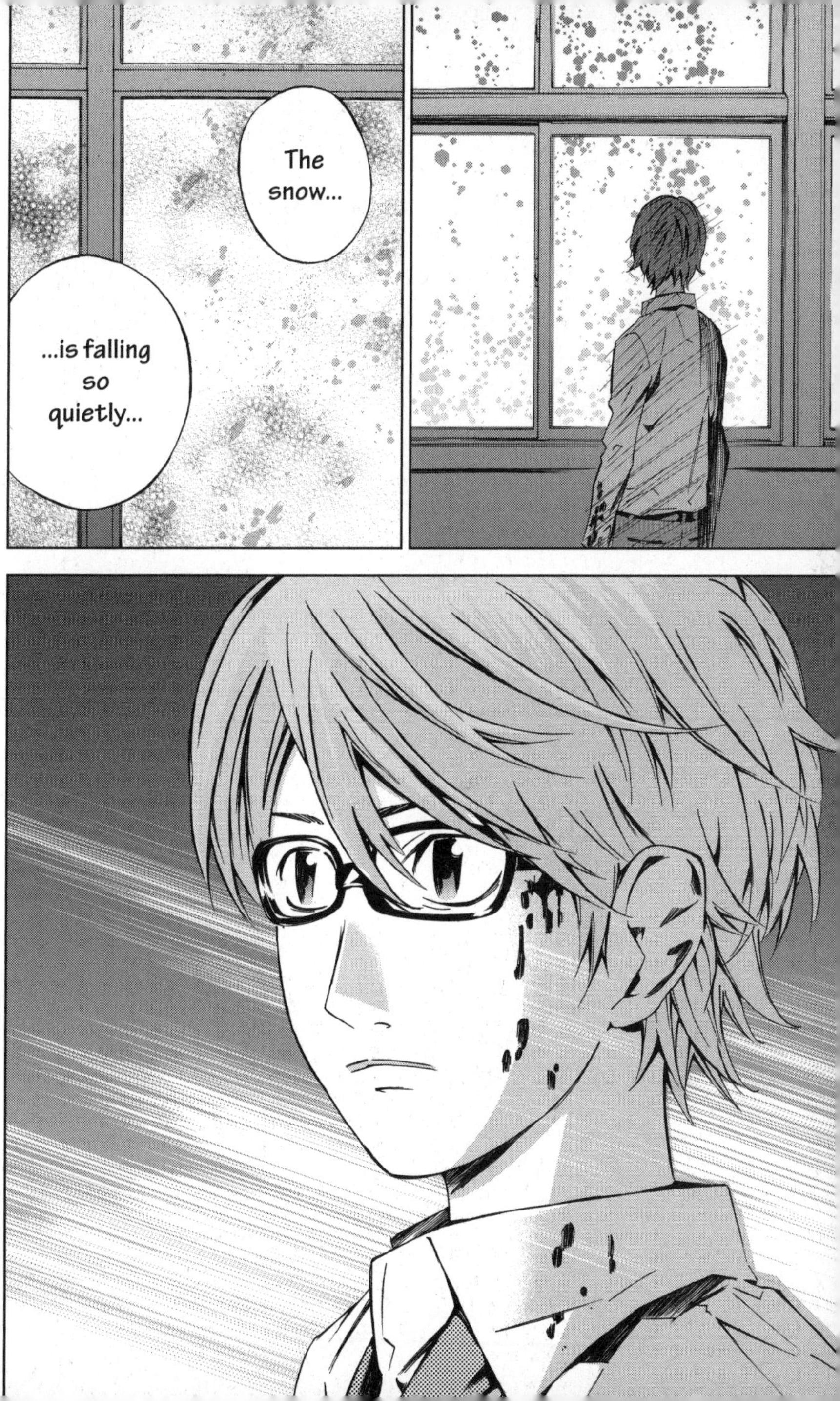
The snow...
...is falling so quietly...

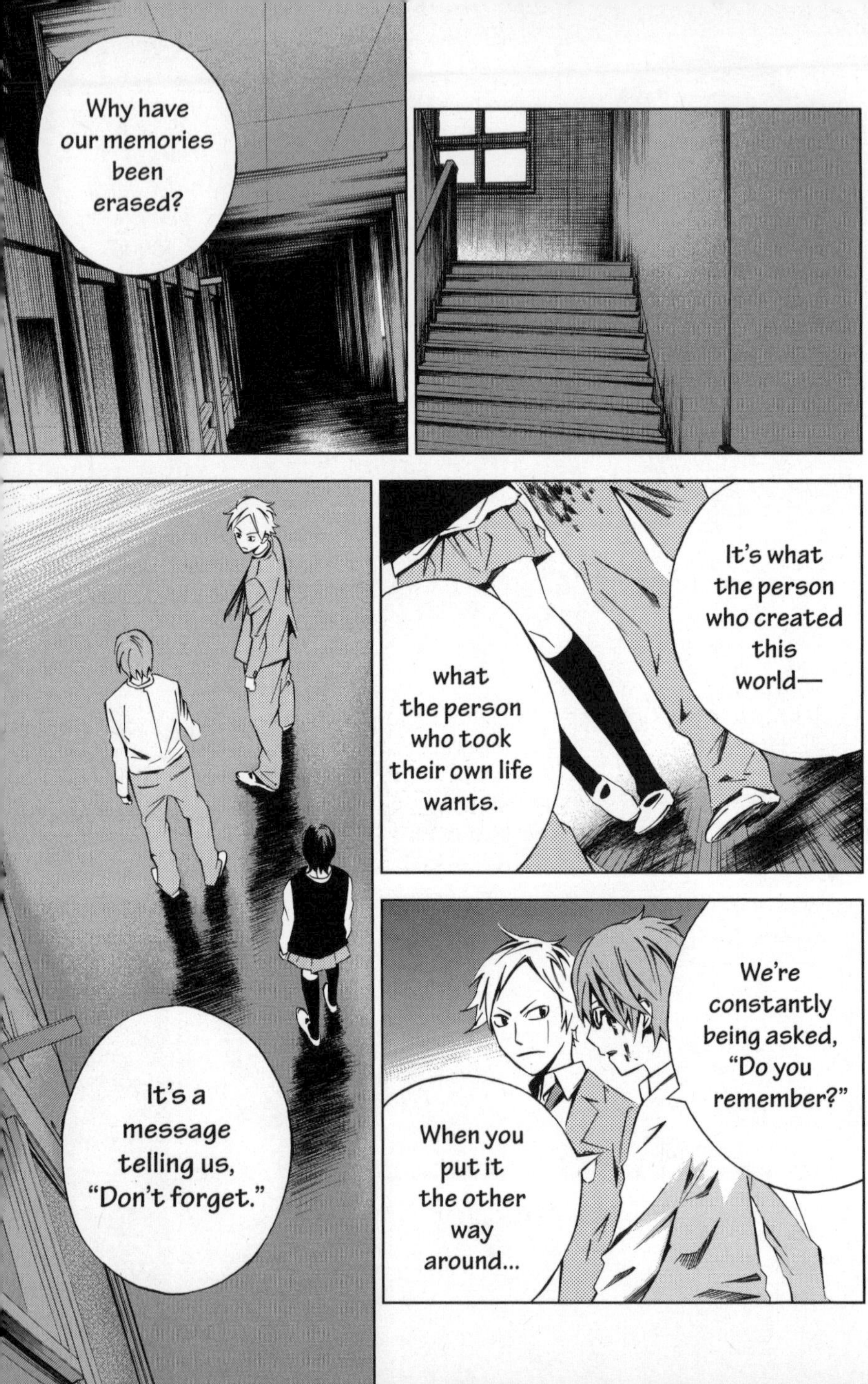
Why have our memories been erased?
It's what the person who created this world—
what the person who took their own life wants.
We're constantly being asked, "Do you remember?"
When you put it the other way around...
It's a message telling us, "Don't forget."

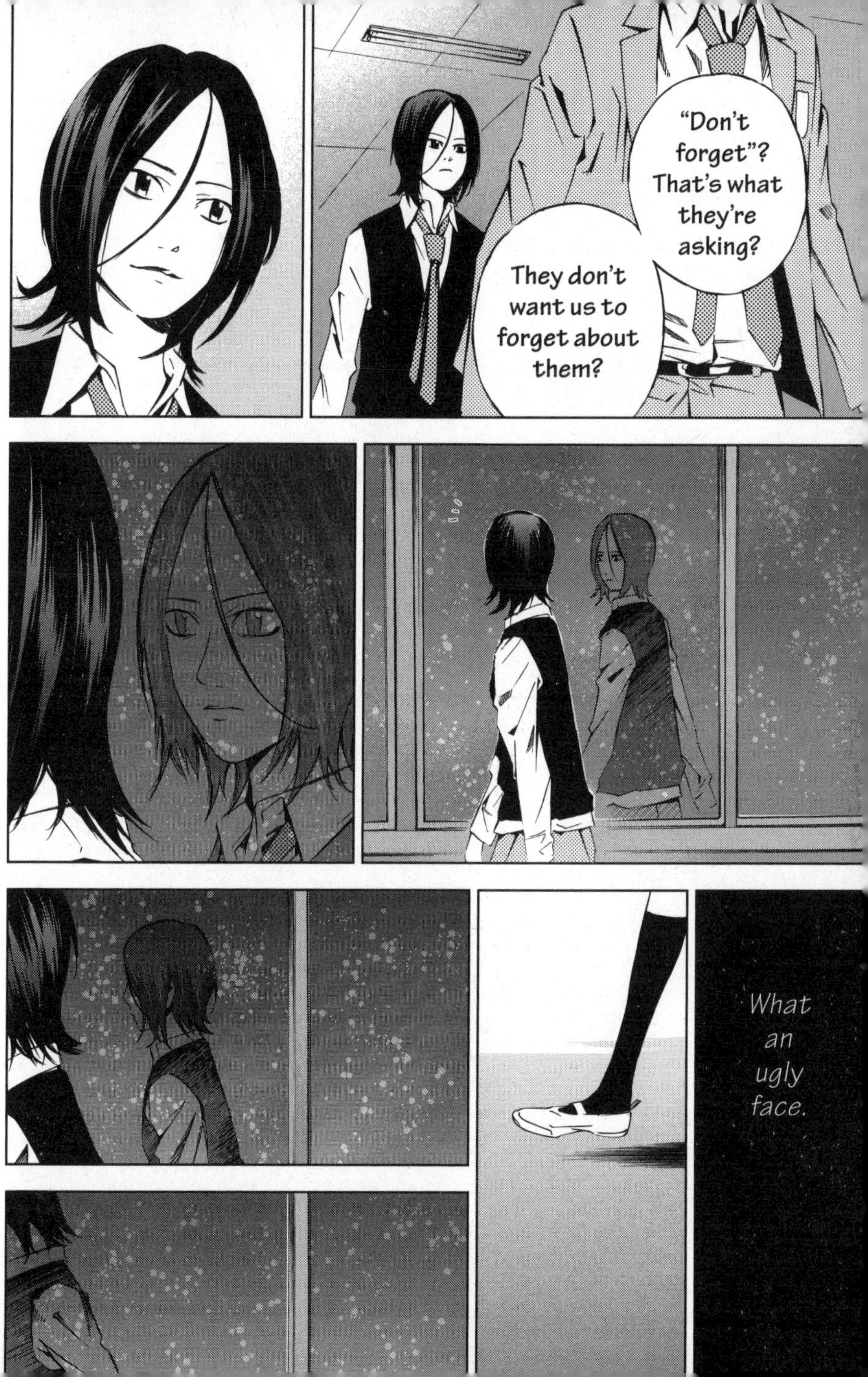
"Don't forget"? That's what they're asking?
They don't want us to forget about them?
What an ugly face.

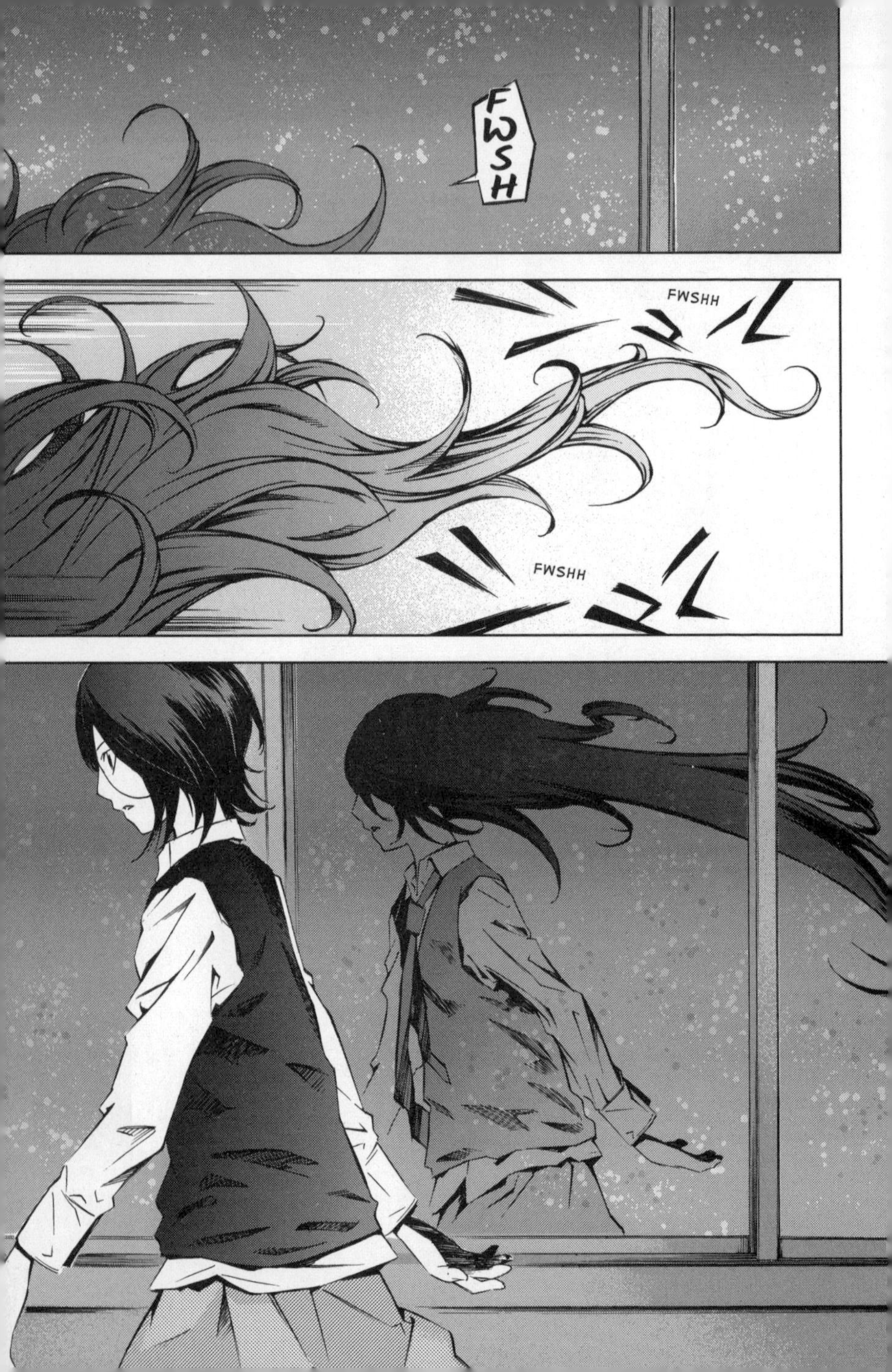
FWSH
FWSHH
FWSHH

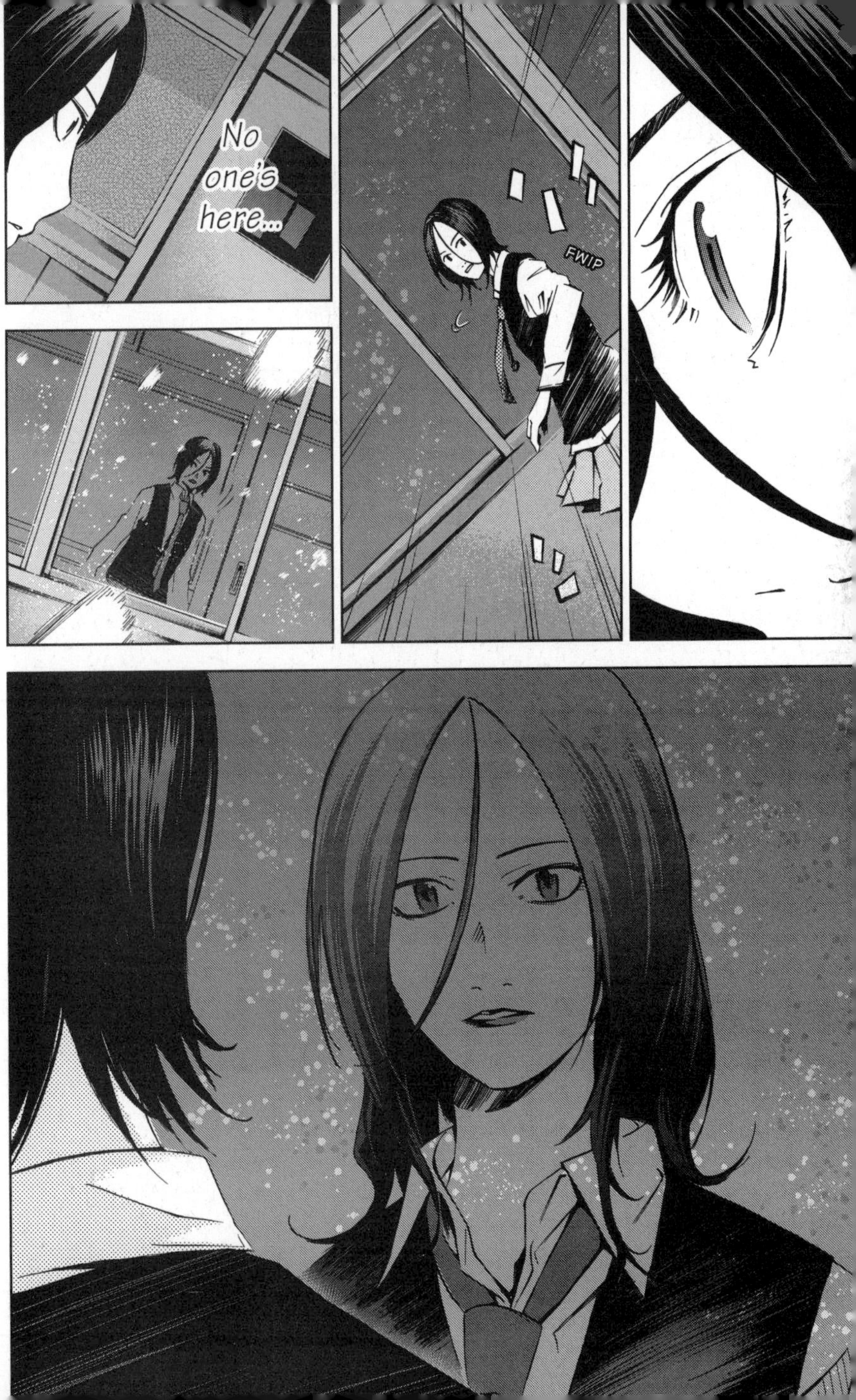

No one's here...
FWIP

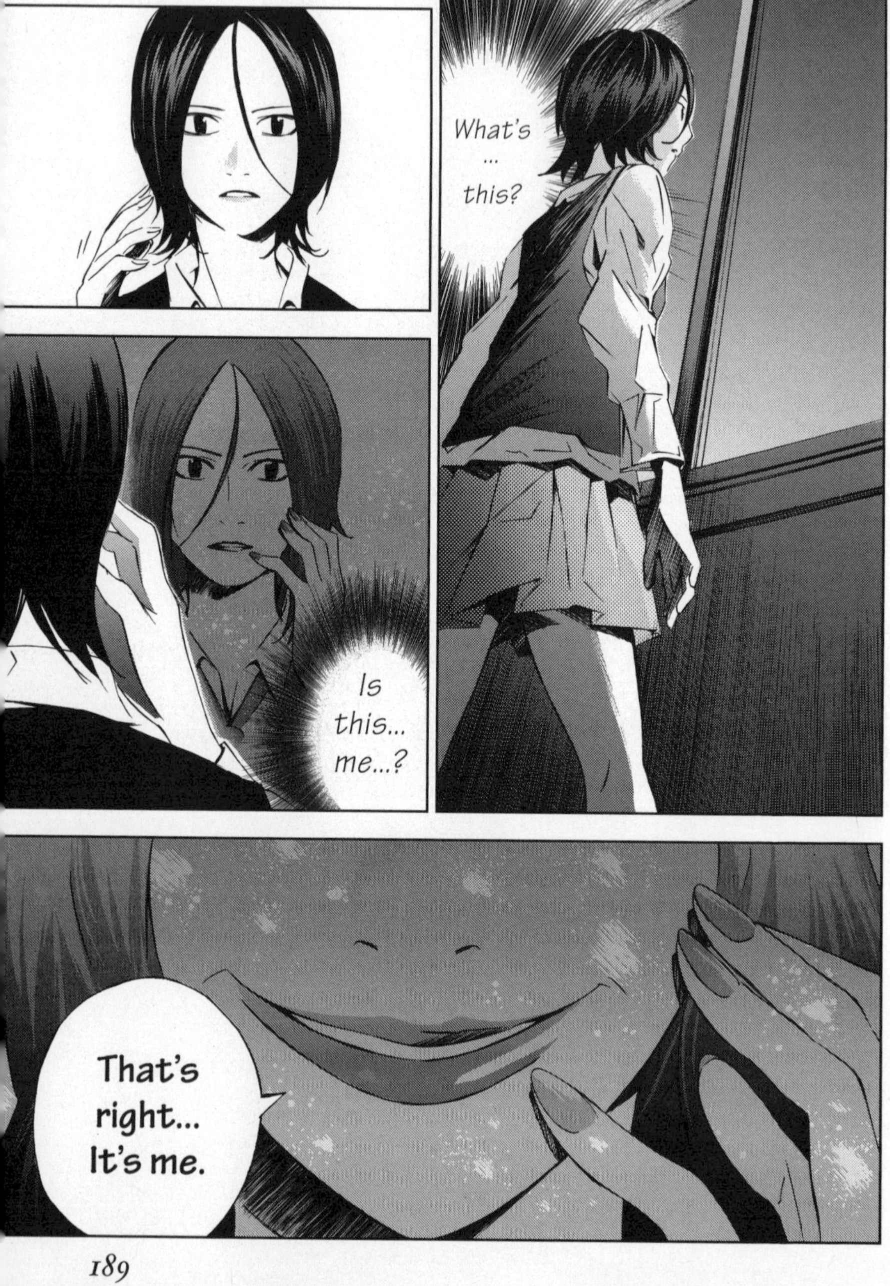
What's ... this?
Is this... me...?
That's right... It's me.

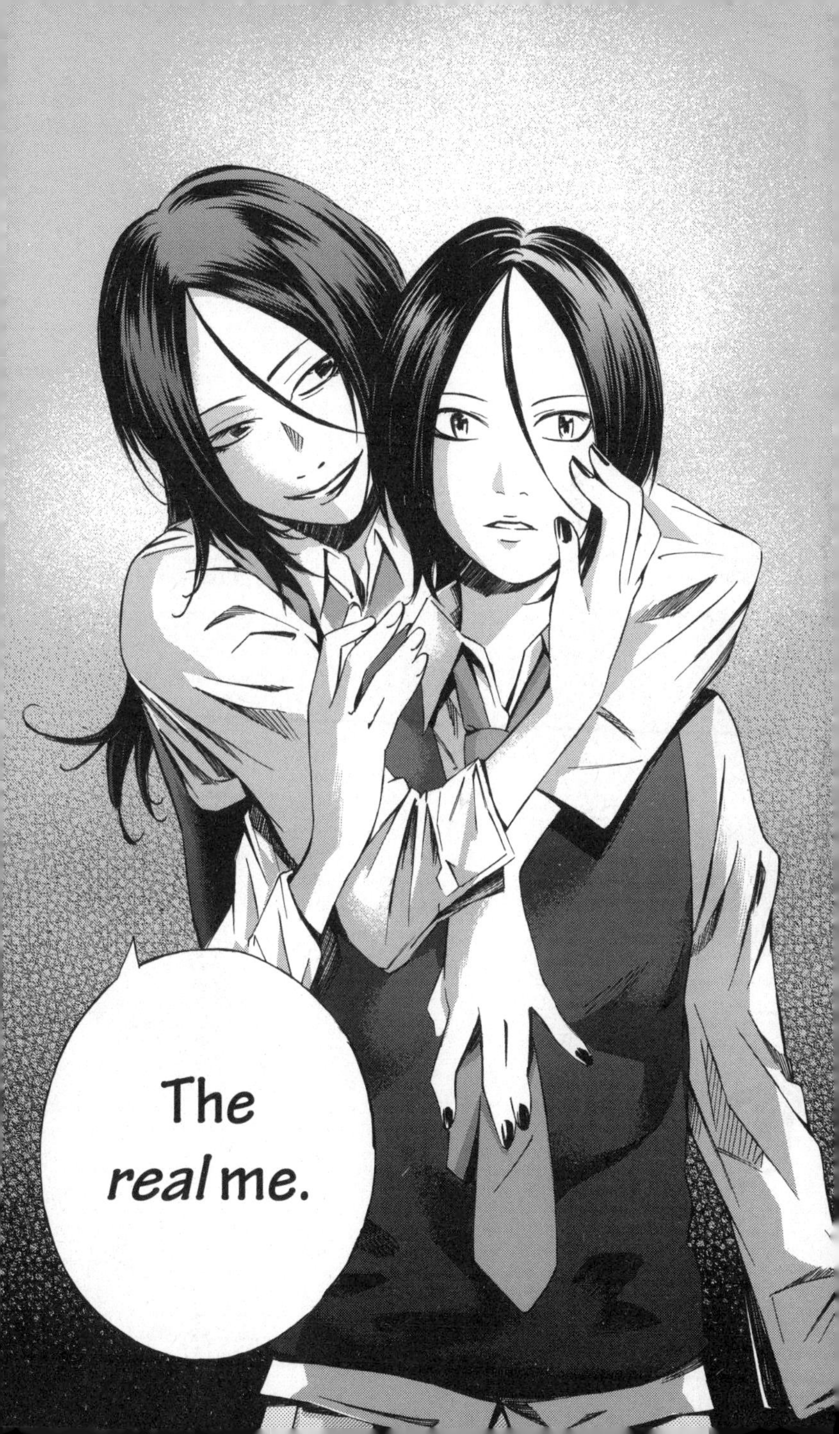
The *real* me.

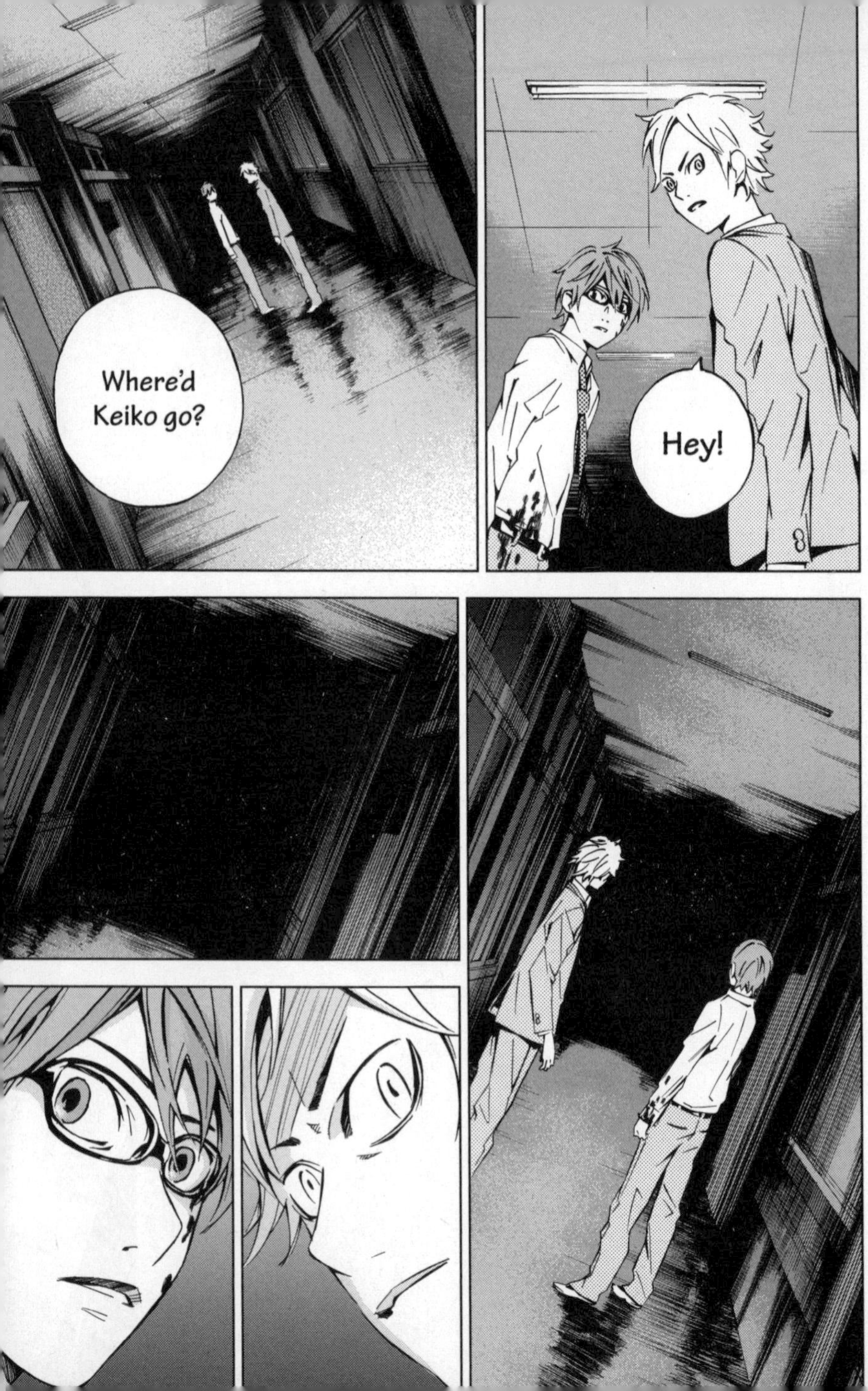
Hey!
Where'd Keiko go?

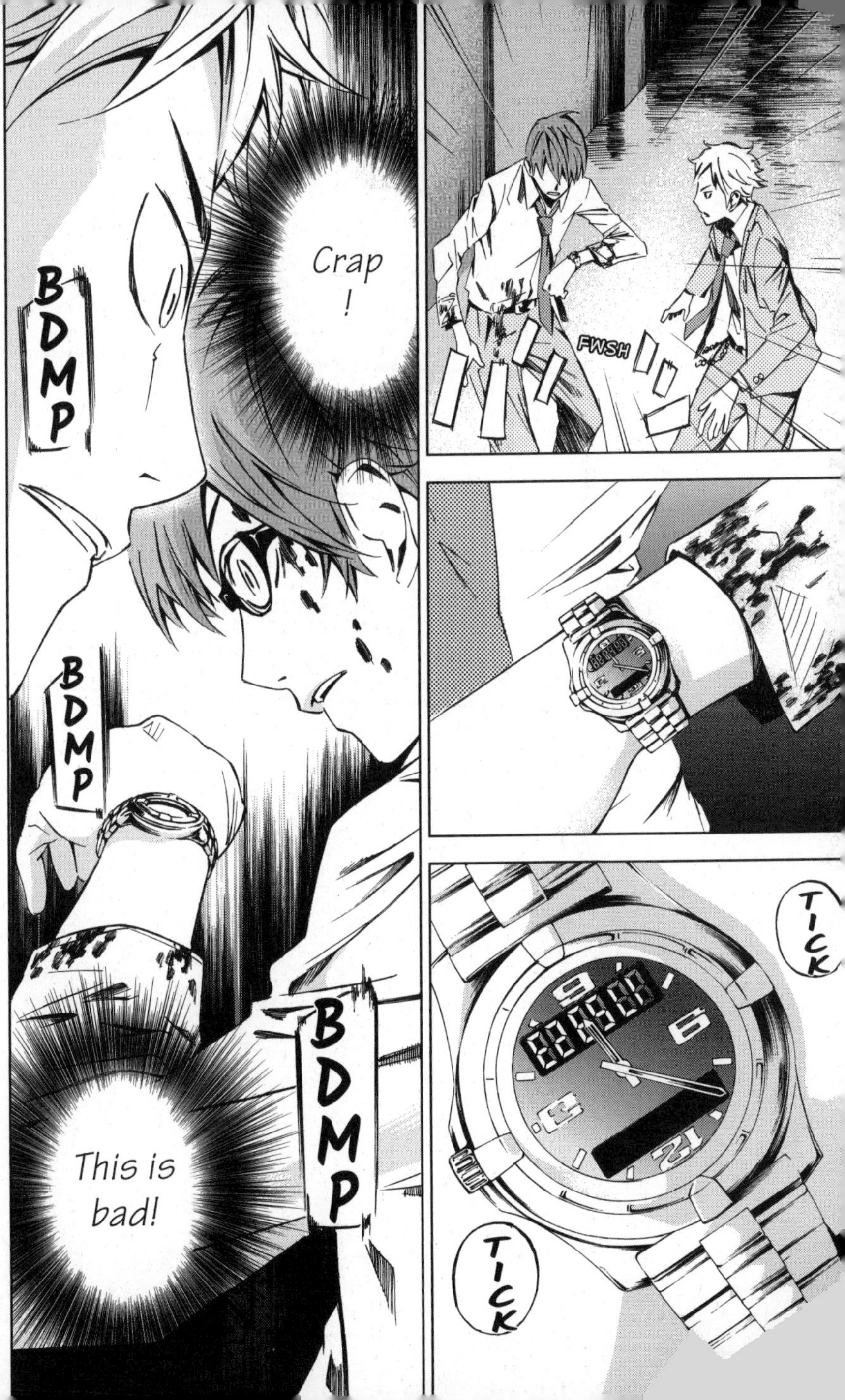
FWSH
TICK
TICK
Crap!
BDMP
BDMP
BDMP
This is bad!

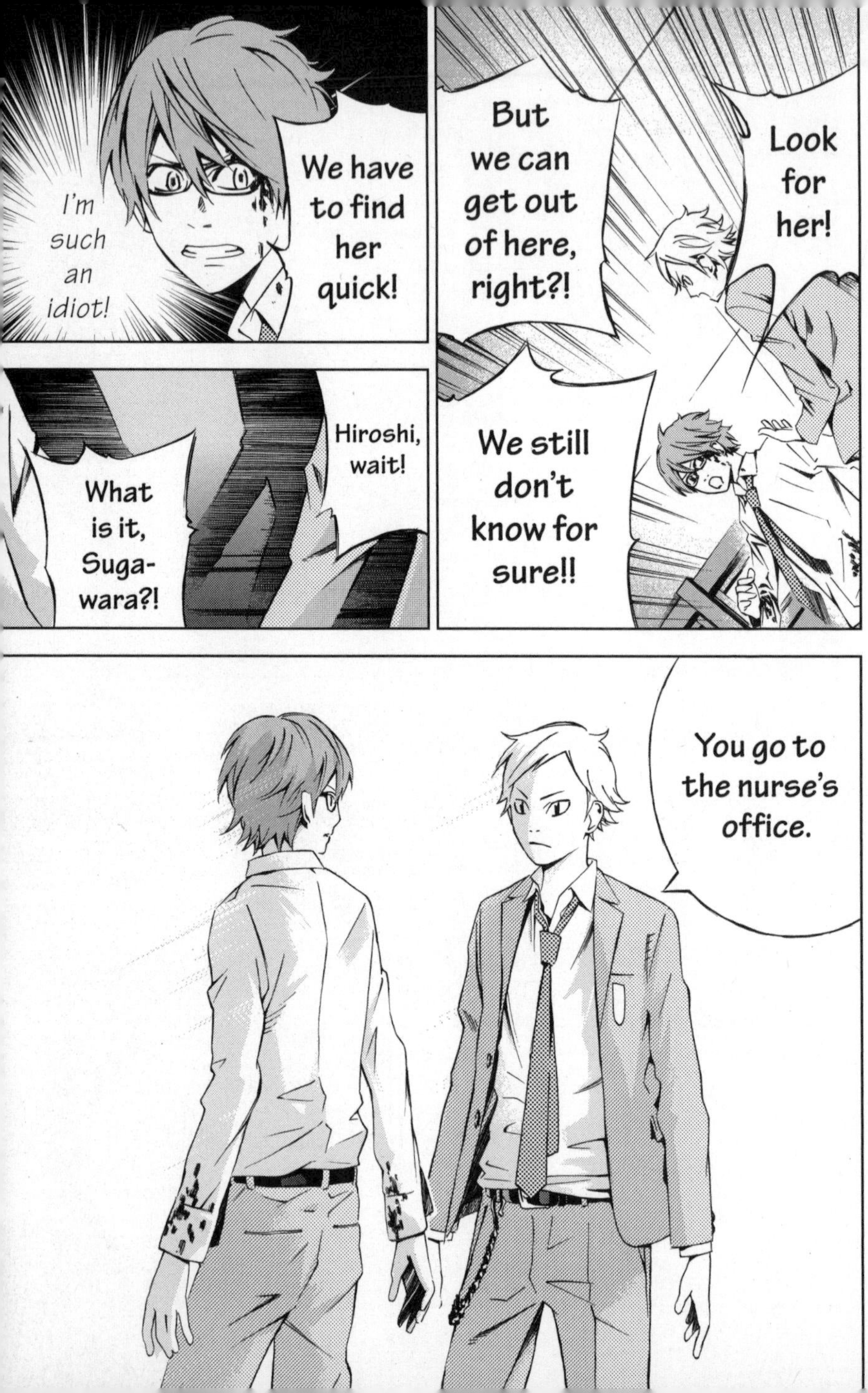
Look for her!
But we can get out of here, right?!
We still don't know for sure!!
We have to find her quick!
I'm such an idiot!
Hiroshi, wait!
What is it, Suga-wara?!
You go to the nurse's office.

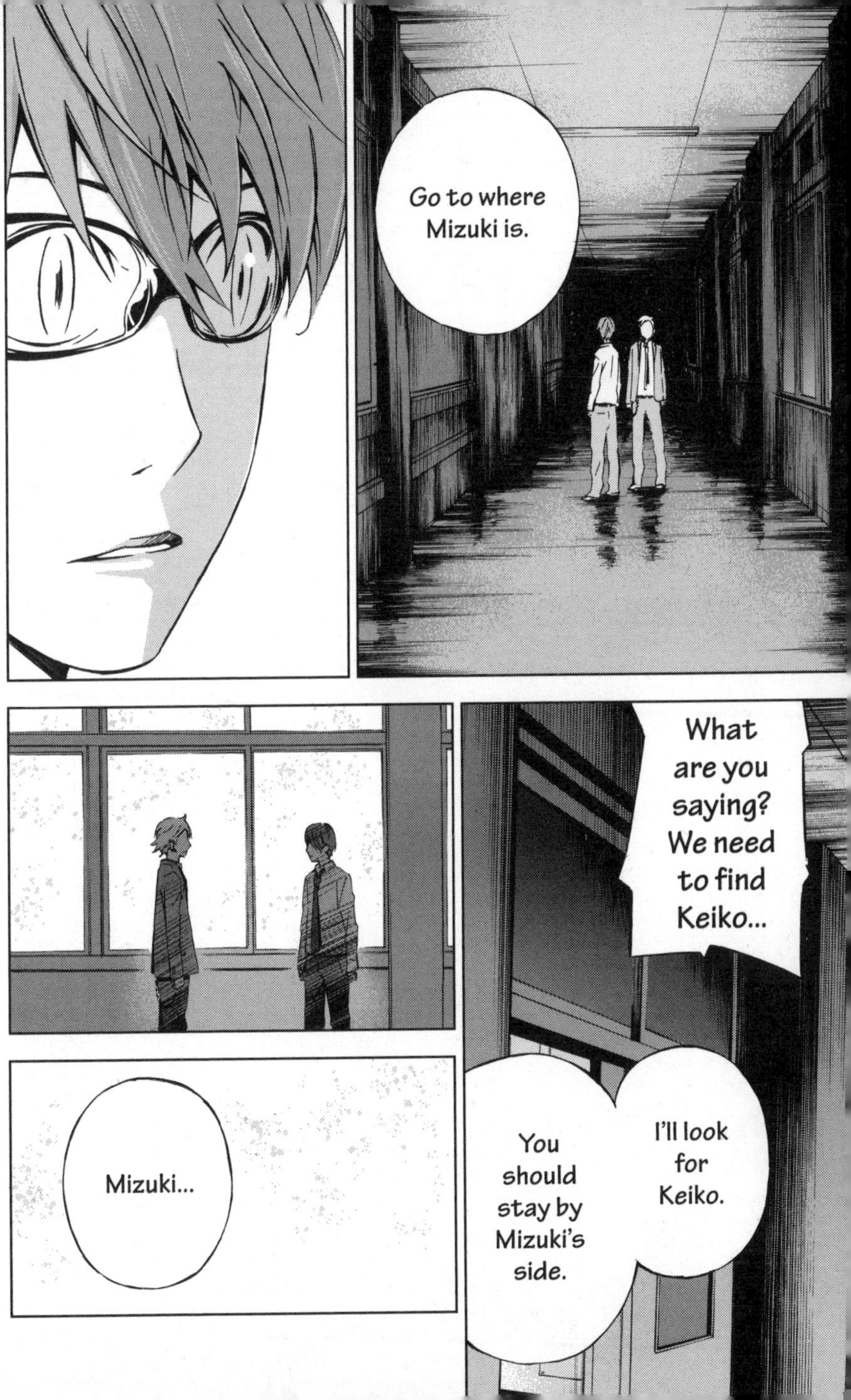
Go to where Mizuki is.
What are you saying? We need to find Keiko...
I'll look for Keiko.
You should stay by Mizuki's side.
Mizuki...

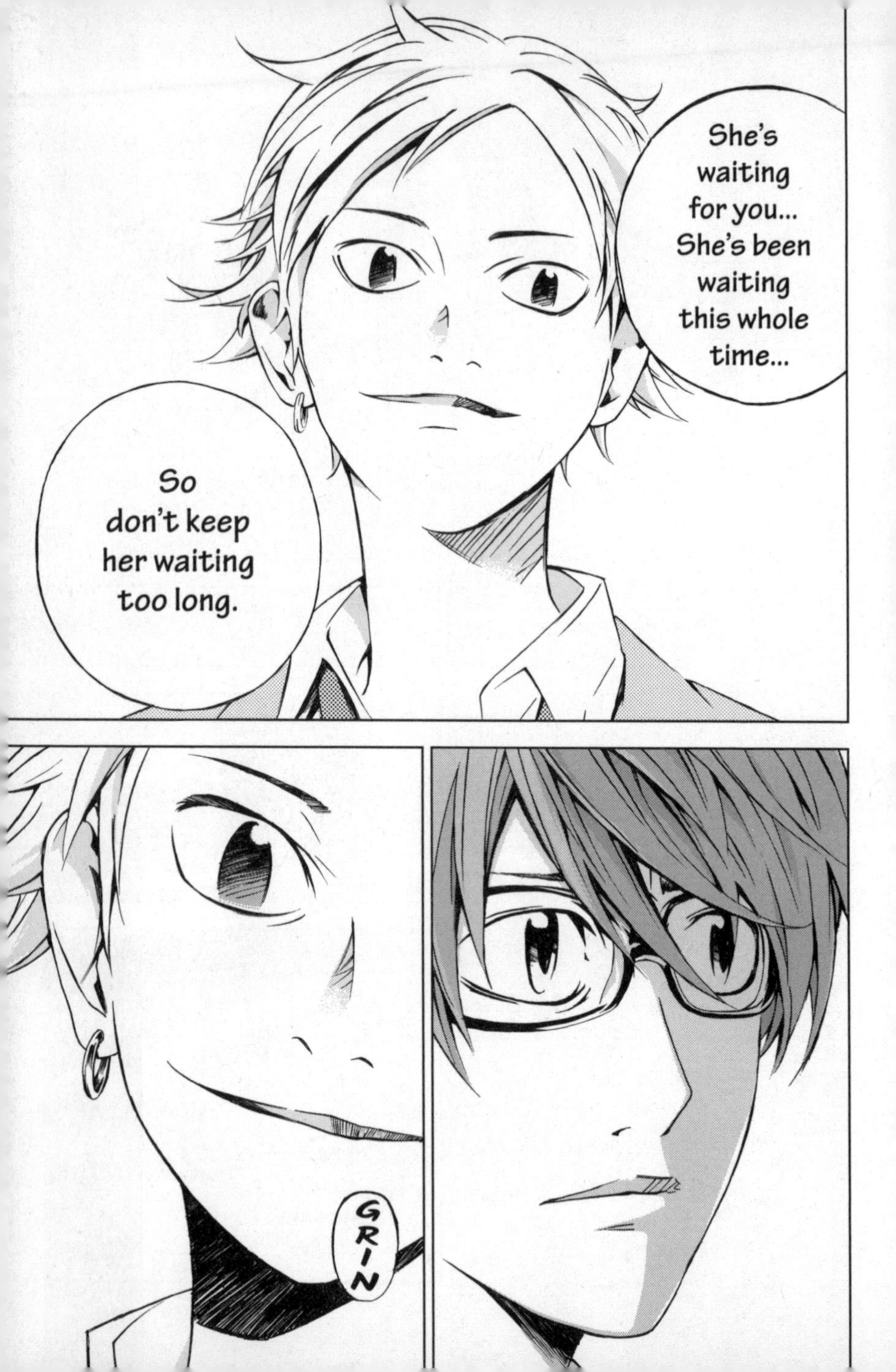
She's waiting for you... She's been waiting this whole time...
So don't keep her waiting too long.
GRIN

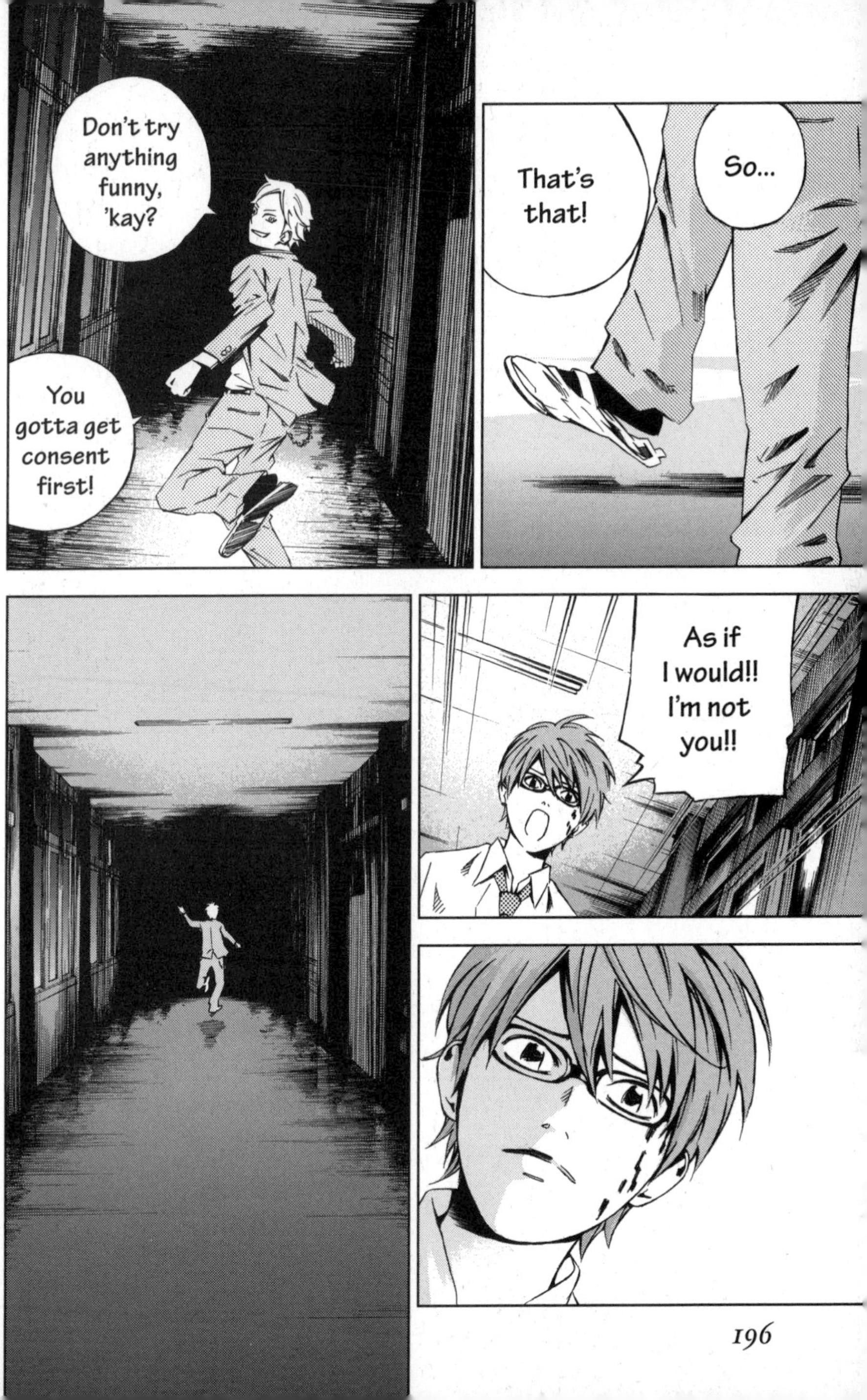
So...
That's that!
Don't try anything funny, 'kay?
You gotta get consent first!
As if I would!! I'm not you!!

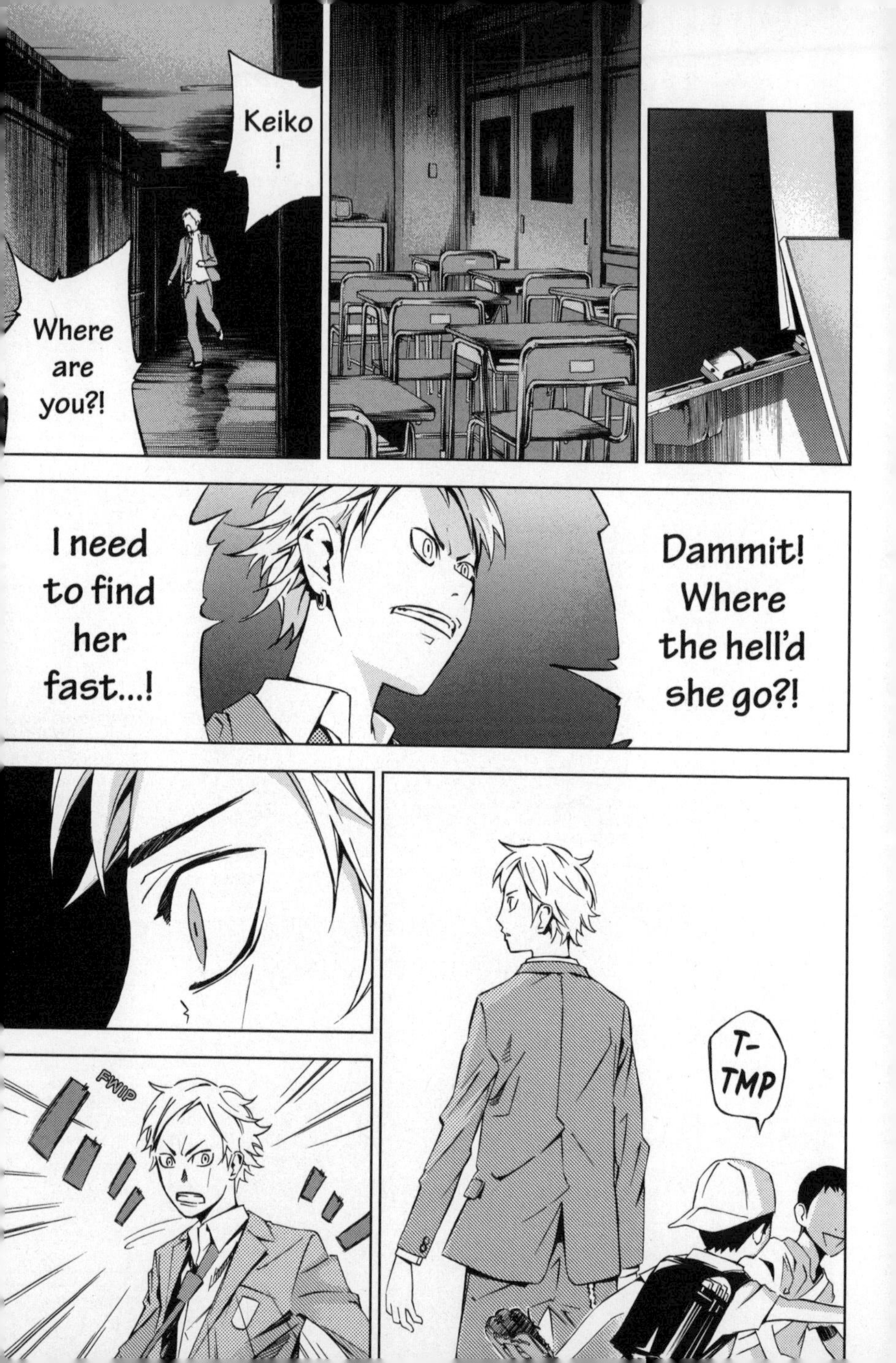
Keiko!
Where are you?!
Dammit! Where the hell'd she go?!
I need to find her fast...!
T-TMP
PWIP

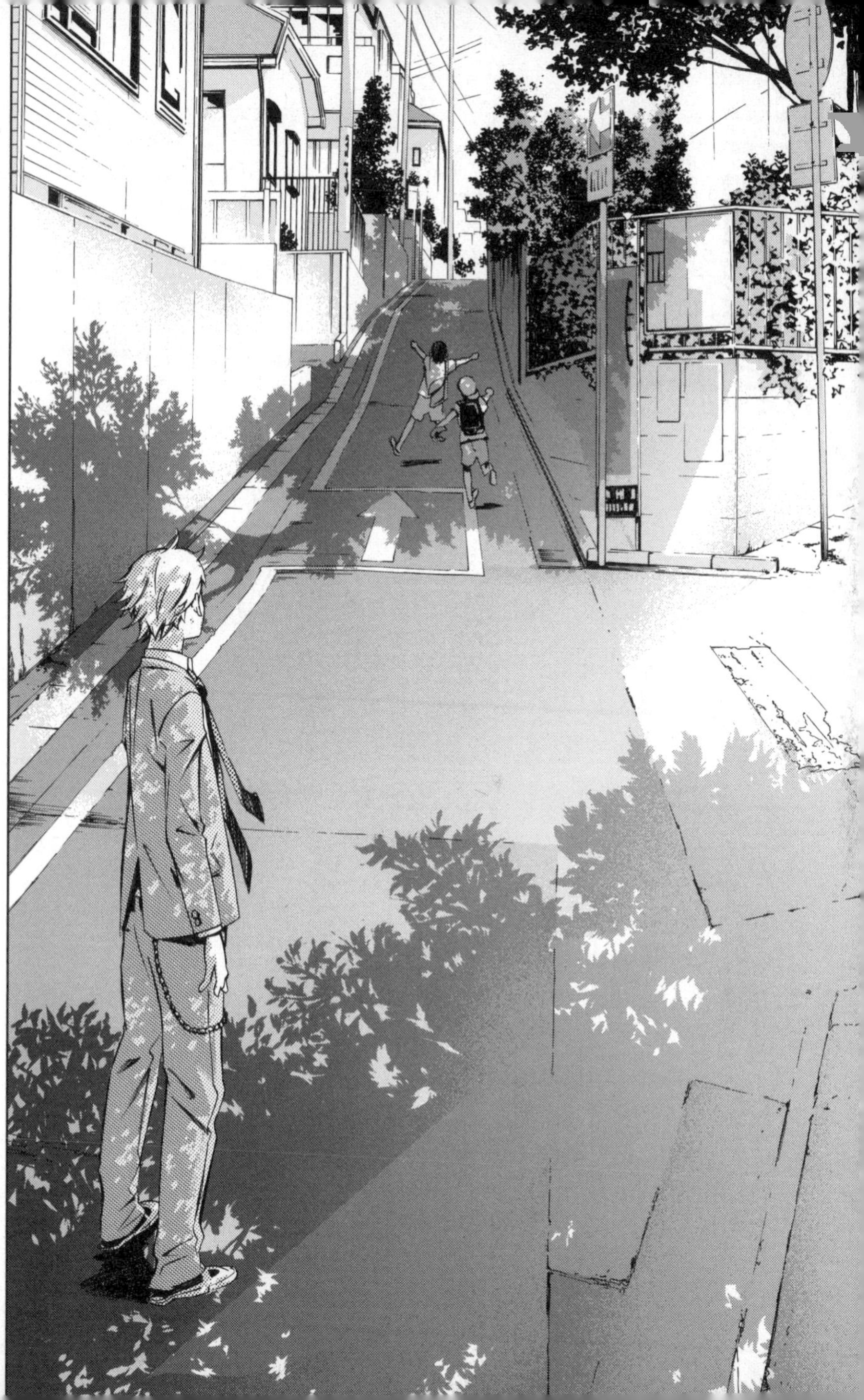

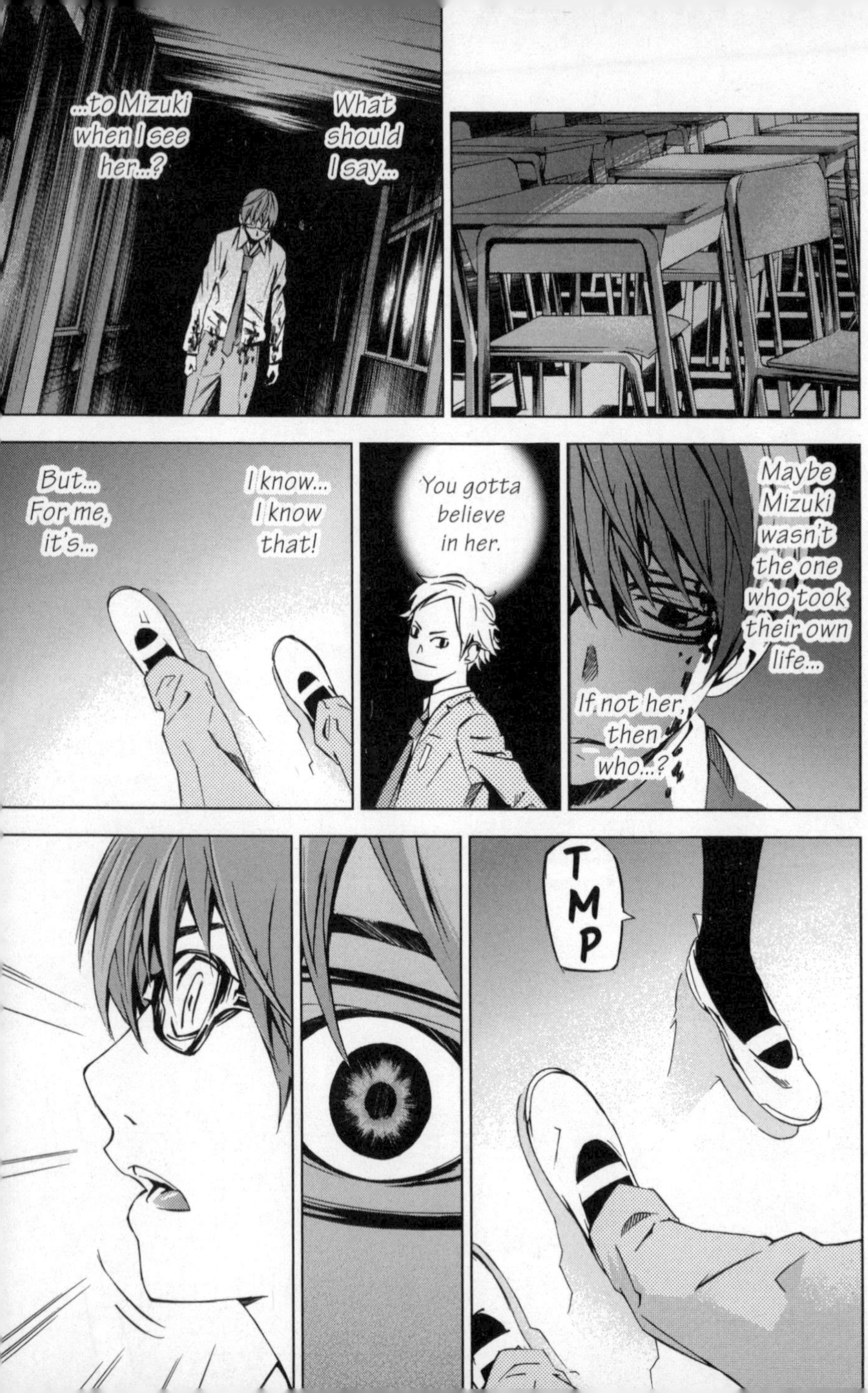
What should I say...
...to Mizuki when I see her...?
Maybe Mizuki wasn't the one who took their own life...
If not her, then who...?
You gotta believe in her.
I know... I know that!
But... For me, it's...
TMP

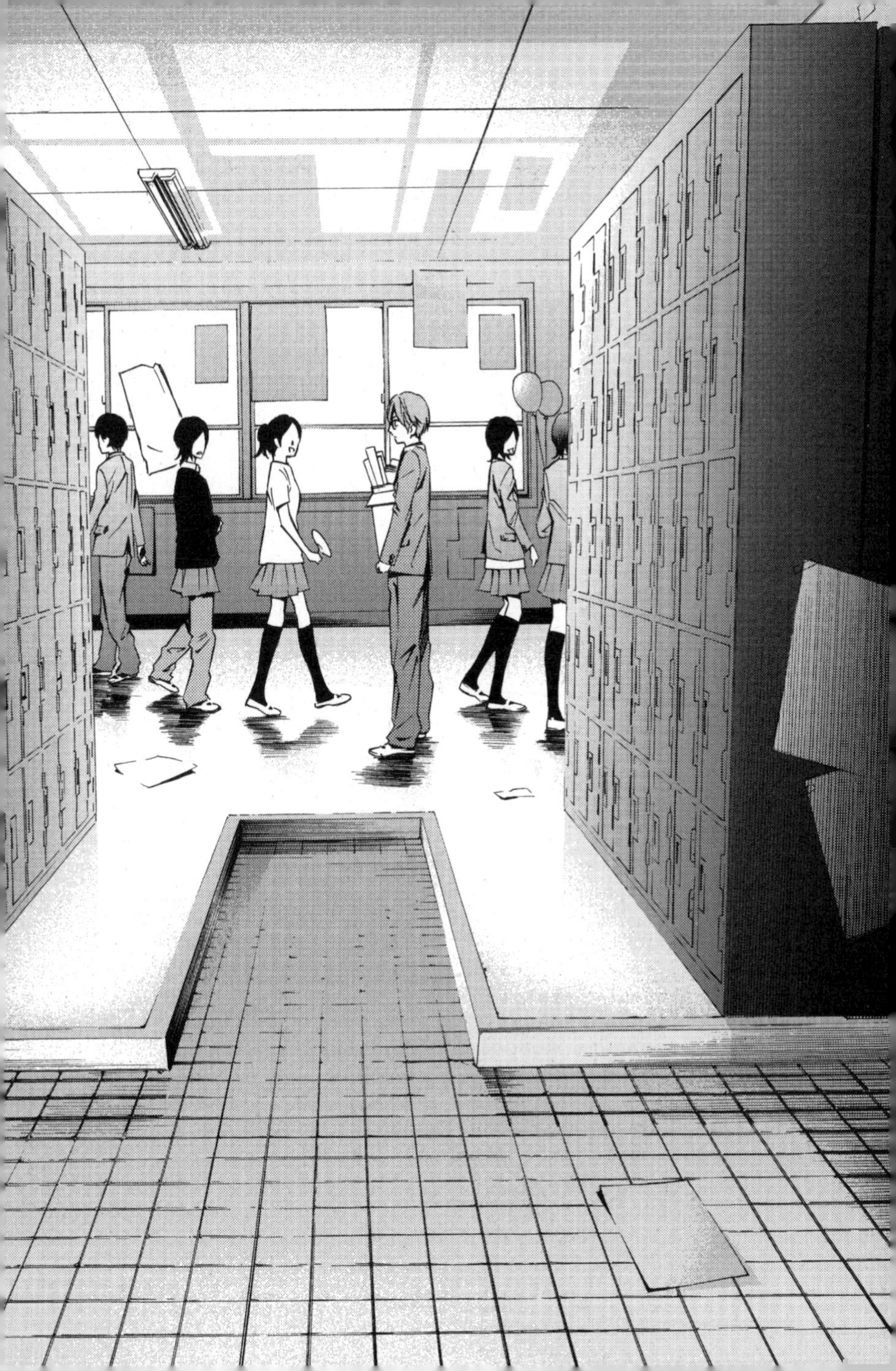

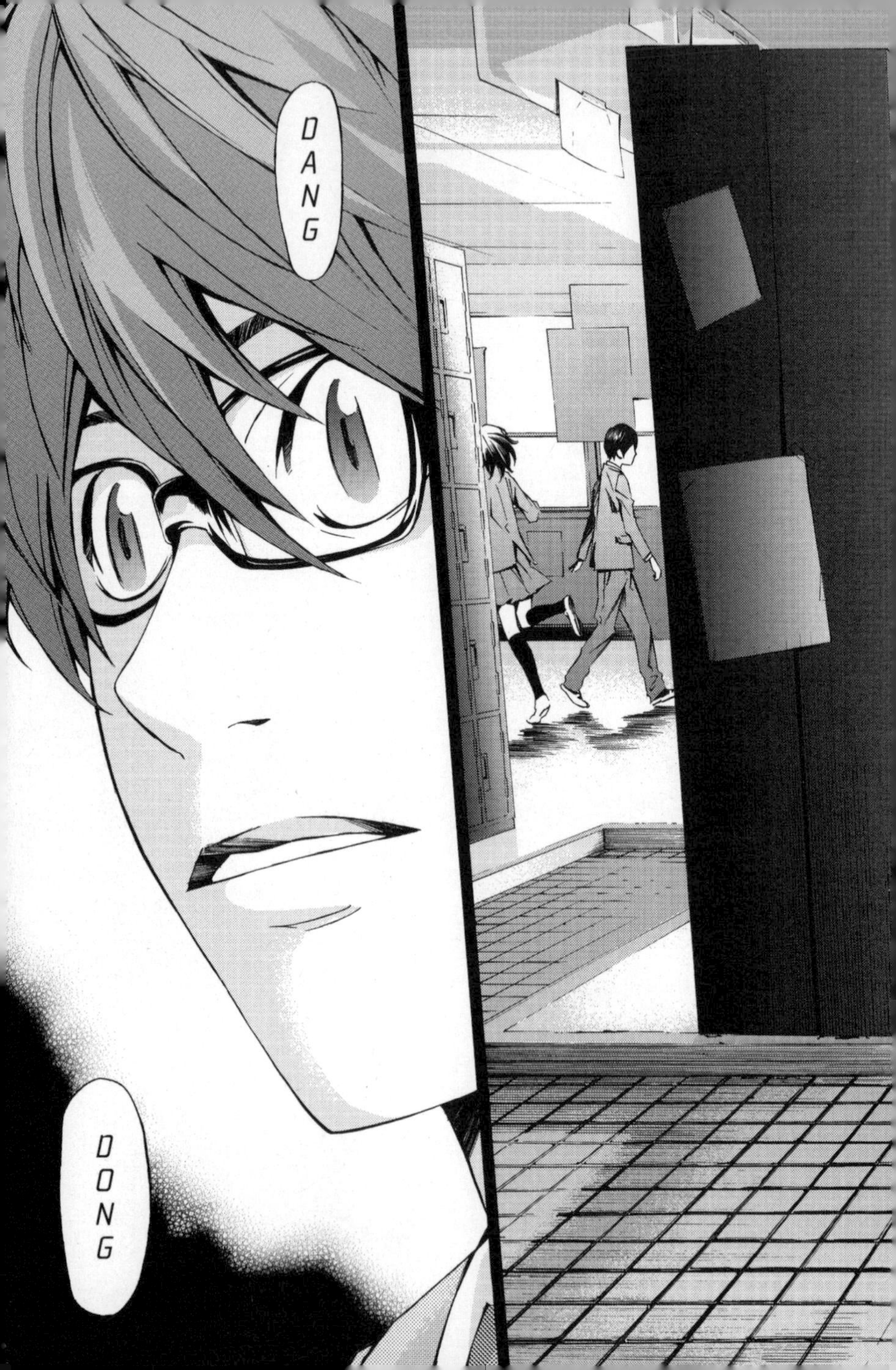
DANG
DONG

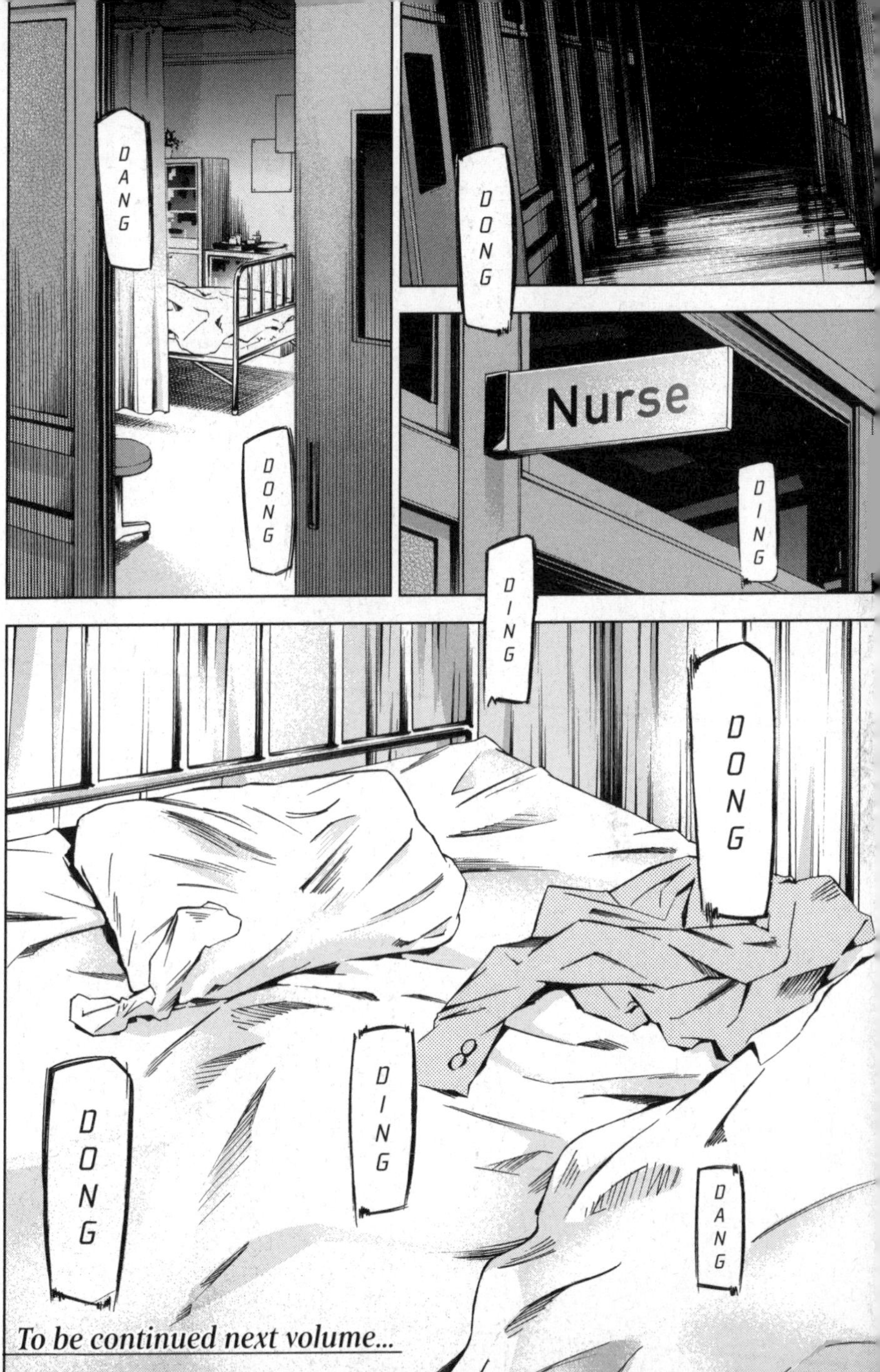

DONG
Nurse
DING
DING
DANG
DONG
DONG
DANG
DING
DONG
To be continued next volume...

A School
Frozen
in Time

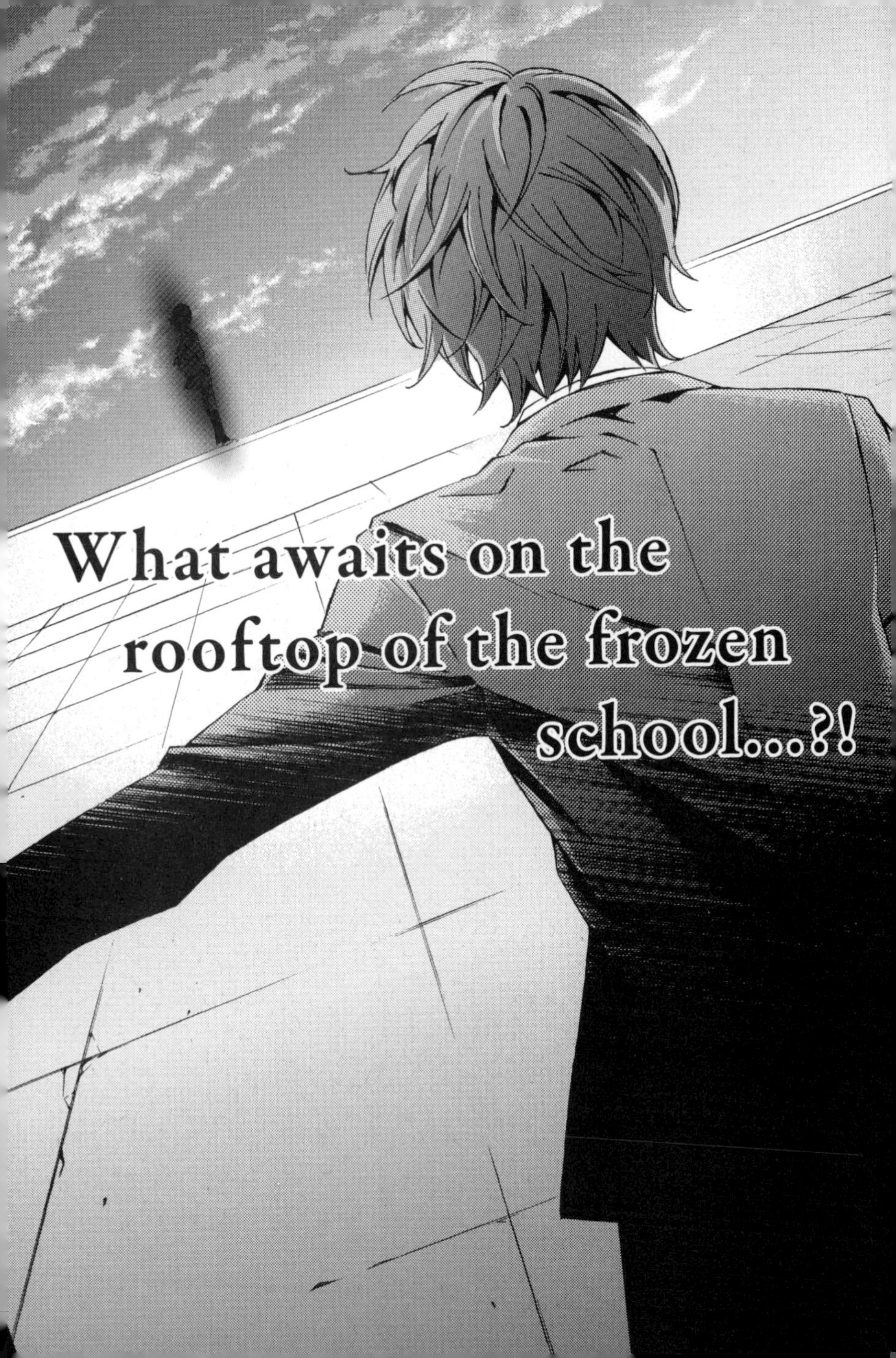
What awaits on the rooftop of the frozen school...?!

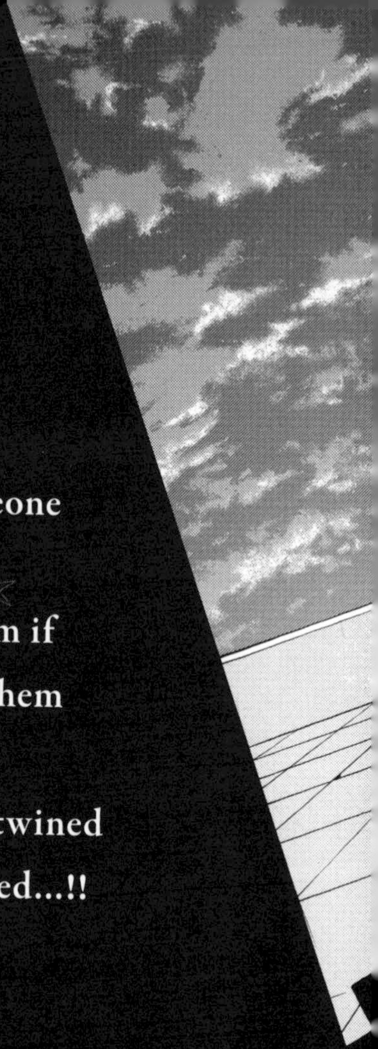

One by one, they disappear...
Only four remain in the sealed-off school building: Keiko, Sugawara, Takano, and Mizuki.
Could the person who jumped from the roof that day be someone amongst them?
Why is that person asking them if they remember *after* robbing them of their memories?
The answers to all of the intertwined mysteries will finally be revealed...!!

A School Frozen in Time

The Final Volume: Volume 4 Coming October 2021

Art by Naoshi Arakawa
Story by Mizuki Tsujimura

"With a huge collection of light novels to keep up with, I currently don't read many full-length novels, but *Anime Supremacy!* has proven itself a must-read for an anime fan like myself.
Well written, informative and charming... 9/10"
-Anime UK News

As three women—a producer, a director, and an animator—survive in a business infamous for its murderous schedules, demoralizing compromises, and incorrigible men, moments of uplift emerge against all odds. More than just a window into an entertainment niche, here's a kickass ode to work.

ANIME SUPREMACY!

MIZUKI TSUJIMURA

Paperback • 416 Pages • $16.95 US/$18.95 CAN
ON SALE NOW!

© Mizuki Tsujimura

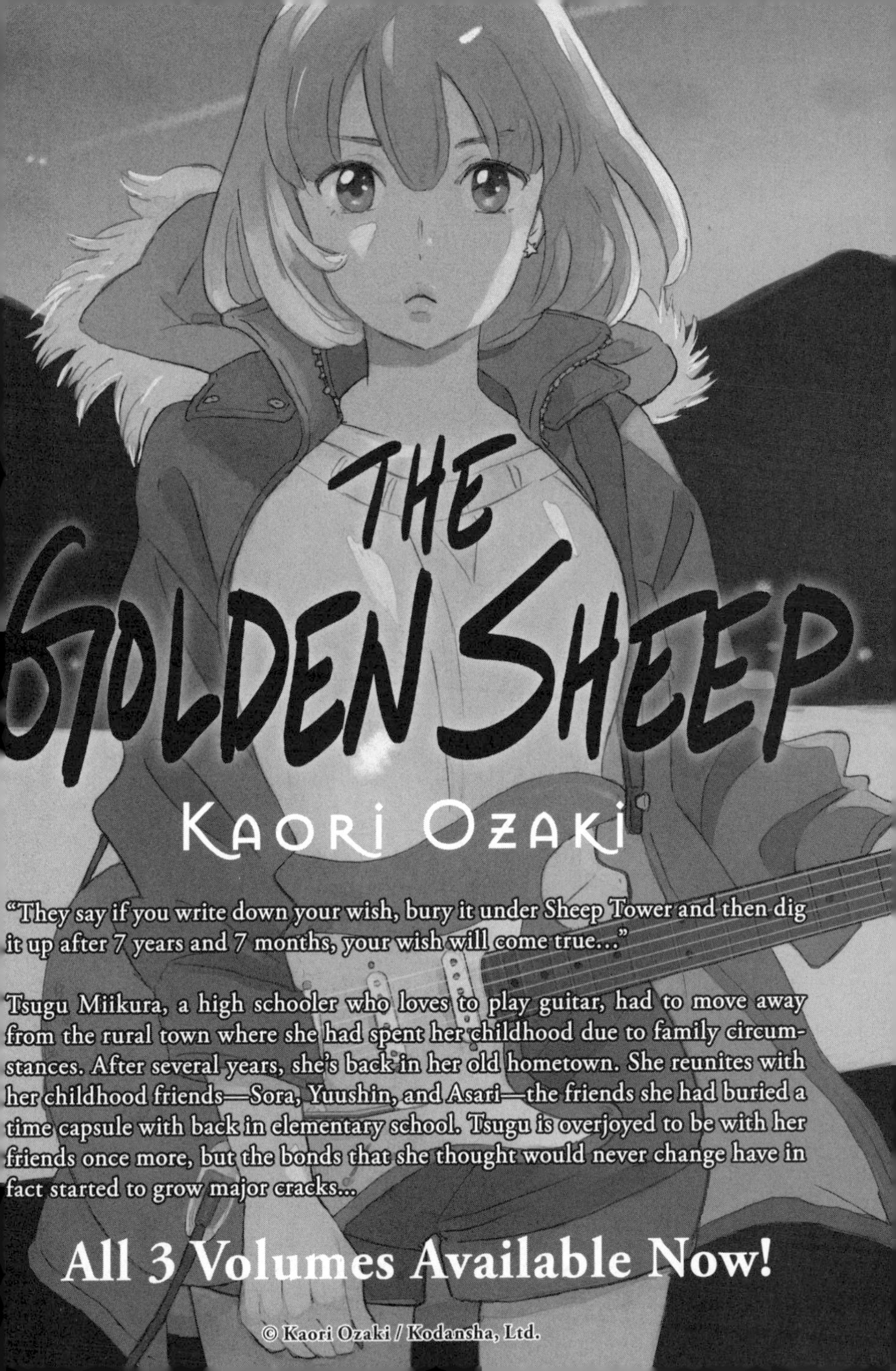
THE GOLDEN SHEEP
KAORI OZAKI
"They say if you write down your wish, bury it under Sheep Tower and then dig it up after 7 years and 7 months, your wish will come true..."
Tsugu Miikura, a high schooler who loves to play guitar, had to move away from the rural town where she had spent her childhood due to family circumstances. After several years, she's back in her old hometown. She reunites with her childhood friends—Sora, Yuushin, and Asari—the friends she had buried a time capsule with back in elementary school. Tsugu is overjoyed to be with her friends once more, but the bonds that she thought would never change have in fact started to grow major cracks...
All 3 Volumes Available Now!
© Kaori Ozaki / Kodansha, Ltd.

Natsuru Nanao, a 6th grader who lives alone with his mother, strikes up an unlikely friendship with the reserved and driven Rio Suzumura. Natsuru plays hookey from soccer camp that summer, and instead of telling the truth to his mother, he spends all his time with Rio and her kid brother at their rickety house, where a dark secret threatens to upend their fragile happiness.

the gods lie.

kaori ozaki

Available Now in Print and Digital!

A School Frozen in Time

volume 3

A Vertical Comics Edition

Editing: Ajani Oloye
Translation: Michelle Lin
Production: Grace Lu
         Tomoe Tsutsumi
Proofreading: Micah Q. Allen

© 2009 Naoshi Arakawa, Mizuki Tsujimura
All rights reserved.
First published in Japan in 2009 by Kodansha, Ltd., Tokyo
Publication for this English edition arranged through Kodansha, Ltd., Tokyo
English language version produced by Vertical Comics,
an imprint of Kodansha USA Publishing, LLC

Translation provided by Vertical Comics, 2021
Published by Kodansha USA Publishing, LLC, New York

Originally published in Japanese as *Tsumetai Kousha no Toki wa Tomaru 3*
by Kodansha, Ltd.
Tsumetai Kousha no Toki wa Tomaru first serialized in *Gekkan Shounen Magazine*,
Kodansha, Ltd., 2008

This is a work of fiction.

ISBN: 978-1-647290-51-1

Manufactured in the United States of America

First Edition

Kodansha USA Publishing, LLC
451 Park Avenue South
7th Floor
New York, NY 10016
www.kodansha.us

Vertical books are distributed through Penguin-Random House Publisher Services.